Shakespeare
The Critical Complex

Series Editors

Stephen Orgel and **Sean Keilen**
Stanford University

A GARLAND SERIES

Series Contents

Shakespeare in the Theater

Edited with an introduction by
Stephen Orgel and Sean Keilen
Stanford University

GARLAND PUBLISHING, INC.
A MEMBER OF THE TAYLOR & FRANCIS GROUP
New York & London
1999

Library of Congress Cataloging-in-Publication Data

Shakespeare in the theater/ edited with an introduction by Stephen
Orgel, Sean Keilen.
    p.   cm. — (Shakespeare, the critical complex ; 8)
    Includes bibliographical references.
    ISBN 0-8153-2968-7 (alk. paper)
    1. Shakespeare, William, 1564–1616—Stage history.
    2. Shakespeare, William, 1564–1616—Dramatic production.
    3. Theater—Production and direction. 4. Theater—History.
    I. Orgel, Stephen. II. Keilen, Sean. III. Series.

PR3091.S364 1999
792.9'5—dc21   99-054097

Printed on acid-free, 250-year-life paper
Manufactured in the United States of America

Contents

Introduction

Shakespeare's plays began their life as scripts, not books, designed to be read only by actors, and thereafter to be realized in the theater for audiences. This volume takes the history of performance to be an essential element in the history of the Shakespearean text. Jackson Barry opens with a pedagogical question: when we teach Shakespeare through a combination of modern editions, films and videotapes, how can we bridge the gap between text and performance? Behind this question lies a larger and more problematic one: what is the responsibility of the performance to the text — to what extent can we ever argue that a particular performance is 'wrong'? Stephen Orgel historicizes the question by considering the Renaissance's notion of the relation of the play to its theatrical environment, probing the limits of the stage Shakespeare imagined through an examination of a group of disparate contemporary visualizations: Serlio's generic settings, the Peacham *Titus Andronicus* drawing, the Swan sketch, Inigo Jones's scene designs. Andrew Gurr pursues the question, asking what Prospero's island 'really' looked like, and how it would have been realized on the stage of the Blackfriars and the Globe.

Steven Urkowitz focusses on the Renaissance actor, excavating a repertory of theatrical gesture from the neglected evidence of the so-called bad quartos, with their clear ties to the living stage and the performing tradition. In the progressive versions of the scripts preserved in these quartos, body language and stage movement are clearly being revised just as dialogue is, and the developing determination of gesture, of the physical presence of the actor, is as essential part of the creative process as the refinement of poetry and the redirection of dialogue.

Jeffrey Knapp and Michael O'Connell are concerned with the place of theater in the England reconstructed by the Reformation. Knapp asks first why theater seemed to moralists incapable of teaching anything but carnality, and second how, despite the force of Reformation ideology, Shakespeare's England nevertheless continued to find in theater a spiritually vital and valuable institution. O'Connell takes a contrary view, calling attention to the radical disruption in both religious and aesthetic theory and practice entailed by the Reformation, and sees as a consequence of this the effective banishment of religion, which had been the overwhelming subject of medieval drama, from the Elizabethan and Jacobean stage.

In a long, brilliant and characteristically speculative meditation, William

Empson undertakes to reconstruct the *Hamlet* of Shakespeare's first audiences, aware as they would have been of the previous 'ur-*Hamlet*' and of the immediate theatrical milieu — aware, that is, of everything about the background and context of Shakespeare's play that is lost to us. The resulting reading really does evoke a lost theatrical world; it remains breathtaking in its freshness and critical daring. Marion Trousdale and Joel Altman too consider the original playgoers and the reception of early performances. Trousdale sees performance as moving beyond the stage and functioning throughout society, a characteristic of the culture as a whole. It was highly charged because acting not only put in question notions of status and degree, but also drew upon and validated deeply felt social practices that themselves might be seen as subversive. Altman suggests that in Shakespeare, dramatic performance and its reception provided a model for articulating and communicating the system of often contradictory fictions that in fact held the social fabric together.

A final group of essays examine the significance of Shakespearean production in later periods. Arthur J. Harris anatomizes the differing forms *King Lear* took when the eighteenth century presented it, and assesses the roles of Colman and Garrick in establishing a version that could be considered standard. Jane Moody describes the development of non-standard, 'illegitimate' performances of Shakespeare in the early nineteenth century, showing how theatrical practice and cultural politics combine in the period to produce a genuinely populist Shakespeare. Mary Nilan analyzes Charles Kean's famous, spectacular *Tempest* of 1857 to show it as the culmination of a century-old debate between text and production. The play, in Kean's realization, was seen as a theater-piece *par excellence*, and was declared, in effect, a triumph of theater over text. Finally, Thomas Clayton surveys representative productions from the Guthrie Theater in the 1960s and 1970s to consider the effectiveness of theatrical strategies that undertake to bring remote texts together with contemporary audiences: setting *Julius Caesar* in a banana republic, for example, or *Measure for Measure* in nineteenth-century Austria-Hungary.

The essays in this volume construct an archeology of theatrical practice in the continuing creation of Shakespeare, considering the place of Shakespeare's theater within society as it changes from Early Modern to modern, the changing social status of playwrights, actors and audiences, the changing character of theatrical patronage and the continuing fact of censorship, and the transformations of theater as an idea, a location, a building, a business, a set of material phenomena.

Shakespeare with Words: The Script and the Medium of Drama

HE teacher of Shakespeare necessarily spends a good deal of time pondering what combination of approaches to the canon, from description of character to rhetorical analysis, will bring his students closest to the material, considerations which sometimes conceal a prior problem common to all drama but particularly plaguing in the case of Shakespeare: where is the play that one would teach? In a day when a major trend in scholarship has been toward Shakespeare on the stage and when chances for a student to see a live or filmed performance of Shakespeare have never been better, a fresh and candid response is indicated to the relationship between the book and the stage as locus of "the play itself." The teacher's deepest concern is probably with the possibility that performance will distort the play he knows in the text, that in its transfer to the theater *Hamlet, King Lear,* or *Macbeth* may gain vividness but lose literary values. This essay attempts to show that the dramatic medium does not in itself distort a play (for it, not the script, is the true place of the play), but that there are, all too frequently perhaps, productions which may clearly be called wrong. Correlatively, this negative judgement may be made on the basis of the most usual instrument available to the student and the teacher—the text—without having to posit this as "the play itself." Finally, the dramatic medium with its squeaking players and gaudy scenes, though by nature uneven and ephemeral, is by no means inimical to most of the highest literary values that may be explicated to a class from the printed page, nor is the printed page, correctly interpreted, a hopelessly inadequate guide to dramatic values.

Plays are readily available in script form while a performance of the same work is likely to be rare, expensive, inconvenient to attend, and of uneven quality, so, in fact, the script stands for the play in the vast majority of learning situations. This long-standing condition has recently been complicated by trends toward a loosening relationship of script to performance which has seen an important segment of the contemporary theater experimenting with the creation of works through group improvisation. When scripts are published for such pieces, as is now the case with two of the outstanding works so created, *The Serpent* by the Open Theatre and *Paradise Now* by the Living Theatre, these scripts may not accurately describe any single performance—even of the originating group. Jean-Claude van Itallie in the introduction to *The Serpent* urges "When other acting groups want to perform *The Serpent* I hope that they will use the words and movement only as a skeleton on which they will put their own flesh."[1] No one will complain much if van Itallie offers such freedom with his own works, but lately many theater groups, especially in university and experimental situations, are proceeding as though they had read such an instruction for the production of the Greek and English classics. Thus a performance of *Oedipus* or *Hamlet* may turn out to resemble the text by Sophocles or Shakespeare only in general story line. In both cases questions arise as to correctness of interpretation (even as to whether this judgment has any relevance), the value of the performance, and the status of the literary artifact—the script—which passes through time and space some record of a play called *Hamlet* or *Paradise Now*.

In order to place this problem in the proper perspective, a few words, in necessarily summary fashion, must be said on the medium of drama. At its simplest the medium in which a play exists is comprised by two or more men in a particular space interacting through and with time. This provides the basis of drama in action and constitutes the ontological place of the play. It is insufficient to discriminate drama as the art of the speaker, for both poetry and narrative depend upon the sense of a speaker even though the lines never need be read aloud or imagined as read aloud. Drama is the art of *several* speakers interacting with one another and with the concrete situation in which they find themselves—a situation which is present, not described.[2] The actions undertaken by these men (requesting, denying, explaining, and so forth) are most often carried on through words. For the playwright, unlike the poet, however, these words are determined by a real physical context, where the players are, for example, surrounded, overheard, or in confrontation. Using the roughly 1200 square feet of the Globe stage, Shakespeare brings two apprehensive sentries into confrontation at twelve o'clock of a bitter cold night *(Hamlet*, I. i). One hundred seventy lines later with a flourish of trumpets he fills this same space with gaily clad courtiers for a state occasion, then, as the Court exits, the contrasting emptiness of this large stage emphasizes the isolation the Prince speaks of in his first soliloquy *(Hamlet*, I. ii). Using the stage and the players in more complex arrangements, Shakespeare produces, for example, the scene in which Malvolio is prompted to fantasies of grandeur while those he names overhear him from their hiding place in the box tree— behind the stage pillars?—*(Twelfth Night*, II. v).

Other things being equal, the better developed and more expressive the language the better the play, but the play as play does not depend upon merely verbal skill, and merely verbal skill will not suffice to make it work. The point is, however, that the best drama by the richness of its situations can create the opportunity—or, better, the necessity—for the greatest literary values

[1] *The Serpent:* A Ceremony Written by Jean-Claude van Itallie in Collaboration with The Open Theatre under the Direction of Joseph Chaikin (New York, 1969), p. xi. See also *Paradise Now:* Collective Creation of The Living Theatre Written down by Judith Malina and Julian Beck (New York, 1971). These plays, based on Genesis and various ritual systems, may be compared with a similarly inspired exercise on *Hamlet* by Joseph Papp. See footnote 6 below.

[2] The medium is not violated if opposing voices are not at every moment present to each other. A soliloquy can be very much an interaction in a concrete situation, as is Hamlet's reaction to his recently departed mother and uncle (I. ii. 129-59) or Macbeth's reaction to the felt presence of Duncan in his banquet chamber (I. vii. 1-28). All Shakespeare citations are to *The Complete Pelican Shakespeare*, ed. Harbage (Baltimore, 1969).

in the speeches which carry the action forward. This may be best demonstrated in *Macbeth*, I. vii where one of the infrequent original stage directions indicates the dramatic design of the action. ("Hautboys. Torches. Enter a Sewer, and divers Servants with dishes and service over the stage. Then enter Macbeth.") Assuming only the minimal features agreed to belong to the Elizabethan stage, a pair of entrances and a few costumed extras, a situation is created which charges the space onto which the actor playing Macbeth enters with a sense of the ongoing banquet located physically and temporally for us by the exit of the servants. Thanks to this silent business the situation needs no description and Macbeth's struggle may begin at its heights with his first words, "If it were done when 'tis done," and develop in a speech rich to overflowing with images and allusions including the naked new-born babe which inspired Cleanth Brooks' well known essay on the imagery of the play.[3] These features are a development of the dramatic medium—the stage with its entrances and exits—allowing Macbeth to be alone for a moment nearby the banquet, then, shortly, to be confronted, guilty in his solitude, by his anxious wife whose comment "He has almost supped. Why have you left the chamber?" (I. vii. 29) snaps us back to the presence established by the crossover of the servants at the beginning of the scene. Her remark also propels the action ahead to the hard decision hammered out in the dialogue of the balance of the scene, always with the physical sense of the banqueting Duncan pressing upon the language, even probably suggesting the images of drink and drunkeness with which Lady Macbeth taunts her recalcitrant thane ("Was the hope drunk . . ." I. vii. 35-38).

The point I would stress for the student is that the scene and its speeches are created out of the possibilities provided by a stage and actors. This is the medium which supplies, for example, the spacial and temporal context which puts such desperate weight on the verbs in "If it were done when 'tis done" and provides trenchancy to the antanaclasis which places the meaning "finished" over against "performed." In any given production this scene may be performed well or badly, but it is in the possibility of performance where this work of art has its true existence, not in the possibility of a solitary reading from the printed page.

Shakespeare teachers will be aware that *Macbeth*, I. vii fits the argument perhaps too readily, is too easy to imagine on a modern Ibsenite stage. The student will need some help moving from this to the slightly different Renaissance sense of performance which included a lively taste for pageantry, debate, and emblematic presentations all of which may seem a betrayal of the medium to a modern director but which, in keeping with medieval traditions, some ambiguous but deep felt notions of *ut pictura poesis,* and a generally much less restrictive sense of what was or was not "a play," seemed very much the materials of the stage to Elizabethans.

The student should be brought to understand precisely the nature of his text in relation to the play for which it stands; briefly that the text preserves the words with which dramatic actions are carried out, though obviously it does not preserve the actions themselves. With the dialogue and a few important

---

[3] The Naked Babe and the Cloak of Manliness," in Brooks' *The Well Wrought Urn* (New York, 1947).

stage directions, however, it is usually possible to recreate the physical situation which brought forth the given words. Despite the examples of scripts, such as that for *The Serpent,* being set down after improvisations, most scripts are still composed before any physical realization of the actions carried in the dialogue has taken place; however, they are composed with such physical realization in mind. Thus a script bears a closer resemblance to an architect's plan than it does to a poem, which is complete in itself on the page. The plan, which may incidentally have some artistic value, really exists only as a diagram for a work partly in another medium (the plan has the same space—scaled down—as the building but does not have the depth, or the various materials with their capacities for sheltering, bearing weight, etc.). Clearly the analogy must not be forced too far, yet its real cogency is sometimes obscured by the following facts. Dialogue, the words of the play, by its very nature forms a large part of drama allowing a script to be more "like" the finished art work than the marks on paper which comprise an architect's plan or a musician's score. This fact is complemented by the fact that most people whether they are familiar with the dramatic medium or not have no trouble reading the words of a play, whereas the plan or the score can be "read" only by persons thoroughly familiar with their medium and who would not take the plan or score to be the work of art itself. In all three cases (of script, plan, and score) anyone sophisticated in the art knows that these are really quite abstract schemata requiring a knowledge of the medium—and frequently of the style—in which they are to be executed for either composition or satisfactory appreciation. Part of teaching Shakespeare consists in conveying the abstract nature of the text as a representation of a work of art, demonstrating that there are pauses, moves, discoveries and so forth which are vital to understanding the play but which are frequently not specifically set forth in the lines. Indeed, students frequently have difficulty obtaining any real enjoyment from playscripts until they are given some insight into what a performance of the script would be like, a difficulty which they experience again when they turn to any drama such as the Oriental which is based upon different conventions of staging.

The student's comfort with the notion of Shakespeare's work as drama is frequently upset by two popular confusions about the function of the actor, confusions which are particularly rife in Shakespeare criticism because theater history records so very many different performances of the same role. These confusions are: the notion of the performer as interpreter and the corollary notion of the performer serving as a transparent medium to pass on a work of art essentially complete in the script. Despite common usage a silent reading of a poem and the production of a play are not comparable acts of "interpretation."[4] The critic is not necessary to the poem and does not add anything to it except in the sense in which he may add understanding of obscure references or words. His "interpretation" is essentially a paraphrase giving his personal understanding of a finished work of art. The actor does not function in this way; in fact, as many symposiums have shown, actors are frequently poor interpreters in this sense. The actor and director do, of course, interpret the play just as any reader would when they are first seeking to understand it, but this is only one part

[4] See Monroe Beardsley's discussion of "interpretation," "performance," and "production." *Aesthetics* (New York, 1958), pp. 9, 56-58.

of the process of rehearsal which, it is insufficiently recognized, is a complicated process of many stages hardly consisting merely of learning to say the lines. The actor, through his work in rehearsals completes a play in a sense quite different from that in which a critic's interpretation could be said to complete a poem, and the spectator or drama critic becomes the true interpreter because he is again offering his personal understanding of a finished work of art.

The differences between the media of poetry and drama should also suggest that critic and actor are not performing comparable acts of interpretation. The ambiguities of a good poem are a deliberate part of its verbal meaning. In performing a play, however, actors obviously must choose between alternative readings of their lines, removing some of the poet's ambiguities from the playwright's arsenal. When a poem is read aloud choices must also be made, but this does not have the same effect as the complete contextualization provided by set, costume, and staging. That drama still retains rich if different grounds for ambiguity has been apparent recently in the Theatre of the Absurd. Since lines and actions are actually performed, not merely described, it is clear what the characters are doing while at the same time the greatest ambiguity surrounds the meaning of these acts, as is frequently the case in Harold Pinter's works.

In the face of inept or perverse productions the sensitive reader is drawn to an ontology of drama which removes the play itself from the physical stage and allows the actors only the function of interpreters or, perhaps more insidiously, communicators of a work which is preserved in its purity somewhere else—an evasion which as I hope to show—is unnecessary. A classic statement of the position which sees the performer as transparent medium may be found in a recent article by James K. Feibleman, where he views the actor as the necessary but ideally neutral agent who should pass on to the audience without additions or distortions a work of art contained somehow in the script, as a good telephone connection passes on a message without introducing any "information" of its own.[5] But in what sense is any artistic medium really transparent? Oil paint has a quality different from that of water color, and John Gielgud has a quality different from that of Marlon Brando. The nature of oil paint does not distort the work of art in the sense of imposing its nature between the idea of the artist and the vision of the spectator nor does a particular actor distort a play simply by his nature as an actor: as a living person with his own peculiar voice and physique. The performer may *seem* transparent because he has in reality always been an integral part of the dramatic work of art—it does not exist without him.

The fact that different performers can take the same role would also seem to suggest transparency, yet when Garrick, Macready, Irving, and Bernhardt played Hamlet they lent to the role a very tangible mark of their own spirit. Thus although to a limited degree interchangeable, the performer is hardly transparent, and once the Prince was cast as, say, Irving, the tightening logic of progressing rehearsals would demand that each aspect of each portrayal become

---

[5] "On the Metaphysics of the Performing Arts," *Journal of Aesthetics and Art Criticism*, XXVIII (1970), 295-99. In the same issue (p. 383) Hilde Hein endorses the view of the performer as transparent medium though this is outside the principal content of her article, "Performance as an Aesthetic Category."

more set, less transparent and general. The realization of this fact allows the student a better sense of what the legendary actors like Garrick, so intimately connected with Shakespeare's name, may actually have contributed.

The confusion is even thicker in the presence of several productions of one script. Although there is an obvious appeal to the position which states that each production of *Hamlet*—indeed, each performance—is a different play. (Consider Barrymore's *Hamlet* with Robert Edmond Jones' sets, and Gielgud's *Hamlet* with Mielziner's sets.) still people have historically wanted to recognize both Barrymore and Geilgud as doing productions of the same work and to say that some productions are in whole or part "wrong." The obvious first ground of unity in these different productions lies in the integrity of the words and actions: have the lines been spoken as written and, for example, is Hamlet fatally wounded in a duel with Laertes? Some latitude is proper since scripts are rarely memorized letter perfect and long scripts like *Hamlet* are frequently played with cuts, even at the Globe. Some stage directions too may be altered with impecunity, especially such interpretive and directorial comments as Shaw and O'Neill frequently introduce (essentially a novelistic device). Yet within reasonable limits it should be possible to recognize the text as intact and the concatenation of events as the same.

This allows for a class of productions best called adaptations, into which the experimental *Hamlets* of Joseph Papp and Charles Marowitz as well as the many recent improvisatory versions of the classics would fall, where lines and/ or events are more or less radically altered.[6] It is quite possible to have a good production of an adaptation and a poor production of the original play. However, since such an adaptation is essentially a modern play based on an older text it can neither be blamed for its deviations nor praised for revivifying the older work.

As in all other works of art there is a depth to great drama which would be expected to be present in a production in addition to a correct rendition of the lines and actions. Such a production will sound the heart of the play by quickening the interactions envisioned by the playwright with a clarity, logic, truth, and passion so that when Hamlet cries,"Now could I drink hot blood" (III. ii. 375) he is not merely speaking louder—or softer—than before but as moved by the actions and words of the others. This will be a production in which all have found in the circumstances of the play and the resources of their own humanity the richest life with which to embody the author's plan. This embodiment will include full use of space and movement and the richest vocal production of the devices of speech the author set out.

If good and accurate performances of the same play may differ considerably, the playwright must obviously be willing to forego the direct control over the medium exercised by the painter or the more precise instructions of a composer or choreographer. Yet many great artists have found satisfaction in their demonstrated skill for creating just those situations and lines which will evoke the richest responses in their performers while leaving to these professionals the freedom to respond as their intuition and depth of feeling dictate. In their very different styles, both Shakespeare and Strindberg have proved their skill for

---

[6] See *William Shakespeare's "Naked" Hamlet: A Production Handbook* by *Joseph Papp* (New York, 1969). A brief description and three pictures of Charles Marowitz' *Hamlet* may be found in his "Notes on the Theatre of Cruelty," *Tulane Drama Review*, XI (1966), 157-59.

6

working through the human capacities of the performer to the lively image no one can achieve without him, the image that is specifically dramatic.

Yet the allowable variance has limits, and it should be possible to designate a performance as incorrect even where all the words and events of the script are present. Such a judgment would be based upon a logic of actions, viewed, of course, with the realization that this is not a preordained mold but an improvisational sense which develops with the developing performance. Thus any production in which it seemed illogical (not improbable) that the lines and events should actually follow from what went before could be called incorrect, a judgment which might well have been passed on a recent university production of *Hamlet* displaying the Prince as a petulant adolescent. Though the interpretation was reasonably sincere for the actor involved, most people sensed it as wrong, since it was apparent that if anyone had behaved the way this Hamlet did, the other characters would hardly have responded with the words and sentiments actually uttered: Shakespeare's words as passed on in the script. Hamlet's soliloquies became a petty whine, yet the human response one senses as appropriate to the situation presented and the words which express it is of a far more noble emotion.

Though quality is not the basic issue here it should be noted that the incorrect production (not the adaptation which, as stated above, is essentially a different play) would probably be a bad production due to the confusions of its breakdowns in logic. Imaginative sets and one or more exciting performances might buoy up parts of the production and, considering the rare perfection of this difficult composite art, allow for a memorable evening in the theater, but overall it would be a failure. On the other hand, a perfectly correct production might be dull if the performers' involvement remained shallow, just the reaction of one prominent Shakespeare scholar and editor to a recent scrupulously "accurate" *Troilus and Cressida*.[7]

Given the limited exposure to Shakespeare most students are allowed—even those who devote a term or a year to such study—only a little of all this can be effectively conveyed. It is probably futile to attempt instruction in acting, drama appreciation, *and* the complexities of even a selected number of the plays. Most knowledgeable teachers will be offering their students excellent explication of the texts and may only want to add, if they do not do so already, an emphasis on the manner in which the values perceivable on the page and commonly called "literary" grow out of a basic dramatic situation contrived in terms of a stage and actors. The example from *Macbeth* above suggests one way in which this might be done. Further, perhaps just a receptive attitude toward Shakespearean performances may be the most effective device, an attitude neither reverential nor scornful but one which acknowledges the excitement of different productions of the one text the class has read while encouraging the student to demand that any given performance make itself as clear and reasonable to him as the acknowledged complexities of the material allow—in short, that the performance bring the abstract script to something he can recognize as life, not false contrivance.

A clumsy production, just because it is a production, does not necessarily

---

[7] See Kenneth Muir's notes on the First World Shakespeare Congress at Vancouver. "Professor Stamm, moreover . . . was so anxious to be true to the text, so unwilling to *impose* an interpretation, that the scenes were flat, static, and uninteresting." *SQ,* XXIII (1972), 137.

give us much true drama, and the silent reader may imaginatively grasp a good deal of the theatricality of the play. However, where the production and the reading fail, they may fail for a similar reason. Especially in Shakespeare and authors commonly regarded as "literary," this reason is frequently a failure to create real interaction among the actors. The actors take the stage and read their lines in the proper order but they do not talk to or listen to those playing the other parts: nothing really happens. The production is monolithic and literary precisely in the way a silent reading might be, where a conventional and surface notion of the "literary" obscures that deeper and more inclusive sense which adds to the meaning of the words their meaning as spoken by and to specific characters in a specific context of actions. The mere *presence* of people or objects on stages goes very little ways toward making drama as, for example, the bed which has become a prominent prop in post freudian productions of *Hamlet* remains literary in its symbolic function until it plays a part as an object of a certain shape and size in the logic of the stage space and in the real use which the actors make of it. Insensitivity to the meaning of the dramatic medium—in this case space and movement—can make the overprominent use of such a symbolic prop as offensive as the overprominent rhyme in a didactic poem.

Many students saw either the stage or film versions of Peter Brook's vivid yet flawed *King Lear*. Maynard Mack's comments on this and other recent experiments with the play provide an example of how even one of our most astute critics can mislead the student as to precisely what they may get out of Shakespeare in the theater.[8] Mack, who confesses to three decades of personal experience with Shakespeare in the theater, is well aware of Lamb's arguments for keeping Shakespeare out of the theater and Granville-Barker's for putting him back. Nevertheless, his criticisms in this section of the book are ultimately based on a notion of each of the productions as reproductions of an independently existing original, the script or "text." Productions are criticized for taking their errant ways "in preference to the author's text" (p. 40), or aside from "the play that Shakespeare wrote" (p. 38). In Herbert Blau's *King Lear*, "Shakespeare's text is left without a function" (p. 36). On the next page, Blau's production notions are held up against "Shakespeare's text" and *"the play itself"* (p. 37, italics mine). In short, the script, or text, for Mack as for Feibleman, becomes the work of art, *the play itself*, and, while Mack obviously does not take the play to be literally the type on the paper, the play is being taken as in the script in the same way the poem is in the book, an analogy which denies the basic nature of the dramatic medium.[9]

The model of an already existing work of art which it is the producer's job to transmit unblemished to an audience—the notion of the transparent medium or the perfect telephone connection which we met above with Feibleman—is suggested by Mack's doubt concerning the Brook and Blau productions

---

[8] *King Lear in Our Time* (Berkeley, 1972), pp. 25-41. Further citations of this book appear in parentheses following the passage.

[9] It should be noted that "text" has certain connotations which "script" does not, for although the two may be synonymous, "text" may also refer to the verbal part of the performed play. However, it is quite a different thing to say that a printer or editor has distorted Shakespeare's text than it is to say that some director has distorted it.

"whether it is Shakespeare's play that *is communicated* by these means" (p. 28, italics mine). A production does not communicate a play. It offers one or more specific performances of that play which, in comparison to other productions or performances (including, if the reader is familiar enough with the dramatic medium, an imaginary performance), may be taken as more or less fully realized and more or less correct in terms of the logic of the developing scene.

Lamb, who really loved both the theater and Shakespeare, was to some extent right in his scepticism about *King Lear* on stage, but this was due to the practical limitations of certain theaters—especially those of the nineteenth century—not to the general nature of the theater as medium. Surely there have been inept productions of this play, and Mack is probably right in finding fault with Charles Laughton's "funny old Father Christmas in a white nightgown, mild and chubby," or Peter Brook's 1962 production in which Lear and his knights destroy Goneril's dining hall in an unjustifiable attempt to rationalize this daughter's casting out of her old father (p. 30). Actually, however, much of the difficulty with the play *King Lear* lies not in the perversity of producers, directors, and actors but in the complexity of Shakespeare's concept, and Mack could, if he had wished, have offered a list of the misreadings made by the critics which would be fully as intimidating as the catalogue of mistaken productions.

If the script is not the work of art itself yet various productions may be said to be incorrect, what place does the written text have in relation to the fully realized drama? Although neither the Quarto nor the Folio texts of *King Lear* —nor any editorial revisions of them—may be said to be "the play itself," they are all we have of Shakespeare's instructions for that play. If the speculation is correct that Shakespeare directed the performances of his plays and if we had transcripts of his remarks in so doing we would obviously have a more complete script. We do, however, have a record of a great deal of the play in having the complete dialogue plus a few important stage directions, and this is, after all, all we have of most plays, including those of our contemporaries.[10] This is probably just as it should be for, as mentioned above, the nature of the playwright's basic material, the actors, is such that they seem to create their performances best when they concretize the specifics of the playwright's situations and the sounds of his words out of their own physical and mental realities. It is in the possibility of these physical realizations that "the play itself" lies. Various productions of *King Lear* (by Macready, Gielgud, Blau, and Brook, for example) give us some idea of what these physical possibilities are. We would not have comprehended the play and Shakespeare would not have written the play without stages and actors to demonstrate the nature of the medium. When we have seen a production we can always return to the script to see if the impression of the dramatic situation we get from reading the dialogue matches the realization we have just seen, but we do this as one would consult a set of directions to see if they have been fully and correctly—even, perhaps, gloriously—carried out, not in the sense in which we return to the Van Gogh original to see if the reproduction we purchased is faithful.

[10] An interesting exception exists in the elaborate "model books" which Brecht provided for some of his plays. See John Willet, ed. *Brecht on Theatre* (New York, 1964), pp. 211-25.

We have progressed to this point on the assumption that Mack was discussing productions of Shakespeare's plays. This, however, is not so in all cases, and where it is not so clarification of just what the object is that he is criticizing may throw some light on that criticism. First, we allowed above for a class of *adaptations*, plays based on another play, perhaps using most of the situation and dialogue of the original but deviating from this enough so that it is in effect a different play. The adaptation may be better or worse than the original— as *King Lear* was better than *King Leir*, and Nahum Tate's *King Lear* was worse than Shakespeare's—but it cannot be condemned for "distorting" an original which it is—perhaps mistakenly—not trying to follow. Clearly Mack is criticizing an adaptation when he blames Charles Marowitz for "directorial reductiveness" (p. 40) in his experimental "collage" *Hamlet*. The case of the Peter Brook-Paul Scofield *King Lear* discussed by Mack is more complex. The fact that "Brook cut Cornwall's servants and their commiseration of Gloucester's fate" (p. 39) together with the other alterations that director made here and there would be enough to put this production technically into the class of adapations, and perhaps that would be an interesting basis on which to deal with it. However, it seems close enough to the original situation and dialogue to be taken as an incorrect production of *King Lear*. If, in a given production, Lear and his retinue are so riotous as to tear apart the dining room of a castle, as they do in the Brook production, yet at a later moment the owner of that castle, Albany, implies he never knew of such riots as he does in Shakespeare's text (I. iv. 264-65), we are coping with an illogical and hence incorrect production. The student truly alive to the medium should be able to recognize such a flaw in a production while at the same time perhaps acknowledging some of the dramatic values that Brook was able to bring out in other scenes.

Much of what Mack has to say about Herbert Blau's 1961 *King Lear* is not based on a production of any kind but upon what Blau *wrote* about his production. The problem here is that the director, Herbert Blau, is playing the critic's game and playing it badly. As Maynard Mack acknowledges (p. 36), much that Blau talked about in his article may not have been discernible in his production.[11] In any case the production is clearly separate from the director's remarks about it. However, a final irony, attaches itself to Mack's criticism of Blau's remarks in which the director imposes what Mack takes to be a Stanislavskian "sub-text" on Shakespeare's play. Blau's extensions in his article of Cordelia's "Nothing" and Lear's response "Nothing will come of nothing" (I. i. 89-90) as a thematic core around which most of the play, including Edgar's disguising and Lear's madness, can be organized is an idea much more congenial to a literary critic like G. Wilson Knight or Robert Heilman than it is to Stanislavsky whose original idea of subtext would hardly have supported the kind of nondramatic interpretations Mack is blaming the Russian director for having inspired in Herbert Blau (pp. 32-37).

We have sighted some small faults in an otherwise exemplary and highly stimulating book—only the first part of which is about performance—to warn the student through the mistakes of the master that this is muddy ground. No

---

[11] The article by Herbert Blau on which much of Mack's criticism is based is "A Subtext Based on Nothing," *Tulane Drama Review*, VIII (1963), 122-32.

10

play, certainly not *King Lear,* may be thought of as fully contained in any *one* production, yet in production we realize as we could not otherwise the dramatic situations which inspire and support all the most subtle values conveyed in the written dialogue. Sometimes even deeply flawed productions may, in a scene, a character, a use of the stage, cast important light on matters ignored in the study. Above all, however, the student should be cautioned to let the performance speak directly to him and to avoid that peculiar form of meta-art: the director's statements about what his play means.

The approach encouraged in these few pages is hardly a new one. Harley Granville-Barker and John Russell Brown, among many others, have maintained a roughly similar stance, but especially as we confront the problem of multiple productions without the necessity of positing each of these as equally valuable or correct, it may offer to teachers, students, and critics a theory with which to take up some of the provocative questions raised by Norman Rabkin in his World Shakespeare Congress paper, "Meaning and Shakespeare":

> Should it not have disturbed critics interested in hypostatizing meaning that no two critics of any play really agree with one another in their formulations, that no two performances reflect identical interpretations or produce uniform responses in their audiences, that all of us return to plays we know intimately to discover that we respond to them in entirely new ways? Is not the disagreement about works of art as significant a fact for the critic as the interpretation he favors? Might a fruitful criticism not begin and end there as validly as it now does with reduction to thematic descriptions of unity?[12]

Scripts are the common medium through which students and teachers share an idea of the play. In most cases the script exists before any production is done and frequently outlasts in its compact integrity the cumbersome and ephemeral performances of it. It is, however, not "the play itself," and not a complete work of art which must be "reproduced" or "communicated." Even its primacy is delusive, for the medium, the possibility of production, must exist before the directions for its use can be composed. Yet the existence of this physical medium with its potential for creating the most complex contexts of speech inspires, even though it does not always fulfill, many extremely subtle literary values both in works for the stage and, by extension, much non-dramatic literature, where the notions of character, tone, scene, etc. are utilized. The consolations of this philosophy point in two directions. One liberates the performance from fault for simply being itself: for not being a transparent medium for conveying a work of art which exists elsewhere. The other liberates the scholar from accepting every aberrant production of a given play simply because it is a production. Teachers and students *can* detect in the text dramatic values which a performance may miss or mistake. Freeing the drama to be bad also frees it for excellence as a separate, responsible, and vital medium whose words and some directions are preserved in the script.

University of Maryland

---

[12] *Shakespeare 1971,* ed. Clifford Leech and J. M. R. Margeson (Toronto, 1972), p. 100.

SHAKESPEARE IMAGINES A THEATER*

STEPHEN ORGEL
English, Johns Hopkins

This essay makes some very speculative observations about the Renaissance's way of conceiving theater, and puts together for comparison and analysis examples that are rarely considered relevant to each other: architectural models, an emblematic frontispiece, eyewitness sketches, Shakespearean scenes. In all these cases, I am interested both in how the stage is imagined to represent its action and in how that action is to be perceived, that is, its relation to an audience.

I

First let us look at three Renaissance artists imagining theaters. In 1545 the Italian architect Sebastiano Serlio devised prototype stage sets for the three traditional kinds of drama: the tragic, the comic, and the satiric or pastoral. These are architectural models designed to be employed in the theater of a noble house in the neo-classic style. Serlio is adapting Vitruvius to the uses of the Italian Renaissance; Vitruvius has a chapter on public theaters, but Serlio assumes that a great house will include a theater of its own. The tragic setting, in Figure 1, consists of palaces and temples, aristocratic and public buildings, and monuments. Its perspective is open, with a triumphal arch at its apex, and beyond the arch a forum of architectural hieroglyphs: pyramid, obelisk, the mysterious embodiments of ancient wisdom. Figure 2, the comic setting, in contrast, consists of middle-class architecture: Serlio says these are merchants' houses, and they clearly belong to a Renaissance Italian cityscape. A shop is visible halfway back on the left, and the perspective is closed by the façade of a Renaissance church with its medieval tower, partly decayed, the only visible link with a monumental past. In the right

* This was first delivered at the International Shakespeare Association Congress, Stratford, 1981. An earlier version of the present essay appears in the proceedings of the Congress (Muir 1983).

Poetics Today, Vol. 5:3 (1984) 549—561

Figure 1. The Tragic Scene, from Sebastiano Serlio, *Architettura*, 1545.

foreground Serlio has placed a brothel, inscribed with the name
Rufia, presumably the madam. No such character figures in any play
of Plautus or Terence; Rufia is in fact not a proper name at all, but
the Italian comedy's generic term for a loose woman (cognate with
ruffian) — Serlio's comedy, if he has one in mind, is modern. The
satiric or pastoral scene, in Figure 3, consists of rustic buildings,
trees, and a mass of birds filling what is visible of the sky. Its huts are
strictly utilitarian, in no recognizable architectural style, and are
visibly overwhelmed by the surrounding nature. This setting makes
no temporal assumptions at all: it is a world that has always been
with us. But, also, its action takes place somewhere altogether
different, in the woods, in nature, without the comforting order
imposed by architectural façades, and barely controlled by symmetry.

For Serlio, then, the tragic is urban, noble, ancient, open, and
mysterious; the comic urban, middle-class, modern, closed, and
rational; the pastoral rustic, humble, timeless, and natural or wild. I
shall return to these prototypes, but here I want to direct our
attention to the fact that the kinds of drama are, for Serlio, inter-
nally consistent and mutually exclusive, both topographically and
chronologically.

14

Figure 2. Serlio, The Comic Scene.

Let us now turn to another Renaissance artist, this time imagining a real play on stage. In 1595 Henry Peacham (or more probably somebody else) did the drawing in Figure 4 of a scene from *Titus Andronicus*. In the center Queen Tamora pleads with Titus for the life of her sons, who kneel on the right, guarded by Aaron the Moor. On the left, two soldiers stand armed with pikes. The stage itself is represented quite schematically — there is simply a line for the front, and no indication of a back façade — but the costumes and properties have been quite vividly rendered, though of course there is no way of knowing whether they are being imagined by Peacham or remembered from a performance. Titus is in Roman dress and the queen is in some sort of generalized royal dress, certainly not either Roman or Elizabethan. The Moor and his prisoners are in simple costumes that might be either Roman or contemporary: the shorts could be either classical bases (military skirts) or Elizabethan puff-pants, the shirt-sleeves of the Moor and the son on the right look Elizabethan, but the son on the left wears the same sort of sash as Titus, and that is clearly intended to be Roman. There is, however, no ambiguity about the two soldiers: they are in full Elizabethan military outfits. Obviously what is important here is not any sense

15

Figure 3. Serlio, The Satiric or Pastoral Scene.

of historical accuracy, or even of consistency, but that the costume be an index to every character's role. Roman general, medieval queen, Elizabethan guardsmen are grouped together in an integral though anachronistic stage picture. If we recall the temporal exclusiveness of Serlio's prototype stages, we shall see that Peacham is expressing a significantly different idea of what and how the theater *represents*.

Now let us look at a Jacobean example, the frontispiece to what is arguably the most far-reaching conception of theater the English Renaissance produced. Figure 5 is the title-page to the Jonson folio of 1616, engraved by William Hole, clearly to Jonson's specifications. It has the form of a triumphal arch. On either side of a central cartouche stand the figures of Tragedy and Comedy; below them are two scenes illustrating the ancient sources of drama, on the left of the *plaustrum*, or cart of Thespis, with the sacrificial goat, the tragedian's prize, tethered to it, on the right a small amphitheater, labeled in Latin *visorium*, with a choric dance in progress. Above Tragedy and Comedy the third of the ancient genres, the satiric or pastoral, is anatomized: on the left a satyr plays a Pan's pipe of seven reeds, on the right a shepherd plays a shaum. Between them is a Roman theater, and above that, at the very top of the arch, stands

16

Figure 4. Henry Peacham (?), a scene from *Titus Andronicus*, 1595 (Harley Papers, Longleat).

Figure 5. William Hole, title page to *The Workes of Benjamin Jonson*, 1616.

17

Tragicomedy, flanked by the tiny figures of Bacchus on the left and Apollo on the right, the two patrons of ancient theater. Jonson's title-page, with characteristic gravity, presents nothing so transient and particular as a scene from a play. It defines the drama in relation to its history and its kinds, and offers a set of generic possibilities.

II

What these very different conceptions of theater appear to have in common is their failure to include an audience. And yet, if we look deeper, their sense of an audience may in fact be taken as a crucial, and indeed a defining, feature and the element that makes them enlightening in relation to Shakespeare. I shall return to these visualizations, but I wish now to consider, briefly, selectively, and very speculatively, Shakespeare conceiving his own theater.

Near the beginning of his career, Shakespeare wrote a play with the problematic of theater at its center, *The Taming of the Shrew*. The drunken Christopher Sly is deceived by a mischievous lord into believing he is an amnesiac aristocrat. He is entertained, in the fashion appropriate to noble houses, with an Italian comedy called *The Taming of the Shrew*. But the play soon bores him, and he sums up his reaction with what turn out to be his final words: " 'Tis a very excellent piece of work . . . would 'twere done."

By dismissing the comedy, however, Sly has annihilated himself. *The Taming of the Shrew* becomes the play, its world expands and fills the stage, and neither Sly nor the mischievous lord is heard of again.[1] It is the play that has dismissed its audience, declaring its autonomy not only of Sly but of its patron, the trifling lord, as well — and of course Shakespeare's drama is not called *The Gulling of Christopher Sly*: it declares its subject to be *The Taming of the Shrew*. But where are we in all this? Clearly not in agreement with Sly, or else the play would not continue. What Shakespeare has done here is to imagine an ideal audience, and then, by a piece of theatrical sleight of hand, turn us into it.

" 'Tis a very excellent piece of work . . . would 'twere done." Plays within Shakespeare plays generally displease their audiences, and always end badly. Hamlet's mousetrap is designed to be offensive; *Pyramus and Thisbe* constitutes a running battle between play and spectators; Cleopatra proleptically disdains her own drama — "Antony/Shall be brought drunken forth, and I shall see/Some squeaking Cleopatra boy my greatness/'I th'posture of a whore" — and disdains its audience as well, "Mechanic slaves/With greasy aprons, rules and hammers"; and Hamlet the playwright and critic

---

1. H. J. Oliver (1982:13–29, 40–43) conclusively refutes the notion that a final scene involving Sly properly belongs in our text of the play and is preserved in the anonymous *Taming of a Shrew*.

Figure 6. Arend van Buchel after Johannes de Witt, the Swan Theater, London, c. 1595 (Univ. of Utrecht Library).

scorns the groundlings to their faces, half the Globe's paying customers. In all these instances, an audience is invented that is conceived to be invidious to the success of the play, and then the uncomprehending or hostile spectators are banished, or the inept or threatening performance is cancelled. This is more than a parodic exorcism or an expression of the playwright's anxieties. It is a way of imagining and defining the *real* audience, on whose deep complicity the success of the drama depends.

Where is the audience in the theater Shakespeare imagines? Serlio and Peacham seem to imagine no audience at all: their visions of theater are confined to the stage. Jonson imagines an audience, but it seems to be an audience of readers for the new classic that his *Works* comprise. Johannes de Witt's drawing of the Swan Theater in 1595 (Figure 6) provides a striking embodiment of the theater of Shakespeare's *Shrew*: the play takes place in an empty playhouse before an imaginary audience; the only visible spectators appear in the gallery of the stage.

19

I want to focus on a scene in which Shakespeare's conception of his audience is particularly problematical, the Dover Cliff scene in *King Lear*. Edgar invents a setting and an imaginary *agon* for Gloucester to perform. It is a scene bewildering in its confusion of false and true, in which the real and the imaginary are indistinguishable. There is nothing in what Edgar says as the scene opens to indicate that his account of the ascent to the cliff and the prospect from it are not the scene's realities; we know about setting and action in this theater by what we are told, and if what Edgar describes were the truth, his lines would read no differently. This perception has led recent criticism to argue that the audience is deceived, just as Gloucester is, into believing that he is in fact being brought to the edge of Dover Cliff, and that we are enlightened only through Edgar's revelation, in an aside, that the setting is all his invention. This theory was first proposed in 1958 by Harry Levin (1976:162–186); it has recently been repeated by James Black (1980:39), and before it becomes doctrine I want to object to it. I want to argue that in fact exactly the opposite is true: that we know from the very beginning of the scene that we are being lied to, and that we are accomplices in the lies.

Levin's thesis takes into account only what Edgar says; it ignores what Gloucester says, and the action, and it is simplistic about the audience. Gloucester and Edgar give contradictory accounts of what is happening on stage, but it is going to be perfectly obvious from the moment of their entrance whether they are struggling to climb uphill or not: any director who tried to deceive the audience on this point would find the scene unstageable. Gloucester's is a perfectly accurate version of what the spectator sees: "Methinks the ground is even" —"Horrible steep," says Edgar. "Hark, do you hear the sea?" —"No, truly," says Gloucester. I would think that the point here is that the action is initially, deliberately, baffling. All we *know* is that Gloucester is obviously telling the truth and Edgar is obviously — on the evidence of our eyes and ears — lying. We know from the beginning, that is, that we are being lied to. Thirty-five lines into the episode Edgar finally takes us into his confidence, just at the point when the vividness and particularity of his description are tempting us to take it for truth, as Gloucester does. It is important for us to be in no doubt that these are lies; and therefore Shakespeare has Edgar confess the falsehood now, explaining it with a piece of odd double syntax: "Why I do trifle thus with his despair/ Is done to cure it." But it is the revelation that is ineffective here; we remain sufficiently convinced of the presence of heights and distances for Gloucester's otherwise baffling fall to work. That is, for the rest of the scene to make sense we must be able to imagine Gloucester on the edge of *something* — if not a physical chasm, at least an emotional one. In the quarto's laconic stage direction, "He

kneels . . . he falls," presumably swooning on the flat platform of
the stage. Since the eighteenth century, the stage convention has
gone the quarto one better and has had Gloucester kneeling on a
little step. What that stage convention says is, but surely he *does* fall.

We never play the scene for what it literally is, blind old Gloucester being duped by Edgar, like Old Gobbo deceived by *his* son for
equally mysterious reasons. We take the fall seriously, with none of
Edgar's detachment; we substitute a little fall for a great one, but we
experience the scene from Gloucester's viewpoint, which is the
viewpoint that Edgar has engineered for him. We stage the scene
effectively, so that Gloucester really can fall: we want the scene to
work. We want it to work precisely because of the extraordinary
effectiveness of Edgar's lies, which are some of the best poetry in
the play. We know them to be lies, and yet we accept them, ignoring
the evidence of our eyes, our ears, the text, just as we accept Edgar's
rationale for his lies, to cure Gloucester's despair. And then as
Gloucester wakes from his swoon, we watch Edgar produce an even
more elaborate set of lies: "Ten masts at each make not the altitude/
Which thou hast perpendicularly fell"; he saw Gloucester accompanied, he says, by a fiend, "his eyes/Were two full moons; he had a
thousand noses,/Horns whelked and waved like the enridgèd sea."
Gloucester's cure requires not the hard truths we might expect, but
outright and even outrageous lies.

They are quintessentially theatrical lies: the Dover Cliff scene is
a paradigm not simply for Shakespeare's stage, but for all theater.
It is a linguistic fact of every Western language that the word for the
imitation of an action — the classic definition of drama — is the same
as the word for the action; both are *act*. In *all* theater the imaginary
is presented as, is taken for, the real. And Edgar's curative theatrical
lies have their roots in Aristotelian catharsis: a *medical* metaphor
described the operation of theater, it purged, and thereby healed,
through pity and terror. By the same token, Gower, the storyteller
of *Pericles*, describes the fantastic legend he is recounting as a
restorative, and the old tales of *The Winter's Tale*, through the
protagonist/audience's willingness to believe in them, heal the
afflictions of his mind and his disordered state.

And, to go a logical step further, there are many places where
Shakespeare puts the audience in Leontes's or Gloucester's position,
lying to us about things we know to be true, misrepresenting action
we have seen taking place. There is, for example, for an audience no
question about whether Hermione is really dead at the end of the
trial scene: Leontes himself demands to see the bodies of his wife
and son, and orders them buried in a single grave. If Mamilius is dead,
so is Hermione. Or again, at the end of *Cymbeline*, when the play
is finally clearing up all its confusions, both Iachimo and Pisanio,
claiming to confess all, produce egregiously (and pointlessly) in-

accurate accounts of their roles in the tragic events of the play. The most blatant instance is surely the famous double time scheme of *Othello*, in which our willingness to believe, like Othello, in the plausibility of a whole sequence of events for which there is literally no time in the play's structure makes the play a serious tragedy rather than a preposterous farce.

What do such examples — examples in which we accept what we know to be untrue — imply about audiences? Obviously not that they are inattentive, but that the drama's reality is infinitely adjustable: that drama for Shakespeare does not create a world. The text itself is unstable. Let us think for a moment about the Elizabethan theatrical companies' unwillingness to see their plays in print. We try to explain this by saying that they are thereby simply protecting their interests, which are dependent on the paying spectator, not the reader; but why is it assumed that if one can read a play one will not go to see it? Italian and French acting companies believed just the opposite — that publication constituted the best advertising, that a good way to arouse interest in a new play was to make the text available; and this seems, on the face of it, more likely to be the truth — truer, that is, to the psychology of audiences. I would think that the English resistance to print goes deeper, to characteristic assumptions about the nature of theater itself: that the script is *essentially* unstable and changes as the performers decide to change it; that it is the property of the performers, not of play-wrights, audiences, or readers; that the *real* play is the performance, not the text; that to fix the text, transform it into a book, is to defeat it. I would think that the textual history of *Hamlet* or *Lear*, or that palimpsest *Macbeth*, bears this out. And when Jonson the playwright wished to assert his control over his drama, he could only do so by publishing it.

If the drama's reality is infinitely adjustable, if drama for Shakespeare does not create a world, what then does it create? What it creates, I would like to suggest, is something the Renaissance would have recognized as an *argument*. This is what critics from Horace to Castelvetro and Sidney mean when they say that mimesis is only the means of drama, not its end. Its end, they assume, is the same as the end of poetry and the other verbal arts, to persuade.

III

Let us now return to our images of the Renaissance theater. I suggest that when they offer an architectural model for the action of a play, as Serlio's stage settings do, that model in fact belies something essential to the Renaissance theater, and in certain ways to the Renaissance notion of art generally, and that is first a basic fluidity or disjunctiveness, and second the extent to which it depends for its truth upon its audience. The parts of a Renaissance play fit together

Figure 7. Inigo Jones, setting for *Artenice* (Racan), 1626
(Devonshire Collection, Chatsworth).

not like architectural structures, but like rhetorical ones; that is, they fit together only in the mind, through the assent — the complicity, really — of the spectator, listener, reader. Peacham's sketch of *Titus Andronicus* is disjunctive in this way: it persuades the viewer of the significance, position, status of its figures; it does not mime a consistent world, what it does is express an action. Its elements fit together only insofar as a viewer interprets and understands them.

The same sort of disjunctiveness will be apparent in any play in a mixed genre that uses for its stage the Serlian model. Serlio's sets look very solid and consistent, and their genres are, as we have observed, mutually exclusive. But consider Figure 7, Inigo Jones's Serlian setting for a court play called *Artenice* in 1626. This elegant drawing has more relevance to the Peacham sketch than is apparent at first glance. The play is one in which the queen is to perform, therefore Jones includes the noble classical architecture and the open perspective of the Tragic Scene; but it is also a comedy, so it includes a merchant's house with its Italian Renaissance loggia; but the queen and her ladies play shepherdesses, so it includes the rustic huts and woods of the Patoral Scene (it is heroical-comical-pastoral). What this means is not that Serlio was conceiving of a drama that was generically pure, but that Serlio's constructs were taken to be analytic, not descriptive. Even the purest of Renaissance

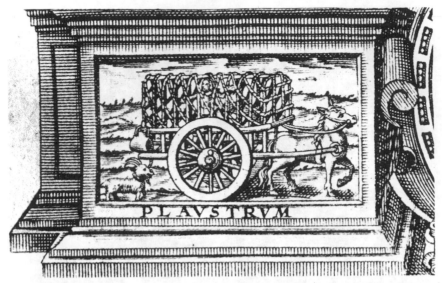

Figure 8. The cart of Thespis, from the title page of Jonson's *Workes*, 1616.

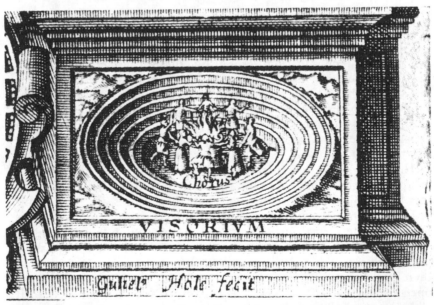

Figure 9. A classical amphitheater, from the title page of Jonson's *Workes*, 1616.

tragedies would have appeared *to an audience* to belong to a mized genre because in performance it would have included *intermezzi* between the acts, or, in England, jigs at the end. As Serlio conceived them, the genres constituted not an idea about the necessary struc-

24

ture of plays, but an idea about the potentialities of theaters to realize the classic forms. And what the models then offered to someone like Inigo Jones was just the opposite of that rigid consistency we find in them: a very fluid set of possibilities.

Finally, let us look again at the statement made by Jonson's title-page to the folio of his *Works*. The architectural model is especially powerful here, and we might expect this doctrinaire classicist to be making a programmatic assertion about the sources of his art and its relation to a classic ideal. To a certain extent the title-page does this; and the viewer participates in the enterprise in an essentially passive way: the parts of the structure, the figures, are all labeled, the effort of interpretation is minimal, and we look on as outsiders — that is, until we look closely. Let us focus on the two plinths. Figure 8 shows Thespis in his cart. He has won the sacrificial goat, the tragedian's prize; this is the founder of tragedy, a figure lost in antiquity and legend. But, in fact, if we look carefully we see that he is in Jacobean dress, a modern playwright — Jonson himself — and clearly one of us. Figure 9 is the amphitheater, labeled *visorium*. To begin with, a linguistic point: *visorium* is not the Roman word for amphitheater. It is not a Roman word at all; it exists in no classical or medieval source, but — like the *Rufia* of Serlio's Comic Scene — is a pure Renaissance coinage. And the chorus that dances within this *visorium* is, like Thespis, Jacobean. Jonson's ambivalence toward, and indeed open hostility to, his theatrical audience is notorious. The audience imagined in the folio is that learned group of understanders, the ideal spectators, who are one with him and who here both observe and enact his drama.

REFERENCES

Black, James, 1980. "*King Lear*: Art Upside-Down," *Shakespeare Survey* 33.
Levin, Harry, 1976 (1958). "The Heights and the Depths: A Scene from *King Lear*," in: *Shakespeare and the Revolution of the Times* (New York: Oxford UP).
Muir, Kenneth et al., 1983. *Shakespeare, Man of the Theater* (Newark, Del.: Univ. of Delaware Press).
Oliver, H. J., 1982. *Introduction to The Taming of the Shrew* (Oxford: The Clarendon Press).

25

THE BARE ISLAND

ANDREW GURR

When Prospero begs the audience not to spell-bind him 'in this bare island' it is not unreasonable to wonder where we are supposed to think we are. From the unique and startling shipwreck scene that set us on shore to that unique and peculiar octosyllabic Epilogue,[1] we have been on an island full of noises and magic that hurt not. At the end, after the 'Exeunt all', the courtiers still in their clothes for Claribel's wedding, the seamen dry again, and Prospero's robe, book and staff all gone, Prospero speaks his last speech bare of his trappings. Is his adjective a transferred epithet? I think not, even in the wake of all the colourful apparel that has just walked offstage. Prospero stands alone on the stage island in the middle of a sea of faces, asking for human breath to blow his sail to Naples, if he is not to be imprisoned on the island. Like Hamlet's ground, that other 'stale promontory', Prospero's stage island has lost its fresh decorations. What, in the original performances, was it bared of, though? A lot of people, certainly, some of them colourfully dressed. Prospero's own props, his magic gown and staff, must have gone too. Was the stage shorn of fabric and colour? Was it all bare boards? Were there no hangings left across the front of the tiring house and Prospero's cell? Was there no painting on the stage posts to make them look like marble as De Witt described them? It would be nice to know. For all the riches of the recent archaeological findings, the Shakespearian mise en scène, the geography of the stage island, is not so much bare as undiscovered.

We can be sure that it was an island, a three-dimensional entity. Thanks largely to the flatness of paper, until very recently the only durable form for recording performance details on, the essential three-dimensional character of the Shakespearian theatre is given too little account in modern thinking. We rely on the invention of perspective to facilitate the use of paper as a representation of the Globe's three-dimensional stage and as a result still use misleading terms like front stage and back stage. Van Eyck's invention of perspective and its ultimate exploitation on the cinema screen condition us to think, if not in two dimensions, then from the position that a two-dimensional picture of a three-dimensional scene invites. Henry Peacham drew the figures he saw on stage in 1595 in Titus Andronicus in a linear spread from 'in front'. De Witt drew his Swan in 1596 from the perspective of a cinema's projection booth. The inescapably two-dimensional form that recording on paper invites seduces us into a two-dimensional mode of thinking. De Witt's actor figures are posed not at the stage 'front' but in the centre of a circle of audience, as near as they can get to 'the middle of the yard', the central point where the Fortune contract ordered its stage to extend. The only audience De Witt's drawing depicts is

---

[1] Stephen Orgel in his Oxford edition of The Tempest notes that this Epilogue is unique in being spoken by a character in the fiction, not an actor in the play.

29

sitting where we now think is 'behind' the actors. Paper pictures are not only two-dimensional but static. They encourage us to think of humans as capable of facing only forwards, in one direction. It would help to think of Prospero's epilogue as spoken by a rotating figure, not a still.

There is a limited but highly specific value in trying to learn more about the original staging of Shakespeare's plays. Theatre is always invented for an occasion. A performance is an event, not a text. Like buildings or stage scenes in pictures, it does not belong naturally on paper.[2] Each new performance of a play that has established itself in a repertory and achieved fixity through print is a new event. The history of theatre is full of plays that died on their first performance and were resurrected successfully a generation or more later. Printed texts of playscripts work against that feature of the play in performance as a transient event or occasion. Each event, and especially each theatrical or performance event, is unique to its moment. It cannot be 'recuperated'. So the exploration of Shakespeare's original staging has to be not a story of texts, even of lost texts, but of their frames, the contexts. Since they are Shakespearian contexts, they are useful when they offer insights that other ways of recuperating the Shakespeare text cannot. So such fragments of evidence about the bare stage island that can be retrieved are worth fitting into the Shakespearian mosaic.

In this exercise what calls for the greatest care is an evaluation of the different kinds of evidence, fragmentary as it all is, and the relative weight that might be attached to one item against the often contradictory indications of the others. What follows is an attempt to give a sense of relative values to the different kinds of evidence about a number of the features that might have stood on Prospero's bare island.

The first consideration is the radically different testimonies from the different amphitheatre playhouses about their shapes. De Witt's drawing of the Swan shows a square stage and a flat

frons with two entry doors, whereas the Rose had a stage in the form of an elongated hexagon, with its *frons* on three angles. The Rose's outside diameter was about 74 feet, while the Globe's seems to have been 99 feet. The closest similarity among all the amphitheatres appears to have been not the stage area but the gallery bays. The Rose, the Globe and the Fortune all seem to have had galleries with bays of about the same size, despite the radical variation in their shapes (square at the Fortune, twenty-sided at the Globe, fourteen-sided at the Rose) and the difference in their overall dimensions. This radical variation in auditorium and stage at the playhouses of the 1590s is at odds with the demonstrable fact that until at least 1594 all the playhouses were treated by the playing companies as interchangeable. The Queen's Men in the late 1580s are recorded at one time or another as playing at every amphitheatre and every inn available to them in London. Not until the Privy Council started designating playhouses for the two approved companies after 1594 could a company expect to have a settled tenure at any playhouse.[3] The Globe and the Fortune were the first playhouses built for particular tenant companies. From this it might be expected that the amphitheatre stages all had similar configurations until 1599. That expecta-

---

[2] It is hardly necessary here to go into the long debate between printed text and performance text, Shakespeare on page and stage, Formalist 'text' against New Historicist 'context'. Harry Berger Jr has put the former case brilliantly in *Imaginary Audition: Shakespeare on Stage and Page* (University of California Press, Berkeley, 1989). The 'performance' case, which I think has more substance, has not yet been thoroughly set out. It lies somewhere between the position Louis Montrose sets out in 'New Historicisms', in *Redrawing the Boundaries: The Transformation of English and American Literary Studies*, eds. Stephen Greenblatt and Giles Gunn (University of Chicago Press, Chicago, 1988), and the position and illuminations that Bernard Beckerman offered long ago in his ur-theoretical *Shakespeare at the Globe 1599–1609* (Macmillan, New York, 1962).

[3] See Gurr, 'Three Reluctant Patrons and Early Shakespeare', *Shakespeare Quarterly*, 44 (1993), 159–74.

30

tion is rubbished by the radical differences of the Rose from its near neighbour the Swan.

The evident difference of one amphitheatre from another complicates the tendency to generalize about the original staging on the basis of internal evidence in the plays. It puts a premium on the value in evidence from stage directions of reconciling the demands in specific plays with the playhouses they were written for. This gives priority most notably to the Rose plays of the 1590s and the Globe plays of the following decade. Such a premium marginalizes the Swan, and that one piece of paper evidence from Utrecht which has ruled thinking about the stages for the last century. It also makes the question of a play's date more important. Plays written before the late 1590s were designed to be staged anywhere. Only the post-1594 plays staged at the Rose, the plays written subsequently for the Globe and the Fortune, and probably in the seventeenth century some plays written for companies settled at the Red Bull and the Cockpit and Salisbury Court hall theatres can be said with any confidence to be designed for a specific venue and its peculiar stage features.

The evidence from the Rose excavation of 1989 has the advantage over other evidence of being what you might loosely call concrete. The paper evidence of De Witt's oddly irregular dimensions in his Swan drawing, and his 'ingressus' from the yard to the galleries, marked in a theatre which we know had at least one stair turret, gives ample ground for us to doubt what we can make of the papers surviving from the time, quite apart from their two-dimensionality. The square stage on the Swan's paper has to be set against the elongated hexagon of the Rose's brick foundations. The large, round, marbled stage posts set so firmly on a line across the middle of the Swan's platform have to be compared with the Rose's small and square pile base abutting the stage 'front'. The three thousand said to cram into the Swan contrast with the two thousand now known to be able to get into the original Rose.

Should the Rose's concrete displace De Witt's paper, or should we acknowledge the likelihood of radically different designs and dimensions for the first two Southwark theatres? In their different ways, whether De Witt's paper or the Rose's brick foundations, both of them offer evidence that is two-dimensional. All the fragments, the Rose dig, the papers of De Witt, Norden, and Hollar, and the play-texts themselves, need to be reassessed in concert. It is no small task. A beginning might be made with a few of the stage features that the uncovering of the Rose foundations throws into question.

THE DISCOVERY SPACE

Two-dimensional pictures of the Shakespearian stage create more problems than they solve, not least that current version of the inner stage, the discovery space. The stage foundations for the Rose, the only recent piece of fresh evidence, give no indication about what Henslowe built for the players to use in 1587 and rebuilt in 1592. The floor plan shows that the Rose probably had a tiring-house front or *frons* with three faces, but there is little to suggest what openings stood in those faces. And a *frons* with three angled walls counters the only other tangible evidence for the Rose's neighbour the Swan of 1595, with its flat-faced two-door wall. Neither piece of evidence helps answer the most vexed question, what occupied the central part of the *frons*. Despite the absence of any central opening at all in De Witt's Swan drawing, the assumption that there was a wide central recess or discovery space has dominated all reconstructions of the *frons*, infecting calculations not only about the entry doors but about the balcony or 'above' and the stage hangings. The long life of the inner stage theory reflects the two-dimensional thinking of earlier theatre historians. Its continuing life, transformed into a long and deep curtained alcove in the centre of the *frons*, dominates thinking about staging. The need to have it has called in doubt the strong evidence that there

31

were lords' rooms over the stage, the location of which in a flat-walled *frons* would prevent the highest-paying customers from seeing any of the set-pieces uncovered in the central alcove. It has also, rather paradoxically, prevented the central opening in the *frons* from being used as an ordinary entry door and has consigned even royal and processional entrances to the flanking doors. It has been invoked as the only access big enough to be used for carrying large stage properties on and off the stage, an assumption that has allowed the two great double doors on each side of the Swan's stage to be replaced with single doors. It now operates as the fall-back position into which are pitched most of the unresolvable puzzles about routine Renaissance staging practices.

De Witt's Swan drawing shows audience sitting in all six of its balcony rooms. The familiar references about Jonson talking to lords who sat over the stage and other casual namings of 'the lords' room over the stage', wherever we put the apostrophe, suggest that De Witt was right to place spectators where they could not see the openings in the *frons*. That is the position for the gallants noted in Everard Guilpin's *Skialetheia* (1598), and at the Globe in Jonson's *Every Man Out*. Dekker mocked Jonson in *Satiromastix* for exchanging courtesies with the gallants in the lords' rooms. Later references to playgoers sitting 'over the stage' come from Dekker in 1607 and E. S. in *c*.1608.[4] Such casual references may be more reliable than stage directions. Privileged access to those rooms by means of the tiring-house back door instead of the common entry doors to the auditorium would offer an amphitheatre equivalence to the means of entry with a stool to sit on the stage that the hall playhouses offered their gallants. I think that this reading of the evidence, consistent as it is, makes a strong case for finding the lords' rooms adjacent to Juliet's central balcony room which later became the music room,[5] and so in a position that prevented the payers of the highest prices from seeing any 'discoveries'. We can speculate endlessly

about the implications of that for the price the lords paid in order to be seen better than they could see, or for the minimization of discovery scenes by the playwrights in order to prevent the lords from feeling deprived.

Some kind of space behind the stage hangings there was for 'discoveries' such as Volpone's gold at the Globe or Faustus in his study at the Rose ('This the man that in his study sits', as the prologue draws back the curtain).[6] Hangings across the *frons* concealed the king and Polonius in *Hamlet*, and later hid the body of Polonius until Hamlet uncovered it. The problems for the over-the-stage watchers in the lords' rooms of viewing what was 'discovered' would have been markedly worse at the Swan than at the Rose, where the angled *frons* might have allowed the viewers in the flanking boxes to see something of what was displayed behind the hangings. The flat plane of the Swan's tiring house front not only makes the watchers above the stage incapable of viewing any 'discovery', but omits any indication of a discovery space between the two large doors of the *frons*. What kind of *frons* the Globe had is a question that can only be answered by excavating under Anchor Terrace, which would require a radical change of policy by English Heritage and is unlikely to happen quickly.

The shape of the alcove (if that is the right word for the part of the tiring-house *frons* from which the players emerged onto the stage: the

---

[4] *Jests to Make You Merry, Non-Dramatic Works*, II.292; E. K. Chambers, *The Elizabethan Stage* II.535.

[5] For the introduction of a music room after 1608 at the Globe in order to accommodate the newly acquired Blackfriars musicians, see Richard Hosley, 'Was there a Music-Room in Shakespeare's Globe?', *Shakespeare Survey 13* (1960), p. 113.

[6] The relation between the 'discovery space' and the stage hangings does no good to the theory that the space may have been a fit-up booth or tent-like structure forward of the *frons*. In any case there would be little room for such a structure on the Rose's broad but shallow stage. This problem also damages Evert Sprinchorn's theory of a raised platform at the rear (see below, note 14).

32

word presupposes a frontal position for the audience, which inhibits thinking of the stage as the centre of a complete circle of spectators), is unclear. The hangings were variously a traverse to be drawn back (*Volpone*) or an arras to hide behind (*Hamlet*). And the space to be 'discovered'? If it was a deep walled-off room, the minimal 390 square feet of free space given the players in the Rose's tiring house would be reduced even further. Comedies required a set of hangings in front of the tiring-house wall, so that the clowns could enter by first sticking their heads through. The evidence for them doing this stretches from 1592 (Nashe) to 1639 (Glapthorne). Such entries needed nothing more than a doorway behind the hangings. Polonius needed little more. The only hint I know of that suggests a size for the discovery space is in the 1647 Folio text of *The Maid in the Mill*, written by Fletcher and Rowley for the Globe in about 1623. It has an anticipatory stage direction at the end of Act 1 which says '*Six Chaires placed at the Arras*'. They have no direct role in the following Act. Were they placed in line? If so, the space for the alcove or discovery behind the arras must have been close to twelve feet, much wider than even the double doorways of De Witt's Swan.

The evidence of Heywood's 1 *If You Know Not Me, You Know Nobody* and its royal 'state', written for the Fortune, supports Fletcher and Rowley's evidence about the Globe with its chair scene. A throne was needed at beginning and end of the play, and for Scene 12 in the middle. Was it permanently positioned on the stage platform? The 'discovery space' is needed for other scenes in the play, notably the bed in Scene 3 and the seven chairs of Scene 5. That raises the whole question of localities on stage and the realism of designated space. In use, a throne obviously designated a throne room or 'presence', and sometimes a lawcourt. If it remained as a passive presence through other scenes, we have to rein in our assumptions about realistic localities and assume that when the dialogue called for a specific locality the

audience shut out of its consciousness the obtrusive properties that did not fit the designated place. The trouble is that just as Shakespeare and other playwrights, and even the stage managers who compiled the seven extant 'plots' of players' comings and goings, often failed to mark exits for their characters they invariably failed to mark exits for their props.

There are a few indicators. One certain thing about the discovery space is that it must have been big enough not just to provide an entryway for ceremonial entrances, but also to carry on and off the largest properties. There was no other form of access to the stage platform. We might also wonder just how many properties of each kind the players had. In that there may be a hint to confirm the belief that properties were not generally left on stage throughout the play. Dekker and Middleton's 1 *The Honest Whore*, written in 1603–4 for the Fortune, like Heywood's 1 *If You Know Not Me, You Know Nobody*, calls for a table in two successive scenes, 3.3 and 4.1. The stage direction for the first runs '*Enter Bellafronte with a Lute, pen, inke and paper being placde before her*'. A table is not specified, but it is hardly likely that the stage hand would have left the writing instruments on the floor. Bellafronte sings to the lute and then starts writing. There is no opportunity for anyone to carry the table off before the next scene. But that, 4.1, opens with a stage direction '*Enter a servant setting out a table, on which he places a scull, a picture, a booke, and a Taper*', traditional devices for a malcontent scene. The writer of this stage direction clearly expected the servant to carry the table in, and for it to be a different table. The first speech in the scene is the servant's address to the table he has just set. Conceivably the writer expected an act break to intervene between one table going out and the other being brought in, but there are no other indications of act breaks in the play, and the Fortune did not use act breaks with any frequency for another decade.

33

SQUARE OR TAPERED STAGES

Even the tangible foundations of the Rose's stage offer a new uncertainty. The row of its foundation bricks, strong enough to support a five-foot high wall though not much more, presumably set the wall high enough to serve as lodging for the joists that supported the stage's planking. Such a solid brick wall would have made unnecessary the Fortune's 'Stadge to be paled in belowe with good, strong and suffi-cyent newe oken bourdes', and also the hang-ings that Heywood said the Roman theatres had around the fore-front of the stage. It was a radically different design from De Witt's Swan, where the dark objects under the stage might be seen as openings in the hangings for devils to run into the yard through the crowd. There is no sign that the Rose's stage foundations had any doorways in them to give the devils access to the yard, and no provision in the Fortune contract of any access from under the stage to the yard.

Besides the conflict of evidence between the Swan's square stage as De Witt presented it and the Rose's irregular hexagon as the archae-ologists found it lies the even larger question of where at the Rose the tiring-house *frons* was set. This has large implications not only for what size of stage each playhouse had but for the capacity of the tiring house behind it. De Witt's Swan gives central place to the stage platform, a huge nearly square space with behind it six (or five) bays of the scaffolding for the tiring house, augmented by the planar surface of the tiring-house front which makes a chord across the polygon of the inner gallery walls. Following Glynne Wickham's reconstruction based on De Witt, Richard Hosley has measured the likely space for the players inside the Swan's tiring house behind the stage front (in a 24-sided structure) at roughly 1045 square feet.[7] Even if the stage was foreshortened by a tiring-house front cutting a chord across the stage-front bays, the Rose evidently had far less space than that. The bays of its polygon were trapezoids

measuring roughly ten feet between the outer and inner walls, with the outer wall measuring sixteen feet and the inner eleven feet.[8] If its tiring-house front was angled, each of its three bays would be more or less eleven feet in length on the inner side with a door in each of the three, angled around the rear of a stage with a total width of thirty-seven feet. The tiring-house space in the three bays behind that would give a floor space of about 390 square feet. If the front ran straight, on a chord across the thirty-seven-foot width of the stage's central line, the backstage space would increase to nearly 630 square feet. This is not a great deal more than the space available for the original stage plat-form if its tiring-house front was angled to follow the three bays. Such a minute tiring-house space, not enlarged noticeably in the 1592 rebuilding, must have suffered further en-croachments too. Space would have been taken up by the stairway up to the balcony or 'above', another stair up to the third-level 'heavens' and its machinery over the stage, and most obtru-sively by the 'discovery space', the walls around the enclosure that made Faustus' study. Walls would be vital if the hangings across the centre of the tiring-house *frons* were not when opened to reveal the entire company in the process of re-costuming itself for the next scenes. Even a 'study' for Faustus as little as six feet wide would cut the tiring house's floor space by another forty or so square feet.

If it followed the larger hexagonal plan, at 475 square feet the Rose's stage area was also markedly smaller than others for which we have measurements – 1200 at the Red Lion, and only slightly less for the stage at the For-tune that replaced the Rose. Such a small stage with its even smaller tiring-house area made the Rose a peculiarly little playhouse by com-

---

[7] See 'A Postscript on the Swan', in 'The Shape of the Globe and the Interior of the Globe', *Renaissance Drama Newsletter*, 8 (Coventry, 1987), 61–78.
[8] Orrell and Gurr, 'What the Rose can tell us', *Antiquity*, 63 (1989), 421–9.

34

parison with its contemporaries. That being so, it is the more remarkable that the 1592 enlargement, increasing the auditorium space by over twenty per cent and demolishing and rebuilding the whole stage area, only negligibly increased the size of the stage platform, giving one extra foot or so from the stage's front edge to the tiring-house *frons*, and nothing to the tiring house area itself. This smallness puts a premium on the question whether the tiring-house front took a straight chord across the thirty-seven feet at the centre of the hexagon or followed the lines of the three bay walls. If it ran straight, the stage area would be reduced by half, and the tiring-house would be enlarged by the same amount. It is difficult to believe that even the thought-to-be-tall Alleyn, whose arrival at the Rose seems to have prompted Henslowe to make his enlargements, would have preferred more backstage space at the expense of a reduced scaffoldage under his stretched footing. There is no sign of any foundation for a straight tiring-house *frons*. It is almost impossible to believe that both the original and the later tiring-houses would not have to compensate for the tapers at each side by having a recessed stage *frons* that followed the walls of the bays at the rear: a stage in the shape of an elongated hexagon, with behind it a small tiring house occupying three gallery bays.

The only points of comparison for this small dimension come from the hall playhouses, which had smaller dimensions all round than the amphitheatres. R. A. Foakes[9] measures the stage of the royal Cockpit-in-Court as a space about 34 feet wide and 16 feet deep at the centre, with the curve of its *frons* cutting the space at the sides to about five feet. The central door space is about four feet, which Foakes notes is hardly enough for the properties that the plays staged there require – *Volpone* and *The Maid's Tragedy*, which call for beds, and the discovery-scenes of *The Duchess of Malfi*. Its curvature and its five doors might be thought to correspond roughly to the Rose *frons* if it followed the three inner walls of the tiring-

house bays. There is little basis for any valid generalizations here. Radical variety in the design of stage areas is the only possible conclusion.

STAGE POSTS

Judging from the archaeological evidence turned up so far, the early Rose may not have had stage posts, though what little evidence there is about plays staged there before the 1592 alterations indicates that it did.[10] The one pile base uncovered in 1989 was added after the new foundation wall for the pushed-back stage was built for the reconstruction of 1592. It must have been meant for a post to uphold the new stage cover. Unless this base covers an earlier cap for the original stage posts, so far undiscovered, there is no sign of any base for a stage post at the first Rose. I think it is conceivable that the new post base was positioned over the old one, which would mean that the original stage posts were positioned seven feet back from the stage front. But that still leaves the 1592 Rose with stage posts right forward by the new stage's edge. These posts were positioned so close to the 'front' line of the stage platform that they would have left little if any room for players to walk round them or hide behind them. It is possible that just enough of the stage's floor timbers protruded forward of the foundation wall to allow the posts to be used for concealment, but the evidence is against it. The erosion line in the original mortar surface of the yard that runs in front of the first stage is too close to the foundation to

[9] R. A. Foakes, *Illustrations of the English Stage 1580–1642* (London, 1985), p. 68.
[10] Gurr, 'The Rose Repertory: What the Plays might tell us about the Stage', in *New Issues in the Reconstruction of Shakespeare's Theatre* (New York, 1990), pp. 119–34. There is also the erosion line across the 'front' of the original stage, matching the depth of the erosion line in the yard that runs round the front of the galleries. These lines were all made by dripping from the thatched roof.

35

allow much room for any substantial protrusion forward of the stage flooring's timbers. That throws doubt on the possibility that the second stage protruded much either. And since they built a new post base for the second Rose the builders could have felt no need to economize by incorporating the old structure. They were free to position the new post wherever the users wanted it.

Stage posts are certainly called for in some of the post-1592 Rose plays. In *Englishmen for my Money*, written by William Haughton for the Rose early in 1598, the clown guides a group of comic foreigners, complaining that they are lost in London, around the stage. One asks 'but watt be dis Post?', and is told it is 'the May-pole on Ivie-bridge going to Westminster'. Their guide then says 'Soft, heere's an other: Oh now I know in deede where I am; wee are now at the fardest end of Shoredich, for this is the May-pole' (lines 1654–61). Two posts identified as maypoles do imply that they were set in enough open space to allow dancing round them. But there might also be a joke built into the visuals in this play, if the characters blundering blindly through the London streets are seen coming dangerously close to the edge of the stage when they encounter the posts. It is necessary to be careful about deducing too much from stage directions. Posts are explicitly invoked for the staging in some plays, and they might have been used for concealment in eavesdropping scenes. But whether they were the mighty structures that De Witt drew is doubtful.

A play written for the Red Bull and acted by the company which once used the Rose provides a test for the evidence from stage directions and text. *Swetnam the Woman Hater*, staged at the Red Bull in about 1619, has two courtroom scenes. To judge from the woodcut on the titlepage of the 1620 quarto, the stage court was set up with a seat for the judge that resembled, and probably was, the same chair of state or throne used for scenes at royal courts. In the woodcut, however, in front of the judge's chair there is a 'bar', behind which the prisoner stands facing the judge and flanked by jury and spectators. Whatever one's qualms about how faithful to the staging the makers of titlepage woodcuts felt it necessary to be, this woodcut does depict the disposition we might expect to see on stage for such scenes of judgement as *Swetnam* 3.1. In that scene, the first of the two judgement scenes, the judge is royal, and the throne would have been placed centrally. An order is given at line 13 to 'Bring to the Barre the Prisoners'. A marginal note at line 31 in the 1620 edition calls for 'A Barre', and 14 lines later a stage direction reads '*The Prisoners brought to the Barre by a Gard*'. It seems reasonable to conclude that this courtroom scene would probably have been staged more or less as in the woodcut, with throne and bar placed centrally. The main difference is that the woodcut depicts the second courtroom scene.

The play's first courtroom scene, in 3.1, is the trial of the lovers. The subsequent populist and feminist call in 5.2 for the trial of Joseph Swetnam is a parodic imitation of the 3.1 formal trial. The woodcut on the *Swetnam* titlepage was clearly intended to depict this scene, with the Queen sitting as judge and the women jurors surrounding the court. In the woodcut Swetnam himself stands at a bar made of a short wooden pillar and two large foils, one stuck in the floor, the other suspended across from its handle to a short pillar. For this burlesque scene the women have taken the men's places, and the courtroom 'bar' is set up explicitly as a home-made affair. Atlanta says

> We want a Barre. O, these two foyles shall serve:
> One stucke i'the Earth, and crosse it from this Tree.
> Now take your places, bring him to the Barre.

This is clearly the scene that should have been depicted in the woodcut, which has swords positioned to make a bar as Atlanta specifies,

36

but no tree.[11] Acts 4 and 5 are full of swords and swordplay, which make the properties the author calls for to set up the improvised courtroom bar apt enough, even in a scene dominated by the women of the play.

The trouble here is the confused and contradictory nature of the evidence. The Swetnam woodcutter might have merged his idea of the 3.1 courtroom with the 5.2 makeshift courtroom, or may have merely used the familiar set for every Jacobean courtroom. Possibly he was not thinking of the stage set at all (which given the windows at the rear seems likely), and just did as he thought fit to show Swetnam at his trial/arraignment. But even the text and stage directions do not make clear how it was staged.

THE 'HEAVENS'

Hamlet's heaven fretted with golden fire is almost certainly a Global phenomenon. The stage traditionally represented the earth, with the heavens above and hell beneath. Faustus and Barabbas went down to a hell under the stage. The stage trapdoor opened Hamlet's grave, which is also the suicided Ophelia's and had been the entry-point for the ghost of his father. It also gives access to Malvolio's hellishly dark cell.[12] William Cartwright's *The Ordinary* (1634–5), a play which may have been written for performance at Oxford but which is soaked in the London plays of the time, has a statement by Moth (3.1.)

> . . . with it my Carcasse entire I bequeathen
> Under my foot to Hell, above my head to
>   heaven.

Nashe had registered a similar three-level cosmos as early as 1591, when the Theatre, the Curtain and the Rose were the only purpose-built amphitheatres in town. In the introduction to the 1591 printing of *Astrophil and Stella*, he wrote

> here you shal find a paper stage streud with pearle, an artificial heav'n to overshadow the fair frame, & christal wals to encounter your curious eyes,

whiles the tragicommedy of love is performed by starlight.[13]

This may or may not mean that the Rose had the same kind of stage cover as the Theatre and Curtain, and therefore had stage posts to support it. John Norden's depiction of the Rose, although he simplified what we now know was a fourteen-sided structure into a hexagon, does show a stage cover in the right position, to the north, where the 1989 excavation confirmed that the stage was. Unfortunately Norden also makes it gable-fronted. This is unlikely. A broad erosion line runs through the mortar flooring across the front of the first stage at the Rose. It appears to have been made by water dripping from the thatch cover over the stage, like the line around the rim of the yard from the gallery roofing. If so, the first stage's cover must have had a penthouse roof sloping down towards the front, like the one De Witt shows at the Swan. A gable front requires a roof that would drain its water sideways, down the flanks of the stage, not across the front. The stage front's erosion line is similar in depth to the lines in the yard's mortar fronting the galleries, though it is much more scuffed. Either Norden was wrong in showing a gable-fronted stage cover, or else the first Rose of 1587 had a stage cover like a penthouse, with its roof ridge running across a chord of the polygon, while the second was altered to give it a ridge at right angles to the northern gallery wall and a gable front, as depicted by Norden. This is a substantial contradiction between different kinds of evidence, more substantial than others because both relate to the same structure. The archaeological evidence seems the more tangible, especially since Norden simplified the

---

[11] See George Fulmer Reynolds, *The Staging of Elizabethan Plays at the Red Bull Theatre 1605–1625* (New York, 1940), pp. 46–7; R. A. Foakes, *Illustrations of the English Stage 1580–1642*, pp. 116–17.

[12] See John Astington, 'Malvolio and the Dark House', *Shakespeare Survey 41* (1989), pp. 55–62.

[13] *Works*, ed. McKerrow, III.329.

37

original fourteen sides of the polygon into six.

'CHRISTAL WALS' AND THE LORDS' ROOMS OVER THE STAGE

Did the richest spectators complete the circuit of audience in the round by sitting on the stage balcony at all the amphitheatres? Nashe knew the Rose and its brave Talbot, and may have had it in mind in the contrasting picture he drew of a stage strewn with pearls and surrounded with see-through walls. A see-through crystal may indicate that he was thinking that some of the crystal-wall gazers were looking from over the stage. An angled tiring-house front would provide a better structure for lords' rooms over the stage if the central space was for the players and the gentry were positioned in the flanking rooms, the angle of which gave at least some view of the stage entrances and the discovery space.

What was on the upper level in the tiring house at the Rose? The post-1592 Rose has a plethora of plays written specifically for it, and we might expect an ample supply of stage directions indicating the furniture that its bare island was equipped with. But stage directions rarely give straight evidence. One in *A Woman Killed with Kindness*, written for Worcester's at the Rose in early 1603, suggests that there may have been a playing space over the stage. It reads '*Enter over the stage* Frankford, Anne and Nicholas' (Scene 5). Wendoll, already on stage, sees them ('There goest thou'), but they do not see him. This is one of the pieces of evidence cited by Allardyce Nicoll for his concept of steps from the yard on each side up to the stage so that players could be seen 'passing over the stage' from one side to the other.[14] The lack of any evidence for steps, or any place for them on a platform with tapered sides, makes it more likely that 'over the stage' meant the same place as the gentlemen's places, the eight-foot-wide central balcony. Using such testimony falls easily into the swirl of circular arguments.

Other stage directions in plays written specifically for the Rose are, mercifully, less ambiguous. In *Englishmen for my Money* a burlesque Romeo and Juliet balcony scene has the Falstaffian lover hoisted up to his love in a buckbasket ('How heavie the Asse is', says his reluctant Juliet) and left suspended in midair while he is mocked and pelted with a cushion (lines 1746–94). The poet assumed the availability of a playing-space 'above' and possibly some form of hoist machinery as well.

The 'lords' rooms' were evidently distinct from the 'twopenny galleries' and even from the 'gentlemen's rooms' noted in the Fortune and Hope contracts. Access to them, unlike the galleries, was through the tiring house. Their position was on the stage balcony, where they are shown in De Witt's Swan drawing. Gentlemen's rooms, probably the ones that Platter notes as costing an extra penny for a cushion and the best view, were the bays closest to the stage at the lowest level of the galleries, to judge from the Hope contract's 'boxes'. The twopenny galleries or rooms were presumably the remaining bays of the polygonal frame stretching around the rest of the gallery circuit. The Fortune contract calls for the gentlemen's rooms and the twopenny rooms to be lined with plaster. At the Rose and probably other amphitheatres both the lords' and the gentlemen's rooms had plastered ceilings, while the lesser gallery bays had no formal ceiling other than the timbers forming the degrees for the level above.

THE *FRONS SCENAE*

Windows in the tiring-house frons

In Foakes's *Illustrations*, four of the scenes shown on the titlepages of play quartos have

---

[14] Evert Sprinchorn, 'An Intermediate Stage Level in the Elizabethan Theatre', *Theatre Notebook*, 46 (1992), 73–94, offers a thoughtful reconsideration of the old case about players 'passing' literally up to and 'over' some structure on the stage, or the stage itself.

38

windows in the rear wall. *Faustus* in 1616 has one, *Swetnam* in 1620 has two, *Bacon and Bungay* in 1630 has one, and *Arden of Faversham* (1633) and *A Maidenhead Well Lost* (1634) both have two. Three of them (*Faustus*, *Swetnam* and *Bacon and Bungay*) have squared floors, like the stage floor in Fludd's Theatrum Orbis. All have flat rear walls, and no tapering sides like the Rose's stage. Against this indication that the illustrators thought of stage rooms as possessing windows, few stage directions for any playhouse offer any function for such windows. Neither De Witt's Swan drawing nor either of Inigo Jones's stage designs for the Cockpit and the Cockpit-in-Court shows windows either. The unison of stage plans and stage directions weighs heavily against the illustrators.

Positioning the stage furniture

Where was the stage furniture positioned on stage in the different playhouses? Where were the royal stage, the row of chairs, the bed and even features such as trees or arbours placed, and where did they stand in relation to the stage posts? There is no evidence that can provide any confident answer to these questions apart from De Witt. His players are at 'stage front', or rather in the centre of the Swan's circuit of audience. The bench the lady sits on is a long way from the tiring house, far enough to give some justification to the arguments that claim the two-line gap between entries and speech that occur in some texts is a measure of how long it took to get from an entry door to the centre-stage or centre-auditorium speaking position.[15] There is a case, too, for thinking that the royal throne or judicial chair of state might have been positioned not facing the 'front' but towards the tiring house where the watching grandees sat. Everyone concerned directly in the royal presence would stand in front of the throne, but lesser beings stood behind. If the throne was placed in the centre of the playhouse it might have faced either way, depending on what players and audience thought their status

was. The only evidence for the positioning of a judicial throne is *Swetnam*'s titlepage, which unequivocally places it facing away from the tiring-house wall. But the reliability of the titlepage illustrators has been called in question once already. There is just not enough evidence to answer this potent question.

Stage hangings

A *frons* with two angles in it, and doors in each of the flanking angles, might suggest that any hangings would front the discovery space in the central section of the wall. Such a positioning would have allowed the hangings to be used not only for discoveries but for entries, especially the clown sticking his head through, a trick recorded of Tarlton before 1588 and of Timothy Reade in the 1630s. One problem with that is Heywood's seemingly unequivocal if anachronistic description, in the *Apology*, of the Roman theatres with curtains of arras tapestry hanging around what he calls the 'forefront' of the stage. His Melpomene laments the loss of the golden age when 'Then did I tread on Arras, cloth of Tissue, / Hung round the fore-front of my stage: the pillars / That did support the Roofe of my large frame / Double appareld in pure Ophir gold: / Whilst the round Circle of my spacious orbe / Was throng'd with Princes, Dukes and Senators' (B2v). She notes elsewhere (F2r) that Rome's stages were 'hung with rich Arras'. Such a general framing for the stage would be appropriate for Dekker's suggestion that the stage could be 'hung with black' for tragedies, but it counters the need for a traverse and a cloth of arras for the Globe in *Hamlet* and *Volpone*. In this case I think the balance of probability lies

---

[15] Mariko Ichikawa and others have noted the frequent incidence in some texts of a two-line interim between characters arriving on stage and starting to speak. See Ichikawa, 'Exits in Shakespeare's Plays: Time Allowed to Exiters', *Studies in English Literature*, 68 (Tokyo, 1992), 189–206.

with the stage directions rather than the vaguer mentions by Heywood and Dekker.

AUDITORIUM ENTRANCES

The size of the auditorium, only 74 feet in outside diameter at the Rose, probably 99 feet at the Globe and the Swan, is as large a factor in calculations about the bare island as the actual stage design. The semiotic potential of a theatre where half the audience is visible to the other half behind Hamlet as he speaks his ostensibly solitary soliloquies has too potent a bearing on the use of the stage island to be set down as a minor consideration. The same is true of the social divisions within the audience. How consistently the workingmen kept themselves to the yard, citizens to the galleries and lords to the rooms over the stage, and what social cachet there was in a gentleman's seat in the gallery near the stage compared with a twopenny gallery bench, are all questions with a bearing on the ways performances were received and responded to. Consideration of the bare island cannot afford to ignore such heavy details as the disposition, geographical and social, of the surrounding sea of theatre audience.

Many assumptions need challenging besides the shape of the stage island. One in particular puts to the test what has been more a conditioning concept or metaphor than an assumption about the design of the amphitheatres. That their development was evolutionary, and that in the forty-seven years between the building of the Red Lion and the Hope the design improved step by step and theatre by theatre is a Darwinian concept that is not very readily supported by the evidence. Building the nine theatres of Elizabethan and Jacobean London was a novel, demanding and infrequent activity, and it is reasonable to expect that each new design would incorporate the best features of its predecessors. That assumption can be tested most thoroughly by a look at the evidence for the means of audience access to the auditorium. Access to the galleries through the

yard or by stair turrets is not a new question, but testing the evidence about it shows up as many contradictions as the geography of the bare island.

Control of access for the spectators, and a means of securing the right payment from them, must always have been a high priority in commercial playhouses. So there is an inherent plausibility in the idea of a consistent development in design from the early buildings which were simple erections of scaffolding around the stage and its yard, and which gave access first through the scaffolding into the yard and then from the yard up into the galleries, into a better system which advantaged the firstcomers. By this theory, in the early system latecomers into the yard would have had to stand at the back, furthest from the stage. If they wanted a seat and a roof they would have to push into the galleries through the firstcomers who, on crowded days, would have used the steps or degrees of the 'ingressus' to sit on. That there would be a consequent jostling for position on the ingressus stairways is not out of keeping with what we know about audience behaviour even in modern theatres where the seating is numbered, and everyone expects a guaranteed place. So the stair turret system, making latecomers enter the galleries from the rear, had the inherent advantage of reducing the occasion for audience aggression. At the same time it reduced the number of gatherers spread through the auditorium and concentrated them in the stair turret lobbies, where they could take money from yard and gallery patrons alike. It is plausible, but the available evidence does not support it.

The Globe's remains exposed in 1989 seem to show the foundations for a stair turret butting onto the outer gallery wall. Lines of bricks are subtended from the centre of two adjacent outer panels of the polygon for eight feet, each of them turning at right angles to run parallel to the main walls and stopping about six feet from each other, well short of the angle that they would form if they met each other. From one

40

side of the two more or less square bays thus enclosed, a pair of walls make a corridor through to the yard. One of these corridor walls runs from outer wall angle to inner wall angle, while the other runs parallel to it at a distance of four feet. If the outer foundations were for a stair turret, the second of the two square bays must have been occupied by a narrow set of stairs less than four feet wide at ground level zigzagging up to each of the three levels of gallery above the ground. At the upper levels these stairs would have given access to lobbies into each gallery on either side of the main wall angle. Such a design is speculative, and it does not fit well with the much narrower flat-fronted lobbies shown in Hollar's drawing of the second Globe. But it is all the concrete evidence we have.

From written accounts it seems that a stair turret system of access to the galleries became current in or before 1600. It is on and after that date that references to the occupants of the 'twopenny galleries' start appearing. This used to bother me a little, because specifying seats in the galleries that cost twopence implied that other seats cost more, and for all William Lambarde's and Thomas Platter's claims that threepence got you a better place and a cushion there are no references to threepenny galleries. The 'twopenny gallery' term must, it seems, have entered with the stair turrets, where the single gatherer at the foot of the stair in the entrance lobby would collect both pennies at the same time. The concept of a 'twopenny' place would not have existed under the old system where patrons entered door by door and gatherer by gatherer, paying one penny at each, unless the 'twopenny gallery' was the place for Platter's cushion, a twopenny access from the one-penny yard separate from the one-penny access to the bare-benched galleries. That would require another single entry-point for such a privileged gallery, where the gatherer collected twopence, which is extremely unlikely and almost impossible in terms of ready access from the yard. We might conjecture that

Lambarde's and Platter's third penny went for a place in a lord's room, or more likely for a cushion in one of the twopenny galleries closest to the stage which qualified as a gentleman's room. The sixpence identified as the price of the lords' rooms is an inference from the prices paid on visits to the Globe by people like Mildmay in the 1620s. That may have been a price peculiar to the lords' rooms at the Globe only after the company's extended use of the Blackfriars had pushed up the social status of their clientele and their prices.

On the face of it, a change in the method for audience access between the early and the later amphitheatres is proclaimed by contemporary testimony. Lambarde, writing before 1596, and Platter writing in 1599, are quite specific. Lambarde wrote that at the Theatre, 'they first pay one pennie at the gate, another at the entrie of the Scaffolde, and the third for a quiet standing'. Platter said

whoever cares to stand below only pays one English penny, but if he wishes to sit he enters by another door, and pays another penny, while if he desires to sit in the most comfortable seats which are cushioned, where he not only sees everything well, but can also be seen, then he pays another English penny at another door.[16]

Such a system of entry does not need stair turrets. The more tangible evidence, both from archaeology and from contemporary pictures, seems to support this. The absence of any turret in the sixty per cent of the Rose's groundplan so far excavated, and the 'ingressus' from the yard to the gallery scaffolding shown in De Witt's Swan drawing both support Lambarde's and Platter's accounts. The Theatre, the Rose and the Swan thus seem to have belonged to the older design of playhouse, without stair turrets. That suggests an evolution in playhouse design, with the more sophisticated form of audience access to the

---

[16] *Thomas Platter's Travels in England*, trans. Clare Williams (London, 1951), p. 167.

41

gallery seats developing later than the system Lambarde and Platter describe.

But it is, of course, not so simple. Against this evidence there are two substantial pieces of evidence that need to be reconciled very carefully against the statements made by Lambarde and Platter. The first is the Utrecht view of the Theatre, which appears to show it with a pair of stair turrets on opposite flanks.[17] The other is the pair of testimonies that the Swan had at least one and probably two examples of the newer form of access. In the 1627 map of Paris Garden Manor[18] the single stair turret on the northeast flank of its polygonal 'Swan' would have made De Witt's 'ingressus' from the yard unnecessary. That is one conflict of evidence. And there is another. However unreliable we think De Witt was the 1627 map might also be questioned, not for its marking of a stair turret but for marking only one. The Hope contract, with all the precision of a building specification, notes that the Swan has plural 'stearcasses . . . without and adjoyninge' its frame. This testimony that the Swan had two stair turrets is at odds with De Witt, with the Paris Garden Manor map and with the Lambarde and Platter evidence.

The Paris Garden Manor map is a problem in another way. Francis Langley when he built his Swan in 1595 close to the Rose was the first impresario to follow Henslowe onto the south bank. His design was evidently larger than Henslowe's since the Swan was claimed to have a capacity of three thousand. Besides its evident differences, the square stage, the planar *frons* and De Witt's testimony to its having walls of flint and timbers painted to look like marble, it may have copied the Rose in the kind of audience access that Henslowe's first playhouse could have had: a single stair turret on its northeastern flank. Until the eastern segment of the Rose's polygon can be excavated, we cannot know for sure that the Rose did not have a stair turret where the Paris Garden map suggests the Swan had one. If so, then Lambarde's and Platter's evidence from 1596 and 1599 about the penny-

by-penny access to the galleries through the yard in the early amphitheatres is quite wrong for the Rose and the Swan. Even De Witt's 'ingressi' could then only be correct if they were built for the few spectators who might be expected to change their minds after first deciding to stand in the yard. A secondary means of access from the yard to the galleries would be useful for when it rained and the penny-payers decided to pay extra to get a roof over their heads, but the opportunity for such second thoughts would intensify the problem of crowding and conflict with the spectators already in position on the access steps. Lambarde, Platter and De Witt all tell a consistent but unconvincing story about audience access.

Worse is to come. James P. Lusardi[19] has argued strongly that Abram Booth's 'The View of the Cittye of London from the North towards the South' (Foakes, *Illustrations*, p. 8), made in the late 1590s, shows that the Theatre had stair turrets. If that is true, and stair turrets were in use as early as 1576, Lambarde and Platter are again contradicted. Neither the Rose, Swan nor the Theatre had the penny-by-penny form of audience entry. Moreover, this means that the stair-turreted Globe, with its framing timbers taken from the Theatre, was built even more like its predecessor than conventional expectation admits.

The obvious advantage of a stair turret for gallery access is twofold: it removes the need to provide stairway space inside the auditorium, where seating space is more profitable, and it admits latecomers to the back of the gallery instead of the front, which is the confrontational access that seems to be required by the step-by-step admission system through the Swan's and the Rose's 'ingressus'. If the

---

[17] See James P. Lusardi, 'The Pictured Playhouse: Reading the Utrecht Engraving of Shakespeare's London', *Shakespeare Quarterly*, 44 (1993), 202–27.
[18] Foakes, *Illustrations of the English Stage 1580–1642*, p. 24.
[19] Lusardi's well-illustrated article considers the stair turrets on page 215.

42

Theatre, the Swan and possibly the Rose all had stair turrets, what playhouses did Lambarde and Platter attend that might have justified their generalizations? Lambarde cited the Bel Savage inn and the baiting house in Paris Garden in his original account of the playhouses, adding the Theatre's name to the list for his 1596 revision. But citing the baiting house raises another question about the Lambarde and Platter testimonies. The baiting-house yards were inaccessible to audiences because they were occupied by the animals. Neither of the Bankside scaffolds shown in the Agas map of 1572 shows any sign of stair turrets, but it seems inherently improbable that their owners would have expected customers to enter through the yard, even if the audience was all required to be in place before the baitings started. Access must have been from the outside, by stairs. The baiting houses must therefore have provided some kind of early model for the stair-turret design of audience access to the playhouse galleries.

Platter must have been even looser than Lambarde in his generalizing, because he certainly went to some amphitheatres which had stair turrets, although he makes no mention of them. Besides at least one visit to a bear-baiting house, where stair turrets were essential, he specified a visit to the Globe ('the house with the thatched roof'), where on 21 September 1599 he saw *Julius Caesar*. We can be fairly sure from the 1989 excavation that the Globe had at least one stair turret. So what led Platter to record a generalization that certainly did not apply to at least two of the amphitheatres he visited? Like the references that appeared in sermons about the decadence of the Theatre long after it was pulled down, Platter may have been repeating out-of-date information the locals had given him, and overlooking his own direct experience. Such a possibility strengthens the case for relying on archaeological concrete rather than written testimonies from the time.

43

'I am not made of stone': Theatrical Revision of Gesture in Shakespeare's Plays

STEVEN URKOWITZ

For the last few months I've been looking for familiar and preeminently visible body-language coded by Shakespeare in the scripts of his plays. I've been finding hundreds of instances of a highly articulate vocabulary of gesture he choreographs for his actors so that they in turn can express more dimensions of recognizable human experience to his audiences.

Most of the actions Shakespeare calls for are relatively easy to find once you decide to look for them. You get what you can from the formal stage directions, of course, and then you hunt for the cues embedded in the dialogue as instructions: 'Give me your hand,' 'Take this purse,' or 'Let us go.' Very soon you start to notice just how much attention Shakespeare pays to the mechanics of gesture and the subtle stylistics of moving actors around and on and off the relatively empty platform stages of the English Renaissance.

But the great surprise for me in these last few months of reading has been seeing just how much of what we call 'character' itself can be determined or altered in a Shakespearean script by changing a movement, or by altering the direction in which a line is spoken, or by assuming a different physical alignment towards other character on stage.

I've found the most interesting evidence in those plays which were first printed in versions radically different from those we are most familiar with now: the earlier and later quartos and First Folio editions of *Hamlet*, *King Lear*, *Richard III*, *Henry V*, *Merry Wives of Windsor*, *Romeo and Juliet* and the Second and Third Parts of *Henry VI*.

For the last fifty to eighty years, people haven't looked very closely at the differences of physical gesture called for in the alternative scripts of these plays. For several reasons, all of which are currently under attack, the earlier versions of these plays were labelled 'bad' quartos. The orthodox story about 'bad' quartos is that Shakespeare didn't write

43

them. Rather, it is fashionable to argue that an anonymous piratical actor or string of actors who had played small roles in Shakespeare's company memorized as much as they could of the plays as they heard them. Then they wrote out all they could recall, confusing and botching up whatever they couldn't remember precisely, and then they sold their faulty memorial reconstructions to printers eager to publish a hot script. So, we are told, the 'bad' quartos only give us Shakespeare transmogrified as through an ass's head, and the 'bad' quarto of *Merry Wives of Windsor*, for example, resembles Shakespeare's *Wives* only as much as Bottom the Weaver's play of Pyramus and Thisbe resembles Ovid's original or Golding's translation. There is a six-foot shelf of monographs, essays and textual notes exclaiming over the worthlessness, the essential un-Shakespearean-ness, of these 'bad' quartos.

Well, having come to the study of Shakespeare with an ass's head installed as original equipment, I have taken to reading these 'bad' quartos. Like Bottom I have had a most rare vision that I will share with you. My Bottomless dream is that the 'bad' texts are not non-Shakespearean but rather very early Shakespearean, and that we can learn wonders about dramatic technique and Shakespeare's artistry by looking for the *differences* between these earliest scripts and their later versions. I propose a kind of differential calculus of theatrical variants, a systematic study of alternative forms of gesture and movement to supplement our already vigorous studies applied to the modes of purely verbal expression in dramatic characters.

From among the many possible examples of differential gestures I might analyse, I've chosen variants found in the roles of three young women: from the histories, Queen Margaret in two versions of the second and third parts of *Henry VI*, from the comedies Anne Page in the Quarto and Folio texts of *Merry Wives of Windsor*, and from the tragedies Juliet in equivalent moments as shown in the first and second Quartos of *Romeo and Juliet*. We will see that in each case either alternative version of a specific gesture or movement will 'work' onstage and be recognized as meaningful by a theatrical audience. We may find, though, that the alternatives may not be imagined with equal ease by *readers* – including many editors of the plays – who are untrained in the interpretation of theatrical scripts. And, incidentally, we may note that either of the alternatives would be accepted unquestionably as 'Shakespearean' if it were the only one we had.

First Queen Margaret. In the opening scene of the 1594 text of *2 Henry VI*, at the first meeting with her husband the king, Margaret presents herself by self-consciously announcing her own modesty and tender spirit [in my italics, marked (A) and (B)]:

The fairest Queene that euer King possest.
KING. Suffolke arise.
Welcome Queene Margaret to English Henries Court,
The greatest shew of kindnesse yet we can bestow,
Is this kinde kisse: Oh gracious God of heauen,
Lend me a heart repleat with thankfulnesse,
For in this beautious face thou hast bestowde
A world of pleasures to my perplexed soule.
QUEENE. *Th'excessiue loue I beare vnto your grace,*
Forbids me to be lauish of my tongue,
Least I should speake more then beseemes a woman: (A)
Let this suffice, my blisse is in your liking,
And nothing can make poore Margaret miserable,
Vnlesse the frowne of mightie Englands King. (B)
KIN. Her lookes did wound, but now her speech doth pierce,
Louely Queene Margaret *sit by my side:* (C)
And vnckle Gloster and you Lordly Peeres,
With one voice welcome my beloued Queene.
ALL. *Long liue Queene Margaret, Englands happinesse.* (D)
QUEENE. We thank you all.
                    Sound Trumpets.
                        2 Henry VI.
                    Quarto (1594), A2^v; 1.1.16-38

Her bridegroom invites her to sit beside him [at (C)], and as far as we can tell she sits. Then the nobles of England greet the new queen while they stand about the royal thrones [(D)]. Margaret's first moments on stage stress decorum, acquiescence to her husband's will, and a posture of repose (albeit formal) within a surrounding context of attentive but upright peers of the realm.

The same moment in the second script of this play, published in the 1623 First Folio, has Queen Margaret announce her boldness rather than her modesty [in my italics, at mark (a)].

The Fairest Queene, that euer King receiu'd.
KING. Suffolk arise. Welcome Queene Margaret,
I can expresse no kinder signe of Loue
Then this kinde kisse: O Lord, that lends me life,
Lend me a heart repleate with thankfulnesse:
For thou hast giuen me in this beauteous Face
A world of earthly blessings to my soule,
If Simpathy of Loue vnite our thoughts.
QUEEN. Great King of England, & my gracious Lord,
The mutuall conference that my mind hath had,
By day, by night; waking, and in my dreames,
In Courtly company, or at my Beades,
With you mine Alder liefest *Soueraigne,*
Makes me the bolder to salute my King,
With ruder termes, such as my wit affoords,

45

> And ouer ioy of heart doth minister. (a)
> KING. Her sight did rauish, but her grace in Speech,
> Her words yclad with wisedomes Maiesty,
> Makes me from Wondring, fall to Weeping ioyes,
> Such is the Fulnesse of my hearts content.
> Lords, with one cheerefull voice, Welcome my Loue.
> ALL KNEEL. *Long liue Qu. Margaret, Englands happines.* (b)
> QUEEN. We thanke you all.
> > Florish
> > Folio (1623), TLN 23-45

Instead of sitting while the nobles salute the Queen, the Folio has Margaret and Henry standing while everyone else onstage kneels before them [at (b)]. Pride of place and dominance become the significant motives made visible to the audience.

Later in the play we have another example of variant gesture affecting the characterization of Margaret. A group of commoners with written petitions appealing for help from Duke Humphrey, the Protector of the Kingdom, inadvertently approach Queen Margaret and her paramour, the Duke of Suffolk. In the earlier text Suffolk reads the petition against his own actions, tears it to pieces, and drives the petitioners away [at my italics, marked (A)]

> SUFFOLKE. I marry this is something like,
> Whose within here?
> > Enter one or two.
> Sirra take in this fellow and keepe him close,
> And send out a Purseuant for his maister straight,
> Weele here more of this before the Kind.
> > Exet with the Armourers man.
> Now sir what yours? Let me see it,
> *Whats here?*
> *A complaint against the Duke of Suffolke for enclosing the commons of long Melford.*
> *How now sir knaue.*
> 1 PET. *I beseech your grace to pardon me, me, I am but a Messenger for the whole town-ship.*
> > *He teares the papers.*
> SUFFOLKE. *So now show your petitions to Duke Humphrey.*
> *Villaines get you gone and come not neare the Court,*
> *Dare these pesants write against me thus.*
> > *Exet Petitioners.* (A)
> QUEENE. My Lord of Suffolke, you may see by this,
> The Commons Joues vnto that haughtie Duke,
> > Quarto, B2ᵛ; 1.3.19-43
> > [my italics]

Suffolk's response is angry and instantaneous, an explosion of irritation.

The equivalent in the Folio has Suffolk again read the petition [at section bracketed and marked (a)], but then, after a delay of five speeches during which a different suit is dealt with, Queen Margaret tears the papers in what seems to be a meditated action [at (b)].

> SUFF. Thy Wise too? that's some Wrong indeede, *What's yours? What's heere? Against the Duke of Suffolke, for enclosing the Commons of Melforde. How now, Sir Knaue?*
> 2 PET. *Alas Sir, I am but a poore Petitioner of our whole Towneship.* (a)
> PETER. Against my Master Thomas Horner, for saying, That the Duke of Yorke was rightfull Heire to the Crowne.
> QUEENE. What say'st thou? Did the Duke of Yorke say, hee was rightfull Heire to the Crowne?
> PETER. That my Mistresse was? No forsooth: my Master said, That he was, and that the King was an Vsurper.
> SUFF. Who is there?
> > Enter Seruant.
> Take this fellow in, and send for his Master with a Purseuant presently: wee'le heare more of your matter before the King.
> > Exit.
> QUEENE. *And as for you that loue to be protected Vnder the Wings of our Protectors Grace, Begin your Suites anew, and sue to him.*
> > Teare the Supplication (b)
> *Away, base Cullions: Suffolke let them goe.* (c) (d)
> ALL. Come, let's be gone. Exit
> QUEENE. My Lord of Suffolke, say, is this the guise? Is this the Fashions in the Court of England?
> > Folio, TLN 404-29 [my italics]

She, not Suffolk, orders the petitioners away [at (c)], and she further commands Suffolk to let them pass from the stage [at (d)]. Here as in the opening scene of the play variant gesture shows Margaret dominating the stage with aggressive strength.

A third variant occurs at the opening of a scene showing the court returning from a hunt with falcons.

> Enter the King and Queene with her Hawke on her fist, and Duke Humphrey and Suffolke, and the Cardinall, as if they came from hawking.
> QUEENE. *My Lord, how did your grace like this last flight?* (A)
> But as I cast her off the winde did rise,
> And twas ten to one, old Ione had not gone out.
> KING. How wonderfull the Lords workes are on earth,
> Euen in these silly creatures of his hands,
> Vnckle Gloster, how hie your Hawke did sore?
> And on a sodaine soust the Partridge downe.
> > Quarto. C1ᵛ; 2.1.1-8
> > [my italics]

47

The Quarto text has Margaret address the opening speech directly to her husband [at (A)]. While she speaks she draws attention almost deferentially towards *his* response. Because she faces the king and has asked him a question needing a reply, Henry functions for the moment as the dominant figure in the group even though Margaret is the one who is speaking.

But the Folio equivalent makes Margaret and her own excitement the centre of attention for all eyes [my italics, at (a)].

> Enter the King, Queene, Protector, Cardinall, and Suffolke, with Faulkners hallowing.
> QUEENE. *Beleeue me Lords, for flying at the Brooke,* (a)
> I saw no better sport these seuen yeeres day:
> Yet by your leaue, the Winde was very high,
> And ten to one, old Ioane had not gone out.
> KING. But what a point, my Lord, your Faulcon made,
> And what a pytch she flew aboue the rest:
> To see how God in all his Creatures workes,
> Yea Man and Mirds are fayne of climbing high.
> Folio, TLN 715-24.

In acting terms, by addressing everyone in the group at once she 'takes the stage.' She makes herself the most important figure. We may not have a specified movement of a hand or leg, but the manifold gestures appropriate to the message 'Look at me!' are among those learned earliest in our childhood (especially memorized by those of us destined to become actors, even by some fated for the profession of teaching).

One last example from Margaret, this one found in the third part of *Henry VI*. The Queen arrives at the court of the King of France as a powerless fugitive seeking his help.

> Enter king Lewis and the ladie Bona, and Queene Margaret, Prince Edward, and Oxford and others.
> LEWIS. Welcome Queene Margaret to the Court of France,
> It fits not Lewis to sit while thou dost stand,
> *Sit by my side*, and here I vow to thee, (A)
> Thou shalt haue aide to repossesse thy right,
> And beat proud Edward from his vsurped seat,
> And place king Henry in his former rule.
> QUEEN. I humblie thanke your royall maiestie,
> And pray the God of heauen to blesse thy state,
> Great king of France, that thus regards our wrongs.
> *3 Henry VI*. Q1 (an octavo volume, 1595),
> C8^v; 3.3.1-16
> [my italics]

In a direct recapitulation of the image of her arrival as a bridge in the court of England, we see the King of France invite her to sit down beside him. Like the earlier moment in the first version of *2 Henry VI* Margaret simply joins the royal figure on a throne or a chair of state. And like the Folio version of the earlier scene, in the Folio text here Margaret instead has a bolder visual gesture:

> Flourish. Enter Lewis the French King, his Sister Bona, his Admirall, call'd Bourbon: Prince Edward, Queene Margaret, and the Earle of Oxford. Lewis sits, and riseth up againe.
>
> LEWIS. Faire Queene of England, worthy Margaret,
> *Sit downe with vs*: it ill befits thy State,   (a)
> And Birth, that thou should'st stand, while Lewis doth sit.
> MARG. No, mightie King of France: now Margaret
> Must strike her sayle, and learne a while to serue,
> Where Kings command. I was (I must confesse)
> Great Albions Queene, in former Golden dayes:
> *But now mischance hath trod my Title down,*
> *And with dis-honor layd me on the ground,*
> *Where I must take like Seat vnto my fortune,*
> *And to my humble Seat conforme my selfe.*   (b)
> LEWIS. *Why say, faire Queene, whence springs this deepe despaire?*   (c)
> MARG. From such a cause, as fills mine eyes with teares,
> And stops my tongue, while heart is drown'd in cares.
> LEWIS. What ere it be, be thou still like thy selfe,
> And sit thee by our side.
>   *Seats her by him.*   (d)
>   Folio, TLN 1720-41 [my italics]

She refuses Lewis's offer and sits down on the stage floor, 'on the ground, / Where I must take like Seat unto my fortune, / And to my humble Seat conforme my selfe.' Lewis reacts to her move with great sympathy [at (c)]. (For a royal person, sitting on the bare earth was a conventional gesture of grave despair: Constance in *King John* [TLN 990-6; II.iv.114], Richard II ['For Gods sake let us sit upon the ground,' F 2v, III.ii.155], and King Lear, in the Quarto text of III.ii.42 which reads 'Alas sir, sit you here?' [F4].) Margaret's daring action draws our eyes to her; she is an arresting presence even in her moments of political weakness. The king eventually raises her to sit beside him at [at (d)]: the thirteen-line interval between his first offer and her acceptance forms a kind of gestural arpeggio, a jazz riff played with the simple action of taking a seat.

I chose these four moments from among hundreds of textual variants relating to Margaret's role in the two versions of the *Henry VI* plays. Now I may be wrong about just who was responsible for these variants. Evidence gets distorted and filtered passing through an ass's head. But whoever set up one or both of these alternative versions, in whatever order they may have been generated and printed, the alternative texts certainly seem to merit our close attention as records of theatrical gesture, Shakespearean or not.

I would like to look briefly at two further examples of similar character changes related to gestures in other plays. These are more speculative, bringing into play my own personal interpretations, more open to dispute. I chose these moments though because I feel they show us a basic quality of Shakespearean characterization, a building-in of multiply-layered personality typically Shakespearean where other playwrights would settle for more broadly outlined patterns of psychological and physical behaviour.

The first of these character variants is found in *Merry Wives of Windsor* when the young gentleman Master Fenton announces his love to Anne Page, asking her to marry him.

> Enter M. Fenton, Page, and mistresse Quickly.
> FEN: *Tell me sweet Nan, how doest thou yet resolue,*
> *Shall foolish Slender haue thee to his wife?*
> *Or one as wife as he, the learned Doctor?*
> *Shall such as they enioy thy maiden hart?*   (A)
> Thou knowst that I haue alwaies loued thee deare,
> And thou hast oft times swore the like to me.
> AN: *Good M. Fenton, you may assure your selfe*
> *My hart is setled vpon none but you,*   (B)
> Tis as my father and mother please:
> Get their consent, you quickly shall haue mine.
> FEN: Thy father thinks I loue thee for his wealth,
> Tho I must needs confesse at first that drew me,
> But since thy vertues wiped that trash away,
> I loue thee Nana, for so deare is it set,
> That whilst I liue, I nere shall thee forget.
> [QUICKLY.] Godes pitie here comes her father.
>   Enter M. Page, his wife, M. Shallow, and Slender.
> PA: M. Fenton I pray what make you here?
> You know my answere sir, shees not for you:
> Knowing my vow, to blame to vse me thus.
> FEN: But heare me speake sir.
> PA: *Pray sir get you gon: Come hither daughter,*
> *Sonne Slender let me speak with you. (they whisper)*   (1)
> QUIC: *Speake to Misteris Page.*   (2)
> FEN. Pray misteris Page let me haue your consent.
> MIS. PA. Ifaith M. Fenton tis as my husband please.
> For my part Ile neither hinder you, nor further you.
> QUIC. How say you this was my doings?
> I bid you speake to misteris Page.
> FEN. Here nurse, theres a brace of angels to drink,
> Worke what thou canst for em, farwell.
>   (Exit Fen.)

QUIC. By my troth so I will, good hart.
PA. *Come wife, you an I will in, weele leaue M. Slender*
And my daughter to talke together. M. Shallow,
You may stay sir if you please.
                    Exit Page and his wife.
SHAL. *Mary I thanke you for that:*
To her cousin, to her.   (4)
SLEN. Ifaith I know not what to say.
AN. Now M. Slender, whats your will?
SLEN. Godeso theres a Iest indeed: why misteris An,
I neuer made wil yet: I thank God I am wise inough for that.
SHAL. Fie cusse fie, thou art not right,
O thou hadst a father.
SLEN. I had a father misteris Anne, good vncle
Tell the Iest how my father stole the goose out of
The henloft. All this is nought, *harke you mistresse Anne.*   (5)
SHAL. He will make you ioynter of three hundred pound a year, he shall
make you a Gentlewoman.
SLEN. I be God that I vill, come cut a long taile, as good as any is in Glos-
tershire, vnder the degree of a Squire.
AN. O God how many grosse faults are hid,
And couered in three hundred pound a yeare?
Well M. Slender, within a day or two Ile tell you more.
SLEND. I thank you good misteris Anne, vncle I shall haue her.
QUIC. M. Shallow, M. Page would pray you to come you, and you M.
Slender, and you Mistris An.
SLEND. Well Nurse, if youle speake for me,
Ile giue you more then Ile talke of.
                    Exit omnes but Quickly.
QUIC. Indeed I will, Ile speake what I can for you,
But specially for M. Fenton:
But specially of all for my Maister,
And indeed I will do what I can for them all three.
            Exit
                    Merry Wives of Windsor
                    Quarto (1602), E4, E4^v, F1; 3.4.1-111
                    [my italics]

In the Quarto text Fenton is the more sophisticated member of the
pair. He teases Anne Page about her other suitors [at (A)]. She is direct
and guileless, like an ostentatiously sincere Arcadian shepherdess [(B)].
Throughout the rest of the scene in the Quarto, specific dialogue-
commands direct characters to move about the stage forming little whis-
pering groups [marked 1,2,3,4,5]. 'Come hither daughter, Sonne Slender
let me speak with you,' says Master Page; 'Speake to Misteris Page,'
says Quickly to Fenton; and Shallow urges Slender 'To her cousin, to
her.' Notice how in the Quarto almost everyone except for Anne Page
and Fenton gives commands that move others around the stage, and with
the exception of Fenton (who stays even after Master Page orders him

away) the orders are followed; those commanded go where they are sent.

The Folio presents different actions and very different characteristics for the *dramatis personae*, though essentially the same narrative material is covered.

Enter Fenton, Anne, Page, Shallow, Slender, Quickly, Page, Mist. Page.
FEN. *I see I cannot get thy Fathers loue,*
Therefore no more turne me to him (sweet Nan.)   (a)
ANNE. Alas, how then?
FEN. *Why thou must be thy selfe.*
He doth obiect, I am too great of birth,
And that my state being gall'd with my expence,
I seeke to heale it onely by his wealth.
Besides these, other barres he layes before me,
My Riots past, my wilde Societies,
And tels me 'tis a thing impossible
I should loue thee, but as a property.   (b)
AN. *May be he tels you true.*   (c)
[FEN.] No, heauen so speed me in my time to come,
Albeit I will confesse, thy Fathers wealth
Was the first motiue that I woo'd thee (Anne:)
Yet wooing thee, I found thee of more valew
Then stampes in Gold, or summes in sealed bagges:
And 'tis the very riches of thy selfe,
That now I ayme at.
AN. Gentle M. Fenton,
Yet seeke my Fathers loue, still seeke it sir,
If opportunity and humblest suite
Cannot attine it, why then *harke you hither*   (I)
SHAL. Breake their talke Mistris Quickly,
My Kinsman shall speake for himselfe.
SLEN. Ile make a shaft or a bolt on't, slid, tis but venturing.
SHAL. Be not dismaid.
SLEN. No, she shall not dismay me:
I care not for that, but that I am affeard.
QUI. *Har ye*, M. Slender would speak a word with you.
AN. *I come to him*. This is my Fathers choice: (II)
O what a world of vilde ill-fauour'd faults
Lookes hadsome in three hundred pounds a yeere?
QUI. And how do's good Master Fenton?
Pray you a word with you.   (III)
SHAL. Shee's comming; *to her Coz:*   (IV)
O boy, thou hadst a father.
SLEN. I had a fahter (M. An) my vncle can tel you good iests of him: pray you Vncle, tel Mist. Anne the iest how my Father stole two Geese out of a Pen, good Vnckle.
SHAL. Mistris Anne, my Cozen loues you.
SLEN. I that I do, as well as I loue any woman in Glocestershire.
SHAL. He will maintaine you like a Gentlewoman.

52

SLEN. I that I will, come cut and long-taile, vnder the degree of a Squire.

SHAL. He will make you a hundred and fiftie pounds ioynture.

ANNE. *Good Maister Shallow let him woo for himselfe.*

SHAL. *Marrie I thank you for it: I thank you for that good comfort: she cals you (Coz) Ile leaue you.* (V)

ANNE. Now Master Slender.

SLEN. Now good Mistris Anne.

ANNE. What is your will?

SLEN. My will? Odd's-hart-lings, that' a a prettie iest indeede: I ne're made my Will yet (I thanke Heauen:) I am not such a fickely creature, I giue Heauen praise.

ANNE. I meane (M. Slender) what wold you with me?

SLEN. Truely, for mine owne part, I would little or nothing with you: your father and my vncle hath made motions: if it be my lucke, so; if not, happy man bee his dole, they can tell you how things go, better then I can: you may aske your father, heere he comes.

PAGE. Now Mr Slender; Loue him daughter Anne.
Why how now? What does Mr Fenter here?
You wrong me Sir, thus still to haunt my house.
I told you Sir, my daughter is disposd of.

FEN. Nay Mr Page, be not impatient.

MIST. PAGE. Good M. Fenton, come not to my child.

PAGE. She is no match for you.

FEN. Sir, will you heare me?

PAGE. No, good M. Fenton.
Come M. Shallow: Come sonne Slender, in; (VI)
Knowing my minde, you wrong me (M. Fenton.)

QUI. *Speake to Mistris Page.* (VII)

FEN. Good Mist. Page, for that I loue your daughter
In such a righteous fashion as I do,
Perforce, against all checkes, rebukes, and manners,
I must aduance the colours of my loue,
And not retire. Let me haue your good will.

AN. Good mother, do not marry me to yond foole.

MIST. PAGE. I meane it not, I seeke you a better husband.

QUI. That's my master, M. Doctor.

AN. Alas I had rather be set quick i'th earth,
And bowl'd to death with Turnips.

MIST. PAGE. Come, trouble not your selfe good M.
Fenton, I will not be your friend, nor enemy:
My daughter will I question how she loues you,
And as I finde her, so am I affected:
Till then, *farewell Sir, she must needs go in,* (VIII)
Her father will be angry.

FEN. Farewell gentle Mistris: farewell Nan.

QUI. This is my doing now: Nay, saide I, will you cast away your childe on a Foole, and a Physitian: Looke on M. Fenton, this is my doing.

FEN. I thanke thee: and I pray thee once to night,
Giue my sweet Nan this Ring: there's for thy paines.

QUI. Now heauen send thee good fortune, a kinde heart he hath: a woman

would run through fire & water for such a kinde heart. But yet, I would my
Maister had Mistris Anne, or I would M. Slender had her: or (in sooth) I
would M. Fenton had her; I will do what I can for them all three, for so I haue
promisd, and Ile bee as good as my work, but speciously for M. Fenton.
Well, I must of another errand to Sir Iohn Falstaffe from my two Mistresses:
what a beast am I to slacke it.

> Exeunt.
>
> *Merry Wives of Windsor.*
> Folio, TLN 1567-1677. [my italics]

Fenton professes his sincerity, beseeching Anne like a simple shepherd,
and Anne Page turns the tables on him. She teases Fenton as the more
sophisticated, joking and courtious lover [(a), (b), (c)]. The gesture only
in the Folio is necessary when Anne breaks the monopoly of move-
commands. Beckoning Fenton to move with her out of hearing of Quickly,
Shallow and Slender, she proposes the first tête-à-tête in the scene [(I)],
and later she drives Shallow away so than she may speak with Slender
alone [(V)]. (Commands and obedience to commands don't follow the
same authoritarian patterns found in the Quarto.) Through her commands-
for-actions and gestures associated with them, Anne Page takes on visible authority as an effective, active person unlike the will-less persona of
her Quarto equivalent.

These variants cohere with scores of others elsewhere in *Merry Wives*.
Similar kinds of changes occur in the roles of Mistress Ford, Mistress
Page, the Host of the Garter and, most of all, Sir John Falstaff and
Master Ford.

Finally one last variant design for a gesture in one more young woman's
role. In the third scene of *Romeo and Juliet* Lady Capulet tells her
daughter about the offer of marriage she has received from the County
Paris.

WIFE: And that same marriage Nurce, is the Theame I meant to talke of:
Tell me Iuliet, howe stand you affected to be married? (1)
IUL: It is an honor that I dreame not off.
NURCE: An honor! were not I thy onely Nurce, I would say thou hadst
suckt wisedome from thy Teat.
WIFE: Well girle, the Noble Countie Paris seekes thee for a Wife.
NURCE. *A man young Ladie, Ladie such a man as all the world, why he
is a man of waxe.*
WIFE: *Veronaes Summer hath not such a flower.*
NURCE: *Nay he is a flower, in faith a very flower.* (A)
WIFE: *Well Iuliet, how like you of Paris loue.* (2)
IULIET: *Ile looke to like, if looking liking moue,
But no more deepe will I engage mine eye,
Then your consent giues strength to make it flie.* (B)
> Enter Clowne.
CLOWNE: *Madilam you are cald for; supper is readie, the Nurce curst in*

the Pantrie, all thinges in extreamitie, make hast for I must be gone to
waite. (C)

> *Romeo and Juliet.*
> Q1 (1597), B4^v-C1; 1.3.63-105.

In the 1597 First Quarto Lady Capulet and the Nurse briefly com-
mend Paris [at (A)], and Juliet very tentatively responds to the idea of
marriage [(B)]. Then a servant enters with urgent calls to hurry the exit of
the Lady and the Nurse, and as far as we can tell from the script the three
women quickly go out together [(C)]. Note that Juliet's mother merely
broaches the ideas of marriage and Paris's attractiveness is single short
speeches, and she says nothing at all about the blessed state of matri-
mony.

The 1599 Second Quarto offers a different constellation of motives
and forces underlying the action.

> OLD LA. Marrie, that marrie is the very theame
> I came to talke of, tell me daughter Iuliet,
> *How stands your dispositions to be married?* (I)
> IULIET. It is an houre that I dreame not of.
> NURSE. An houre, were not I thine onely Nurse, I would say thou hadst
> suckt wisedome from thy teate.
> OLD LA. *Well thinke of marriage now,* yonger then you (II)
> *Here in Verona, Ladies of esteeme,*
> *Are made alreadie mothers by my count.*
> *I was your mother, much vpon these yeares*
> *That you are now a maide,* thus then in briefe: (III)
> *The valiant Paris seekes you for his loue.* (a)
> NURSE. A man young Lady, Lady, such a man as all the wold. Why hees a
> man of waxe.
> OLD LA. Veronas Sommer hath not such a flower.
> NURSE. Nay hees a flower, in faith a very flower.
> OLD LA. What say you, can you loue the Gentleman? (IV)
> *This night you shall behold him at our feast,*
> *Reade ore the volume of young Paris face,*
> *and find delight, writ there with bewties pen,*
> *Examine euery married liniament,*
> *And see how one an other lends content:*
> *And what obscurde in this faire volume lies,*
> *Finde written in the margeant of his eyes.*
> *This precious booke of loue, this vnbound louer,*
> *To bewtifie him, onely lacks a Couer.*
> *The fish liues in the sea, and tis much pride*
> *For faire without the faire, within to hide:*
> *That booke in manies eyes doth share the glorie*
> *That in gold claspes locks in the golden storie:*
> *So shall you share all that he doth possesse,*
> *By hauing him, making your selfe no lesse.* (b)
> NURSE. Lo lesse, nay bigger women grow by men.

55

OLD LA. *Speake briefly, can you like of Paris loue?*   (V)
IULI. Ile looke to like, if looking liking moue.
But no more deepe will I endart mine eye,
Then your consent giues strength to make flie.
          Enter Serving.
SER. Madam the guests are come, supper seru'd vp, *you cald, my young*
Lady askt for, the Nurse curst in the Pantrie, and euerie thing in extremitie:
I must hence to wait, I beseech you follow straight.   (c)
MO. We follow thee, *Iuliet the Countie staies.*
NUR. *Go gyrle,* seeke happie nights to happie days.   (VI)
          Exeunt.
          Q2 (1599), B4^v-C1.
          [my italics and underlining]

Lady Capulet stresses her status as Juliet's mother and her own superior experience [in the second line and at (a)]. She praises Paris with wild extravagance, concentrating almost exclusively on his physical appearance [at (b)]. And she is short-tempered and pushes repeatedly for an immediate reply [at (II), (III), (IV) and (b)]. Juliet gives the same tentative response, but it stands fraily against a very hard-sell sales pitch. The urgent call from a servant again prompts the exit from the scene, but in this version he also specifically calls for Juliet with the other two women [at (c)].

The gesture that I read in the final moment of the scene is only implied, subtly suggested by the last two speeches. I believe that Lady Capulet and the Nurse have to repeat the servant's commands to Juliet because she hangs back, unwilling to rush into the pressured whirl of courtship, sexuality and marriage proferred by her mother. First the servant calls on her to move, then her mother, and then the Nurse. If Juliet were to leap eagerly toward the exit the last two speeches would be unnecessary. The gesture here is a non-move, a stillness, a hesitant and mute resistance.

Scores of other variants in this text systematically exaggerate the coercive pressures mounted by the Capulets on their daughter. As we saw Anne Page as a more independent character in the second version of *Merry Wives*, here we see Juliet under tighter constraint, like

a wantons bird,
That lets it hop a litle from his hand,
Like a poore prisoner in his twisted gives,
And with a silken threed, plucks it back againe,
So loving Jealous of his libertie.
          [Q2,D4-D4^v; II.ii.177-81]

In the balcony scene Juliet feels this constraining love towards Romeo, modelling it on the stresses and forms we can observe in her own destructively-protective familial affections. The tiny gesture of hesitation and acquiescence I read in the differential text of this scene reflects the tragic and fundamentally passive helplessness of Juliet's character as it is amplified in the Second Quarto version.

* * * *

As a boy in high school, when I was asked to read Shakespeare's plays I hated the task. They lay dead on the page, or they were mumbled aloud by my hyperesthetic English teacher, and they seemed emotionally bleak, a language expressively so heavy that I could connect them to nothing I had ever known. The words as words and the poetry as poem seemed completely alien. But now, when I teach these playscripts to similarly distanced students, I find that they begin to respond fully when we pay attention to Shakespeare's dialogue as coded action. The movement demanded or simply suggested in the poetry appeals directly to our shared experience as people. The movement makes the poetic action recognizable. The gestural variants I've just examined with you seem to me to demonstrate how Shakespeare probed for more and more compelling and evocative gestures for his actors, hoping, I believe, to create a more binding sympathy between player and audience.

Finally I suggest that a differential calculus of gestural variants is a necessary tool for anyone charged with editing or criticizing Shakespeare's texts. And I offer that a calculus of gesture would go far to open the complex and kinetic phenomena of Shakespeare's plays to the huge audience now exposed to them as opaque school-texts and as cultural icons carved in mute stone.

Hofstra University

57

THE IDOLATROUS EYE: ICONOCLASM, ANTI-THEATRICALISM, AND THE IMAGE OF THE ELIZABETHAN THEATER

BY MICHAEL O'CONNELL

In 1583, seven years after the first public theater was built in London, Philip Stubbes declared that all stage plays are "sucked out of the Devills teates, to nourish us in ydolatry heathenrie and sinne."[1] A few months earlier Stephen Gosson, in his second attack on the stage, compared playgoing with the eating of meat sacrificed to idols, against which St. Paul had cautioned the Corinthians: "If we be carefull that no pollution of idoles enter by the mouth into our bodies, how diligent, how circumspect, how wary ought we to be, that no corruption of idols, enter by the passage of our eyes & eares into the soule?"[2] Again and again the Elizabethan anti-theatrical writers hurl the charge of idolatry against the stage. The charge is a strange one, for the drama of the period is what we would recognize as secular, having nothing obvious to do with worship—and hence with the false worship of idolatry. Behind the attack appears to lie a religious preoccupation, one that surfaces as well in an obverse way when Reformed writers attack what they see as the theatricality of Catholic worship. John Rainolds, the learned Oxford divine and a popular university preacher, charged that "Popish priests . . . have transformed the celebrating of the Sacrament of the Lords supper into a Masse-game, and all other partes of Ecclesiastical service into theatrical sights." He sees this as precisely analogous to the way the gospel was "played" instead of preached in the traditional mystery plays.[3] That such writers saw theater, even what we consider secular theater, in religious terms may explain the extraordinary vehemence of their opposition and why they could not be satisfied with reform. For although such anti-theatrical writers as John Northbrooke, Anthony Munday, Stubbes, and Gosson inveigh against what they see as the dangerous moral corruption of the London theaters, there is for them no question of regulating behavior in the playhouses or censoring what was played on their stages. Only a complete extirpation of all theaters and playing would satisfy them. In this North-

279

brooke, who in 1577 was the first to write against the stage, is typical of those who would follow him: stage plays and interludes "are not tollerable nor sufferable in any common weale, especially where the Gospell is preached," and he would exclude all actors, along with witches, sorcerers, and other notable sinners, from receiving the sacrament.[4]

In his recent and masterful study, *The Antitheatrical Prejudice*, Jonas Barish records that the bitterest opposition to the theater coincides with periods when the theater most flourishes. In ancient Greece the accomplishments of the great tragedians brought on Plato's anti-theatrical reaction; in Renaissance England the vehement attacks of the Puritans came as the public theaters opened with the work of a generation that would include Marlowe and Shakespeare; and in seventeenth-century France the artistry of Racine and Molière evoked the unremitting hostility of the Jansenists. The one exception to this pattern that Barish finds is the medieval drama. For despite the "abundance and energy of medieval theatrical culture, no sustained body of anti-theatrical writing survives from the Middle Ages."[5] The one medieval attack on the stage that Barish discusses, a fourteenth-century sermon of Lollard inspiration attacking miracle plays, is therefore an exception, an oddity of the age. There is obvious plausibility in Barish's explanation why the vigorous medieval drama was, if not immune, then largely free from opposition. The theater of the Middle Ages originated in the ritual of the Church and took its life from the mysteries of faith that maintained the culture. Its central subject was the biblical story of man's salvation.

But to explain the medieval embrace of the stage thus is to raise immediate questions about the opposition to it that occurs after the Reformation. For not only was much Elizabethan drama based on materials that sustained the culture, but as printed texts even the fictional works from which stage comedies and romances derived were not subject to an attack of comparable vehemence. The most curious fact of all, however, is that in post-Reformation England it was the biblical drama that provoked the most bitter, sustained—and successful—opposition. That a popular and vernacular biblical drama should be assailed by the left wing of the English Reformation requires explanation, for to an even greater degree than in the preceding two centuries the religious life of the culture took its sustenance from the Bible. On the face of it nothing would appear to have been more educationally useful to the goals

Iconoclasm and the Elizabethan Theater

of the reformers than suitably revised versions of the mystery cycles. That the biblical drama was Catholic in origin scarcely accounts for its rejection. Virtually all church buildings in England had been constructed for Catholic worship, but this proved no inhibition to their being adapted and used for Protestant worship. Similarly, the *Book of Common Prayer* in large part translated and reshaped the liturgy and rites inherited from the Catholic past. In nearly all cases the new wine of the English Reformation was successfully decanted into the old bottles of the Catholic past. But in the case of the biblical drama the bottle was decisively smashed and the pieces successfully hidden away for several centuries.[6] And the secular drama, though it not only survived but triumphed in the generation of playwrights who emerged in the 1590s, was subjected to a sustained religious attack for the first time in centuries—indeed for the first time, it seems, since the Church Fathers had warned Christians against Roman drama more than ten centuries before.

I wish to advance an argument not so much competing with as complementing Barish's to explain the nature of Elizabethan anti-theatricalism. Barish is entirely persuasive in his account of how anxiety about the fluid, protean self implied by theatricality stands as a constant behind Western anti-theatricalism.[7] But what of the specifically religious content of these attacks on the nascent public theaters, particularly the concern over idolatry? And why was the most extreme hostility directed toward biblical drama? What in the psychological climate of the late sixteenth century made drama seem so threatening to the left wing of English Protestantism? My answer to these questions is rooted in some historical particulars of the century, in attitudes toward the perceptual faculties, those structuring agents of human knowledge, and in the ways these attitudes were formed in reaction to the previous century. I see a comparatively sudden shift in the way perceptual faculties were valued and deployed between the late Middle Ages and the culture of the Reformation and shall argue that this shift led to a profound change in the religious aesthetic of the Reformation. This alteration of perceptual/aesthetic values, along with the psychic anxieties identified by Barish, stands behind the opposition to the emerging theater of the English Renaissance. An equally important question concerns the way drama, particularly as it was shaped by its most self-conscious practitioners, formed its identity in response to this attack upon it as idolatry. Identity, whether in individuals or in

Michael O'Connell   281

institutions, comes not only of what fosters but what opposes. Because apparently secular drama was attacked in religious terms, we must be open to the possibility that it may define itself in similar terms. To this end I want to conclude with a tentative exploration of the contrasting ways Shakespeare and Jonson defined their dramaturgy in response to this post-Reformation alteration of perceptual values.

I

The charge of idolatry came in part *ex origine*: Northbrooke and Gosson both argue that plays were first devised to honor the false gods of the Gentiles at their festivals and because of this retain the taint of idolatry.[8] But more significantly, plays were idolatrous as well in that they were ἐίδωλα, images, things seen. "For the eye," Gosson writes, "beeside the beautie of the houses, and the Stages, [the playwright] sendeth in Gearish appearell, maskes, vauting, tumbling, dauncing of gigges, galiardes, morisces, hobbehorses; showing of judgeling castes, nothing forgot, that might serve to set out the matter with pompe, or rather the beholders with varietie of pleasure."[9] Its appeal to the eye, they are persuaded, is what makes the theater so vivid, so effective in fixing itself in the mind. Anthony Munday voices what is a common fear—as well as a backhanded tribute to the power—of the stage. "There commeth much evil in at the eares, but more at the eies, by these two open windowes death breaketh into the soul. Nothing entereth in more effectualie into the memorie, than that which commeth by seeing, things heard do lightlie passe awaie, but the tokens of that which wee have seen, saith Petrarch, sticke fast in us whether we will or no."[10] Theater, in fact, overpowers by the fulness of its sensual appeal; one is surrounded by speech, motion and gesture. When Ben Jonson makes his Puritan Zeal-of-the-Land Busy call the puppets of Bartholomew Fair "that idol, that heathenish idol . . . a beam in the eye of the brethren," he is repeating both the actual language of the anti-theatrical writers and expressing their abhorrence of the powerful visual appeal of playing.

This conviction about the power of the theater should lead us to ask why it was not seized upon as an effective tool for the educational aims of the Reformation, why it was instead condemned as idolatrous and popish. An earlier generation of English reformers did in fact make tentative use of the stage as such a persuasive and polemical tool. In the late 1530s and the '40s, the

Iconoclasm and the Elizabethan Theater

time of John Bale's dramatic activity, Cromwell and Cranmer had fostered Protestant interludes and moralities as a means of publicizing reformed doctrine.[11] But the fate of the mystery cycles shows most clearly the difficulty felt by the next generation of Elizabethan churchmen, and particularly the left wing of the Church, in squaring the stage with religious objectives. Like the *Book of Common Prayer*—and with even less theological strain[12]—the plays could have been adapted if the impulse to use them had existed among Elizabeth's influential churchmen. The plays themselves are comparatively light in doctrinal comment on the issues that divided Christendom: their doctrine bears rather on the larger concerns of fall and salvation, God's judgment and mercy, and man's moral choices in response to this drama of his redemption. Marian plays, to be sure, formed a part of the cycles, but these could have been eliminated with no decisive loss to the power of the whole. And similar alterations in the plays dealing with the sacrament of the altar could have conformed their teaching to the new order of things.

But the plays were doomed to a thorough suppression by the Elizabethan church and government, and from the methods employed and the attitudes expressed in the suppression, we can see that the antipathy toward biblical drama ran far deeper than mere disagreement with the doctrinal formulations expressed in them. In fact, the surviving records indicate that attempts by the civic authorities to alter their traditional cycles to conform to doctrinal change were met by an implacable ecclesiastical determination to end their performance altogether, however they were revised. When the York cycle was played for the first time in Elizabeth's reign, in 1561, some of the pageants concerning the Virgin were excised, and when it was given for what would be the last time in 1569, some 50 passages had been altered.[13] The following year saw Edmund Grindal appointed archbishop of York. A Marian exile in Strasbourg and a Calvinist in theology, Grindal had as bishop of London urged the banning of plays during the plague of 1564, adding that it would suit him if plays were banned forever because of their profanation of the Word of God.[14] Grindal took an active role in suppressing the traditional biblical drama in the North. At York the civic authorities were cautious enough to have their Paternoster play "perused, amended, and corrected" before it was played in 1572, but in spite of their precautions, Grindal later called for the copy of the play to be delivered to him. Some three

Michael O'Connell   283

years later a delegation of citizens went to the archbishop to ask for the return of "all suche play bookes as pertayne to this cittie now in his graces custody." (Gardiner theorizes that the Creed play had also been impounded). The citizens' hope was that the archbishop would appoint some learned divine to oversee and correct the plays. But his grace simply kept the plays and did not return them. In 1579 an attempt was made to revive the Corpus Christi cycle, but again efforts to have the plays overseen and amended came to nothing more than the apparent archiepiscopal impounding of that text as well (Gardiner, 75–77). What the central government and church authorities wanted, clearly, was not a biblical drama in conformity with reformed theology, but no biblical drama at all.

This is confirmed by the rest of the record in the North. Gardiner's account of Chester (79–81) also shows popular support for the plays in the face of official opposition. Grindal sent a letter to stop the performance of the Corpus Christi plays there in 1571, but the mayor, John Hankey, allowed them to go forward with the claim that the archbishop's inhibition had come too late. Three years later another mayor, Sir John Savage, like Hankey a loyal Protestant, took the precaution of having the plays corrected and amended before he allowed them to be performed again. But he was acting against a direct prohibition from Grindal and the Earl of Huntington, the Lord President of the North. After his mayoralty, Savage was called before the Privy Council to answer for his apparent defiance. His defense, as well as that of Hankey, came in a letter from the succeeding mayor stating that both had been acting on behalf of the alderman of the city in consideration of the benefit the citizens derived from the performance of their ancient cycle plays. The document that expresses the decision to suppress the Wakefield plays in the spring of 1576 gives what must have been the official sentiment behind the suppression of the biblical drama. The ecclesiastical commission of York, having learned of the city's intention to stage the plays, stated "that there be many thinges used which tende to the derogation of the Maiesty and glorie of God, the prophanation of the sacraments and the maunteynance of superstition and idolatry." It was therefore decreed that no play or pageant be played "wherein the Maiestye of God the Father, God the Sonne, or God the Holie Ghoste or the administration of either the Sacramentes of baptisme or of the Lordes Supper be counterfeyted or represented, or anythinge plaied

284   *Iconoclasm and the Elizabethan Theater*

64

which tends to the maintenaunce of superstition and idolatrie or which be contrarie to the lawes of God or of the realme" (Gardiner, 78).

The real issue, then, is representation. The charges against the mystery plays are that they *represent* God and *counterfeit* the life of Christ and the institution of the sacraments. This explains why the guilds and aldermen of the various towns were fighting a losing battle in attempting to preserve their plays by adjusting the doctrine expressed in them and excising the Marian pageants. For the real sticking point was not Marian, ecclesiastical or eucharistic dogma, but the physical portrayal of the divine. And while it may have been just possible to reduce the God of the Old Testament plays to an offstage voice, there is no way that the heart of the cycles, the life, death and resurrection of Christ, could have been played without an actor portraying Christ. The real center of the altered religious aesthetic which separates the latter half of the sixteenth century from a time forty or fifty years earlier when the cycles were last played without interference—and indeed which separates the townspeople in some cases from their ecclesiastical governors—is the physical, visual portrayal of the sacred.

While inveighing against theater in general, the London antitheatrical writers save their most enthusiastic invective for the religious stage. Munday considers it "of all abuses . . . the most undecent and intollerable" that sacred matters should be prophaned by actors.[15] What disturbs him and Stubbes is not only that Scripture is enacted but that it is treated with artistic license. In bringing biblical narratives to stage life, the playwrights of the mystery cycles had been free to elaborate and humanize the figures of sacred history. Both comedy and pathos serve to bring the narratives closer to the emotional life of an audience. Noah's wife, at the last minute, decides she wants nothing to do with shipboard life. And Joseph reacts with the jealousy and anger that any man would who discovers that his betrothed, whom he had thought chaste, is with child. To Munday this elaboration means that "the reverend word of God, & histories of the Bible . . . are so corrupted with the actors gestures of scurrilitie, and so interlaced with uncleane, and whorish speeches" that it is wholly impossible to derive any moral or spiritual benefit from the plays. Stubbes reprehends "the bawdry, scurrility, wanton showes, and uncomely gestures" which he believes prophane the Word of God in the religious drama.[16] If none of the mystery cycles had survived, we

Michael O'Connell   285

would imagine from such sixteenth-century descriptions that some bizarre form of biblical pornography had been served up on the medieval stage.

These attitudes toward the biblical drama, officially expressed by suppression and unofficially by the invective of the anti-theatrical writers, stand diametrically opposed to those which had prevailed in the previous two centuries. And it is in fact only in our own time, when the plays have again been performed and their dramatic power in part rediscovered (though one may feel that only a beginning has been made) that we have emerged from the shadow of this Elizabethan condemnation. Behind the condemnation lies a two-fold alteration in religious sensibility. There is first the vigorous rejection of the idea that God, Christ, or the sacred events of biblical history should be physically represented. And secondly—the reverse of the same coin—there is a new literalism in the attitude toward scripture. As Walter Ong has argued, the Bible was present to medieval culture in a largely oral mode: "the culture as a whole assimilated the biblical word not verbatim but as oral culture typically assimilates a message, thematically and formulaicly; tribally rather than individually, by contrast with post-typographical culture."[17] The biblical drama of the mystery cycles was far less concerned with *literal* fidelity to the words of Scripture than with emotional engagement with its patterns of fall and redemption, judgment and salvation. The story of Abraham and Isaac, for example, is elaborated from a brief and strikingly unemotive scriptural text into a dialogue that emphasizes the human pathos of their situation and Isaac's self-submission to his father's terrible duty. At the end of the play its prefigurement of the Father's sacrifice of *his* Son is made explicit, and the theological pattern is given thereby an emotional emphasis it would not otherwise possess.

With the Reformation comes an insistence on *scriptura*, on what is written—and only what is written. God's self-revelation is to be found in the exact words of a text. Ong links this to the development of typography, which made exact, unvarying texts possible and lent increased confidence to the "word-in-space." A consequence was an alteration of the psychological structures for assimilating the word.[18] The written word became the norm of truth. In the case of the mystery plays, the words of Scripture had been a point of departure for dramatic elaboration, though this elaboration was consonant with traditions of interpretation. Such elab-

Iconoclasm and the Elizabethan Theater

oration would clearly become suspect when religious truth was perceived to reside in exact texts. This altered status of the word clearly stands behind the intense dislike on the part of the anti-theatrical writers for the interpolations and adaptations of biblical narrative in the cycle plays. Stubbes shows this in the extraordinary interpretation he gives to the beginning of St. John's Gospel in order to condemn players of religious drama: "In the first of *John* we are taught, *that the word is God, and God is the word.* Wherefore, whosoever abuseth this word of our God on Stages, in Playes and Enterludes, abuseth the majesty of God in the same, maketh a mocking stocke of him, and purchaseth to himself eternal damnation."[19] The abuse worthy of damnation that Stubbes discovers in the mystery plays is not, of course, anything that to a modern eye (or ear) smacks of irreverence or irreligious mockery; it is simply the attempt to find and portray the emotional life of the biblical narratives. And to the medieval sensibility they were clearly more narrative, more story, than text. To Stubbes it is a text that has been tampered with—amplified, versified, then enacted with all the visual and aural embellishment that actors must use. His antipathy to such adaptation leads him to the heterodox identification of the *Logos* with the word of scripture, rather than with the preexistent Christ; he turns the words of the text into the Word toward which words can only point. In this he merely gives slight exaggeration to the role the reformers had assigned Scripture as the sole connecting link between man and God; only in the words of a written text was the Word to be encountered. Expressed in the heightened form Stubbes here gives it (and common enough in polemical contexts), the position can be defined as logolatry, the reverse of the coin of idolatry of which Catholicism stood accused by the Reformation.

II

While the opposition to secular drama was confined by and large to the left wing of the Reformation in England—the party that would evolve toward Puritanism—the opposition to religious drama was official policy. This opposition is symptom and part of a larger change in the religious aesthetic, a change which comes of a comparatively sudden and far-reaching shift of attitude toward the perceptual faculties in worship. We can find its ultimate source in the crisis in the relation of image and word that came with the Reformation; there developed a deep-seated anxiety about the role

Michael O'Connell   287

of the visual, especially in worship, but in other religious contexts as well. Until that point the relation between image and word had remained generally untroubled in the Western church.[20] Christianity, like the Judaism from which it emerged, obviously takes its life from verbal narratives and teaching; at its center is verbal remembrance—initally oral, but in written form from the second half of the first century—of the life and teaching of Christ. Though largely aniconic at first, because of its Judaic roots, Christianity appears to have accepted visual portrayal of Christ, and later of martyrs and saints, from the early centuries. By the fourth century visual art had a definite role in Christian worship. The best-known Western challenge to images came at the end of the sixth century when Serenus, bishop of Marseilles, removed and destroyed images in a church to prevent their worship. Gregory the Great commended his concern for idolatry but forbade the removal and destruction of images. His defense of images would become the classic one in the West: that visual representations were the "books" of the illiterate, and to this end their instructive, nonidolatrous use should be encouraged. In the East, of course, the use of images met more serious challenge in the series of iconoclastic controversies of the eighth century. Stephen Gero has called these controversies "an undeniable foreshadowing of some aspects of the Protestant Reformation."[21] And indeed at their peak in the 760s and 770s the attacks against images extended also, almost inevitably, to the doctrine of the intercession of the saints and the cult of relics. The Second Nicean Council resolved the question by defending icons and defining their nonidolatrous use; it also distinguished the worship due to God alone (*latria*) from the honor accorded to saints (*dulia*). The Gregorian and Nicean defenses of images would remain largely effective until the Reformation. In tracing subsequent incidents of iconoclasm in the Western church, W. R. Jones concludes that they were isolated attacks by religious radicals on a system of devotion which most Europeans found emotionally and doctrinally satisfying.[22] It is not until the 1520s that the visual element in worship is subjected to sustained and decisive attack.

To understand the Reformation reaction it is necessary to realize the extent to which worship and devotion in the late Middle Ages were expressed in visual, sensual form. Religious experience tended toward physical manifestation—the pilgrimage, the procession, the mystery cycles, veneration of the Sacrament, elab-

288   *Iconoclasm and the Elizabethan Theater*

orate devotions to the saints—to a degree that may appear excessive to modern sensibility. The extraordinary growth of the cult of relics fostered pilgrimages, the object of which was the sight of the saint's bones or the richly decorated tomb that held them. When shrines of the Virgin became the major centers of pilgrimage, as they did in the late Middle Ages, it was usually a statue that provided the focus of devotion.[23] The cult of the saints created the need, increasingly in the fifteenth century, for vividly rendered paintings and statues. The practice of elevating the Host, making it visible to the congregation, became widespread in public worship about the middle of the thirteenth century. The monstrance, for displaying the Host, came into use in the following century. Indeed, the visual worship of the Eucharist, which would so deeply trouble the reformers, is a striking feature of late medieval sacramental devotion. To *see* the Host became a principal concern of worshippers, and in cities people would sometimes go from church to church to witness the elevation as often as possible. Glass chalices were also called for so the laity also might see the wine which had been made the Blood of Christ.[24]

There may appear in such devotion an excessive embracing of the merely superficial, the trappings and rags (sometimes literally) of religion. It is a piety that seems to satisfy spiritual need by physical expression. Huizinga, to whom we owe vivid descriptions of late medieval piety, expresses what is a likely modern reaction to such devotion:

> The naive religious conscience of the multitude had no need of intellectual proofs in matters of faith. The mere presence of a visible image of things holy sufficed to establish their truth. No doubts intervened between the sight of all these pictures and statues— the persons of the Trinity, the flames of hell, the innumerable saints—and belief in their reality. All these conceptions became matters of faith in the most direct manner: they passed straight from the state of images to that of convictions, taking root in the mind as pictures clearly outlined and vividly colored, possessing all the reality claimed for them by the church, and even a little bit more.[25]

His last phrase in particular emphasizes what is the usual modern assumption about such late medieval religious expression: that it is an excess of the illiterate and simple. The problem here is the same one Peter Brown addresses in terms of late antiquity: a false distinction between what is assumed to be "popular religion" and that practiced by an intellectual elite.[26] There can be no doubt that theologically inexpert worshippers brought more literal assumptions to their devotions, both before the Reformation and after. But aside from the cautions against idolatry in the use of images and criticism of the excesses of pilgrimages and relic-mongering, there is little evidence that the educated did not also derive satisfaction from modes of worship and devotion in which the visual and sensuous played an important part. Princes and churchmen made pilgrimages as well as the humble. In England the cult of the saints and the veneration of images were defended against Lollard sentiment by such learned theologians as Reginald Pecock.[27] And aside from the austere Cistercians, monastery churches were not less given to visual elaboration and display than cathedral or parish churches, and indeed were more likely than the latter to possess important relics. The difference, if there is one, is more a matter of degree—or an understanding of the theological underpinnings—than basic disagreement about the forms of religious expression. Here, as in the Reformation, the learned instructed the unlearned.[28]

In his largely negative account of late medieval religious practice, Huizinga focuses on the excesses of this highly sensuous and physical devotion—the avidity for relics and pilgrimages, the multiplicity of saints and their elaborately clad statues, and a pervasive and arbitrary system of symbolism for all the gestures and acts of everyday life. But what is important to realize is that the same physically expressive devotion that underlay these practices also gave rise to the highly developed painting and sculpture of the period, to architecture of unequaled grace and majesty, to stained glass, to vestments, reliquaries, and chalices of exquisite craftsmanship. Huizinga refers to the tendency "to give concrete shape to every conception," to express thought through an embodied image.[29] What is at work here is what may be called a strongly incarnational sense of religious experience, a habit of understanding which incarnates spiritual values and longings in forms immediately accessible to human senses and emotions. The fifteenth-century devotional painting of Northern Europe illustrates this most clearly: events in the life of Christ or in the lives of the Virgin and the saints are portrayed in such a way as to render them fully accessible to immediate human experience. The sorrow on the face of the Virgin in a Deposition from the Cross is that of a mother who has lost her son, and the vividness of the painted image conveys that directly, the visual bypassing verbal expression in its effect. The enacted emotions in the figures of sacred history in the mystery plays are a similar case in point.

But even such nonrepresentational arts as architecture attempted to embody the sacred in physical images. Indeed, the Gothic cathedrals and monastery churches of Northern Europe may provide the most complete illustration of this medieval desire to express the sacred in physical terms. For these are, above all, expressive buildings, and even in modern nonbelievers they are capable of evoking the awe and wonder the builders intended. They were not conceived abstractly or simply to give visual pleasure. As Otto von Simson and others have shown, the buildings were designed according to geometric principles by the following of which the medieval architect believed he was imitating the Creator.[30] Using such principles, the Gothic architect could apply the very laws that order heaven and earth. In this way the sanctuary he built not only would become a model of the cosmos in its imitation of the order of the visible world, but it would express an image of the perfection of the world to come. The fabric of the material church thereby portrays the spiritual church, the universal church that encompasses heaven and earth and extends in time from the creation to the last judgment.[31] The cruciform plan of most Gothic churches establishes them further as representative of the mystical body of Christ, a symbolic identification entirely consistent with the idea that they represent the universal church. Even the disposition of the sculpture both within and without expresses visibly the relation of the whole company of heaven to the worshippers themselves. One may well feel that the symbolism in the hierarchic arrangement of the images far outweighed its use as a *biblia pauperum*; it was not for the illiterate only but for all the faithful to sense their place in a grand scheme of patriarchs, prophets, apostles, saints, and angels. The luminosity that Von Simson establishes as a central principle of Gothic architecture expresses a theology of light that follows St. John's Gospel in identifying the Light of Christ with the divine creative force. Thus what had earlier been painted or portrayed in mosaic in the image of the Christus Pantocrator was given new symbolic expression in the light that literally enlightens the world imaged in the church.[32] That the holy was embodied visibly, through stone, glass, and wood, would be everywhere felt in the light and space and the structural perfection of such a building.

Michael O'Connell   291

There is moreover a kind of incarnational logic in the relation of saints' relics to the symbolic drama performed in every medieval church. Most cathedrals and the churches of large monastic foundations contained, or had been founded on, the physical remains of a martyr. In late medieval practice it became indispensable for the dedication of an altar, even in parish churches, that it contain the relic of a martyr.[33] As the symbolic enactment of Christ's sacrifice on Calvary, the Mass would thus be performed over or near the remains of a martyr who had in his own death reenacted this sacrifice. The relation thereby expressed between Christ and the martyrs points toward an incarnational understanding that accords the saints a participation in the sacrificial victory of Christ. It is not that they become sharers exactly in the act of redemption. But the incarnational relationship implied in the cult of the saints, as the reformers were shrewd enough to intuit, does suggest that Christ's role as human and divine redeemer flows over into other mediators between God and man.[34] In this sense Christ's unique identity may appear compromised in the recognition that those who imitated him in life and death may also be channels of divine favor. The association of relics with the Mass implies some such imaginative understanding that theology could not articulate, let alone endorse.

I suggest this theological dimension to the highly physical expression of late medieval piety in order to indicate the interconnectedness of the seemingly separate Reformation challenges to icons, relics, the intercession of the saints, liturgical ceremony, and the real presence in the Eucharist. It should also be apparent that these challenges must be understood as aimed ultimately at more than the superficial elements of religious expression, that behind them lies the question of how the divine is to be experienced. Is the divine to be understood as continually incarnated through sacralized elements of the human world? Has the Incarnation of Christ so transformed the physical that it may provide access to the sacred? Or is it idolatrous to seek the divine in the physical, the Creator in the creature? Is the Incarnation to be understood solely in terms of Christ and experienced primarily in language and through texts that may be traced back to historical contact with him? Without itself articulating the connections, the Reformation would attack the diverse manifestations of the more open incarnationalism of medieval religion—and so successfully that much of the substance of its critique has survived the intervening centuries.

That this critique was inextricably bound up with the logocentrism of the humanist program will be apparent in a brief tracing of its history. Significantly, Luther's attitude toward the aesthetics of worship, visual art and music in particular, remained largely positive, while that of his followers more directly influenced by humanism turned sharply negative. Huldrych Zwingli stands as the central figure of this latter development. But between Luther and Zwingli the logocentric theology of Erasmus is of crucial importance in clarifying and making explicit those tendencies toward a word-centered religious culture released by the development of typography. His attacks on pilgrimages, relics, and the cult of the saints in the *Colloquies* are well known. Of equal importance here is his celebration of the vividness and power of Christ's image as it is discovered in the text of Scripture and his consequent depreciation of the efficacy of the visually rendered image to devotion. In the *Paraclesis* Erasmus goes so far as to wonder whether the Christ who is portrayed in the printed gospels does not live "more effectively" than when he dwelt among men.[35] For Christ's contemporaries, Erasmus asserts, saw and heard less than readers may see and hear in the text Erasmus has just edited. In the written gospels Christ is "so fully present" that one would see less if he looked upon him with his own eyes. This devaluation of the actual Incarnation in comparison with the textual record of it may not be a fully considered position of Erasmus; it seems in context rather an expression of the enthusiasm of presenting the first typographical edition of the Greek New Testament to the world. But it does illustrate the intensity of his conviction that Christ was to be encountered most fully in the word, and not in any visual form.

Erasmus himself was never an actual iconoclast, of course, and he was not unresponsive to visual art.[36] In *The Godly Feast* Eusebius, the host, points out the frescoes on the walls of his garden and chapel. But this exception in a sense proves the rule: the figures in each picture "speak" in the verbal labels painted alongside, usually trilingually in Latin, Greek, and Hebrew; visual images are thus dominated by their learned verbal accompaniment. Elsewhere Erasmus shows himself highly suspicious of the devotional use of art and gives the opinion that it would be pref-

Michael O'Connell 293

erable to have no images but the crucifix in churches.[37] A very revealing moment in this contest of word and image occurs in Erasmus's catechism for adults.[38] The student in the dialogue wonders whether the honor that the second commandment implies should be given to the *name* of God might conflict with the prohibition of idolatry in the first commandment. For a word naming God is as much a created thing as an image, and in honoring a word one may perhaps be giving idolatrous worship to a man-made object. The master, Erasmus's spokesman, answers this easily: one does not bow one's head or knees to the word or voice of man, but to Him whom the word signifies; a word is nothing like an image, and there is no peril that a word should be taken for the thing represented. It is necessary, moreover, that God should be declared, and for this use the speech of man was given to him. A medieval theologian such as Pecock, however, could just as easily apply this reasoning to images: in the reverence accorded an image, not the paint or wood but the person represented is honored, and there is no danger that a mere representation may be taken for the living person.[39] Later Thomas More would stand his friend's defense on its head: if we agree to reverence the verbal symbol for God, it is illogical to fear idolatry in reverencing the visual symbols.[40] A recent scholar of Erasmus's logocentrism notes this changed emphasis: "The religious pedagogy of the medieval centuries, which relied on the visual image, is succeeded by the humanist doctrine of the published text. . . . The humanist persuasion that an eloquent text orates reality expands in Erasmus to a lively faith in the real presence of Christ as text."[41] "Christ as text," for Erasmus, replaces the painted, sculpted Christ, and for succeeding reformers Christ's real presence as text would eclipse his real presence in the visible, tactile Eucharist.

It is in Zwingli's career in Zurich that this Erasmian logocentrism first reaches full iconoclastic expression. Educated in humanist discipline, Zwingli was a thorough-going Erasmian before he became a reformer. He spent two years immersed in the study of Erasmus's works and later would date his conviction that Christ was the sole mediator between God and man from his reading of a poem by Erasmus.[42] Zwingli's attitudes toward the aesthetics of worship achieve such rigor and consistency that through him we can witness this Erasmian hegemony of word over image becoming cultural fact. Zwingli sets in motion the forces to which Erasmus had given expression, but at the same time he appears more an indicator, a barometric needle pointing toward a tendency in the culture, than a cause of this shift of thinking.

In January of 1519 Zwingli began his tenure as "people's priest" in the Great Minster of Zurich in humanist fashion by giving a series of discourses on the Gospel of St. Matthew, expounding "the complete plain text without any of the accretions of scholastic interpretation" (Potter, 60). More discourses followed on the New Testament, based always on the principle of *sola scriptura*. Zwingli began the Reformation in Zurich this same year with an attack on the cult of the saints. Much of what followed—attacks on fasting, clerical celibacy, the Mass and the Eucharist, the papacy and episcopal authority—fit the Lutheran mold, though Zwingli was always careful to insist on his independence from Luther. Zwingli's first original contribution to the course of the Reformation came in January of 1523 when in the list of his *Sixty-Seven Conclusions* (for public disputation in Zurich) he attacked the use of music in worship. The attack comes in the context of a rigorously logical discussion of prayer, in which he maintains that no prayer can be pleasing to God but that which comes directly from the heart. All choral singing, therefore, artificial and public as it is, cannot be true prayer. He also finds that music is nowhere commanded in Scripture to be part of worship. The real issue, as we might expect, is the split between word and music in devotional singing: one cannot concentrate on the full sense of the words and sing well (Garside, 49). Music divides one from verbal content and thus cannot be true prayer. What is fascinating about Zwingli's rejection of music in worship is that he was not a tone-deaf despiser of an art he could not understand or enjoy but, as Garside has shown, particularly accomplished in music and able to play a variety of instruments well (7–26, 73–77). His rejection of music, moreover, was centered entirely on worship, and he himself continued to play for private recreation. Equally interesting is how quickly and completely Zurich was convinced of the correctness of Zwingli's rejection of musical worship: a year later, by decree of the ruling council, the organs were silenced, and a year after that the Roman Mass was sung for the last time and replaced with an entirely spoken communion service. In 1527 the organs were completely removed from the churches and destroyed. Though vocal music was again permitted after 1598, organs would not be returned to the churches of Zurich until well into the nineteenth century (Garside, 61–62).

Michael O'Connell 295

Zwingli's rejection of images came later in the same year. It was the product of the same rigorous logic and scriptural literalism which he had applied to prayer. The second commandment had forbidden *all* images as idolatrous, and in his prohibition Zwingli applied the commandment not only to churches but to all public places and even to private homes (Garside, 149). Only representations of historic events were excepted, and these could not be placed in churches. Though Zwingli's position on images was not unopposed, the response of the ruling council of the canton was even swifter than with music. Within a few weeks it was decreed that all the paintings with moving panels be shut and that no images or reliquaries be carried in procession. Six months later the removal of all images was ordered. Every statue was removed from its niche and broken up, all paintings were taken down and burned, all frescoes were chipped off, all crucifixes removed, and every vessel, image and votive lamp on the altars was taken down and melted. Even the carved choir stalls were removed and burned. Then the walls were whitewashed. When the operation was completed, a pious if reactionary Zuricher who had made his pilgrimage to Compostela said of the Great Minster, "There was nothing at all inside and it was hideous." But Zwingli could exult, "In Zurich we have churches which are positively luminous; the walls are beautifully white!" (Garside, 159–60). The Word could now be read and preached with no competition from the idolatrous eye.

Zwingli's attitudes toward devotional music and art were, as Garside has argued (39–43), part of a comprehensive understanding of worship. He aimed to eliminate everything sensual from it that he could. Even public worship, though necessary, was potentially suspect because it could be a setting for display and hypocrisy. Christ's injunction to pray in secret (Matthew 6:6) became for Zwingli the ideal toward which all worship should tend. If for a moment we consider public liturgy as a form of drama, we can see here a point at which Barish's argument and my own coincide. At the same time Zwingli wishes to clear the stage of all sensual distraction, eliminating as well the "costuming" of vestments, he grows scrupulous about the self who acts a part in public worship. The discrepancy between the interior self and the self who speaks or sings a part in a liturgy creates anxiety about hypocrisy. The self who is "played" in public worship may not be the same self one encounters in the privacy of meditation. A psychology that can accept the necessity, or even the utility, of such playing—or is not so self-conscious as to take particular notice of it—will accept the role that a liturgical celebration thrusts upon it. But a self not so constituted will need reassurance that the role is not a role. Bare walls can reflect back to a worshipper a self unmediated by distracting or competing human images. A service in which language alone is allowed, without images, music, gestures or vestments, better induces the reflection in which the single self may be encountered. The stripping of the theatrical from worship, then, corresponds both to a general anxiety toward the visual and to a need to bring public worship toward a simplicity in which self-reflection is a major goal.

Though Zwingli's strictures on music were not so universally applied—Calvin would allow hymns that were scripturally based—his position and example in purifying worship of visual elements would be followed throughout all of Northern Europe, especially where the Swiss Reformation was influential. In England this process would occur late and with a gradualism typical of the course of the Reformation there, but with a general acceptance that argues an atmosphere prepared in advance by the humanist culture of the previous two decades. In *Utopia*, published some twenty years before any actual iconoclasm in England, More has his Utopians worship in churches which are dark—for "they think that excessive light makes the thoughts wander"—and completely free of images.[43] (In the next decade, of course, More would defend images, relics, and the cult of saints against Tyndale in his *Dialogue Concerning Heresies*.) By 1536, when Hugh Latimer, newly made bishop of Worcester, attacked images and relics before Convocation, the climate was such that Convocation would readily agree to regulate images more strictly. The beginning of the dissolution of the monasteries that same year can be seen as the first outbreak of widespread iconoclasm in England.[44] The dissolution was obviously the result of numerous political, economic, and religious factors, but that iconoclastic sentiment was among them is clearly indicated by the fate of the buildings and the way the furnishings were disposed of. Most of the 650 monastic churches, images of the heavenly kingdom and symbolic models of the cosmos, were systematically destroyed or allowed to collapse when stripped of their roof lead and timber. Clearly the symbolic system and the habits of perception that had fostered it had virtually disappeared by the late 1530s. Except for isolated instances, most

Michael O'Connell   297

notably the Pilgrimage of Grace, there appears to have been little popular opposition to the dismantling of these hundreds of buildings and the dispersal of their furniture and ornaments.

That we are dealing with a pervasive change in habits of thought and perception is confirmed by the virtual cessation in the building of parish churches in England after the 1520s.[45] The previous two centuries had witnessed a vigorous program of ecclesiastical building; numerous Perpendicular Gothic parish churches spread throughout England testify still to this century and more of enthusiastic building. The building and renovation continued into the first two decades of the sixteenth century before abruptly ending. This near general halt in church building would last a century and a half, until the latter half of the seventeenth century.

Iconoclasm became royal policy in 1547 under Somerset's protectorate and with the concurrence of Archbishop Cranmer. Although a royal proclamation in July of that year continued to make the distinction between images that were used merely as "remembrances" and those that were idolatrous, in practice the distinction was impossible to maintain. In London the iconoclasm was general; the images in St. Paul's and most of the parish churches were pulled down and broken, and many of the churches were then whitewashed. Later the Privy Council ordered all images to be taken down and removed. After Somerset's fall, the order was made statute law in the same bill that established the *Book of Common Prayer*.[46] In some places images were withdrawn to be hidden away in hope of a reversal of iconoclast policy, but the more general response was the destruction of statues or their decapitation to prevent the saints' recognition. Stone altars, which contained martyrs' relics, were removed and replaced with wooden communion tables. Much stained glass was removed, though often it was saved for want of a clear replacement to keep out the weather. In many cases the word literally effaced the image: frescoes and painted rood screens were whitewashed and then covered with scriptural verses. In the Norfolk church of St. Mary's Priory in Binham the old painted figures have since become visible beneath the whitewash and texts from Tyndale's New Testament.[47]

While Mary's reign temporarily reversed this iconoclastic policy, it again prevailed, though with less overt destruction in the Elizabethan church. The only visual ornament allowed was the royal arms where the rood had once stood. A moveable communion

Iconoclasm and the Elizabethan Theater

table was to be available for placement in the nave or west end of the church, but the rest of the church furnishings were arranged to accommodate a congregation assembled to listen. If iconoclastic enthusiasm had been the nemesis of the church fabric in the 1540s, now it was simply neglect and the depredations of covetous gentry.[48] Opposition to idolatry was a frequent pretense for raiding the ornamentation of country churches. By many accounts the state of Elizabethan churches was such that if a Rip van Winkle had returned from the beginning of the century, he might have suspected that the worshippers had gone collectively blind.

III

In itself the attack of the anti-theatrical writers would not necessarily have influenced the self-understanding of the Elizabethan theater. But that attack was, as this account of Reformation iconoclasm indicates, part of a larger cultural movement that necessarily affected the development of something so dependent on the visual as drama. Students of the sixteenth century are well aware of the ways Tudor governments displaced religious ritual in their own extensive use of pageantry and display. But as Louis Montrose has argued, theater represents something separate from, indeed in an anthropological sense counter to, these authorized structures of social control. It is instead an innovation frequently seen as threatening to orthodox moral or religious order.[49] As such, its identity was formed amidst this deep anxiety about visual representation and ritual. The anxiety is well represented in language: phrases like "painted shows" and "colors of rhetoric" convey a pejorative, or at best ambivalent, sense of the visual. Distrust of appearance is virtually an article of faith in the humanist poetics. It becomes indeed the mainspring of Spenser's allegory. There the word *seems* almost invariably leads to the apprehension of visual deception; only the poet's own morally charged language and close attention to what characters *say* enable a reader to negotiate this world where what *is* must be discovered beneath what *seems*. In this poetics language is represented as the only reliable index of reality.

Theater cannot afford to be so mistrustful of what appears. Every bit as much as what is heard, its stock in trade is what is seen. The sumptuous costuming of the Elizabethan and Jacobean stage makes amply clear that the lack of scenic decoration did not mean indifference to visual display. One line of its development, the

Michael O'Connell 299

Stuart masque, would become so intensely visual that Ben Jonson's notorious quarrel with Inigo Jones can be understood as centering exactly on this losing battle the word there waged with the multiplicity of arts appealing to the eye. The public theaters, of course, did not yield to this dominance. They remained true to their original design as playing spaces affording maximum scope to verbal art. But this should not obscure the fact that contemporaries, and not only the anti-theatrical writers, testified to the powerful impression made on the eye as well as the ear of playgoers. In its self-understanding the stage cannot be expected simply to have evaded this pervasive anxiety in the religious and humanist culture. As it defined and defended itself, it had of necessity to confront the question of what part the visual had in its identity. The contrasting responses of Jonson and Shakespeare to this need show how acute this problem of definition was.

Barish has described Jonson's always ambivalent, frequently hostile relationship to the stage he wrote for; without exaggeration he characterizes it as "a deeply rooted anti-theatricalism."[50] Something of Jonson's hostility came of his contentious temperament. But it was founded intellectually on his primary allegiance to humanist culture. Richard Helgerson has recently shown how large a part this allegiance played in Jonson's creation for himself of a laureate identity *against* his identity as a man of the theater.[51] Even when promoting or defending his stage works, as he constantly does, Jonson appears seldom able to allow a play to be a play. In his prefaces and prologues he insists on them frequently as *poems*. Mockery of the physical requirements of staging, predominantly the movement and visual effects required by an audience for whom a play was not a poem but a show, also pepper the prefatory explaining he found essential to his identity as a playwright. His insistent hope that readers would find in his plays what mere audiences had missed reached its logical end when he printed them in his *Works* of 1616, a gesture of self-presentation as characteristic of Jonson as it was innovative for the stage. Erasmus's insistence on the higher truth of the verbal, printed edition of Christ finds a significant counterpart in Jonson's valuation of the printed texts of his plays against their theatrical incarnations.

With his brilliant stage caricatures of the Puritans, Jonson met the attack on the theaters head-on. In the final act of *Bartholomew Fair* he ridicules the attack effectively as Zeal-of-the-land Busy rails against the idolatry of the puppet theater, only to be confuted

Iconoclasm and the Elizabethan Theater

in his disputation with a puppet. And yet even that play appears deeply ambivalent about the spectacle of theater. It portrays the theatrical in the gaudiness, the tawdriness even, of the fair with its gingerbread and hobbyhorse vendors, pickpockets, pig booth, and puppet show—and in doing so comes close to conceding the Puritan argument. Only the simple-minded or foolish in the play are allowed to be whole-hearted partisans of puppet show and fair. Justice Overdo, with his classical allusions and desire to correct social enormities, reminds us most of Jonson, and in his suspicion of the fair he becomes the unwitting ally of Busy. What the play accomplishes is an uneasy and, for Jonson, rare concession to popular taste and the need for spectacle. Overdo is reminded of his first name, "you are but Adam, flesh and blood," and the claims of a flesh-and-blood audience are finally acknowledged, though not wholly approved.

Intensified perhaps by the quarrel with Inigo Jones, Jonson's cross-grained dislike of the theatrical seems to have increased rather than decreased in the latter part of his writing for the stage. If Puritans would have worshippers avoid the distraction of the visual to attend to the word of Scripture, Jonson wanted them to attend to his own words. The prologue to *The Staple of News* not only distinguishes between the poet and those who perform his words on stage but seems indeed to hanker after a blind audience:

> For your own sakes, not his, he bad me say,
> Would you were come to hear, not see a play.
> Though we his actors, must provide for those
> Who are our guests here, in the way of shows,
> The maker hath not so; he'd have you wise,
> Much rather by your ears, than by your eyes.[52]

This comes but as an extreme version of what Jonson in one way or another always wanted: near exclusive attention to the verbal element of the mixed art that theater is. His anxiety about spectacle points emphatically to the problem of definition that humanism and the Reformation created for theater. While his greatest stage creations are masters of deceiving the eye, characters for whom the costume change is as essential as breathing, he could never rest easy in this power of the stage. For all the vigor of his satire of the Puritans, a part of him remained as convinced as they that sight distracted the mind from the truth of the word.

Without Jonson's primary allegiance to humanist values, Shake-

Michael O'Connell   301

speare could assert the equal claim of the eye in the epistemology of theater. It is obvious that throughout his career he was far less anxious than Jonson about the status of theater in relation to humanist canons of literary definition. But in his most self-reflexive plays he insists in a positive way on the identity of theater as a visual art. Though *Midsummer Night's Dream* may appear in the lovers' plot to express the debility of sight, Puck's control of their eyes becomes an obvious analogue of the playwright's power over his audience. Through the anointing and reanointing of eyes we sense the need for our own complicity in the processes by which theater practices on the faculty of sight. It is fear of visual disguise that leads the mechanicals into the comic rending of theatrical illusion when Bottom suggests that the actors had better confess their real identities. A similar concern also leads them to the wonderfully inept stage images of Wall and Moonshine. Though much of the humor of *Pyramis and Thisbe* remains impervious to analysis, we may sense that some of it comes of the half-literate status of the mechanicals. Clearly Prologue has been tripped up by the punctuation of a written text, and in subject and rhetoric the mechanicals' play may seem to parody humanist concerns by handing them over to ill-suited scholars. But Bottom impresses, and indeed achieves his status as the imaginative center of the play, by his ability to give himself up to vision. His child-like eagerness to accept and enter into what he sees sets him off not only from the lamely joking court audience of the mechanicals' play but also from the detached if sympathetic Theseus. When Bottom exclaims on his fairy vision, we may properly take the confused synesthesia as a Shakespearean judgment of the relative importance of the various senses to the theatrical experience: "The eye of man hath not heard, the ear of man hath not seen, man's hand is not able to taste, his tongue to conceive, nor his heart to report, what my dream was" (*MND*, 4.2.210–14).[53] And as a deformation of the text of St. Paul, Bottom's formulation would have an easily calculated effect on textual literalists.

A moment of primary significance to the question of theatrical self-definition occurs when Hamlet protests the reality of his appearance; "Seems, madam? nay, it is, I know not 'seems' " (*Hamlet*, 1.2.76). His costume, his gestures, his face, and his actions may indeed seem, may be visual signs "that a man might play," but with him they are coterminous with his inward state, with his essential reality. It is a feature of the play that the theatrical metaphor becomes so completely identified with Hamlet's consciousness—and ultimately with ours—that the play can be said to achieve meaning only in terms of the metaphor. Shakespeare takes a strange risk by identifying his theater with the action and setting of the play. Hamlet (or the actor playing Hamlet?) refers to the stage directly when he points down to it and calls the ghost "this fellow in the cellerage" (1.5.151). He likewise gestures to the physical features of the Globe when he directs Rosencrantz and Guildenstern's attention to "this goodly frame, the earth . . . this most excellent canopy the air, look you, this brave overhanging firmament, this majestical roof fretted with golden fire" (2.2.297–301). Even "Hercules and his load," the Globe's icon, breaks into our awareness in the gossip about theatrical fashion that follows. It is a risk, obviously, because such attention may intrude too insistently into the fiction and distract from its acceptance; self-reflexivity is not in itself the only end of *Hamlet*. And yet Shakespeare finds it essential to identify his medium, theater, in all its physicality and visual appearance, with what the play comes to mean. One wonders if there is some idea of the double epistemology of theater implied in the double performance of The Murder of Gonzago, first as a mime, then with language (and Hamlet's own forcing commentary). Does the doubling suggest a kind of primacy of physical personification, which in turn leads to theatrical completion when language is added?[54] The words *show* and *tell* dominate the brief connecting dialogue of Hamlet and Ophelia (3.2.141–46). The stylization of each version, mimed and spoken, works to focus attention on them as complementary modes of conveying understanding.

As has been frequently enough noted, Hamlet is obsessed with mere seeming. There is something paralyzing about his intense consciousness of the distinction between what seems and what is. He achieves his revenge only when he can accept his own metaphor, can accept his role as a role and become, in both senses, an actor. In a larger sense this means that theater itself, including appearance, all the *seems* of costume, gesture, and spectacle, must be accepted. The realizing of the metaphor includes the building itself, the "goodly frame" whose cellerage, stage, and canopy comprise the world. The literal redundancy of Fortinbras's final command, "Bear Hamlet like a soldier to the stage," is but a final example of the identification of *seems* and *is* that permeates the central metaphor of the play.

Michael O'Connell   303

Confidence in what is seen—extending even to what to Jonson's eye were impermissibly spectacular effects—characterizes Shakespeare's dramaturgy in the second half of his career. It is not of course that he sets eye against ear in reaction to Jonson. But he is able to employ masque-like scenes and stage effects with none of Jonson's anxiety about theatrical essence. This becomes especially true of the romances, those plays Jonson mocks in the induction to *Bartholomew Fair* as making nature afraid with their "servant monsters . . . tales, tempests, and such like drolleries."[55] Any number of scenes might illustrate this confidence, but the one that involves the greatest dramatic risk is also the one that most emphatically responds to the linkage I have described between iconoclasm and anti-theatricalism. I refer of course to the final scene of *The Winter's Tale*. The transformation of a seeming statue into a living, breathing woman, one whom the audience as well as the characters have thought sixteen years dead, is a theatrical stroke of unparalleled boldness.[56] We have learned to read the scene, and indeed the play, as one involving a high degree of self-reflexivity on Shakespeare's part. Inevitably we associate Shakespeare's art with what is said of the supposed sculpture, "who, had he himself eternity and could put breath into his work, would beguile Nature of her custom, so perfectly he is her ape" (5.2.97–99). The issue of idolatry is raised early in the scene when Perdita asks to kneel before the statue—"do not say 'tis superstition"—and to kiss it. What is significant for my argument is the way the scene insists on faith in what is seen. As spectators, we are at one with Leontes in our ignorance of the statue's truth; his increasing wonder is ours as well. As Paulina intensifies the mystery about the statue, she insists on the necessity of Leontes's faith, but in speaking to the court, she appears to evoke the audience's faith as well:

> It is requir'd
> You do awake your faith. Then, all stand still.
> On; those that think it is unlawful business
> I am about, let them depart.

> (5.3.94–97)

Leontes's response to her is both a command to the court and, when we reflect on it, a judgment of the audience: "Proceed; / No foot shall stir." As theatrical performance testifies, the faith and complicity of the audience are also at stake; if anyone stood to

Iconoclasm and the Elizabethan Theater

leave, one senses, the play itself could not proceed. Though Paulina's words direct Hermione's movements, we are required primarily to believe in, and are affected by, what is seen; it is music, rather than words, that becomes the main accompaniment—and intensification—of the visual moment. The effect on an audience is analogous to religious experience: an act of faith is required for the enactment of the seeming miracle. In its quasi-religious enactment, the scene appears to realize the worst fears of the antitheatrical writers: it presses its audience into idolatry, at least for the moment we assent with Leontes to whatever reality the statue may mysteriously possess. An audience's reward, of course, is the statue's incarnation into full theatrical life. The dramatist does possess the advantage of breath over the sculptor, breath that in a moment will issue in blessing over Perdita. Shakespeare does not counter, finally, but embraces the charge of idolatry.

It is no accident that modern criticism has frequently responded to this scene with frankly religious terminology. We are aware of the distinction between drama and religious ritual, but the play's own symbolic terms and the demands it makes upon its audience appear to blur the boundary. Montrose in particular calls attention to ways Shakespeare brings religious rites and magic into his plays to explore "the affinities between the theatrical playing space, the ecclesiastical sacred space, and the charmed circle":

> It is precisely by means of the boldest theatricality that the climax of *The Winter's Tale* is transformed into a rite of communion. The audience on the stage and the audience in the theatre are atoned by the great creating nature of Shakespeare's art—an art fully realized only when it is incarnated by human players. If we take the attackers and defenders of the theatre at their word, and if we credit our own experience as playgoers, we may be willing to consider the possibility that a Jacobean audience could experience as intense an emotional and intellectual satisfaction from a performance of *The Winter's Tale* as from a divine service.[57]

Though the play is formally secular, the critical terms here set it closer to the incarnational religious aesthetic I described as the basis of medieval art. The combination of the final scene's frankness as spectacle, its rich emotional appeal, and our sense that ultimate human concerns are being addressed by its overcoming of tragedy and death conveys a powerful sense of transcendence. It is surely for this reason that the words rite and ritual figure continually in our critical discussions, even though the scene nei-

Michael O'Connell   305

ther enacts a ritual properly speaking nor even portrays one. The words, however, seem the only ones available to us to describe our sense of the physical conveying the transcendent, of outward signs effecting inner transformations. The playwright incarnates characters who enact and incarnate a Nature instinct with forgiving benevolence.

IV

Glynne Wickham has emphasized the continuities both in stage-craft and the structuring of plays between the medieval drama and that of Shakespeare and his contemporaries. It should not surprise us that some of these continuities were even literal; he cites the case of churches in the 1560s and 70s selling off their vestments to provincial acting companies for costumes.[58] Whether or not it was the same satin or brocade that passed from a priest's cope to a player's costume, we can sense at least figural continuity in the puritan discomfort at the richness and display of stage apparel. So too with architectural metaphor. If sacred buildings were no longer claimed as models of the cosmos, one playhouse at least boldly assumed the reversion of that title. Frances Yates has suggested that the Globe could have advanced its claim even in the geometry of its design.[59] Like the architects of Gothic cathedrals, the builders of the Globe may have employed a symbolic geometry to define a relation between its structure, the microcosm of man, and the macrocosm of the world. Such a symbolic Vitruvian geometry for the design of the Globe is conjectural, but support for the *idea* of the perfect theater as symbolic image of the cosmos comes from Thomas Heywood's *Apology for Actors* (1612). There Julius Caesar's round theater in the Campus Martius is described as a detailed model of the universe, its canopy ("which wee call the heavens") containing moving stars and planets and circumscribed with all the lines dividing the heavenly zones. Its seating hierarchically grouped the entire society of imperial Rome, from emperor to *plebs*. "In briefe, in that little compasse were comprehended the perfect model of the firmament, the whole frame of the heavens, with all grounds of astronomical conjecture."[60] If in its motto the Globe proclaimed "Totus mundus agit histrionem," it also meant to make the obverse claim: in the names assigned its various components, it clearly asserted that all the stage is a world. What was no longer claimed for ecclesiastical buildings, what was

Iconoclasm and the Elizabethan Theater

no longer allowed in the temporal universality of the mystery plays was taken as inheritance by Shakespeare's theater.

The Elizabethan and Jacobean theater was not a neutral cultural institution. The attacks upon its beginnings and its fate in 1642 make this amply clear. It was seen by an influential part of the intellectual elite as an antagonist and competitor of the progressive religious culture. To an articulate part of that elite it appeared religiously atavistic, dangerously so, and able to appeal to sensibilities that should properly have atrophied in the reform of religion. The popularity of the London theaters testifies to the survival of those sensibilities, even as the reform was successful in eliminating them from worship. Theater was not worship, but as a cultural institution, its roots lay deep in the centuries in which it had performed a religious function. Its status was ambiguous in the late sixteenth and early seventeenth centuries—not religious in the same sense it had been, and yet, in the terms by which the culture defined it, not secular either. Because of its subsequent history—and here perhaps the interruption in 1642 was decisive—we are accustomed to treat theater as an aesthetic and secular institution. From this perspective the work of Shakespeare and his contemporaries impresses us with its difference from the recently banished medieval stage. But from a cultural perspective we are more likely to see continuities, a mending of the rents in the social and religious fabric. What would it mean to our sense of the Elizabethan and Jacobean stage, one wonders, that from this anthropological perspective it could be viewed as a competing—idolatrous—religious structure?

University of California, Santa Barbara

NOTES

[1] Stubbes, *The Anatomie of Abuses* (London, 1583), sig. [Lvi].

[2] Gosson, *Playes Confuted in five Actions* (London, 1582?), sig. [B. 8ʼ].

[3] Rainolds, *Th'overthrow of Stage-playes* (London, 1599), 161.

[4] Northbrooke, *Spiritus est vicarious Christi in terra: A Treatise wherein Dicing, Dauncing, Vaine playes or Enterludes . . . are reproved* (London, 1577), 58.

[5] Barish, *The Antitheatrical Prejudice* (Berkeley and Los Angeles: Univ. of California Press, 1981), 66.

[6] See Harold C. Gardiner, S. J., *Mysteries' End: an Investigation of the Last Days of the Medieval Religious Stage* (New Haven: Yale Univ. Press, 1946).

[7] Barish is primarily concerned with what connects the outbreaks of Western antitheatricalism. He sees it as "too widespread, too resistant to changes of place and time to be ascribed entirely, or even mainly, to social, political, or economic factors" (116–

Michael O'Connell   307

17). Such recurrent prejudice against playing rests on the Stoic ideal of stasis in the personality and "belongs to a conservative ethical emphasis in which the key terms are those of order, stability, constancy, and integrity." From such an emphasis, theater may seem deeply threatening in its basic premise that men may play different selves and that we may be spectators at an event in which a fiction is enacted as if it were real. Rather than dealing with a centered, stable self, we assist at a process in which a true self has been cast off, even if temporarily, in favor of a fictive self. Barish's argument thus can elucidate Renaissance anti-theatricalism in particular, for the Stoic ideal of a self resistant to change—perhaps in therapeutic reaction to the psychic change bred by the Reformation—had a powerful hold on the sixteenth century.

[8] Northbrooke, 69; Gosson, sig. [B.8ᵛff].

[9] Gosson, sig. E.1.

[10] Munday, A second and third blast of retrait from plaies and Theaters (London, 1590), 95–96.

[11] E. K. Chambers, The Elizabethan Stage, 4 vols. (Oxford: Clarendon Press, 1923), 1:240–42; Gardiner, 51–59.

[12] On that theological strain see Horton Davies, Worship and Theology in England: from Cranmer to Hooker, 1534–1603 (Princeton: Princeton Univ. Press, 1970) 165–226.

[13] Gardiner, 72–74 and n. 47.

[14] Glynne Wickham, Early English Stages, 1300–1660, 3 vols. (London: Routledge and Kegan Paul, 1959–81), 2:77.

[15] Munday, 104.

[16] Stubbes, 102.

[17] Ong, The Presence of the Word: Some Prolegomena for Cultural and Religious History (New Haven: Yale Univ. Press, 1967), 269.

[18] Ong, 272; Stephen J. Greenblatt has given a vivid account of the psychological effects of printed books in the religious culture of the 1520s (Renaissance Self-Fashioning from More to Shakespeare [Chicago: Univ. of Chicago Press, 1980], 74–114).

[19] Stubbes, 102.

[20] See W. R. Jones, "Art and Christian Piety: Iconoclasm in Medieval Europe," in The Image and the Word, ed. Joseph Gutmann (Missoula, Mont.: Scholars Press, 1977), 75–105.

[21] "Byzantine Iconoclasm and the Failure of a Medieval Reformation," in Gutmann, 54.

[22] Jones, 95.

[23] J. C. Dickinson, An Ecclesiastical History of England: the Later Middle Ages (London: Adams and Charles Black, 1979), 37; Dickinson points to "the intense and widespread appreciation of the visual arts" which characterized every level of medieval society (411).

[24] Davies, 140; Lionel Rothkrug, "Popular Religion and the Holy Shrines," in Religion and the People, ed. James Obelkevich (Chapel Hill: Univ. of North Carolina Press, 1979), 28–29, 35–37.

[25] Huizinga, The Waning of the Middle Ages (1924; rpt. New York: Doubleday Anchor, 1954), 165.

[26] Brown, The Cult of the Saints: its Rise and Function in Latin Christianity (Chicago: Univ. of Chicago Press, 1981), 12–22.

[27] See the Repressor of Overmuch Blaming of the Clergy, part 2, chapters 2 to 6, in Rerum Britannicarum Medii Aevi Scriptores, Rolls Series 19, ed. Churchill Babington (London: Longman, Green, Longman and Roberts, 1860), 136–75.

[28] When outbreaks of iconoclasm came in the 1520s, they were led not by the theologically sophisticated or the reformers themselves but by laymen, for the most part illiterate or barely literate, who had listened to the aniconic arguments of their social and intellectual superiors.

[29] Huizinga, 152.

[30] Otto von Simson, *The Gothic Cathedral: Origins of Gothic Architecture and the Medieval concept of Order* (New York: Pantheon, 1956), 35–39.

[31] George Lesser, *Gothic Cathedrals and Sacred Geometry*, 3 vols. (London: Tiranti, 1957–64), 1:147–48; an example of the architectural expression of time may be seen in the ceiling bosses of Norwich Cathedral (late fifteenth century), which portray the events of sacred history from the creation at the west end to the last judgment at the east.

[32] Von Simson, 39.

[33] *New Catholic Encyclopedia* (New York: McGraw-Hill, 1967–79), s.v. "Relics."

[34] See in particular Peter Brown's sensitive description of the beginnings in late antiquity of this association of the martyrs and their relics with Christ's triumph over death (Brown, 69–84, esp. 72).

[35] "Qui quod pollicitus sese semper nobiscum fore usque ad consummationem seculi, in his litteris praecipue praestat, in quibus nobis etiamnum vivit, spirat, loquitur, pene dixerim, efficacius quam cum inter homines versaretur" (*Omnia Opera*, ed. Joannes Clericus, 6 vols. Leiden, 1703–6; rpt. Hildescheim: Georg Olms, 1961), 5:142E.

[36] See Erwin Panofsky, "Erasmus and the Visual Arts," *JWCI* 32 (1969): 200–227.

[37] *Dilucida et pia explanatio symboli*, in *Omnia Opera*, 5:1187D; the work was translated into English c. 1533 as *A Playne and godly exposition or declaration of the commune Crede*; see especially sigs. T.v–vi.

[38] Erasmus, *Omnia Opera*, 5:1189A; *Playne and godly exposition*, sigs. T.viii^v–U.i^v.

[39] Pecock, *Repressor*, part 2, chapter 3, in *Rerum Britannicarum*, 19:148–49.

[40] *Dialogue Concerning Heresies*, in *Complete Works of St. Thomas More*, vol. 6, ed. Thomas Lawler, Germain Marc'hadour, Richard Marius (New Haven: Yale Univ. Press, 1981), part 1, 39–40.

[41] Marjorie O'Rourke Boyle, *Erasmus on Language and Method in Theology* (Toronto: Univ. of Toronto Press, 1977), 83.

[42] See Charles Garside, *Zwingli and the Arts* (New Haven: Yale Univ. Press, 1966), 33–39, 94; and G. R. Potter, *Zwingli* (Cambridge: Cambridge Univ. Press, 1976), 71.

[43] *Utopia*, in *Complete Works*, vol. 4, ed. Edward Surtz, S.J., and J. H. Hexter, 231–33.

[44] John Phillips, *The Reformation of Images: Destruction of Art in England, 1535–1660* (Berkeley and Los Angeles: Univ. of California Press, 1973), 53–54, 61–69.

[45] See Hugh Braun, *Parish Churches: their Architectural Development in England* (London: Faber and Faber, 1970), 151.

[46] Phillips, 89–97.

[47] Phillips, 96, figs. 24a and b.

[48] Davies, 358–59, 370–71.

[49] Louis A. Montrose, "The Purpose of Playing: Reflections on a Shakespearean Anthropology," *Helios*, n.s. 7 (1980): 51–74.

[50] Barish, 132.

[51] Helgerson, *Self-Crowned Laureates: Spenser, Jonson, Milton and the Literary System* (Berkeley and Los Angeles: Univ. of California Press, 1983), 101–84.

[52] *The Staple of News*, Prologue, 1–6; I quote from the Everyman's Library edition of *The Complete Plays*, 2 vols., ed. Felix E. Schelling (London: Dent, 1910), 2:349.

[53] All citations of Shakespeare are from *The Riverside Shakespeare*, ed. G. Blakemore Evans (Boston: Houghton Mifflin, 1974). For a discussion of the extent of the synaesthesia in the language of the play, see Garrett Stewart, "Shakespearean Dream-play," *ELR* 11 (1981): 44–69.

[54] In experimental modes the theater seems frequently to insist on the primacy of the visual and physical; I think particularly of the experiments of The Living Theater

Michael O'Connell   309 in the late 1960s and of Antonin Artaud, *The Theater and Its Double*, trans. Mary Caroline Richards (New York: Grove, 1958), 37–41, 86–87.

35 *Bartholomew Fair*, Induction, 11.

36 In exploring the tradition of the metamorphosis of sculpture into persons (and the reverse), Leonard Barkan emphasizes that Shakespeare has gone to some trouble — and dramatic risk — to fashion the recognition scene *as* an apparent transformation of a statue ("'Living Sculptures': Ovid, Michelangelo and *The Winter's Tale*," *ELH* 48 [1981]: 639–67).

37 Montrose, 62.

38 Wickham, 2:35–40.

39 Yates, *Theatre of the World* (Chicago: Univ. of Chicago Press, 1969), 125–35.

60 Heywood, *An Apology for Actors* (London: the Shakespeare Society, 1841), 35.

310   *Iconoclasm and the Elizabethan Theater*

JEFFREY KNAPP

Preachers and Players
in Shakespeare's England

But to have divinity preach'd there! did you ever dream of such a thing?
—Shakespeare, *Pericles* (c. 1608)

To MANY A GODLY ELIZABETHAN, the new public theaters and the
newly purified church were enemies in a war that the theaters seemed to be winning. Such pious antagonism toward the English stage marked a revolutionary
change from the time of Miracle and Morality plays, when the Catholic church
had welcomed the services of players; and it even marked a change from earlier
days in the Reformation, when Protestant clergymen had embraced the English
stage so wholeheartedly as to appear its "driving force."[1] Perhaps the most influential figure among these earlier Reformers, and a playwright himself, John
Foxe, had gone so far as to assert that "players, printers, [and] preachers" were
"set up of God, as a triple bulwark against the triple crown of the pope, to bring
him down" (1563);[2] and yet only a few years after the construction of the first
permanent playhouses, the Theater and the Curtain (1576), the compiler of *A
Second and Third Blast of Retrait from Plaies and Theaters* (1580) called upon "every
true soldier of Jesus Christ" to join him in his assault upon "the chapel of Satan,
I mean the Theater," "to the suppressing of those which fight against [God's]
word."[3]

What was it about the new theaters that had suddenly made plays seem
capable of teaching the people nothing "but that which is fleshly and carnal?"[4]
The vast concourse of people to these theaters, and the opportunities for idleness,
debauchery, and sedition that such mass audiences generated, were of course
high on the list of reasons why the stage was now said to be inimical to true religion, although the more outrageous offenders against the gospel, according to
the theaters' opponents, were the players themselves. Not only were they said to
engage in every imaginable vice both on and off the stage, but they had begun
staging their plays, or rather "waging their battle," "on the Sabbath day the more
conveniently to destroy the souls of the children of God" (*Blast*, 58). The resulting
competition between player and preacher could at times seem outrageously
direct. In 1596, for instance, a group of citizens from the Blackfriars district of
London petitioned the Privy Council to stop construction of a playhouse to be
built "so near" their church "that the noise of the drums and trumpets will greatly
disturb and hinder both the ministers and parishioners in time of divine service

REPRESENTATIONS 44 • Fall 1993 © THE REGENTS OF THE UNIVERSITY OF CALIFORNIA and sermons."[5] The author of the *Blast* claimed the players had already taken their attack much further, and actually invaded "every Temple of God, and that throughout England," with their performances, "so that now the Sanctuary is become a players' stage" (77–78). But the most oft-cited evidence in Elizabethan England that the players had set out to undermine the church was the sheer popularity of the players in comparison to the church. "Woe is me!" one scandalized observer among many exclaims, "The play houses are pestered, when churches are naked; at the one it is not possible to get a place, at the other void seats are plenty" (1587).[6]

For the reformed clergy (a number of whom took up the attack on the stage in their sermons), the mortification produced by this outrush of patrons from church to theater must have been acute.[7] Preachers may always have fretted about the size of their audience; yet these were exceptional days, when the Word, buried for centuries beneath the "dumb show" of Catholic ritual, had at last been restored to a "miserable and hungry people."[8] Why then were there so few takers? To the author of the first printed attack on the public theaters, the preacher John Northbrook (1577), the paradox is stunning: "There was never more preaching, & worse living, never more talking and less following, never more professing, and less profiting, never more words and fewer deeds, never truer faith preached and less works done, than is now" (*Treatise*, 145).[9] For Northbrook, as for other pious commentators, this deplorable state of affairs was not to be imputed "unto the preaching of God's word," however, but rather "unto the wickedness and perverse nature of man's corruption." The fact that "many can tarry at a vain Play two or three hours, when as they will not abide scarce one hour at a Sermon," was said to show only how "great is our folly, to delight in vanity, and leave verity, to seek for the meat that shall perish, and pass not for the food that they shall live by for ever" (67). Indeed, the greater passion of the English people for players rather than preachers is, Northbrook concludes, only one of the many signs "whereby we may easily gather, that the day of judgment is not far off" (146).

Other Elizabethans put more of the blame on the preachers. After all, the Reformation did not uproot Catholicism or even "heathenism" from Elizabethan England overnight; many parishioners loathed their preachers (especially their puritan preachers) precisely for the new religion they were preaching.[10] But to a remarkable extent the hostility of parishioner to preacher appears to have been fueled by a hatred of preaching per se. Puritans such as Northbrook may have associated this resistance to sermons with unregeneracy—"If the Preacher do pass his hour but a little," a country bumpkin is told in George Gifford's *Briefe Discourse* (1582), "your buttocks begin for to ache, and ye wish in your heart that the Pulpit would fall" (the bumpkin replies, "Ye may guess twice before ye guess so right")— but others recognized the need to moderate the godly fixation on sermonizing.[11] As the historian Christopher Haigh notes, some divines turned to catechism for help. The failure of preachers in this duty, writes the catechist Robert Cawdrey, "is in very deed the cause why their preaching taketh so little effect amongst their parishioners." To Cawdrey's mind, the difference that catechism made was rhetorical: it could feed people the sort of "meat" that "their nature and capacity was able to digest and conceive."[12] The conservative minister Leonard Wright (1589) thought a more basic accommodation to the carnality of one's flock was in order. Far less disdainful than Northbrook of his parishioners' appetite for "the meat that shall perish," Wright observed that Christ "did both feed the souls of his sheep, with heavenly doctrine, and examples of virtuous living, and their bodies with material food of barley loaves and fishes"—and, according to Wright, it was Christ's material food that "did more win the people's hearts, than all his wonderful miracles and divine Sermons which they saw and heard." Hence, Wright concludes, we "shall find that a mean learned Parson of an honest conversation, keeping a good house in his Parish, shall persuade and profit more in coming to one dinner, than the best Doctor of divinity which keepeth no house shall do by preaching a dozen solemn sermons."[13]

Along with these milder supplements to preaching came the more direct solution of reforming the preacher. For the godly, this meant ridding England's pulpits of the "dumb dogs" who could do little more than read prepared services; the true preachers were those dedicated ministers, in lamentably short supply, who sermonized their flock "as the spirit moved them."[14] Yet critics of the puritans argued that the preacher should rightly be moved by the plight of his parishioners' buttocks as well. When Wright complains of those preachers who "stand so long about instructing the souls, as though they had forgotten the people had any bodies, who do not so much edify as tedify" (*Summons*, 46–47), he may well be recalling the advice of the influential rhetorician Thomas Wilson (1553), who similarly cautions sermonizers not to think that their spiritual zeal alone will suffice to spread the gospel.[15] Wilson recommends that the preachers take a more rhetorical—indeed, a more theatrical—approach to their calling:

Except men find delight, they will not long abide: delight them, and win them: weary them, and you lose them for ever. And that is the reason, that men commonly tarry the end of a merry play, and cannot abide the half hearing of a sour checking Sermon. Therefore, even these ancient preachers, must now and then play the fools in the pulpit, to serve the tickle ears of their fleeting audience, or else they are like some times to preach to the bare walls, for though the spirit be apt, and our will prone, yet our flesh is so heavy, and humors so overwhelm us, that we cannot without refreshing, long abide to hear any one thing. (27)

"They are like some times to preach to the bare walls": for those Elizabethans who shared Wilson's sentiments, the theater's power to empty the church might well have seemed to stem just as much from the preachers' intemperate spirituality as from the carnality of the people.[16]

In fact, Wilson's chastisement of preachers tempts us to see even the players in a different light. Northbrook would agree that players had become more popular than preachers because the players and not the preachers were willing to "play the fools"—but what if some players intended their folly to be edifying, as Wilson had recommended? What if, in other words, some Elizabethans came to prefer the theater to the established church because they believed the player had *subsumed* the preacher's role? Surprisingly, Northbrook himself suggests this possibility, though he treats it with contempt. So ardent for playgoing have the people become, he writes, "that they shame not to say and affirm openly, that Plays are as good as Sermons, and that they learn as much or more at a Play, than they do at God's word preached" (66). The author of the *Blast* raises and rebukes the same argument: try to withdraw playgoers "from the Theater unto the sermon, [and] they will say, By the preacher they may be edified, but by the player both edified and delighted" (91).[17] Yet after all, nothing could have been more traditional for the English stage than to serve as a platform of religious instruction; why, with the rise of permanent theaters, should that function have simply vanished without a trace?

At one point in modern literary criticism, when it seemed to some scholars as if any reference to religion in an Elizabethan play disclosed a Christian polemic, the answer was easy: the theaters never really had abandoned their religious roots; plays truly had been as good as sermons. Over the past three decades, however, in reaction against the simplifications and also the piety of this critical school, literary historians have generally responded to the problem of the Elizabethan theater's religious heritage by tracing the merely formal or histrionic survival of religious plots, themes, and types upon an increasingly naturalistic stage. This secularizing approach has hardened into an orthodoxy at least as dogmatic and far more pervasive than the scholarship it discredited. Insofar as recent critics have even raised the possibility of a religious Elizabethan theater, their arguments have moved in two skeptical directions. Scholars such as Glynne Wickham have concluded that the Elizabethan theater was indeed "effectively divorced from religion," but they ascribe this rupture to state censorship, not to theatrical depravity.[18] Another group of critics, including Louis Montrose and Stephen Greenblatt, have argued that the Elizabethan theater continued to satisfy if not a religious then a ritualist craving in its audience.[19] According to these critics, the Elizabethans found in the new secular theaters a "substitute" for the "rituals and ceremonial forms of pre-Reformation culture" (Montrose, 59); Shakespeare may have transformed "religious ideology" into fiction, but his audience embraced the "evacuated rituals" of his theater as simply "preferable to no rituals at all" (Greenblatt, *Shakespearean Negotiations*, 126–27).

I want to argue, however, that neither an increasing naturalism on the Elizabethan stage, nor an evacuation and then appropriation of religious mystique by that stage, need have been secularizing operations. As for the state censorship to which the players were subjected, such repressiveness may simply have had the effect of driving the theater's religion underground. Frankly scriptural plays did in any case continue to be performed on the public stage; the cast of Thomas Lodge and Robert Greene's *A Looking Glasse for London and England* (c. 1590) even includes two Old Testament "preachers," Hosea and Jonah, who repeatedly exhort London to "repent, amend, repent."[20] What's more, during the Marprelate controversy (1588–90), the Church of England actually licensed the "chapel of Satan" to take on a preacherly function, in defense of the prelacy.[21] My goal in this essay is to suggest how, in less obvious cases as well, Elizabethans were capable of regarding the theater as a spiritually valuable institution. My model will be Shakespeare, especially his final Elizabethan history, *Henry V*.

In plays written both before and after *Henry V*, Shakespeare openly satirizes puritan spirituality: like many of his contemporaries, he loves to ascribe a voracious carnality to the puritan who "scarce confesses / That his blood flows; or that his appetite / Is more to bread than stone."[22] Less often remarked are Shakespeare's similar, though subtler, critiques of Catholicism, some of which I will try to detail here. Most scholars interpret such demystifications in Shakespeare as further evidence of his secularism; but I will argue that Shakespeare regards his exposure of puritan and papist carnality as serving a religious purpose, in promoting a less repressive and thus more durable spirituality.

For Shakespeare, in fact, the carnal spectacles of the theater are better than demystifying: they are sacramental. In other words, Shakespeare believes that his audience can draw spiritual strength from their carnal experience of the theater, and *Henry V* shows that this belief has strong affinities with mainstream English Protestant conceptions of the eucharist.[23] Catholics claimed that the host was literally transubstantiated into Christ's body, and that the priest in breaking holy bread thus reinstantiated Christ's sacrifice; English Protestants viewed the eucharist as a visible sign of invisible grace, a memorial of a sacrifice whose spiritual effects communion made more accessible. Shakespeare alludes to this eucharistic controversy in *Henry V* when one character pessimistically asserts that "men's faiths are wafer-cakes" (2.3.45); according to an army of Protestant writers, papist faith was not only as brittle as wafer-cakes but as small, reduced to an idolatrous belief in a "wafer god."[24] Following those Protestants who instead treated the petty materiality of the wafer as proof that the eucharist *represented* Christ, *Henry V* suggests that the carnal spectacles of the theater sacramentally highlight, rather than obscure, the operations of the spirit precisely because those spectacles are so conspicuously inadequate to the tales of "*Non nobis* and *Te Deum*" (4.8.121) they represent.

Combined with the theater's popularity, this insufficiency of the stage to its grand subject matter undermines not only papist idolatry, Shakespeare presumes, but clerical elitism generally. In *Henry V*, I will argue, pretensions to exclusive spiritual powers allow the clergy and even the king to treat French and English soldiers as "sacrifices" (4.prologue.23) to their own carnal interests. But the Chorus to *Henry V* insists that Shakespeare's players could not so much as represent clergy and king without the imaginative participation of the audience. Framing his histories as far less homiletic than sacramental experiences, Shakespeare suggests to his audience that the process of spiritual edification must necessarily be communal and must necessarily include the flesh; while by locating the real sacramental action of the theater less on the stage than in the mind,[25] he also encourages his auditors to take responsibility for their own spiritual welfare. For Shakespeare, in short, the new public theaters seem to have represented a marvelous device not to "fight against God's word," as some preachers claimed, but to save it from the preachers.

I

If asked to compare Shakespeare to such outspokenly religious contemporaries as Spenser and Donne, even those critics who detect a spark of religion in Shakespeare would have to admit that he did not like to preach. In one important respect, of course, the comparison is unfair: neither Spenser nor Donne faced the kind of censorship regarding their religious views that by 1606 prevented Shakespeare from even mentioning "the holy Name of God or of Christ Jesus, or of the Holy Ghost or of the Trinity" in his plays.[26] Nonetheless, to most recent critics Shakespeare's apparent reticence about Christian doctrine has seemed a matter less of state imposition than of personal choice. Throughout his extensive survey of Shakespeare's theological allusions in *Shakespeare and Christian Doctrine* (1963), Roland Mushat Frye, for instance, claims that there is not so much as a thread of religious polemic to be found anywhere in Shakespeare's plays. According to Frye, in fact, the plays not only fail to "furnish us evidence of Shakespeare's religious orientation," but the little theology they do invoke always proves "contributory to the drama, and not vice versa." Speaking for more than a generation of Shakespeare critics, Frye concludes that "the mirror of Shakespearean drama was held up to nature, and not to saving grace."[27]

And yet not once in his exhaustive study does Frye consider the most obvious evidence in Shakespeare for his "religious orientation"—his representations of churchmen. The omission is both more surprising and more revealing than secularizing critics such as Frye would lead us to believe, because in Shakespeare's plays, as David Bevington reminds us, "anticlericalism is staple."[28] The opening scene of what is possibly Shakespeare's first history play, *1 Henry VI*, sets the anticlerical pattern for the rest. In the midst of a funeral procession for Henry V, the Duke of Gloucester accuses the Bishop of Winchester of having prayed for Henry's death, and, when Winchester in turn charges Gloucester with disobedience to "God and religious churchmen" (1.1.40), the exasperated Gloucester exclaims,

Name not religion, for thou lov'st the flesh,
And ne'er throughout the year to church thou go'st
Except it be to pray against thy foes.
                         (1.1.41–43)

The audience does not have long to wait before learning whether Gloucester's attack is justified. In the scene's final speech, after the lay noblemen have hurried off the stage on state business, Winchester like the medieval stage-vice turns to the audience to protest,

Each hath his place and function to attend:
I am left out; for me nothing remains:
But long I will not be Jack out of office.
The king from Eltham I intend to steal,
And sit at chiefest stern of public weal.
                         (173–77)

One could hardly imagine English history introduced with a more antiprelatical slant.

Why does Shakespeare make his first historical villain a bishop? Some scholars would assign *1 Henry VI* to the late 1580s, the very period in which the anti-episcopal "Martin Marprelate" waged his pamphlet war. Winchester was, moreover, the bishopric held by one of Martin's prime targets Thomas Cooper, whom Martin accused of "most godless proceedings."[29] For a critic like Bevington, committed to the notion that Shakespeare's anticlericalism was "notably mild" (201) for its day, an alliance between Shakespeare and the outrageously derisive Martin would be unthinkable. Yet the next installment of Shakespeare's histories, *2 Henry VI*, paints an even fiercer portrait of Winchester than the first: he is shown helping to arrange Gloucester's murder and then dying, terrified and unrepentant, in the same bed as his victim. Marprelate would have been hard-pressed to match the grotesque mixture of foolery and repugnance that Shakespeare inscribes on the very face of his expiring prelate: "See how the pangs of death do make him grin!" (3.3.24).

Of course, the mere fact of Shakespeare's satirizing one particular bishop (and a Catholic bishop at that) does not in itself demonstrate that Shakespeare had any religious objections to bishops. In explicit support of Frye, Bevington claims that on the contrary Shakespeare's attitude toward Winchester is essentially "non-theological" (202), because Shakespeare "attacks the bishop for moral crimes and political meddling, not for doctrine" (201). Yet one might just as easily argue that Shakespeare excludes specific doctrinal complaints against his bishop so as to include both past (Catholic) and present (Protestant) irreligious Winchesters within the scope of his satire.[30] Winchester's lack of enthusiasm for theology is in any case part of Gloucester's opening grievance against him; and when

Gloucester and Winchester once again wrangle in *2 Henry VI*, it is the king who tries to pacify them with doctrine—"blessed are the peacemakers on earth"—only to have the bishop characteristically pervert that doctrine: "Let me be blessed for the peace I make / Against this proud Protector with my sword!" (2.1.34–36).

Shakespeare may drop this element of downright caricature from his later representations of English bishops, as Bevington maintains, but he never abandons the dark comedy of episcopal militarism. The first speech by the Bishop of Carlisle in *Richard II*, for example, does sound far more pastoral than any speeches of Winchester, as Carlisle offers heavenly encouragements to a king faced with rebellion:

> Fear not, my lord, that Power that made you king
> Hath power to keep you king in spite of all.
> The means that heavens yield must be embrac'd,
> And not neglected; else heaven would,
> And we will not. Heaven's offer we refuse,
> The proffered means of succors and redress.
> (3.2.27–32)

And yet another lord, interpreting for Carlisle, immediately highlights the element of mystification in Carlisle's otherworldly rhetoric: "He means, my lord, that we are too remiss, / Whilst Bullingbrook, through our security, / Grows strong and great in substance and in power" (33–35). What the bishop counsels when he speaks of heavenly aid, in short, is nothing other than swift military action.

In the later *2 Henry IV*, so much more audaciously bellicose is the rebellious Archbishop of York that many of the passages concerning him in the play appear to have been censored.[31] The first of these passages begins with familiar irony: "The gentle Archbishop of York is up / With well-appointed pow'rs" (1.1.189–90). In *Richard II*, Henry IV had praised Carlisle for the "high sparks of honor" (5.6.29) he exhibited, for his gentility rather than his religion; and here the characterization of York as a "gentle" rebel can escape sounding incongruous only if he is understood to be aristocratically, rather than benevolently, gentle. Yet Shakespeare is no longer content simply to correlate a bishop's militarism with his high social position. For the first time in the history plays, he has a character articulate a theory of episcopal warfare. The speaker in question, a retainer of Hotspur's father Northumberland, explains why he thinks York will succeed in his rebellion where Hotspur had failed. Hotspur

> had only but the corpse,
> But shadows and the shows of men, to fight;
> For that same word, rebellion, did divide
> The action of their bodies from their souls,
> And they did fight with queasiness, constrain'd.
> (1.1.192–96)

REPRESENTATIONS

98

York, on the other hand, "turns insurrection to religion."

> Suppos'd sincere and holy in his thoughts,
> He's follow'd both with body and with mind;
> And doth enlarge his rising with the blood
> Of fair King Richard, scrap'd from Pomfret stones;
> Derives from heaven his quarrel and his cause;
> Tells them he doth bestride a bleeding land,
> Gasping for life under great Bullingbrook,
> And more and less do flock to follow him.
> (1.1.201–209)

From *1 Henry VI* to *2 Henry IV*, Shakespeare has charted a steady progression in episcopal support for violence: first Winchester the faithless brawler, then Carlisle the sanctifier of war, then York the sanctifier of war who himself engages in warfare.

Yet if in one respect the bishop in *2 Henry IV* (who describes himself as intending not to break peace but to establish it; 4.1.85–86) represents only a more sophisticated version of the bishop in *1 Henry VI* (who clownishly threatened to make peace with his sword), in another respect York is strikingly different from his predecessors. With no apparent interest in their flocks, both Winchester and Carlisle promoted violence only before an elite group, the aristocracy, whereas York when he is up in "ill-beseeming arms" (84) resumes his pulpit to address the common people. As Prince John complains to him,

> it better show'd with you
> When that your flock, assembled by the bell,
> Encircled you to hear with reverence
> Your exposition on the holy text
> Than now to see you here an iron man, talking,
> Cheering a rout of rebels with your drum,
> Turning the word to sword and life to death.
> (4.2.4–10)

Yet this new urge in a bishop to "publish" (1.3.86) the blessings he bestows on war does not indicate some new episcopal populism: in another probably censored passage, York derides the common people as, among other things, "sick," "giddy," and "unsure," a "beastly feeder," or "common dog" that "wouldst eat thy dead vomit up / And howl'st to find it" (87–108). Episcopal war remains a "gentle" business; York only shows how a bishop can employ the "vulgar heart" (90) against one's aristocratic rivals.

The final play in the sequence of Shakespeare's Lancastrian histories, *Henry V*, opens by partially recapitulating this transition from an episcopal militarism that is personal and overtly elitist to one that is public and covertly elitist. The action of the play begins with a private conference between two prelates, the

Preachers and Players in Shakespeare's England

Bishop of Ely and the Archbishop of Canterbury, who bemoan a parliamentary bill that would "strip" the clergy of "all the temporal lands, which men devout / By testament have given to the Church" (1.1.9–11). Canterbury himself lists the benefits to the commonwealth that this confiscation would fund, among them "a hundred almshouses right well supplied" for the "relief of lazars, and weak age / Of indigent faint souls past corporal toil" (15–17). His one hope that the "commons" (71) will not have their way with the clergy turns out to be the king, "a true lover of the holy Church" (24), whom the Archbishop has bribed by pledging Harry an enormous sum to help him finance his planned conquest of France. The next scene takes place at court, and turns this shabby backroom deal into a pious public spectacle. Canterbury delivers a learned disquisition on French legal history that ends by assuring Harry of his just title to the French crown; both Canterbury and Ely then exhort Harry to "forage in blood of French nobility" (1.2.110) as his warlike ancestors have, "in aid whereof" the clergy will provide him with the "mighty sum" already mentioned in the previous scene. Once again Shakespeare's bishops have gone from secret conspirators to open propagandists for war, though this time the same characters fill both roles and thus conspicuously fuse the interests of the church with the bloodshed it promotes.

Yet the bishops of *Henry V* do not entirely synthesize the disparate characters of their predecessors. Although they do continue to "incite" (1.2.20) their king to violence, they no longer preach war, as York once had, to the common people. That office passes to the king. In fact, so zealously does Harry absorb both the church's money and its sanctifications of violence that after the second scene the bishops drop out of the play altogether. Immediately following Canterbury's final lines, Harry begins to speak of conquering France "by God's help" (1.2.222), "by God's grace" (262), with "God before" (307)—a theme he never tires of reiterating throughout the play. It is now the king who counsels his courtiers to "deliver / Our puissance into the hand of God, / Putting it straight in expedition" (2.2.189–91); and, once the wars in France are under way, it is again the king who inspires his soldiers: "Follow your spirit; and upon this charge / Cry, 'God for Harry, England, and Saint George'!" (3.1.33–34). After the triumph at Agincourt, Harry's public acknowledgments of God's part in the war effort grow even stronger. As soon as the French herald tells him that the English have carried the day, Harry exclaims, "Praise be God, and not our strength, for it" (4.7.82), and later he has it "proclaimed through our host" that it is death "to boast of this, or take that praise from God / Which is his only" (4.8.112–19). The night before, during a debate with common soldiers, Harry had already made the best case in the histories for believing that God approves of war—the biblical argument that war is God's "beadle" or "vengeance" (4.1.162), His scourge for punishing sin. But of course this theory does not let Harry off the hook for leading his soldiers into war; as Christ explains in a warning often quoted by Elizabethan writers to explicate the moral status of a scourge, "it must needs be that offenses shall come, but woe be to that man, by whom the offense cometh."[32] The bishops begin the play by confessing their interest in war to be self-serving; and, while Harry may sound, and truly be, more devoutly inclined than they, both he and his fellow debaters agree that the war he elsewhere calls "well-hallowed" (1.2.293) is "his cause" and "his quarrel" (4.1.122–23) alone.[33]

Earlier in the play, Harry had himself underscored the need to mistrust "glist'ring semblances of piety" (2.2.114); but then Shakespeare throughout *Henry V* takes every opportunity to highlight the monstrous incongruity of yoking "blood and sword and fire," as the bishops do, to professions of "spirituality" (1.2.131–32). The Duke of Burgundy, for instance, likens soldiers to "savages" who do nothing "but meditate on blood" (5.2.59–60). The Chorus puts a better face on this monomania when he claims that "honor's thought / Reigns solely in the breast of every man" (2.prologue.3–4) in the English army. Yet even this idealization of their militarism allows the English soldiers no room for thoughts of religion: as Harry's disputant Williams says of his comrades, "How can they charitably dispose of anything, when blood is their argument?" (4.1.142–43). If Harry's piety gilds over such bloodymindedness, the paint cracks and peels in the scenes of the lower classes that Shakespeare continually intersperses with scenes of their betters. To the braggadocio Pistol, for example, the point of war is only "to suck, to suck, the very blood to suck!" (2.3.50). His fellow lowlife Nim "scorns to say his prayers, lest 'a should be thought a coward" (3.2.36–37). The captains of Harry's army, an intermediate class in the play, make such brutality look if anything more appalling by their crude appeals to religion. "God's plud" (3.2.19)—that is, by God's blood—are the first words of the Welsh captain Fluellen, though the past master at this sort of blasphemy is the Irish captain MacMorris: "I would have blowed up the town, so Chrish save me law" (3.3.34); "There is throats to be cut, and works to be done, and there ish nothing done, so Christ sa' me law" (54–55); "So Chrish save me, I will cut off your head" (72–73). Pistol's version of these oxymoronic oaths pares them to the bone. When Bardolph blocks an impending duel between Pistol and Nim, promising "by this sword" to kill the first man who draws, Pistol remarks, "Sword is an oath, and oaths must have their course" (2.1.95–97). The joke is that Pistol translates *sword* into *'s word*, "by God's word," and thus literally enacts the sacrilege of which Prince John in *2 Henry IV* had accused the Archbishop of York—"turning the word to sword."[34]

The most straightforward demystification in the play of Harry's holy war, however, is a war crime that ironically reflects Harry's absorption of both the bishops' money and their piety: Harry's old companion Bardolph robs a church. Pistol cannot believe that Fluellen would let Bardolph be hanged for such a crime; the only thing Bardolph stole, Pistol protests, was a minor accessory of Catholic ritual, a "pax of little price" (3.6.45). Whatever the rules of military discipline, the marked contrast between Bardolph's petty theft and the enormous sum that

Henry extorted from the church does make Bardolph's punishment seem excessively harsh. The fact that a "pax," of all things, should become grounds for hanging only strengthens Pistol's case. It is not just that *pax* means "peace," or even that, as a component of the mass, the pax helped celebrate the heavenly pardon won for humanity by Christ's sacrifice; the irony of Bardolph's theft is that he steals what already in some sense belongs to him, though not to him exclusively—a share of communion.

This aspect of Bardolph's crime links him both with Harry and, more tellingly, with Harry's bishops, who regard the "temporal lands" of the church as their own "possession" (1.1.8).[35] For Protestant writers, in fact, the reason such "merchandise" as Bardolph's pax had been invented in the first place was to facilitate the clergy's plunder of the church. In one antipapist tract after another, Protestants attacked the "thievish" Catholic mass as a travesty of communion, "a sacrament rather of hate and dissension than of love and unity," designed to secure "a certain special privilege" for the Catholic priesthood.[36] In Thomas Becon's account (1563), these "massmongers" are not content to wear special robes, stand behind rails, and conduct their service in a language the people do not understand; they actually bar the people from fully partaking of the eucharist, instead offering them only an inedible pax to kiss: "While the boy or parish-clerk carrieth the *pax* about, ye yourselves alone eat up all and drink up all" (*Displayeng*, 279). Bardolph may have stolen a pax, and Harry "a greater sum / Than ever at one time the clergy yet / Did . . . part withal" (*Henry V*, 1.1.80–82), but the worse "church-robbers" in *Henry V* are the clergy themselves, who have not only appropriated the church from the people but sponsored "hate and dissension" with its resources.[37]

Oddly enough, Harry's own church-robbery thus turns out to be an old trick of his, the kind of "good jest" he had supposedly repudiated upon becoming king—that is, to "rob the thieves" (*1 Henry IV*, 2.2.94, 96). Though thwarting the will of the commons, his confiscations from the bishops do after all confer some benefits on his people, by helping to break the episcopal monopoly not just on church wealth but on church piety as well. We have already seen how Harry adopts York's public religion in preaching war to his soldiers, but Harry takes his populism a good deal further than York had. The Chorus is inspired to his highest commendation of the king ("Praise and glory on his head!") when the night before Agincourt Harry "goes and visits all his host, / Bids them good morrow with a modest smile / And calls them brothers, friends, and countrymen" (4.prologue.31–34). Twice in the play we hear Harry himself voice this egalitarian regard for his soldiers: "For there is none of you so mean and base / That hath not noble luster in your eyes" (3.1.29–30); "For he today that sheds his blood with me / Shall be my brother; be he ne'er so vile, / This day shall gentle his condition" (4.3.61–63). The deaths in battle of two noble Englishmen, Suffolk and York, seem not only to realize this promise of a blood brotherhood but to cast a religious glow over it: as an English lord recalls it, the dying York takes the already dead Suffolk

> by the beard, kisses the gashes
> That bloodily did yawn upon his face,
> And cries aloud, "Tarry, dear cousin Suffolk.
> My soul shall thine keep company to heaven.
> Tarry, sweet soul, for mine, then fly abreast,
> As in this glorious and well-foughten field
> We kept together in our chivalry."
>
> (4.6.13–19)

Harry's gift to his soldiers, this set piece appears to claim, is to liberate a holy-seeming communion from the confines of the church to the open battlefield.[38]

The less "pretty" (28) the picture of a soldiers' brotherhood in the play, however, the more egalitarian it looks. The French herald speaks of princes who "lie drowned and soaked in mercenary blood" (4.7.71); what he sees mixing "nobles" with "common men" (69) is the same power that for Harry turns mean and base soldiers noble, or in Exeter's eyes makes heaven as much a "yokefellow" (9) to chivalry as York is to Suffolk: violence. The English produce their own unseemly yet emphatic mixture of noble and commoner when Williams challenges Harry to a duel, although Harry dodges this threat to himself and his position by causing Fluellen to act as his substitute.[39] Other characters too use scapegoats to displace the leveling effects of violence. Bardolph reminds the dueling Nim and Pistol that "we must to France together. Why the devil should we keep knives to cut one another's throats?" (2.1.86–87). A companion of Williams employs this reasoning on Williams and Harry: "Be friends, you English fools, be friends. We have French quarrels enough" (4.1.212–13). Only the vanquished in the play prove capable of envisioning a peace or unity that is not realized through the sacrifice of some outsider. In the play's closing moments, the French king and queen foresee an end to even larger structures of exclusion than class: the queen prays for ties so close between the French and the English "that English may as French, French Englishmen, / Receive each other" (5.2.352–53), a communion the French king calls a "Christian-like accord" (338). Yet Harry's final words in the play make little reference to these internationalist pleas. Though heroically capable of forging bonds between piety and egalitarianism, Harry never transcends the war-mongering that enables him to forge those bonds in the first place. The only occasion on which he approximates an inclusive vision of French-English relations is when he playfully tempts his future wife, the French princess Katherine, with the thought of a renewed Crusade: "Shall not thou and I, between Saint Denis and Saint George, compound a boy, half-French half-English, that shall go to Constantinople and take the Turk by the beard?" (200–202). The anticlericalism of the history plays may suggest Shakespeare's longing for a religion that

Preachers and Players in Shakespeare's England

would be inclusive and pacifist rather than elitist and bellicose; but the last of these plays seems to leave us with the image of a communion broadened from clergy to congregation, from paxes to peace, only when first sanctified by violence.

II

Harry's wartime egalitarianism is, however, not the only alternative to a prelatical church in the play. Although the movement from church to court in the opening scenes of *Henry V* has long been a major topic of scholarly discussion, critics have less carefully examined the remarkable transition from prologue to play that precedes it. Perhaps that is because this transition is so much more jarring: instead of the heroic military struggles that the prologue's Chorus leads us to expect ("O for a Muse of fire!"), the first scene of *Henry V* places us in the midst of an episcopal conspiracy. Yet, when compared to the smooth modulation of this conspiracy into Harry's war effort, the very discontinuity of prologue and first scene seems to speak well of the Chorus; and indeed throughout the prologue the Chorus expatiates on an institution holding so little in common with either the church or the court that it will come to represent a moral standard against which both episcopal and kingly piety can be judged. This alternative institution is the theater.

The most striking difference between the theater as the Chorus manifests it and the church as the bishops manifest it is the theater's openness. In the prologue, this is both a literal and a figurative feature: literal, because the theater is open-air, a "wooden O" (1.prologue.13); figurative, because the Chorus openly admits the theater is nothing but a wooden O. Both forms of openness reverberate throughout the prologue, as the Chorus repeatedly apologizes for the "unworthy scaffold" (10) upon which "flat unraised spirits" (9) have presumed to stage Harry's story. These are the sort of derogatory terms that antitheatricalists loved to apply to the theater, belittling players as "poor, silly, hunger-starved wretches" who "are so base-minded, as at the pleasure of the veriest rogue in England, for one poor penny, they will be glad on open stage to play the ignominious fools for an hour or two together" (Pierce, *Marprelate Tracts*, 330). Yet in similarly depreciating the players of *Henry V* as mere "ciphers" to the "great account" they have theatricalized, the Chorus actually supplies the audience with terms for preferring the players to the bishops whom the audience will meet in the first scene: secretive and covetous aristocrats who translate the great account of Harry's story into a "mighty sum" of hoarded treasure, the bishops, that is, make "open" and "poor" sound like virtues. Indeed, the Chorus's apologies for the theater broaden its antiprelatical implications even beyond the scaffold and the players. He regrets that the theater lacks not only "a kingdom for a stage" and "princes to act" upon it but an audience composed of "monarchs" (3–4). This is nearly the class of audience the bishops come to address in scene 2, with an earl their lowest ranking auditor; but the same inclusive mixture of "mean and gentle" that "behold" (4.prologue.45–46) Harry before Agincourt is presumably what fills the seats of the theater that now beholds him anew.

It is as such an accessible "king of good fellows" (5.2.233) that Harry himself helps sharpen the contrast between the theater and the church throughout the play. He even points the way toward seeing the theater as an alternative site of spiritual edification. Half of the bishops' first scene is devoted to their astonishment at the extraordinary "reformation" (1.1.34) in Harry's character since his accession to the throne. "Never was such a sudden scholar made" (33), exclaims Canterbury, who considers this change in Harry a nearly miraculous "wonder,"

> Since his addiction was to courses vain,
> His companies unlettered, rude, and shallow,
> His hours filled up with riots, banquets, sports,
> And never noted in him any study,
> Any retirement, any sequestration
> From open haunts and popularity.
>
> (53–59)

The members of the audience who have previously witnessed the two parts of *Henry IV* know better than to think that Harry's "addiction to courses vain" allowed him no time for "study," but then as spectators of Harry's time spent in "open haunts" and as frequenters of such haunts themselves, the audience has a double advantage over the bishops, who not only differentiate "study" from "popularity" but never deign to mix with the people.

On a number of occasions in *Henry V*, Harry himself expounds the lessons that "courses vain" have taught him. The most basic of these lessons is to view anyone and anything, no matter how contemptible, as a possible source of edification. "God Almighty!" Harry exclaims on the morning of Agincourt, "There is some soul of goodness in things evil, / Would men observingly distil it out" (4.1.3–5). The immediate example Harry has in mind is his enemy, a "bad neighbor" who "makes us early stirrers" (6); more important, Harry says, the French "are our outward consciences, / And preachers to us all, admonishing / That we should dress us fairly for our end" (8–10). "Thus," Harry concludes, "may we gather honey from the weed / And make a moral of the devil himself" (11–12).

If even the French and the devil can be seen as "preachers," then surely so can the denizens of "open haunts." But what does Harry think they preach? His debate with Williams and his companions leads Harry to soliloquize on what is by this point in his story an old theme for him, the surprising lack of difference between king and commoner: "What have kings that privates have not too, / Save ceremony, save general ceremony?" (4.1.225–26). Harry speaks as dismissively of this "idol Ceremony" (228) as Protestants did of the idolatrous ceremonies that obscured the Truth while exalting the Catholic (and, to Marprelate, the episcopal) clergy above the people. The balm, the scepter, the ball, the sword. the mace, and all the rest of royal pomp are for Harry so many disguises that fail to hide not only how "the King is but a man" (99) but also how much better off the common man is in comparison to the king. For the commoner's "gross brain" allows him to sleep, whereas Harry the scholar-king must always keep the sort of "watch" (270–71) that this very meditation of Harry's exemplifies. Yet here of course is the royal difference Harry had first seemed to question. The comparison between king and commoner, a moral Harry gathered from the weeds of popular haunts, has taught him to discount as little more than props not only the ceremonial accoutrements that distinguish the king from the commoner but also the mortal body that assimilates him to the commoner. What really sets the king apart from the commoner, Harry thus implies, must be the king's uncommon brain, his marvelous capacity for watching and learning.

Again and again in the play Harry sermonizes on the insignificance of all but immaterial distinctions. In a lighter version of his ceremonial catalogue the act before, Harry reminds his future wife Katherine that "a good leg will fall, a straight back will stoop, a black beard will turn white, a curled pate will grown bald, a fair face will wither, a full eye will wax hollow, but a good heart, Kate, is the sun and the moon" (5.2.157–60). What makes the body less valuable to Harry than the "brain" or "heart" is not only the body's mutability but the mind's power to exploit this mutability: comforting Sir Thomas Erpingham on the subject of his listless troops, Harry assures him that "when the mind is quickened, out of doubt / The organs, though defunct and dead before, / Break up their drowsy grave and newly move / With casted slough and fresh legerity" (4.1.20–23). This is the basis of Harry's appeal to his army throughout the war—"All things are ready if our minds be so" (4.3.71)—and it easily modulates for Harry into the piety that leads him to declare, after the outnumbered English at Agincourt defeat the French, "O God, thy arm was here, / And not to us, but to thy arm alone / Ascribe we all" (4.8.104–6).

Such antimaterialism is famously anticipated by the Chorus, who repeatedly exhorts the audience to translate the obvious material deficiencies of the theater into an "imaginary puissance" (1.prologue.25). Yet if Harry and the Chorus both derive a lesson in the power of the immaterial from their experience of open haunts, the audience served by the Chorus seems better able to appreciate this lesson than Harry's subjects can.[40] The only king in the play to have mixed with commoners, Harry is in a unique position to compare classes, and he capitalizes on his special knowledge so successfully that he comes to be regarded with awe: "When he speaks," Canterbury marvels, even "the air, a chartered libertine, is still" (1.1.48–49). Although Harry's preaching may help liberate such immaterial power and its attendant mystique from the church, Harry alone remains, as his precursor York was said to be, "the very opener and intelligencer / Between the grace, the sanctities of heaven" and the "dull workings" (2 Henry IV, 4.2.20–22) of his auditors. The theater, by contrast, makes the mixture of king and commoner a sight for all the audience to see; it even turns Harry's soliloquy on the subject into a public spectacle. Just as Harry demystifies the bishops' privileged relation to spirituality, so the theater demystifies the esoteric scholarship of the king.[41]

This new communal access to a previously restricted knowledge has, as Joel Altman has shown, specifically eucharistic overtones in the Henriad. The audience of the plays "participates" in Harry's experience as communicants were said to "participate" in Christ; the exclusive hold of the clergy on a spiritual power commodified into lands and paxes gives way, it seems, to the more inclusive and also immaterial communion enabled by the play. If Harry's antimaterialism sets this reformation in motion, the antimaterialism of the Chorus advances it even further along Protestant lines. Especially in the context of clergymen desperate to save their privileges, the Chorus's Harry-like insistence on the physical inadequacies of the theater—"imperfections" that the audience must "piece out" with their "thoughts" (1.prologue.23)—recalls standard Protestant polemic against the Catholic church. Just as the Chorus claims that Harry's soldiers at Agincourt are "pining and pale" wretches before Harry inspires them, and that the theater's representation of Agincourt will amount to only "four or five most vile and ragged foils" unless the audience agrees to "eke out" such props with their "working" thoughts (3 and 4.prologue), so the Reformers claimed that the church and its paraphernalia would be "of little price" (as Pistol says of the pax) without the spiritual investments of God and each individual worshipper. "I so make division between the Spirit and sacraments," writes Calvin (trans. 1561), for instance, "that the power of working remain with the Spirit, and to the Sacraments be left only the ministration, yea and the same void and trifling without the working of the Spirit: but of much effectualness, when he inwardly worketh and putteth forth his force."[42]

Catholics objected to this Protestant denial of any intrinsic spiritual efficacy to the sacraments in the same terms that Stephen Greenblatt applies to Shakespeare's representations of Christian ceremonies: they argued that the Protestants "do evacuate and make of none effect the sacraments."[43] But Protestants routinely countered that it was rather the papists who had robbed the sacraments of their true substance, turning the Lord's Supper, as John Jewel (1562) argued, into "a stage-play, and a solemn sight; to the end that men's eyes should be fed with nothing else but with mad gazings, and foolish gauds."[44] The prologues to Henry V suggest that Shakespeare wants to help redeem the spirituality not only of the sacraments but of stage-plays too. When the Chorus advises the spectators of Henry V that they should be "minding true things by what their mock'ries be"

(4.prologue.53), he exhorts them to invest what seem like empty signs with something more substantial—to treat open haunts, material communions, the flesh, in other words, as vehicles for an immaterial force.[45]

Shakespeare seems to expect that this conversion will be facilitated not only by the audience's participation in Harry's extraclerical piety but also by the Chorus's repeated belittlement of the stage. From the first prologue of *Henry V*, the Chorus subordinates both Harry and the players who represent his story to the imaginative capacities of the audience, "For 'tis your thoughts that now must deck our kings" (1.prologue.28). This sort of self-deprecation was, in principle, the job of every Protestant preacher: to make plain, as James Pilkington (1560) cautions, that "it is not we that speak, when we speak any truth: but it is the Holy Spirit of God that speaks in us, whose instruments we be."[46] Yet the manifest alternative in *Henry V* to the bishop or king who encourages his auditors to treat him idolatrously is the player, not the preacher, as the Chorus shows. He humbly asks the audience to "admit" (1.prologue.32) him to a public office that, unlike "king" or "bishop," lasts only as long as the run of the play; and he relegates himself, along with every other stage-herald of "true things," to the status of a mockery.

But then Harry is equally as self-deprecating as the Chorus; what's more, he employs his humility, as the Chorus does not, for overtly pious ends. The Chorus himself tells us how Harry, "being free from vainness and self-glorious pride," refused to have his war-worn armor paraded through London, "giving full trophy, signal, and ostent / Quite from himself to God" (5.prologue.17–22). If even this ostensibly modest king proves committed to retaining a privileged hold on spirituality, why should we believe that the far less religious-sounding Chorus is not at least as interested in exclusivity and self-empowerment? After all, although he may appear, like a good Protestant, to place the burden of spiritual action where it belongs—onto the "working" thoughts of each auditor—the Chorus also occasionally stresses, like a good Catholic, the mediatory power of the players. Having claimed in the first prologue, for instance, that his auditors must fill in the play's temporal gaps with their thoughts, he nevertheless adds that he will "supply" this function (28–32); or again, in the second prologue he declares that the players, not the thoughts of the audience, will "convey" the audience to France and back, "charming the narrow seas / To give you gentle pass" (37–39). Most revealing, *Henry V* is hardly as unsatisfactory a play as the Chorus makes it out to be, a fact Shakespeare highlights for his audience when, in likening Pistol to the "roaring devil i'th' old play" (4.4.64), he contrasts the primitive religious stage to his own more sophisticatedly naturalist theatrical illusions. Why, then, shouldn't we regard the Chorus's abasement before the mental power of the audience as simply a means of flattering his auditors and absorbing them in the play? This is certainly the view of players that the author of the *Blast* favors: he claims that "the principal end of all their interludes" is only "to juggle in good earnest the money out of other men's purses into their own hands" (115–16).

According to the antitheatricalists, in other words, one should respond to Shakespeare's intimations of piety just as Gloucester had responded to Shakespeare's first episcopal villain: "Name not religion, for thou lov'st the flesh."

This charge is a significant problem for Shakespeare, so significant, in fact, that the story of Shakespeare's career-long response to it would require another essay to unfold. Yet *Henry V* provides at least the outlines of a defense of the theater's carnality, for the whole thrust of Shakespeare's stage-religion is to reject the *violent* opposition between spirit and flesh that the bishops promote from one side and Harry from the other. Harry's spirituality may be egalitarian, allowing him to glimpse a noble luster even in the eyes of the mean and base, but, as we have seen, the inclusiveness of his piety goes only so far: it thrives on a warfare waged not just between the English and the French but also between the spirit and the flesh. Comparing Harry to his forebears, the French king, Charles, treats these two enmities in Harry as if they were one:

> Witness our too-much-memorable shame
> When Crécy battle fatally was struck,
> And all our princes captived by the hand
> Of that black name, Edward, Black Prince of Wales,
> Whiles that his mountant sire, on mountain standing,
> Up in the air, crowned with the golden sun,
> Saw his heroical seed and smiled to see him
> Mangle the work of nature and deface
> The patterns that by God and by French fathers
> Had twenty years been made.
>
> (2.4.53–62)

The strange confusion here of Edward III smiling on his heroical seed and of God well pleased with his Son suggests that Charles too conflates spirituality with warfare; more specifically, Charles rewrites the spirit's mingling with the flesh in Christ as a spirited mangling of "the work of nature." For the French as for the English king, in other words, a spirit "fleshed" (50) is one that has been given a taste for trouncing the flesh, not redeeming it.

If the Chorus also belittles the flesh in comparison to the spirit, he does not encourage the same murderous opposition between the two. In one respect his more moderate approach reflects the fictionality of the violence he introduces: unlike Harry's Agincourt, of course, Shakespeare's "brawl ridiculous" (4.prologue.51) causes no physical harm. Conversely, the persuasive naturalism of Shakespeare's fictions suggests that, no matter how paltry the theater and, by analogy, the flesh may be, the audience requires both in order to sustain its "imaginary puissance." Yet the difference between Shakespeare's theatrical spirit and Harry's military one runs still deeper. When Harry encounters the "lank lean cheeks and war-worn coats" of his "poor" troops, he extols the ability of spirit and Spirit to crush the opposing French; but when the Chorus considers the four or five most vile and ragged foils of his players, he is led only to pray for the audience's "pity" (4.prologue.22, 26, 49). In other words, the Chorus regards the material inadequacy of the theater as forming the basis of a plea for spiritual aid and fellowship. Insofar as Shakespeare's theater succeeds in catering to the carnal impulses of the audience, this plea grows only more persuasive: with its own money and pleasure at stake, the audience has, after all, a vested interest in pitying the players' weak efforts.

Yet the fellowship between flesh and spirit that Shakespeare aims to encourage through the experience of *Henry V* depends on more than a matching fellowship between stage and audience: it depends as well on a fellowship encouraged *within* the audience. In the play, the English achieve a Christian-like accord amongst themselves only by venting their pitiless antagonisms onto the French; in the theater, Shakespeare may accept that his audience requires a scapegoat for its own pacification and unification, but he denies that the audience's relation to this scapegoat need be violent. Once again he appears to imagine his auditors playing the communicants to the eucharist of his historical drama. That is, he seems to think that, as a stage for two kinds of immaterial violence—the represented violence of Harry's wars and the violence done to Harry's wars in representing them—*Henry V* provides the audience as "unbloody" a sacrifice as the eucharist was thought to supply in recalling Christ's death.[47]

That Shakespeare believed his audience could achieve some form of communion through the spiritual sacrifices inspired by his theater is implied by the Chorus's first apology for the play. We have already seen how the Chorus begins *Henry V* with a wish for a fully royal theater; the reason he desires such a theater, he explains, is that he wants "the warlike Harry" to appear "like himself"—that is, as a god of violence, who would

> Assume the port of Mars, and at his heels
> Leashed in like hounds, should famine, sword, and fire
> Crouch for employment.
>
> (1.prologue.5–8)

"But pardon, gentles all." This brief line epitomizes the sort of moral adjustment the audience is asked to make throughout the play. Confessing himself unable to stage Harry's superhuman violence, the Chorus at the same time begs the audience to forgo its own violence. In fact, he offers this very self-sacrifice of the audience as precisely its compensation for the players' shortcomings. Unlike an all-royal theater, the audience may be socially diverse, and unlike Harry it may lose the opportunity for murder; here as in the rest of Shakespeare's histories, aristocracy and warfare go hand in hand. Yet, the Chorus suggests, the audience gains by these losses a sublimely coherent identity after all, a unity transcending class, in which "all" come to share a gentility that embraces rather than excludes, that pardons rather than kills.[48] Even some Protestant divines would have regarded such a communion as literally sacramental: Tyndale (c. 1533) argues that because it transpires "even in our own selves," forgiveness represents "more sensible and surer" a sacrament than either baptism or the Lord's Supper.[49] In ending the prologue on this communal note, beseeching his auditors "gently to hear, kindly to judge, our play" (32–34), the Chorus prepares those auditors to regard the theater as not only a more open, cheap, and egalitarian site of "participation" than the clergy-run church they will next encounter, but, above all, a more *peaceable* institution.

Why then does the Chorus not say so much outright? Apparently, his indirection is, for Shakespeare, one more sign of the saving difference between players and preachers. In defense of the bitter dissensions sparked by their sermonizing, many puritans proudly recalled the scriptures that Winchester and Pistol mangle, about Christ's coming to bring not peace but a sword; the author of *A Dialogue, Concerning the Strife of Our Church* (1584) maintains that in any case godly preachers never disrupt more than "a cursed unity and a wicked love, which is in the flesh" (61).[50] Yet Shakespeare so values the communality of the theatrical experience—values it, indeed, before any particularity of doctrine—that he has the Chorus explicitly address no more controversial a spiritual issue than the powers of the imagination. This is not the supposed transcendence of dogma, the displacement of religion by literature, for which modern critics have praised Shakespeare; what gives the *appearance* of an aestheticizing skepticism in his plays is rather Shakespeare's increasing conviction that, for religion's sake, doctrinal controversies must be muted. Sacrificing preacherly goals to what he considers the necessarily prior objective of a theatrical community, Shakespeare even allows the hawkish members of his audience a provisional confidence in his militarism, and offers his play as a (pardonable) scapegoat when that confidence is repeatedly betrayed.[51]

Such faith in communion as the strongest basis for edification pits Shakespeare against more than the factiousness that godly preaching could generate. The reformer Miles Coverdale (1593) extols the sacraments for distributing not only Christ's love but his power as teacher to all participants: "Christ with these outward tokens thought to couple and knit together the members of his holy church in obedience and love one towards another; whereby they knowing one another among themselves, might by such exterior things stir and provoke one another to love and godliness."[52] In presenting *Henry V* as an "outward token" that is nondoctrinal and thus obviously free of the need for any privileged "exposition on the holy text" like York's,[53] Shakespeare seems intent on fostering an even more radical alternative to clerical elitism than Coverdale envisions. Indeed, much of the theater's beauty for Shakespeare seems to lie in its plain *inadequacy* to the task of edification. Gone is the didactic religiosity "i'th' old play." With the aid, not the impediment, of a state censorship that keeps preachers off the stage, the theater as Shakespeare sees it now helps register the difference between the

Spirit and any vehicle that would lay some special claim to it. No longer must the people wait for a bishop, king, or even Chorus to play the preacher and, in the process, assume the port of Mars; rather, Shakespeare suggests, the people can learn how to edify each other—stirring and provoking one another, as Coverdale says, but to love and godliness.[54]

It is not just by inspiring pity that Shakespeare seems to think the physical limitations of the theater capable of promoting this reformed communion: a "cockpit" in which "the very casques" of Agincourt cannot be "crammed" literally forces intimacy on a socially disparate audience. At one point the Chorus appears to suggest that the physical limitations of England too, "model to thy inward greatness, / Like little body with a mighty heart" (2.prologue.16–17), have this same incorporating effect. Yet the Chorus evokes this conception of England just as he is about to inform us of some treasonous Englishmen who had been hired by the French to murder Harry; one of these assassins was even Harry's occasional "bedfellow" (2.2.8). Clearly the intimacy encouraged by physical limitations has its limitations. But then the Chorus had called England only a "model" to its inward greatness; like the theater, in other words, the little body of the English isle is no more than a "mockery," an outward and unworthy token that does not measure up to the spiritual truth it signifies. Insofar as the "little place" (1.prologue.16) of the theater takes the part of little England in Shakespeare's history plays, then, it may help convert England into a spiritual allegory, but it also weakens England's claims to intrinsic spiritual virtue. As I have tried to demonstrate, however, Shakespeare stops short of insisting that such material "imperfections" as the English isle possess *no* spiritual significance whatsoever. In resisting what he considers the clerical and kingly tyrannies that would turn the word to sword, Shakespeare's history plays support a "gentler" moral: one in which the "fleshly and carnal" cannot be excluded from the project of redemption ("so Chrish save me"), even if they must always remain as "ciphers to this great account."

Notes

I would like to thank the following friends and colleagues for greatly improving this essay: Paul Alpers, Oliver Arnold, John Coolidge, Stephen Greenblatt, Dorothy Hale, Richard Helgerson, Steven Knapp, Nancy Ruttenburg, and Ramie Targoff.

1. John N. King, *English Reformation Literature: The Tudor Origins of the Protestant Tradition* (Princeton, N.J., 1982), 275; the playwright-clergymen named by King are John Bale, Thomas Becon, John Foxe, William Baldwin, Nicholas Udall, and Nicholas Grimald.
2. John Foxe, *The Acts and Monuments* (1563–83), ed. Stephen Cattley and George Townsend (1837–41, 1843–49), 8 vols. (New York, 1965), 6:57; quoted in E. K. Chambers, *The Elizabethan Stage*, 4 vols. (Oxford, 1923), 1:242, n. 1. For evidence that Elizabeth's

government encouraged Protestant propaganda on the stage in 1559–1560, see ibid., 1:243–44.

3. [Anthony Munday (?) and] Salvianus, *A Second and Third Blast of Retrait from Plaies and Theaters*, ed. Arthur Freeman (New York, 1973), 58–59, 89.

4. John Northbrook, *A Treatise Wherein Dicing, Dauncing, Vaine Playes or Enterluds With Other Idle Pastimes etc. Commonly Used on the Sabboth Day, Are Reproved* (1577?), ed. Arthur Freeman (New York, 1974), 62.

5. Quoted in Chambers, *Elizabethan Stage*, 4:320.

6. Quoted in ibid., 4:304.

7. The preacher John Stockwood (1579) speaks of "the often and vehement outcrying of God his Preachers against" the theaters; *A Very Fruiteful Sermon Preched at Paules Crosse* (London, 1579), 24. Cf. *Blast*, A4v; and Stephen Gosson, *Playes Confuted in Five Actions* (1582), in *Markets of Bawdrie: The Dramatic Criticism of Stephen Gosson*, ed. Arthur F. Kinney (Salzburg, 1974), 149. Paul's Cross seems to have been a popular venue for these protests. See the Paul's Cross sermons by John Walsall (*A Sermon Preached at Pauls Crosse* [London, 1578]) and Thomas White (*A Sermon Preached at Pawles Crosse* [London, 1578]); and the two by Stockwood (*A Sermon Preached at Paules Crosse* [London, 1578]; and *A Very Fruiteful Sermon*). An antitheatrical Paul's Cross sermon by a preacher named Spark is mentioned in the preface to the *Blast* (A3v).

8. Thomas Becon, *A Comparison Betwene the Lordes Supper, and the Popes Masse* (1563), ed. John Ayre, *Prayers and Other Pieces* (Cambridge, 1844), 378.

9. Chambers thus underestimates the issue when he suggests that "a touch of professional *amour propre* gave its sting to the conflict" between player and preacher (1:256). The theater was, of course, not the only perceived rival to the church. Other commonly cited adversaries were dice, cards, piping, dancing, and the alehouse; see Patrick Collinson, *The Religion of Protestants: The Church in English Society, 1559–1625* (Oxford, 1982), 203–7.

In a number of influential essays, Christopher Haigh has recently argued that, during the second half of Elizabeth's reign, the apparent inefficacy of Elizabethan preaching became an open scandal: "It was clear to the ministers, as it must surely be to historians, that the preaching-campaign had produced only a small minority of godly Protestants, leaving the rest in ignorance, indifference, or downright antipathy"; "The Church of England, the Catholics and the People," in Haigh, ed., *The Reign of Elizabeth I* (London, 1984), 209, cf. 205–14; "Anticlericalism and the English Reformation," in Haigh, ed., *The English Reformation Revised* (Cambridge, 1987), 73–74; and "Puritan Evangelism in the Reign of Elizabeth I," *English Historical Review* 92 (1977): 30–58, passim. But Haigh tends, I think, to overestimate clerical disillusionment with preaching; for a more balanced account, see Collinson, "The Elizabethan Church and the New Religion," in Haigh, ed., *Reign*, 169–94, passim; and Collinson, *Religion*, 195–241. For other Tudor versions besides Northbrook's of "the hoary complaint that the preacher is not regarded," see J. W. Blench, *Preaching in England in the Late Fifteenth and Sixteenth Centuries: A Study of English Sermons, 1450–c. 1600* (Oxford, 1964), 124–25, 237–38, 272–73, 309–10, and 324. For uncommon confidence that preaching had begun (1587) to make such "places of sin" as the theater "more empty than before," see the *Seconde Parte of a Register, Being a Calendar of Manuscripts Under That Title Intended for Publication by the Puritans About 1593*, ed. Albert Peel, 2 vols. (Cambridge, 1915), 2:219.

10. See Christopher Haigh, "The Continuity of Catholicism in the English Reformation," in *English Reformation Revised*, 176–208. Nonconformists joined the attack as well:

reflecting on the poor results of established preaching, Henry Barrow (c. 1590) comments, "It is unsound milk that giveth no increase to the body in 30 years' space"; *A Brief Discoverie of the False Church*, in *The Writings of Henry Barrow, 1587–90*, ed. Leland H. Carson (London, 1962), 501.

11. George Gifford, *A Briefe Discourse of Certaine Points of the Religion, Which Is Among the Common Sort of Christians, Which May Be Termed the Countrie Divinitie* (London, 1582), 26r.

12. The first quotation, cited by Haigh, "Church," 209, appears in the 1604 edition of Robert Cawdrey's *A Short and Fruitfull Treatise, of the Profite and Necessitie of Catechising* (B6v); the second quotation appears in the 1580 edition (A6v). Haigh also cites much of the homiletic literature to which I refer.

13. *A Summons for Sleepers. . . . Hereunto is annexed, A Patterne for Pastors* (London, 1589), 51.

14. I quote the seminal puritan complaint on the subject, the *Admonition to the Parliament* (1572) of John Field and Thomas Wilcox; in *Puritan Manifestos: A Study of the Origin of the Puritan Revolt*, ed. Walter Howard Frere and Charles Edward Douglas (1907; reprint ed., London, 1954), 22, 11. For a careful accounting of the established clergy by puritan writers, see the "Survey of the Ministry" (1586) in the manuscript *Second Parte of a Register* (2:88–174). Under the heading of "What duty is performed" by the minister surveyed, the only interest of the surveyors is whether and how often that minister preaches—and the most common entry is "n.-p.," "no preacher."

15. "The preachers of God, mind so much edifying of souls, that they often forget, we have any bodies. And therefore, some do not so much good with telling the truth, as they do harm with dulling the hearers"; Thomas Wilson, *The Arte of Rhetorique* (1553; rev. ed., 1560), ed. Thomas J. Derrick (New York, 1982), 278.

16. Nothing irritated puritans so much as the sort of accommodative preaching Wilson recommends. Thomas Cartwright (1572) denounces those "profane preachers" who mix "merry tales" in their sermons; *A Second Admonition to the Parliament*, in Frere and Douglas, eds., *Puritan Manifestos*, 109–10; just as the author of *A Dialogue, Concerning the Strife of Our Churche* (London, 1584) attacks the minister who "can occupy a pulpit an hour or two with fine tales and Fables, and pretty jests to make the people laugh" (56; cf. Gifford, *Briefe Discourse*, 48r).

17. Cf. Philip Stubbes, *An Anatomie of Abuses* (1583; rev. eds. 1583, 1584, 1595), ed. Arthur Freeman (New York, 1973), L7v; Henry Crosse, *Vertues Common-wealth* (London, 1603), Q2r; Lake, *Probe*, 268; Robert Milles, *Abrahams Suite for Sodome* (London, 1612), D6r; and *A Shorte Treatise Against Stage-Playes* (1625), in *The English Drama and Stage Under the Tudor and Stuart Princes, 1543–1664*, ed. William Carew Hazlitt (London, 1869), 237–40. It is not hard to guess why opponents of this view are the only ones to record it. When it was alleged (1610) that the musician and theatrical entrepreneur Philip Rosseter had voiced such an opinion, he was called before the bishop of London; see Edgar I. Fripp, *Shakespeare Man and Artist*, 2 vols. (1938; London, 1964), 2:750 (my thanks to Karl Wentersdorf for helping me track this reference down).

No amount of sermonizing by the players would have mollified the antitheatricalists, who were more appalled by the presence of religion on the public stage than by its absence. As Northbrook declares, "It is better that spiritual things be utterly omitted, than unworthily and unreverently handled and touched" (*Treatise*, 65). To put religion on the stage was, these writers assumed, "to mingle scurrility with Divinity," which the antitheatricalists variously explained as mixing the sacred with "Paganism" (Crosse, *Vertues Common-wealth*, P3r) or with "filthy, lewd, & ungodly speeches" (*Blast*, 114). But for some the very *staging* of religion counted as the most objectionable mixture, because it subjected "spiritual things" not only to carnal shows but to the base players. Thus Gosson, for instance, allows biblical drama that is intended to be read, not played; *Playes Confuted*, 177–78.

18. Glynne Wickham, *Early English Stages, 1300–1600*, vol. 2, *1576–1660*, part 1 (London, 1963), 19.

19. Louis Montrose, "The Purpose of Playing: Reflections on a Shakespearean Anthropology," *Helios* n.s. 7 (1980): 51–74; and Stephen Greenblatt, "Shakespeare and the Exorcists," *Shakespearean Negotiations: The Circulation of Social Energy in Renaissance England* (Berkeley, 1988), 94–128. See also Michael O'Connell, "The Idolatrous Eye: Iconoclasm, Anti-Theatricalism, and the Image of the Elizabethan Theater," *English Literary History* 52 (1985): 279–310. C. L. Barber takes a similar position on the theater's appropriation of the sacred: "The new theater's secular personages could be invested with meanings cognate to those that had entered into worship"; "The Family in Shakespeare's Development: Tragedy and Sacredness," in *Representing Shakespeare: New Psychoanalytic Essays*, ed. Murray M. Schwartz and Coppelia Kahn (Baltimore, 1980), 196. Unlike Montrose and Greenblatt, however, Barber also argues that the tragedies derive their pathos in large part from the failure of the theater to make good the loss of Catholic ritual (see esp. 196–97). This view is elaborated in Barber and Richard Wheeler's *The Whole Journey: Shakespeare's Powers of Development* (Berkeley, 1986).

20. Thomas Lodge and Robert Greene, *A Looking Glasse for London and England*, ed. George Alan Clugston (New York, 1980), 200. For the survival of scriptural drama in the permanent theaters, see Lily B. Campbell, *Divine Poetry and Drama in Sixteenth-Century England* (1959; reprint ed., Berkeley, 1961), 238–60; and Ruth H. Blackburn, *Biblical Drama Under the Tudors* (The Hague, Neth., 1971), 160–91. Blackburn notes that a resurgence in such drama seems to have begun around 1587.

21. The best introduction to this strange episode in the history of Elizabethan religion and drama is Charles Nicholl, *A Cup of News: The Life of Thomas Nashe* (London, 1984), 62–79.

22. This is the Duke's description of the "precise" Angelo in *Measure for Measure* (1604). In the two parts of *Henry IV* (1596–98?), Falstaff (whom Shakespeare originally named after a proto-Protestant martyr, Sir John Oldcastle) mocks holier-than-thou puritan cant.

   Except in the case of *Henry V*, for which I have used Gary Taylor's edition (Oxford, 1982), I cite throughout *The Riverside Shakespeare*, ed. G. Blakemore Evans et al. (Boston, 1974).

23. I am not the first to argue that *Henry V* is a sacramental play. See Joel Altman's superb essay, "'Vile Participation': The Amplification of Violence in the Theater of *Henry V*," *Shakespeare Quarterly* 42 (1991): 1–32, which anticipates my argument about *Henry V* in many respects.

24. For perhaps the most extraordinary rendering of the charge that Catholics worship nothing more than "a thin wafer-cake," see Thomas Becon, *The Displayeng of the Popishe Masse* (1563), in *Prayers and Other Pieces*, 278–79. The Protestant resonance of Shakespeare's "wafer-cakes" is noted by Gary Taylor in his edition of *Henry V* (Oxford, 1984), 144.

   Shakespeare more fully alludes to a Protestant view of the eucharist when Fluellen forces Pistol to eat a leek and Gower comments to Pistol, "Will you mock at an ancient tradition, begun upon an honorable respect, and worn as a memorable trophy of predeceased valor . . . ?" (5.1.63–66). The difference between this violently imposed nationalist communion and what Shakespeare considers a more truly spiritual communion will be the burden of my paper.

25. Cf. "Play with your fancies, and in them behold" (3.prologue.7); "Work, work your thoughts, and therein see" (25).

26. "An Act to Restrain Abuses of Players" (27 May 1606), in Chambers, *Elizabethan Stage*, 4:338–39.

27. Roland Mushat Frye, *Shakespeare and Christian Doctrine* (Princeton, N.J., 1963), 271, 13, 267.

28. David Bevington, *Tudor Drama and Politics: A Critical Approach to Topical Meaning* (Cambridge, Mass., 1968), 201.

29. William Pierce, ed., *The Marprelate Tracts: 1588, 1589* (London, 1911), 399.

30. The prelate of the *Henry VI* plays may even have reminded Shakespeare and his audience of a third bishop of Winchester, Stephen Gardiner, whose "proud and glorious spirit," "stubborn contumacy against the king, and malicious rebellion against God and true religion," had been denounced by Foxe, *Acts*, 6:24. For the story of Gardiner's vicious dealings with a Lord Protector and young king of his own, see ibid., 6:24–266. Gardiner appears as Bishop of Winchester in Shakespeare's *Henry VIII*.
    In her discussion of *King John*, Virginia M. Vaughan also argues that Shakespeare's "tendency to ignore specific doctrine" allows him to attack "the venality of the established church" in general, "whether Catholic or Protestant"; but she differs from me in claiming that what motivates Shakespeare's assault on the church in *King John* is his secularist loyalty to the state: "*King John*: A Study in Subversion and Containment," in Deborah Curren-Aquino, ed., *King John: New Perspectives* (Newark, Del., 1989), 70.

31. For the case that the play was censored, see Janet Clare, *"Art Made Tongue-Tied by Authority": Elizabethan and Jacobean Dramatic Censorship* (Manchester, 1990), 68–70.

32. Matthew 18.7 (Geneva version). For the Elizabethan theory of the scourge, see Roy Battenhouse, *Marlowe's Tamburlaine: A Study in Renaissance Moral Philosophy* (Nashville, Tenn., 1941), 13–15 and 108–13; and Eleanor Prosser, *Hamlet and Revenge* (1967; 2nd ed., Stanford, Calif., 1971), 202, who quotes Harry on war.

33. For those members of the audience who had previously witnessed Harry's father advise him to protect his crown by busying "giddy minds / With foreign quarrels" (*2 Henry IV*, 4.5.213–14), Harry's selfish motives would of course be all the plainer. I do not mean to argue, however, that the war truly is Harry's cause alone: the second scene of the play shows how Harry's clergy, his aristocracy, and even his fellow monarchs press him to declare war. I will shortly examine the social bonds that not only lead to war but are supported by it.

34. Taylor, *Henry V*, 128, notes the pun in "sword." Pistol elsewhere adopts the more direct blasphemy of his captains as part of a comic pretension to a higher class: "Oui, couper la gorge, par ma foi" (4.4.33).

35. Shakespeare also emphasizes the profiteering of the Catholic clergy later in the play, when Harry, meditating on his father's murder of Richard II, tells us he has "five hundred poor"

> in yearly pay,
> Who twice a day their withered hands hold up
> Toward heaven to pardon blood. And I have built
> Two chantries, where the sad and solemn priests
> Sing still for Richard's soul.
> (4.1.286–90)

Harry promises to "do" still "more," yet he also adds a Protestant-sounding qualification about the ultimate inefficacy of good works: "Though all that I can do is nothing worth,/Since that my penitence comes after all,/Imploring pardon" (290–93). For a more open attack on the Catholic view of pardon, see *King John*, 3.1.162–71.

36. Thomas Becon, *A New Catechisme* (1564), ed. John Ayre, in *The Catechism of Thomas Becon, with Other Pieces* (Cambridge, 1844), 239, cf. 300–301; Becon, *Displayeng*, 281; Nicholas Ridley, *Certein Godly, Learned, and Comfortable Conference Betwene N. Rydley and H. Latimer* (1556), ed. Henry Christmas, in *The Works of Nicholas Ridley* (Cambridge, 1841), 123.

37. John Jewel, *An Apologie, or Aunswer in Defence of the Church of England* (1562), trans. Lady A[nne] B[acon] from *Apologia Ecclesiae Anglicanae* (1562), in *Works*, 4 vols., ed. John Ayre (Cambridge, 1845–50), 3:63. Jewel uses the phrase to characterize the papists' sacrilegious corruption of the Lord's Supper into a "private" ceremony. Cf. Ridley's long attack on the papists as church-robbers, especially in regard to the mass, in *A Frendly Farewel* (1559), in *Works*, 398–405.

38. Fluellen too clothes warfare in the "ceremonies," "cares," "forms," "sobriety," and "modesty" (4.1.72–74) that Harry has helped to lift from the church.

39. After causing Williams to relate the story of his challenge, Henry suggests to Fluellen that Williams's adversary may be "a gentleman of great sort, quite from the answer of [Williams's] degree." Fluellen responds to this caution with an egalitarianism he considers licensed by dueling: though Williams's enemy "be as good a gentleman as the devil is, as Lucifer and Beelzebub himself," argues Fluellen, "it is necessary, look your grace, that he keep his vow and his oath" (4.7.129–33). For another version of class distinctions associated with the devil or false religion generally, see Pistol's response to the "O Seigneur Dieu!" of his frightened French prisoner: "O Seigneur Dew should be a gentleman" (4.4.6–7).

40. For a reading of the play that treats the analogy between King and Chorus as an equation, see Lawrence Danson, "*Henry V*: King, Chorus, and Critics," *Shakespeare Quarterly* 34 (1983): 27–43.

41. Introducing his manuscript life of Elizabeth (1603), John Clapham writes, "The affairs of princes are no fit subject for every private man's pen: their projects and consultations are imparted but to few"; "Certain Observations Concerning the Life and Reign of Queen Elizabeth," in *Elizabeth of England*, ed. Evelyn Plummer Read and Conyers Read (Philadelphia, 1951), 31. But Shakespeare not only undertakes the affairs of his princes as his subject; he also imparts their projects and consultations to many.

The potentiality of the Renaissance English theater to demystify kingship has been powerfully underscored by Franco Moretti in "The Great Eclipse: Tragic Form as the Deconsecration of Sovereignty" (1979), in *Signs Taken For Wonders: Essays in the Sociology of Literary Forms*, trans. Susan Fischer, David Forgacs, and David Miller (1983; rev. ed., London, 1988), 42–82; and by Stephen Orgel in "Making Greatness Familiar," *Genre* 15 (1982): 41–48; see also David Scott Kastan, "Proud Majesty Made a Subject: Shakespeare and the Spectacle of Rule," *Shakespeare Quarterly* 37 (1986): 459–75. Recently, however, this view has come under vigorous attack by Richard Helgerson, who argues that Shakespeare's history plays increasingly work not to empower the audience but to "efface, alienate, even demonize all signs of commoner participation in the political nation"; *Forms of Nationhood: The Elizabethan Writing of England* (Chicago, 1992), 214. Helgerson contrasts Shakespeare's histories with those produced in Philip Henslowe's theater, which Helgerson considers far more populist in part because the Henslowe histories "lack the elaborate genealogies that are such a prominent feature

Preachers and Players in Shakespeare's England

in all of Shakespeare's English histories. And they pay almost no attention to the strategies by which power is achieved and maintained" (238). But this unwillingness to probe into the affairs of princes (which Helgerson somewhat exaggerates) is precisely what Moretti and Orgel would associate with a conservative theater. To grasp their point, take a dramatist who contrasts even more sharply with Shakespeare than Henslowe's dramatists do. Not once in Ben Jonson's plays for the public theater does a king appear on the stage; yet for a more exclusive audience Jonson wrote masque after masque celebrating the virtues of the reigning monarch. Shakespeare's history plays may consistently focus upon the personal and political dealings of royalty, yet these plays (in which kings more often than not fare quite badly) were produced in the public theater; for the praise of the reigning monarch, Shakespeare never wrote a single masque.

42. John Calvin, *The Institution of Christian Religion* (London, 1561), trans. T[homas]. N[orton]. from *Institutio Christianae Religionis* (1536–59), 4.14.9. Altman makes the same point; "'Vile Participation,'" 19, n. 50.

43. Heinrich Bullinger, *Fiftie Godlie and Learned Sermons*, trans. by H. I. (1577) from *Sermonum Decades Quinque* (1549–51), ed. Thomas Harding, in *The Decades of Henry Bullinger*, 4 vols. (Cambridge, 1849–52), 4:313.

44. Jewel, *Works*, 3:64. For other references to the theatricality of Catholic sacraments, see Jonas Barish, *The Antitheatrical Prejudice* (Berkeley, 1981), 159–65.

45. To support his claim that Shakespeare's plays merely empty out religion, Greenblatt cites *King Lear*. Having masterfully demonstrated how the play suits the anti-Catholic purposes of a Protestant polemicist such as Thomas Harsnett, who argues that Catholic exorcism, and Catholicism generally, are nothing more than theater, Greenblatt nevertheless concludes that *Lear* finally undermines Harsnett, because "there is no saving institution" in the play against which the "evacuated rituals" of Catholicism "may be set"; *Shakespearean Negotiations*, 127. Yet this assessment of Lear's tragedy disregards, I think, the setting of the play: where in a pagan Britain hundreds of years prior to Christ's birth was such a "saving institution" to be found? Greenblatt further discounts the Protestant implications of his argument when he remarks in the story of Edgar and Edmund the traces of "an allegory in which Catholicism is revealed to be the persecuted legitimate elder brother forced to defend himself by means of theatrical illusion against the cold persecution of his skeptical bastard brother Protestantism" (121). Yet Protestants routinely represented *their* faith as the old one, with Catholicism a later heresy. In Jewel's *Certain Sermons* (1583), for instance, Catholic ceremonies are said to be "base-born" (*Works*, 2:991)—like Edmund—while the true "sacraments that Christ left for our most comfort have been miserably mangled and defaced" (994)—like Edgar. Following this new set of identifications, one could argue that Edgar's theatrical defense typologically anticipates the better Protestant device of a theater that employs illusion to rescue the truth. This reading is untenable for Greenblatt only because he assumes, with the antitheatricalists, that religion must be "purged of theater" (*Shakespearean Negotiations*, 127) in order to survive.

46. *The Works of James Pilkington*, ed. James Scholefield (Cambridge, 1842), 84.

47. Cf. Jewel's account (1565) of the holy communion as an "unbloody sacrifice" in his *Replie Unto M. Hardinges Answer*, *Works*, 2:734–35: e.g., "Our christian sacrifices in the gospel, because they are merely spiritual, and proceed wholly from the heart, are called unbloody" (734).

48. Altman argues just the opposite about the communion inspired by *Henry V*: he maintains that it *joins* "audience to soldiery" ("'Vile Participation,'" 16) rather than differ-

entiates the two. Thus Altman associates the Chorus's repeated characterization of the audience as "gentles" with Harry's promise to his troops that any English soldier who sheds his blood at Agincourt "shall gentle his condition." Yet there is nothing oxymoronic about the Chorus's fusion of gentleness with pardon, whereas Harry's fusion of gentleness with bloodshed strikes the same jarring note as the references to the "gentle" rebel York do in *2 Henry IV*.

49. William Tyndale, *An Exposicion Uppon the V. VI. VII. Chapters of Mathew*, in *Works*, 3 vols., ed. Henry Walter (Cambridge, 1848–50), 2:91. John Bradford (1562) more cautiously maintains that to pardon "such as offend us is *as* a sacrament," "for as certain as we are that we pardon them that offend us, so certain should we be that thou dost pardon us, whereof the forgiving our trespassers is, as it were, a sacrament unto us"; *Godlie Meditations*, in *The Writings of John Bradford*, 2 vols., ed. Aubrey Townsend (Cambridge, 1848–53), 133 (the first quotation, with my emphasis, is from a marginal note added to the 1567 edition).

The Protestant emphasis on the significatory function of the sacraments seems to have generated a good deal of confusion among the godly about what counted as a sacrament and why the sacraments were necessary to one's spiritual life. Like Tyndale and Bradford, many English reformers confined the sacraments to a special category of signs that "do exhibit and give the thing that they signify indeed"; John Hooper, *A Briefe and Clear Confession of the Christian Faith* (1581), in *Later Writings of Bishop Hooper*, ed. Charles Nevinson (Cambridge, 1852), 45. But in what sense were the sacraments thought to "give" grace? The performative theory shared, I am arguing, by Shakespeare, in which the sacraments convey the real presence of Christ by promoting a community of worshippers, was a secondary solution to the problem. Most writers preferred to argue that Christ was *spiritually* present in the Lord's Supper, though the fear of papist idolatry usually reduced this claim to the studied obscurity of Bradford, who declares that Christ's real spiritual presence is such "as reason knoweth not and the world cannot learn, nor any that looketh in this matter with other eyes, or heareth with other ears, than with the ears and eyes of the Spirit and of faith"; "Sermon," 96–97; see Clifford William Dugmore, *The Mass and the English Reformers* (London, 1958), esp. 202–47. However, during a similarly unhelpful explication of the sacraments, in which he argues that the Lord's Supper sets Christ "before us even as he was crucified upon the cross," Jewel (1565) seems to associate the real presence with precisely what, in the context of the mass, scandalizes him: the peculiarly *dramatic* nature of sacramental representation; *Works*, 1:448. Cf. his more conventional but still revealing statement in the *Apology* that the Lord's Supper places Christ's sacrifice "as it were, before our eyes"; *Works*, 3:62.

A simpler alternative to the corporal presence of the Catholics was proposed by the Swiss reformer Ulrich Zwingli, who argued that the sacraments should be regarded as nothing more than signs; yet, as I have noted, Elizabethan Protestants generally sided with their Catholic adversaries in rejecting such an "evacuation" of the sacraments. If the body and blood of Christ were not somehow conveyed in the bread and wine of the Lord's Supper but resided in the interpreting faith of the communicant alone, they argued, why should a believer bother to eat the bread or drink the wine at all? As an imaginary interlocutor in Roger Hutchinson's *Faithful Declaration of Christes Holy Supper* (1560) puts it, "We may receive his body without the sacrament, wheresoever we be, if we believe upon him; whether we be in the field, or in the town, or in our beds"; *Works*, ed. John Bruce (Cambridge, 1842), 243. Hutchinson responds with the strongest defense of the sacraments in the Protestant arsenal: "It is not enough to receive [Christ's body] spiritually, we must receive it also sacramentally; for both receipts be required and commanded, and Christ himself with his apostles used both for our erudition, example, and instruction" (244). Shakespeare may have accepted this argument from scriptural authority and agreed that the spiritual receipt of Christ's body in the field, town, bed, or theater was "not enough," but he seems to have believed that the community achieved in the theater was at least a better start for Christians than the sort of communion practiced in a preacherly or a prelatical church.

50. Championing the contentiousness of the godly preacher, Gifford asks, "Will ye charge Christ and his Gospel, because as he sayeth, he came not to send peace, but a sword, to set the father against the son?" (*Briefe Discourse*, 47v). Cf. John Bate, *The Portraiture of Hypocrisie* (London, 1589), 15–17. Reginald Scot (1584) complained to church officials in Kent of some puritan ministers who "stick not to affirm that the note of a good preacher is to make debate, according to Christ's Matt. 10"; *Second Parte*, 1:233; cf. 238; cited in Collinson, *Religion*, 108. For conflicts generated by or focused upon activist Protestant preachers in Renaissance England, see Haigh, "Church," 214–17.

51. The strongest evidence in the play against viewing Shakespeare as a pacifist is his famous comparison of Harry to Essex in the final prologue, when the Chorus asks the audience to imagine the citizens of London flocking to "their conqu'ring Caesar,"

> As, by a lower but loving likelihood,
> Were now the General of our gracious Empress—
> As in good time he may—from Ireland coming,
> Bringing rebellion broached on his sword,
> How many would the peaceful city quit
> To welcome him!
>
> (5.prologue.28–34)

Most critics read this passage as praise of Essex, although it states only that London's citizens *would* welcome Essex, not that they *should* welcome him. What's more, the passage suggests the same demystifying account of warfare that runs through the rest of the play, with the difference that London appears "peaceful" here in contrast to an Irish rather than a French scapegoat. I do not want to deny, however, that the passage, and the play as a whole, may *sound* like celebrations of militarism.

52. Miles Coverdale, *Fruitfull Lessons* (1593), in *The Writings and Translations of Miles Coverdale*, ed. George Pearson (Cambridge, 1844), 411. For the same point made in a more general context, see, e.g., the homily "Against Strife and Contencion" (1547): "We cannot be jointed to Christ our head, except we be glued with concord and charity, one to another"; *Certain Sermons or Homilies* (1547) and *A Homily Against Disobedience and Wilful Rebellion* (1570): *A Critical Edition*, ed. Ronald Bond (Toronto, 1987), 192.

53. According to Thomas Rogers in his authorized exposition of the Thirty-Nine Articles, *The English Creede* (1585–87), not even church sacraments required homiletic accompaniment: Rogers cites as an "error" the belief that "the sacrament is not a sacrament if it be not joined to the word of God preached"; *The Catholic Doctrine of the Church of England*, ed. J.J.S. Perowne (Cambridge, 1854), 271.

54. This extraclericalism was shared by the radical Protestant sect known as the Brownists. Attacking the preachers of the established church, the Brownist writer Henry Barrow argues that "this exercise of prophecy belongeth to the whole church, and ought not to be shut up in this manner amongst the priests only, the people being shut out either to speak or hear"; *Brief Discoverie*, 529; see 529–33. Yet if Shakespeare agrees with the

separatists that "preaching is not tied to the pulpit" (Robert Browne, *A True and Short Declaration* [1584], in *The Writings of Robert Harrison and Robert Browne*, ed. Albert Peel and Leland H. Carson [London, 1953], 410), he is also conservatively opposed to the separatists' zeal for preaching, not to mention their expulsion of the impure from congregation and communion.

For an account of Shakespeare's theater as a model of *political* consent, see the forthcoming work of Oliver Arnold.

HAMLET WHEN NEW

By WILLIAM EMPSON

ONE feels that the mysteries of Hamlet are likely to be more or less exhausted, and I have no great novelty to offer here, but it has struck me, in the course of trying to present him in lectures, that the enormous panorama of theory and explanation falls into a reasonable proportion if viewed, so to speak, from Pisgah, from the point of discovery by Shakespeare. To do that should also have a relation with the impressions of a fresh mind, meeting the basic legend of the play at any date. I was led to it from trying to answer some remarks of Hugh Kingsmill, in *The Return of William Shakespeare*, who said that Hamlet is a ridiculously theatrical and therefore unreal figure, almost solely concerned with scoring off other people, which the dialogue lets him do much too easily, and attractive to actors only because "they have more humiliations than other men to avenge." A number of critics seems to have felt like this, though few have said it so plainly; the feeling tends to make one indifferent to the play, and over-rides any "solution of its problems," but when followed up it leads to more interesting country. I discussed it in my book *Complex Words*, pp. 66-9, by the way, but only so far as suited the theme of the book, a theme I am ignoring here. It seems to give a rather direct route to a reconsideration of the origins, along which one might even take fresh troops into the jungle warfare over the text.

The experts mostly agree that Kyd wrote a play on Hamlet about 1587, very like his surviving *Spanish Tragedy* except that it was about a son avenging a father instead of a father avenging a son. The only record of a performance of it is in 1594, un-

123

der conditions which make it likely to have become the property of Shakespeare's company; jokes about it survive from 1589, 1596, and 1601, the later two regarding it as a standard out-of-date object. A keen sense of changing fashion has to be envisaged; when Shakespeare's company were seduced into performing *Richard II* for the Essex rebels they said they would have to be paid because it was too old to draw an audience, and it wasn't half as old as *Hamlet*. A gradual evolution of *Hamlet*, which some critics have imagined, isn't likely under these conditions. We have to consider why Shakespeare re-wrote a much-laughed-at old play, and was thus led on into his great Tragic Period, and the obvious answer is that he was told to; somebody in the Company thumbed over the texts in the ice-box and said "This used to be a tremendous draw, and it's coming round again; look at Marston. All you have to do is just go over the words so that it's *life-like* and they can't laugh at it." Kyd had a powerful but narrow, one might say miserly, theatrical talent, likely to repeat a success, so his *Hamlet* probably had a Play-within-the-Play like the *Spanish Tragedy*; we know from a joke it had a Ghost; and he would have almost all the rest of the story as we know it from the sources. For all we know, when Shakespeare created a new epoch and opened a new territory to the human mind, he did nothing but alter the dialogue for this structure, not even adding a scene. The trouble with this kind of critical aproach, as the experienced reader will already be feeling with irritation, is that it can be used to say "That is why the play is so muddled and bad." On the contrary, I think, if taken firmly enough it shows how, at the time, such a wonderful thing as Shakespeare's *Hamlet* could be conceived and accepted.

The real "Hamlet problem," it seems clear, is a problem about his first audiences. This is not to deny (as Professor Stoll has sometimes done) that Hamlet himself is a problem; he must be one, because he says he is; and he is a magnificent one, which has been exhaustively examined in the last hundred and fifty years. What is peculiar is that he does not seem to have become one till towards the end of the eighteenth century; even Dr. Johnson, who had a strong natural grasp of human difficulties, writes about Hamlet as if there was no problem at all. We are to think, apparently, that Shakespeare wrote a play which was extremely successful at the time (none more so, to judge by the references), and continued to hold the stage, and yet that nearly two hundred years had to go by before anyone had even a glimmering of what it was about. This is a good story, but surely it is rather too magical. Indeed, as the Hamlet Problem has developed, yielding increasingly subtle and profound reasons for his delay, there has naturally developed in its wake a considerable backwash from critics who say "But how can such a drama as you describe conceivably have been written by an Elizabethan, for an Elizabethan audience?" Some kind of mediating process is really required here; one needs to explain how the first audiences could take a more interesting view than Dr. Johnson's, without taking an improbably profound one.

The political atmosphere may be dealt with first. Professor Stoll has successfully argued that even the theme of delay need not be grasped at all by an audience, except as a convention; however, Mr. Dover Wilson has pointed out that the first audiences had a striking example before them in Essex, who was, or had just been, refusing to make up his mind in a public and alarming manner; his attempt at revolt might have caused civil war. Surely one need not limit it to Essex; the Queen herself had long used vacillation as a major instrument of policy, but the habit was becoming unnerving because though presumably dying she still refused to name a successor, which in itself might cause civil war. Her various foreign wars were also dragging on indecisively. A play about a prince who brought

disaster by failing to make up his mind was bound to ring
straight on the nerves of the audience when Shakespeare re-
wrote *Hamlet*; it is not a question of intellectual subtlety but of
what they were being forced to think about already. It seems
to me that there are relics of this situation in the text, which
critics have not considered in the light of their natural acting
power. The audience is already in the grip of a convention by
which Hamlet can chat directly to them about the current War
of the Theatres in London, and then the King advances straight
down the apron-stage and urges the audience to kill Hamlet:

> *Do it*, England,
> For like the hectic in my blood he rages,
> And *thou* must cure me.

None of them could hear that without feeling it was current
politics, however obscure; and the idea is picked up again, for
what seems nowadays only an opportunist joke, when the Grave-
digger says that Hamlet's madness won't matter in England,
where all the men are as mad as he. Once the idea has been
planted so firmly, even the idea that England is paying Dane-
geld may take on some mysterious weight. Miss Spurgeon and
Mr. Wilson Knight have maintained that the reiterated images
of disease somehow imply that Hamlet himself is a disease, and
this gives a basis for it. Yet the audience might also reflect that
the character does what the author is doing—altering an old
play to fit an immediate political purpose. This had to be
left obscure, but we can reasonably presume an idea that the
faults of Hamlet (which are somehow part of his great virtues) are not only specific but topical—"so far from being an
absurd old play, it is just what you want, if you can see what
is at the bottom of it." The insistence on the danger of civil
war, on the mob that Laertes does raise, and that Hamlet could
raise but won't, and that Fortinbras at the end takes immediate
steps to quiet, is rather heavy in the full text though nowadays

often cut. Shakespeare could at least feel, when the old laugh-
ingstock was dragged out and given to him as a new responsibility, that delay when properly treated need not be dull; considered politically, the urgent thing might be not to let it get
too exciting.

Such may have been his first encouraging reflection, but the
political angle was not the first problem of the assignment, the
thing he had to solve before he could face an audience; it was
more like an extra gift which the correct solution tossed into his
hand. The current objection to the old play *Hamlet*, which
must have seemed very hard to surmount, can be glimpsed in
the surviving references to it. It was thought absurdly theatrical. Even in 1589 the phrase "whole Hamlets, I should say
handfuls, of tragical speeches" treats Hamlet as incessantly
wordy, and the phrase of 1596, "as pale as the vizard of the
ghost which cried so miserably at the Theatre, like an oyster
wife, Hamlet Revenge," gets its joke from the idea that her
dismal bawling may start again at any moment, however sick of
her you are (presumably she is crying her wares up and down
the street). The objection is not against melodrama, which they
liked well enough, but against delay. You had a hero howling
out "Revenge" all through the play, and everybody knew he
wouldn't get his revenge till the end. This structure is at the
mercy of anybody in the audience who cares to shout "Hurry
Up," because then the others feel they must laugh, however
sympathetic they are; or rather, they felt that by the time
Shakespeare re-wrote *Hamlet*, whereas ten years earlier they
would only have wanted to say "Shush." This fact about the
audience, I submit, is the basic fact about the re-writing of
Hamlet.

The difficulty was particularly sharp for Shakespeare's company, which set out to be less ham than its rivals, and the Globe
Theatre itself, only just built, asked for something impressively

new. And yet there was a revival of the taste for Revenge Plays in spite of a half-resentful feeling that they had become absurd. Now Kyd had been writing before the accidental Destruction of the Spanish Armada, therefore while facing a more immediate probability of conquest with rack and fire; the position had remained dangerous, and the Armada incident didn't seem as decisive to them as historians make it seem now; but I think the wheel seemed to be coming round again, because of the succession problem, so that we ought not to regard this vague desire to recover the mood of ten years earlier as merely stupid. I suspect indeed that the fashion for *child* actors, the main complaint of the Players in *Hamlet*, came up at this moment because children could use the old convention with an effect of charm, making it less absurd because more distanced.

Shakespeare himself had hardly written a tragedy before. To have had a hand in *Titus Andronicus*, ten years before, only brings him closer to his current audience; his own earlier tastes, as well as theirs, were now to be re-examined. *Romeo* does not suggest an Aristotelian "tragic flaw." As a writer of comedies, his main improvement in technique had been to reduce the need for a villain so that the effect was wholly *un*-tragic, and meanwhile the series of History Plays had been on the practical or hopeful theme "How to Avoid Civil War"; even so he had manoeuvred himself into ending with the cheerful middle of the series, having written its gloomy end at the start. What Shakespeare was famous for, just before writing *Hamlet*, was Falstaff and patriotic stuff about Henry V. *Julius Caesar*, the play immediately previous to *Hamlet*, is the most plausible candidate for a previous tragedy or indeed Revenge Play, not surprisingly, but the style is dry and the interest mainly in the politics of the thing. One can easily imagine that the external cause, the question of what the audience would like, was prominent when the theme was chosen. If Essex came into the

background of the next assignment, Shakespeare's undoubted patron Southampton was also involved. I am not trying to make
him subservient to his public, only sensitive to changes of taste
in which he had an important part; nor would I forget that the
misfortunes of genius often have a wild luck in their timing. But
he must have seemed an unlikely person just then to start on a
great Tragic Period, and he never wrote a Revenge Play afterwards; we can reasonably suppose that he first thought of *Hamlet* as a pretty specialized assignment, a matter, indeed, of trying
to satisfy audiences who demanded a Revenge Play and then
laughed when it was provided. I think he did not see how to
solve this problem at the committee meeting, when the agile
Bard was voted to carry the weight, but already did see how
when walking home. It was a bold decision, and probably decided his subsequent career, but it was a purely technical one.
He thought: "The only way to shut this hole is to make it big.
I shall make Hamlet walk up to the audience and tell them,
again and again, 'I don't know why I'm delaying any more than
you do; the motivation of this play is just as blank to me as it
is to you; but I can't help it.' What is more, I shall make it
impossible for them to blame him. And *then* they daren't
laugh." It turned out, of course, that this method, instead of
reducing the old play to farce, made it thrillingly life-like and
profound. A great deal more was required; one had to get a
character who could do it convincingly, and bring in large
enough issues for the puzzle not to appear gratuitous. I do not
want to commit the Fallacy of Reduction, only to remove the
suspicion that the first audiences could not tell what was going
on.

Looked at in this way, the plot at once gave questions of very
wide interest, especially to actors and the regular patrons of a
repertory company; the character says: "Why do you assume *I*
am theatrical? I particularly hate such behavior. I cannot help

my situation. What do you *mean* by theatrical?" Whole areas
of the old play suddenly became so significant that one could
wonder whether Kyd had meant that or not; whether Hamlet
really wants to kill Claudius, whether he was ever really in
love with Ophelia, whether he can continue to grasp his own
motives while "acting a part" before the Court, whether he is
not really more of an actor than the Players, whether he is not
(properly speaking) the only sincere person in view. In spite
of its great variety of incident, the play sticks very closely to
discussing theatricality. Surely this is what critics have long
found so interesting about Hamlet, while an occasional voice
like Kingsmill's says it is nasty, or Professor Stoll tries to save
the Master by arguing it was not intended or visible at the time.
But, so far from being innocent here, what the first audiences
came to see was whether the Globe could re-vamp the old
favorite without being absurd. To be sure, we cannot suppose
them really very "sophisticated," considering the plays by other
authors they admired; to make *The Spanish Tragedy* up-to-
date enough for the Admiral's Company (which was paid for in
September, 1601, and June, 1602, in attempts to catch up with
Shakespeare's *Hamlet* presumably—indeed I think with two
successive *Hamlets*) only required some interesting "life-like"
mad speeches. But that they *imagined* that they were too sophisticated for the old *Hamlet* does seem to emerge from the
surviving jokes about it, and that is all that was required. We
need not suppose, therefore, that they missed the purpose of
the changes; "he is cunning past man's thought" they are more
likely to have muttered unwillingly into their beards, as they
abandoned the intention to jeer.

As was necessary for this purpose, the play uses the device of
throwing away dramatic illusion much more boldly than Shakespeare does anywhere else. (Mr. S. L. Bethell, in *Shakespeare
and the Popular Dramatic Tradition,* has written what I take to

be the classical discussion of this technique.) A particularly
startling case is planted early in the play, when the Ghost
pursues Hamlet and his fellows underground and says "Swear"
(to be secret) wherever they go, and Hamlet says

> Come on, you hear this fellow in the cellarage,
> Consent to swear.

It seems that the area under the stage was *technically* called the
cellarage, but the point is clear enough without this extra sharp-
ening; it is a recklessly comic throw-away of illusion, especially
for a repertory audience, who know who is crawling about among
the trestles at this point (Shakespeare himself, we are told),
and have their own views on his style of acting. But the effect
is still meant to be frightening; it is like Zoo in *Back to Me-
thusaleh,* who says "This kind of thing is got up to impress you,
not to impress me"; and it is very outfacing for persons in the
audience who come expecting to make that kind of joke themselves.

Following out this plan, there are of course satirical misquo-
tations of the Revenge classics, as in "Pox! leave thy damnable
faces and begin. Come—'the croaking raven doth bellow for
revenge' " (probably more of them than we realize, because we
miss the contrast with the old *Hamlet*); but there had also to
be a positive dramatization of the idea, which is given in Hamlet's scenes with the Players. Critics have wondered how it
could be endurable for Shakespeare to make the actor of Hamlet upbraid for their cravings for theatricality not merely his
fellow actors but part of his audience (the term "groundlings"
must have appeared an insult and comes nowhere else); but
surely this carries on the central joke, and wouldn't make the
author prominent. I agree that the Player's Speech and so
forth was a parody of the ranting style of the Admiral's Company (and when Hamlet praised it his actor had to slip in and

out of real life, without turning the joke too much against the Prince); but even so the situation is that the Chamberlain's Company are shown discussing how to put on a modern-style Revenge Play, which the audience knows to be a problem for them. The "mirror" was being held close to the face. As to the talk about the War of the Theatres, people were curious to know what the Globe would say, and heard its leading actor speak for the Company; they were violently prevented from keeping their minds on "buried Denmark." What is technically so clever is to turn this calculated collapse of dramatic illusion into an illustration of the central theme. The first problem was how to get the audience to attend to the story again, solved completely by "O what a rogue" and so forth, which moves from the shame of theatrical behavior and the paradoxes of sincerity into an immediate scheme to expose the King. Yet even here one might feel, as Mr. Dover Wilson said (with his odd power of making a deep remark without seeing its implications), that "the two speeches are for all the world like a theme given out by the First Violin and then repeated by the Soloist" —Hamlet has only proved he is a better actor, and indeed "rogue" might make him say this, by recalling that actors were legally rogues and vagabonds. We next see Hamlet in the "To be or not to be" soliloquy, and he has completely forgotten his passionate and apparently decisive self-criticism—but this time the collapse of interest in the story comes from the Prince, not merely from the audience; then when Ophelia enters he swings away from being completely disinterested into being more disgracefully theatrical than anywhere else (enjoying working up a fuss about a very excessive suspicion, and thus betraying himself to listeners he knows are present); next he lectures the Players with grotesque hauteur about the art of acting, saying that they must always keep cool (this is where the word *groundlings* comes); then, quite unexpectedly, he fawns upon Horatio as a man who is not "passion's slave," unlike himself, and we advance upon the Play-within-the-Play. The metaphor of the pipe which Fortune can blow upon as she pleases, which he used to Horatio, is made a symbol by bringing a recorder into bodily prominence during his moment of triumph after the Play scene, and he now boasts to the courtiers that he is a mystery, therefore they cannot play on him—we are meant to feel that there are real merits in the condition, but he has already told us he despises himself for it. Incidentally he has just told Horatio that he deserves a fellowship in a "cry" of players (another searching joke phrase not used elsewhere) but Horatio only thinks "half of one." The recovery from the point where the story seemed most completely thrown away has been turned into an exposition of the character of the hero and the central dramatic theme. No doubt this has been fully recognized, but I do not think it has been viewed as a frank treatment of the central task, that of making the old play seem real by making the hero life-like.

Mr. Dover Wilson rightly points out the obsessive excitability of Hamlet, as when in each of the scenes scolding one of the ladies he comes back twice onto the stage, each time more unreasonable, as if he can't make himself stop. "But it is no mere theatrical trick or device," he goes on, "it is meant to be part of the nature of the man"; and meanwhile psychologists have elaborated the view that he is a standard "manic-depressive" type, in whom long periods of sullen gloom, often with actual forgetfulness, are followed by short periods of exhausting excitement, usually with violence of language. By all means, but the nature of the man grows out of the original donnée; his nature had (first of all) to be such that it would make the old story "life-like." And the effect in the theatre, surely, is at least prior to any belief about his nature, though it may lead you on to one; what you start from is the *astonishment* of Hamlet's incessant changes of mood, which also let the one actor combine in himself elements which the Elizabethan theatre usually separates (e.g. simply tragedy and comedy). Every one of the soliloquies, it has been pointed out, contains a shock for the audience, apart from what it says, in what it doesn't say: the first in having no reference to usurpation; the second ("rogue and slave") no reference to Ophelia, though his feelings about her have been made a prominent question; the third ("To be or not to be") no reference to his plot or his self-criticism or even his own walk of life—he is considering entirely in general whether life is worth living, and it is startling for him to say no traveller returns from death, however complete the "explanation" that he is assuming the Ghost was a devil; the fourth ("now might I do it pat") no reference to his obviously great personal danger now that the King knows the secret; the fifth ("How all occasions do inform") no reference to the fact that he can't kill the King now, or rather a baffling assumption that he still can; and one might add his complete forgetting of his previous self-criticisms when he comes to his last words. It is this power to astonish, I think, which keeps one in doubt whether he is particularly theatrical or particularly "life-like"; a basic part of the effect, which would be clear to the first audiences.

However, the theme of a major play by Shakespeare is usually repeated by several characters in different forms, and Hamlet is not the only theatrical one here. Everybody is "acting a part" except Horatio, as far as that goes; and Laertes is very theatrical, as Hamlet rightly insists over the body of Ophelia ("I'll rant as well as thou"). One might reflect that both of them trample on her, both literally and figuratively, just because of their common trait. And yet Laertes is presented as opposite to Hamlet in not being subject to delay about avenging his father or to scruples about his methods; the tragic flaw in Hamlet must be something deeper or more specific. We need therefore to consider what his "theatricality" may be, and indeed the reader may feel I am making too much play with a term that Elizabethans did not use; but I think it makes us start in the right place. The Elizabethans, though both more formal and more boisterous than most people nowadays, were well able to see the need for sincerity; and it is agreed that Shakespeare had been reading Montaigne about how quickly one's moods can change, so that to appear consistent requires "acting," a line of thought which is still current. But to understand how it was applied here one needs to keep one's mind on the immediate situation in the theatre. The *plot* of a Revenge Play seemed theatrical because it kept the audience waiting without obvious reason in the characters; then a theatrical *character* (in such a play) appears as one who gets undeserved effects, "cheap" because not justified by the plot as a whole. However, theatrical behavior is never only "mean" in the sense of losing the ultimate aim for a petty advantage, because it must also "give itself away"—the idea "greedy to impress an audience" is required. Now the basic legend about Hamlet was that he did exactly this and yet was somehow right for it; he successfully kept a secret by displaying he had got one. The idea is already prominent in Saxo Grammaticus, where it gives a triumphant story not a tragic one; and "the Saxon who could write" around 1200 is as genuine a source of primitive legend as one need ask for. I am not sure whether Shakespeare looked up Saxo; it would easily be got for him if he asked, when he was given the assignment, but Kyd would have done it already; we think of Kyd as crude, but he was a solidly educated character. If Shakespeare did look up Saxo he only got a firm reassurance that his natural bent was the right one; the brief pungent Latin sentences about Hamlet are almost a definition of Shakespeare's clown, and Mr. Dover Wilson is right in saying that Shakespeare presented Hamlet as a kind of generaliza-

tion of that idea ("they fool me to the top of my bent" he remarks with appalling truth). Here we reach the bed-rock of
Hamlet, unchanged by the local dramas of reinterpretation; even
Dr. Johnson remarks that his assumed madness, though enter-
taining, does not seem to help his plot.

Kyd would probably keep him sane and rather tedious in
soliloquy but give him powerful single-line jokes when answer-
ing other characters; the extreme and sordid pretence of madness implied by Saxo would not fit Kyd's idea of tragic decorum. I think that Shakespeare's opening words for Hamlet,
"A little more than kin and less than kind," are simply repeated
from Kyd; a dramatic moment for the first-night audience, because they wanted to know whether the new Hamlet would be
different. His next words are a passionate assertion that he is
not the theatrical Hamlet—"I know not seems." Now this
technique from Kyd, though trivial beside the final Hamlet,
would present the inherent paradox of the legend very firmly:
why are these jokes supposed to give a kind of magical success
to a character who had obviously better keep his mouth shut?
All Elizabethans, including Elizabeth, had met the need to
keep one's mouth shut at times; the paradox might well seem
sharper to them than it does to us. Shakespeare took care to
laugh at this as early as possible in his version of the play. The
idea that it is silly to drop hints as Hamlet does is expressed by
Hamlet himself, not only with force but with winning intimacy,
when he tells the other observers of the Ghost that they must
keep silence completely, and not say "I could an I would, there
be an if they might" and so on, which is precisely what he does
himself for the rest of the play. No doubt he needs a monopoly
of this technique. But the first effect in the theatre was another
case of "closing the hole by making it big"; if you can make
the audience laugh *with* Hamlet about his method early, they
aren't going to laugh *at* him for it afterwards. Instead they

can wonder why he is or pretends to be mad, just as the other characters wonder; and wonder why he delays, just as he himself wonders. No other device could raise so sharply the question of "what *is* theatrical behavior?" because here we cannot even be sure what Hamlet is aiming at. We can never decide flatly that his method is wrong, because the more it appears unwise the more it appears courageous. There seem to be two main assumptions, that he is trying to frighten his enemies into exposing themselves, and that he is not so frightened himself as to hide his emotions though he hides their cause. I fancy Shakespeare could rely on some of his audience to add the apparently modern theory that the relief of self-expression saved Hamlet from going finally mad, because it fits well enough onto their beliefs about the disease "melancholy." But in any case the basic legend is a dream glorification of both having your cake and eating it, keeping your secret for years, till you kill, and yet perpetually enjoying boasts about it. Here we are among the roots of the race of man; rather a smelly bit perhaps, but a bit that appeals at once to any child. It is ridiculous for critics to *blame* Shakespeare for accentuating this traditional theme till it became enormous.

The view that Hamlet "is Shakespeare," or at least more like him than his other characters, I hope falls into shape now. It has a basic truth, because he was drawing on his experience as actor and playwright; these professions often do puzzle their practitioners about what is theatrical and what is not, as their friends and audiences can easily recognize; but he was only using what the theme required. To have to give posterity, let alone the immediate audiences, a picture of himself would have struck him as laying a farcical extra burden on an already difficult assignment. I think he did feel he was giving a good hand to actors in general, though with decent obscurity, when he worked up so much praise for Hamlet at the end, but you are meant to be dragged round to this final admiration for Hamlet, not to feel it all through. To suppose he "is Shakespeare" has excited in some critics a reasonable distaste for both parties, because a man who models himself on Hamlet in common life (as has been done) tends to appear a mean-minded neurotic; whereas if you take the *plot* seriously Hamlet is at least assumed to have special reasons for his behavior.

We should now be able to reconsider the view which Professor Stoll has done real service by following up: Hamlet's reasons are so good that he not only never delays at all but was never supposed to; the self-accusations of the Revenger are always prominent in Revenge Plays, even classical Greek ones, being merely a necessary part of the machine—to make the audience continue waiting with attention. Any problem we may invent about Shakespeare's Hamlet, on this view, we could also have invented about Kyd's, but it wouldn't have occurred to us to want to. In making the old play "life-like" Shakespeare merely altered the style, not the story; except that it was probably he who (by way of adding "body") gave Hamlet very much better reasons for delay than any previous Revenger, so that it is peculiarly absurd of us to pick him out and puzzle over *his* delay. I do not at all want to weaken this line of argument; I think Shakespeare did, intentionally, pile up all the excuses for delay he could imagine, while at the same time making Hamlet bewail and denounce his delay far more strongly than ever Revenger had done before. It is the force and intimacy of the self-reproaches of Hamlet, of course, which ordinary opinion has rightly given first place; that is why these legal arguments that he didn't delay appear farcical. But the two lines of argument are only two halves of the same thing. Those members of the audience who simply wanted to see a Revenge Play again, without any hooting at it from smarter persons, deserved to be satisfied; and anyhow, for all parties, the suspicion that Hamlet was a coward or merely fatuous had to be avoided. The ambiguity was an essential part of the intention, because the more you tried to translate the balance of impulses in the old drama into a realistic story the more peculiar this story had to be made. The old structure was still kept firm, but its foundations had to be strengthened to carry so much extra weight. At the same time, a simpler view could be taken; whatever the stage characters may say, the real situation in the theatre is still that the audience knows the revenge won't come till the end. Their own foreknowledge is what they had laughed at, rather than any lack of motive in the puppets, and however much the motives of the Revenger for delay were increased he could still very properly blame himself for keeping the audience waiting. One could therefore sit through the new *Hamlet* (as for that matter the eighteenth century did) without feeling too startled by his self-reproaches. But of course the idea that "bringing the style up to date" did not involve any change of content seems to me absurd, whether held by Shakespeare's committee or by Professor Stoll; for one thing, it made the old theatrical convention appear bafflingly indistinguishable from a current political danger. The whole story was brought into a new air, so that one felt there was much more "in it."

This effect, I think, requires a sudden feeling of novelty rather than a gradual evolution, but it is still possible that Shakespeare wrote an earlier draft than our present text. To discuss two lost plays at once, by Kyd and Shakespeare, is perhaps rather tiresome, but one cannot imagine the first audiences without forming some picture of the development of the play, of what struck them as new. Mr. Dover Wilson, to whom so much gratitude is due for his series of books on *Hamlet*, takes a rather absurd position here. He never edits a straightforward Shakespeare text without finding evidence for two or three

layers of revision, and considering them important for a full understanding of the play; only in *Hamlet*, where there is positive evidence for them, and a long-recognized ground for curiosity about them, does he assume they can be ignored. He rightly insists that an editor needs to see the problems of a text as a whole before even choosing between two variant readings, and he sometimes actually asserts in passing that Shakespeare wrote earlier drafts of *Hamlet*; and yet his basis for preferring Q2 to F is a picture of Shakespeare handing in *one* manuscript (recorded by Q2) from which the Company at once wrote out *one* acting version (recorded by F), making drastic cuts and also verbal changes which they refused to reconsider. He says he is not concerned with "sixteenth century versions of Hamlet," a device of rhetoric that suggests a gradual evolution, too hard to trace. I am not clear which century 1600 is in (there was a surprising amount of quarrelling over the point in both 1900 and 1800), but even writing done in 1599 would not be remote from 1601. I postulate one main treatment of the play by Shakespeare, first acted in 1600, and then one quite minor revision of it by Shakespeare, first acted in 1601, written to feed and gratify the interest and discussion which his great surprise had excited the year before. To believe in this amount of revision does not make much difference, whereas a gradual evolution would, but it clears up some puzzling bits of evidence and I think makes the audiences more intelligible.

Mr. Dover Wilson's two volumes on *The Manuscript of Shakespeare's Hamlet* are magnificently detailed and obviously right most of the time. I am only questioning this part of his conclusions: "we may venture to suspect that (always assuming Shakespeare to have been in London) *Hamlet* was not merely a turning-point in his career dramatically, but also marks some kind of crisis in his relations with his company." The idea that Shakespeare wasn't in London, I take it, is inserted to allow for the theory that he was in Scotland drafting his first version of *Macbeth*, which need not delay us. The cuts for time in the Folio seem to be his main argument, because he ends his leading volume (*Manuscript*, p. 174) by saying that Shakespeare discovered his mistake if he imagined that the Company would act such a long play in full. "If" here is a delicacy only, because the purpose of the argument is to answer critics who had called our full-length *Hamlet* "a monstrosity, the creation of scholarly compromise" between rival shorter versions. I agree with Mr. Dover Wilson that Shakespeare did envisage a use for this whole text. But Mr. Dover Wilson had just been giving an impressive section (pp. 166-170) to prove that some of the Folio cuts are so skilful that Shakespeare must have done them himself—perhaps unwillingly, but at least he was not being ignored. Another part of the argument for a quarrel is that the producer "did not trouble to consult the author when he could not decipher a word or understand a passage," but this section argues that Shakespeare did make a few corrections in the Prompt Copy, when a mistake happened to lie near the bits he had looked up to make his cuts. Surely this makes the author look culpably careless over details rather than in a huff because he hadn't been consulted over details. Another argument uses errors which are unchanged in the quartos and folio to suggest that the Company repeated the same bits of petty nonsense blindly for twenty years. But Mr. Dover Wilson also argues that the Prompt Copy used for the Folio was "brought up to date" in later years, at least on such points as the weapons fashionable for duelling; the same might apply to some slang terms which were already out of date when the Folio was published, though he labors to restore them now from the Quarto. I think he presumes an excessive desire to save paper in this quite wealthy company; they are not likely to have kept the same manuscript Prompt Copy of their most popular play in constant use for twenty years. There would have to be a copying staff, in any case, to give the actors their parts to learn from. The baffling question is how the Folio *Hamlet* with its mass of different kinds of error could ever occur; and the theory of Mr. Dover Wilson is that it was badly printed from a copy of the Company's (irremovable) Prompt Copy made by a Company employee who was careless chiefly because he knew what was currently acted, so that his mind echoed phrases in the wrong place. Surely I may put one more storey onto this card castle. Heming and Condell, I suggest, set this man to copy the *original* Prompt Copy, which so far from being in current use had become a kind of museum piece; they tried to get a basic text for the printer, and only failed to realize that it isn't enough in these matters to issue an order. The basic object to be copied had neither the later corrections nor the extra passages which had been reserved for special occasions, and the interest of the man who copied it is that he could scribble down both old and new errors or variants without feeling he was obviously wrong. It seems improbable that the Globe actors, though likely to introduce corruptions, would patiently repeat bits of unrewarding nonsense for twenty years; my little invention saves us from believing that, without forcing me to deny that Mr. Dover Wilson's theory has produced some good emendations.

We cannot expect to recover a correct text merely from an excess of error in the printed versions of it; and in no other Shakespeare play are they so confused. But surely this fact itself must have some meaning. I suggest that, while Shakespeare's *Hamlet* was the rage, that is, roughly till James became king without civil war, it was varied a good deal on the night according to the reactions of the immediate audience. This would be likely to make the surviving texts pretty hard to print from; also it relieves us from thinking of Shakespeare as frustrated by the Company's cuts in his first great tragedy. Surely any man, after a quarrel of this sort, would take some interest in "at least" getting the printed version right. No doubt there was a snobbery about print, to which he would probably be sensitive, and also the text belonged to the Company; but neither question would impinge here. The Company must have wanted a large text for the Second Quarto, and even the most anxious snob can correct proofs without attracting attention. Indeed there was at least one reprint of it (1611), and probably two, during his lifetime; they can be observed trying to correct a few mistakes, but obviously without help from the author. You might think he fell into despair over the incompetence of the printers, but they could do other jobs well enough, and were visibly trying to do better here. The only plausible view is that he refused to help them because he wouldn't be bothered, and I do not see how he could have felt this if he had been annoyed by the way *Hamlet* had been mangled at the Globe. I think he must have felt tolerably glutted by the performances.

Critics have long felt that the First Quarto probably contains evidence for a previous draft by Shakespeare which is hard to disentangle. I am not trying to alter the points of revision usually suggested, and need not recall the arguments in their lengthy detail; I am only trying to give fresh support for them against Mr. Dover Wilson's view that Q1 is a perversion of the standard Globe performance. One must admit, on his side, that a text published in 1603 cannot be trusted to be unaffected by changes in the performance supposedly made in 1601; the idea that this was a travelling version, suited to audiences less experienced than the Globe ones, seems a needed hypothesis as well as one suggested by the title-page. Also, though often weirdly bad in detail, it is a very workmanlike object in broad planning; somebody made a drastically short version of the play which kept in all the action, and the effect is so full of action that it is almost as jerky as an early film, which no doubt some audiences would appreciate. There seems no way to decide whether or not this was done independently of the pirating reporters who forgot a lot of the poetry. The main change is that the soliloquy "To be or not to be" and its attendant scolding of Ophelia is put before the Player scene, not after it; but a producer wanting a short plain version is wise to make that change, so it is not evidence for an earlier draft by Shakespeare. The variations in names might only recall Kyd's names, perhaps more familiar in the provinces. What does seem decisive evidence, and was regularly considered so till Mr. Dover Wilson ignored rather than rebutted it, is that this text gives a sheer scene between Horatio and the Queen alone, planning what to do about Hamlet's return to Denmark; surely this would be outside the terms of reference of both the potting adapter and the pirating hack. The text seems particularly "cooked up" and not remembered from Shakespeare; but then, what these people wanted was "action," and it is less like action to have Horatio report Hamlet's adventures than to let the hero boast in person; and it is not inherently any shorter. Also this change fits in with a consistently different picture of the Queen, who is not only made clearly innocent of the murder but made willing to help Hamlet. Mr. Dover Wilson does not seem to deal with this familiar position beyond saying "Shakespeare is subtler than his perverters or his predecessors," assuming that the Q1 compiler is his first perverter; and he argues that the Queen is meant to appear innocent even of vague complicity in the murder in our standard text of *Hamlet*. But surely it is fair to ask what this "subtlety" may be, and why it deserves such a fine name if it only muddles a point that was meant to be clear. Why, especially, must the Queen be given an unexplained half-confession, "To my sick soul, as sin's true nature is . . . ," a fear of betraying guilt by too much effort to hide it? Mr. Richard Flatter, I think, did well to emphasize how completely this passage has been ignored by critics such as A. C. Bradley and Mr. Dover Wilson, whose arguments from other passages to prove that she was meant to seem innocent are very convincing. Surely the only reasonable view is that Shakespeare in his final version wanted to leave doubt in the minds of the audience about the Queen. You may say that the adapter behind Q1 simply got rid of this nuisance, but you are making him do an unlikely amount of intelligent work. It is simpler to believe that he is drawing on an earlier version, which made the Queen definitely on Hamlet's side after the bedroom scene.

Mr. Dover Wilson used to believe in two versions by Shakespeare and apparently does so still, or if not he must be praised for giving the evidence against his later view with his usual firmness. Harvey's note praising a *Hamlet* by Shakespeare, he recalls, needs to predate the execution of Essex in February 1601, whereas the remarks about the War of the Theatres, and perhaps a hint at the seige of Dunkirk in the soliloquy "How all occasions do inform against me," belong to the summer of that year. If we are to believe in a revision for 1601, then, it should include these items, and probably the rest of the soliloquy, also the new position for "To be or not to be" and the scolding of Ophelia, and a number of changes about the Queen, not long in bulk. The idea that the main text was written before the death of Essex and the revision after it should perhaps have more meaning that I can find; perhaps anyway it corresponds to a certain darkening of the whole air. But there is no need to make this revision large or elaborate; the points just listed seem to be the only ones we have direct evidence for, and are easily understood as heightening the peculiar effect of *Hamlet* for a public which had already caught on to it. May I now put the matter the other way round: I do not believe that our present text of *Hamlet*, a weirdly baffling

thing, could have been written at all except for a public which
had already caught on to it.

The strongest argument is from the soliloquy "How all occasions."* Mr. Dover Wilson says that the Company omitted
this "from the very first" from the Fortinbras scene, "which
was patently written to give occasion to the soliloquy." But no
producer would leave in the nuisance of an army marching across
the stage after removing the only point of it. Fortinbras had
anyway to march his army across the stage, as he does in Q1
as well as F, and presumably did in Kyd's version. The beginning of the play is a mobilization against this army and the end
a triumph for it; the audience thought in more practical terms
than we do about these dynastic quarrels. But that made it all
the more dramatic, in the 1601 version, to throw in a speech
for Hamlet hinting that the troops at Dunkirk were as fatuous
for too much action as he himself was for too little. It is only
a final example of the process of keeping the old scenes and
packing into them extra meaning. What is reckless about the
speech is that it makes Hamlet say, while (presumably) surrounded by guards leading him to death, "I have cause and will
and strength and means To do it," destroying a sheer school of
Hamlet Theories with each noun; the effect is so exasperating
that many critics have simply demanded the right to throw it
away. Nobody is as annoying as this except on purpose, and
the only reasonable view of why the speech was added is that
these Hamlet Theories had already been propounded, in long
discussions among the spectators, during the previous year. But
the bafflement thrown in here was not the tedious one of making
a psychological problem or a detective story insoluble; there
was a more obvious effect in making Hamlet magnificent. He
finds his immediate position not even worth reflecting on; and
he does get out of this jam, so you can't blame him for his
presumption at this point. His complete impotence at the mo-

*I discuss the other changes in the second part of this essay.

ment, one might say, seems to him "only a theatrical appearance," just as his previous reasons for delay seem to have vanished like a dream. Here as elsewhere he gives a curious effect,
also not unknown among his critics, of losing all interest for
what has happened in the story; but it is more impressive in
him than in them. By the way, I would like to have one other
passage added by Shakespeare in revision, the remarks by Hamlet at the end of the bedroom scene (in Q2 but not F) to the
effect that it will only cheer him up to have to outwit his old
pals trying to kill him; this seems liable to sound merely boast-
ful unless afterwards proved genuine by his private thoughts,
but if the soliloquy is being added some such remark is needed
first, to prepare the audience not to find it merely unnatural.

One might suppose that this dream-like though fierce quality
in Hamlet, which became perhaps his chief appeal two centuries
later, was only invented for the 1601 revision. I think one can
prove that this was not so. The moral effect is much the same,
and hardly less presumptuous, when he insists at the end of the
play on treating Laertes as a gentleman and a sportsman, though
he has already told the audience (in high mystical terms) that
he is not such a fool as to be unsuspicious; and the moral is at
once drawn for us—this treatment unnerves Laertes so much
that he almost drops the plot. The fencing-match no less than
the Play Scene is an imitation which turns out to be reality,
but that is merely a thing which one should never be surprised
by; Laertes ought still to be treated in the proper style. "Use
them after your own honour and dignity; the less they deserve,
the more merit is in your bounty"; this curious generosity of
the intellect is always strong in Hamlet, and indeed his main
source of charm. One reason, in fact, why he could be made so
baffling without his character becoming confused was that it
made him give a tremendous display of top-class behavior, even
in his secret mind as expressed in soliloquy. Now the paradoxi-

cal chivalry towards Laertes (which commentators tend to regard as a "problem" about how much Hamlet understood) is well marked in Q1, which fairly certainly didn't bother about the 1601 revision. On the other hand it wouldn't be in Kyd's version, because Kyd wasn't interested in this kind of startlingly gentlemanly behavior, as well as not wanting to use it as an explanation of the delay. It really belongs, I think, to the situation of continuing to claim a peculiar status as an aristocrat after the practical status has been lost, like Dukes in Proust; the casual remark by Hamlet in the graveyard that all the classes are getting mixed seems to me to have a bearing on his behavior. By the way, the reason why Hamlet apologizes to Laertes merely by claiming to be mad, which many commentators have felt to be a shifty way to talk about his killing of Laertes' father (since we have seen that that was not done when mad), is that he is uneasy about the incident "I'll rant as well as thou"; to have scuffled with Laertes while they both kicked the body of his sister in her grave was disgustingly theatrical, and he is ashamed of it. This seems to him much more real than having caused the deaths of both father and sister, a thing he couldn't help, and even when dying beside Laertes he refuses to admit any guilt for it. To have allowed his situation to make him theatrical is serious guilt, and (according to Q2) he snatches the occasion to throw in a separate apology to his mother, for the way he behaved to *her* on the occasion when Polonius happened to get killed. This emphasis on style rather than on one's incidental murders seems now madly egotistical, but it would then appear as consistently princely behavior. It seems clear that Shakespeare used this as a primary element in his revivification of Hamlet.

In this kind of way, he got a good deal of mystery into his first version of *Hamlet*, starting with the intention of making it life-like. Then, when the audiences became intrigued by this mystery, he made some quite small additions and changes which screwed up the mystery to the almost torturing point where we now have it—the sky was the limit now, not merely because the audiences wanted it, but because one need only act so much of this "shock troops" material as a particular audience seemed ripe for. No wonder it made the play much too long. The soliloquy "How All Occasions" is a sort of encore planned in case an audience refuses to let the star go, and in the big days of *Hamlet* they would decide back-stage how much, and which parts, of the full text to perform when they saw how a particular audience was shaping. This view gives no reason to doubt that the whole thing was sometimes acted, ending by torchlight probably, with the staff of the Globe extremely cross at not being allowed to go home earlier. I am not clear how much this picture alters the arguments of Mr. Dover Wilson from the surviving texts, but it clearly does to a considerable extent. Everyone says that the peculiar merit of the Elizabethan theatre was to satisfy a broad and varied clientele, with something of the variability of the Music Hall in its handling of the audience; but the experts do not seem to imagine a theatre which actually carried out this plan, instead of sticking to a text laid down rigidly beforehand. It is unlikely to have happened on any scale, to be sure, except in the very special case of *Hamlet*. But if you suppose it happened there you need no longer suppose a quarrel over some extras written in for occasional use. And there is the less reason to suppose a quarrel, on my argument, because the Company must have accepted Shakespeare's 1601 revision as regards both Ophelia and the Queen, for example treating the new position for "To be or not to be" as part of the standard Prompt Copy, eventually recorded in the Folio. (One would never swap back the order of scenes "on the night.") I imagine that this excitement about the play, which made it worth while keeping bits for special audiences, had already died down by 1605, when the Company sent plenty of Shakespeare's manuscript to the printer (as Mr. Dover Wilson says) just to outface the pirate of Q1; one no longer needed to keep extras up one's sleeve. But I should fancy that the claim on the title-page, "enlarged to almost as much again as it was," does not only refer to the extreme shortness of the pirate's version; advertisements even when lying often have sources of plausibility, and it would be known that a few of the Globe performances had also been almost recklessly enlarged.

The criticism of *Hamlet* has got to such a scale that it feels merely pokey to say one thing more; a library on the topic would completely fill an ordinary house. But I feel that the line of thought I have been following here is one which many recent critics have taken, and yet without their taking it as far as it will go.*

*Part II of Mr. Empson's essay will appear in the next issue.

HAMLET WHEN NEW (PART II)

By WILLIAM EMPSON

THE first part of this essay argued that the 1600 Globe audiences would have laughed at the Kyd version of *Hamlet* simply because they could shout "Hurry Up"; thus the first problem for Shakespeare in re-writing it was to find how to stop them, by making the delay itself a subject of interest. From this point of view, I maintained, it is reasonable to revive the idea that he wrote two versions of *Hamlet*, and that the mangled First Quarto gives indirect evidence about the first one; an idea common among Victorian critics, but blown upon since then by Sir Edmund Chambers and Professor Dover Wilson. The first version, for 1600, solved the technical problem so well that it established Hamlet as a "mystery" among the first audiences; then a minor revision for 1601 gratified this line of interest by making him a baffling one and spreading mystery all round. Thus the soliloquy "How all occasions," which seems to defy the commentators deliberately, was written as an extra for audiences especially fascinated by Hamlet; our full text was meant to be used sometimes but not regularly. These assertions, I would claim, fit in with the textual evidence, which is very confusing, better than anything else; but the main reason for believing them is that they explain how such an extraordinary play could get written at all. We need some picture of the first audiences even to understand what was intended.

I assume, then, that the First Quarto gives evidence about the first draft, so that the main changes for the second concern Ophelia and the Queen; whom I will consider in turn. The scolding of Ophelia by Hamlet, and the soliloquy "To be or not to be" before it, were put later in the play. The main pur-

pose in this, I think, was to screw up the paradoxes in the character of Hamlet rather than to affect Ophelia herself. I tried
to describe in the first part of this essay a sort of Pirandello sequence in his behavior from meeting the Players to the Recorder
scene, which raises problems about whether he is very theatrical
or very sincere, and this is much heightened by putting his hys-
terical attack on Ophelia in the middle of it; especially beside
the utter detachment of "To be or not to be," which J. M.
Robertson found so incredible in its new position as to demand
grotesque collaboration theories. The first version by Shakespeare must have carried the main point of this sequence, because
even the First Quarto makes him take an actual "pipe" after
the Play scene and use it to claim he is a mystery ("though you
can fret me, yet you cannot play upon me"); but this was a
crucial part to "heighten" if you wanted to heighten the mystery
as a whole.

One might also feel that the change had another purpose;
combined with the new doubts about the Queen it gives the play
a concentrated anti-woman central area. In any case, the worst
behavior of Hamlet is towards Ophelia, whether you call it theatrical or not; the critics who have turned against him usually
seem to do so on her behalf, and his relations with the two women raise more obvious questions about whether he is neurotic
than the delay. The first question here is how Shakespeare
expected the audience to take the scolding of Ophelia, admitting
that an audience has different parts. We can all see Hamlet has
excuses for treating her badly, but if we are to think him a hero
for yielding to them the thing becomes barbaric; he punishes her
savagely for a plot against him when he has practically forced
her to behave like a hospital nurse. I feel sure that Mr. Dover
Wilson is getting at something important, though as so often
from a wrong angle, when he makes a fuss about adding a stage
direction at II, ii, 158, and insists that Hamlet must visibly
overhear the King and Polonius plotting to use Ophelia against

him. No doubt this is better for a modern audience, but we need to consider the sequence of changes in the traditional play. In our present text, even granting Mr. Dover Wilson his tiny stage direction, what Hamlet overhears is very harmless and indeed what he himself has planned for; it was he who started using Ophelia as a pawn, however much excused by passion or despair. Kyd, I submit, would give solid ground for Hamlet's view that Ophelia is working against him; the merits of Kyd, as I am assuming all along, have nothing to do with leaving motives obscure. She would do it highmindedly, in ringing lines, with distress, regarding it as her duty since her lover has become mad, and never realizing what deep enmity against him she is assisting; but still she would do something plain and worth making a fuss about. Hamlet's scolding of her for it would follow at once. The agile Bard, with gleaming eye, merely removed the adequate motivation for the scolding of Ophelia, a habit to which he was becoming attached. Then for his revision he took the scolding far away even from the trivial bit of plotting, no more than was essential to explain the sequence, that he had left in for his Hamlet to overhear; thus making Mr. Dover Wilson's view harder for a spectator to invent. One can respect the struggle of Mr. Dover Wilson to recover one rag of the drapery so much needed by Hamlet, but if this was the development the Globe Theatre is not likely to have given any.

We should recall here, I think, the rising fashion in the theatres for the villain-hero, who staggers one by being so *outré*, and the love-poems of Donne, already famous in private circulation, which were designed to outrage the conventions about chivalrous treatment of women. Also the random indecency of lunatics, a thing the Elizabethans were more accustomed to than we are, since they seldom locked them up, is insisted on in the behavior of Hamlet to Ophelia whether he is pretending or not. The surprising instruction of the Ghost—"Taint not thy mind" —was bound to get attention, so that one was prepared to think

his mind tainted.   I think the Shakespeare Hamlet was meant
to be regarded by most of the audience as behaving shockingly
towards Ophelia, almost too much so to remain a tragic hero; to
swing round the whole audience into reverence for Hamlet before he died was something of a lion-taming act. This was part
of the rule that all his behavior must be startling, and was only
slightly heightened in revision.   But to see it in its right proportion we must remember another factor; the theatre, as various
critics have pointed out, clung to an apparently muddled but no
doubt tactical position of both grumbling against Puritans and
accepting their main claims. The Victorians still felt that Hamlet was simply high-minded here. D. H. Lawrence has a poem
describing him with hatred as always blowing and snoring about
other folks' whoring, rightly perhaps, but in Hamlet's time this
would feel like the voice of lower-class complaint against upper-
class luxury, as when he rebukes the Court for too much drink.
All Malcontents rebuked luxury; this aspect of him would not
need to be "brought out."

Here I think we have the right approach to another Victorian
view of Hamlet, of which Bernard Shaw is perhaps the only
representative still commonly read: that he was morally too advanced to accept feudal ideas about revenge, and felt, but could
not say, that his father had given him an out-of-date duty; that
was why he gave such an absurd excuse for not killing the King
at prayer. (Dr. Johnson thought it not absurd but too horrible
to read.) Without this obscure element of "discussion drama,"
Shaw maintained, the nineteenth century would never have found
Hamlet interesting; and of course Shaw would also feel it high-
minded of him to be a bit rough with the women in a Puritan
manner. This Hamlet Theory has been swept away by ridicule
too easily, and I was glad to see Mr. Harbage defend it recently with the true remark that no moral idea was "remote
from the Elizabethan mind", indeed, the most available source
for *Hamlet*, the version by Belleforest, itself objects in princi-

ple to revenge. The word "feudal" needs to be removed (as so often); it is royal persons who cannot escape the duty of revenge by an appeal to public justice; this is one of the reasons why they have long been felt to make interesting subjects for plays. But I think Shakespeare's audiences did regard his Hamlet as taking a "modern" attitude to his situation, just as Bernard Shaw did. This indeed was one of the major dramatic effects of the new treatment. He walks out to the audience and says "You think this an absurd old play, and so it is, *but I'm in it*, and what can I do?" The theatrical device in itself expresses no theory about the duty of revenge, but it does ask the crowd to share in the question. No wonder that one of the seventeenth-century references, dropped while describing someone else, says "He is like Prince Hamlet, he pleases all."

This trait of his character has rightly irritated many critics, most recently perhaps Senor Madariaga, whose lively book on Hamlet has at least the merit of needing some effort to refute it. He finds him a familiar Renaissance type of the extreme "egotist," as well as a cad who had been to bed with Ophelia already. The curious indifference of Hamlet to the facts does make him what we call egotistical, but this would be viewed as part of his lordliness; "egotism," I think, is only a modern bit of popular psychology, quite as remote from medical science as the Elizabethan bit about "melancholy" and much less likely to occur to the first audiences. The argument that Hamlet has been to bed with Ophelia gives an impression of clearing the air, and I think greatly needs refuting; I am glad to have a coarse enough argument to do it without being suspected of undue chivalry. We need a little background first. Senor Madariaga points out that the corresponding lady in the sources did enjoy Hamlet's person on a brief occasion, and argues that the audience would take the story for granted unless it was firmly changed; he then easily proves that the actress of Ophelia can make all references to her virginity seem comic, but this doesn't prove

she was meant to. The only "source" which most of the audience would know about is the play by Kyd which we have lost,
and there is a grand simplicity about the drama of Kyd which
is unlikely to have allowed any questionable aspect to his hero.
The legend itself, I agree, gives Hamlet a strong "Br'er Fox"
smell, and Shakespeare had a nose for this, but the tradition of
the theatre would let him assume that Ophelia represented pure
pathos and was somehow betrayed. Kyd would be likely to introduce the idea that this lady, who is undignified in the sources,
had a high position and was regarded as Hamlet's prospective
Queen. Shakespeare gave this a further twist; he implies at
her first appearance that her brother and father are angling to
make her Queen; they don't say that to the girl, and still less to
Hamlet's parents, but we need not believe their over-eager pro-
testations about the matter; the situation is a well-known one for
the audience. (The placid lament of the Queen over the grave
of Ophelia, that she had expected her to marry Hamlet, sounds
as if she had long known it was in the wind.) They both tell
her that the urgent thing is not to go to bed with him too quickly,
and the audience will assume that this important family plan is
being carried through; unless, of course, she leers and winks as
Senor Madariaga recommends, but that would only make her
seem a fool. The impact of the poetry that introduces the character has a natural right to interpret her; it is hauntingly beautiful and obviously does not interpret the father and brother
who speak it:

> The chariest maid is prodigal enough
> If she unmask her beauty to the moon

and so forth; the whole suggestion is that she must hold off
from Hamlet, as part of her bid for grandeur, and yet that
tragedy may come of it. However, I agree that these vast poetic gestures towards all human experience could easily suggest

just the opposite, that she is sure to have done what she is advised against; a more definite argument is required. In the Play scene, when Hamlet is offensively jeering at her for her supposed lust, and she is trying to laugh it off (pathetically and courageously; it is unfair of Senor Madariaga to say this proves she is used to such talk), she says "you are keen, my lord, you are keen," meaning to praise his jokes as high-minded general satire against the world, though they are flat enough bits of nastiness, and he answers:

It would cost you a groaning to take off my edge.

Now the conviction that it is fun to make a virgin scream and bleed was far too obvious to the Elizabethans for this to mean anything else; I can imagine alternatives, but do not believe in them and will wait for them to be advanced by some opponent. The point is not that Hamlet's remark has any importance on the stage, but that the first audiences took for granted one view of her or the other, from the production if not from the tradition (an ambiguity here, I think, would only confuse the production), whereas we have to learn what they took for granted by using details which at the time merely seemed to fit in. This detail, I submit, is enough to prove they assumed her to be a virgin.

I am not trying to whitewash Hamlet; he is jeering at the desires of the virgin which he is keen to excite and not satisfy, and this is part of what sends her mad. But to jeer at a prospective Queen for having yielded to him already would be outside the code; the more loose the actual Court habits were (a point Senor Madariaga uses) the more ungentlemanly it would seem, and Hamlet never loses class, however mad. He also keeps a curious appeal for the lower classes in the audience as a satirist on the upper class, as I have tried to describe; even here, some of the audience would probably enjoy having jeers against an aggressively pure young lady whose family are angling for a grand marriage; but for this purpose too he needs to be unworldly rather than to have been to bed with her already. What seems more important to us is his "psychology," and that gives' the same answer; the whole point of his bad temper against her, which he builds up into feverish suspicions, is that it arises because she has shut him out, not because she has yielded to him. In the Nunnery scene, when he runs back for the second time onto the stage because he has just thought of a still nastier thing which he can't bear not to say, he says "I have heard of your paintings, too," heard that women in general paint their faces. It is almost a Peter Arno drawing. He calls her obscene because all women are (like his mother) and a prostitute because she is plotting against him (like a nurse). To allow any truth to his accusations against her seems to me throwing away the whole dramatic effect.

But of course there is a grave solemn truth, never denied, which is simply that Ophelia did want to marry him and ought not to have been accused of lust for it. Senor Madariaga regards her behavior when mad as proof of incontinence when sane, an idea which strikes me as about equally remote from an Elizabethan audience and a modern doctor. She sings a song in which the man says to the woman "I would have married you, as I promised, if you had not come to my bed," which seems to ask for application to her own case; but many of the parallels in her mad talk work by opposites; indeed the agony of it (as in the mad speeches added to *The Spanish Tragedy*, for instance) is that we see her approaching recognition of the truth and then wincing far away again. "They say a made a good end" is her comment on the father who died unshriven, and "Bonny sweet Robin is all my joy" deals with her appalling lover before she walks out to death. Well might she reflect that the girls in the ballads, who came to a simpler kind of disaster by giving too early, met a less absolute frustration than the girl who held off because she was being groomed for queen-hood; and surely this idea is the point of her vast farewell: "Come, my coach; . . . Good night, good ladies". But we can argue more directly than from the poetry of the thing. When she brings out this ballad the wicked King, who never falls below a certain breadth of sentiment, says "Pretty Ophelia," a quaintly smoking-room comment which directly tells the audience what to feel. Soon after, her brother echoes the word in a rage, saying that even in the madness forced upon her by Hamlet she turns Hell itself to favour and to prettiness, but the King saw that "pretty" is right at once. Recently I was being asked by a student in Peking what to make of the

> long purples
> Which liberal shepherds give a grosser name
> But our cold maids do Dead Men's Fingers call them.

Why are the obscene thoughts of these peasants necessary in the impossible but splendid description of her death? At the time, I could only say that the lines seemed to me very beautiful, and in the usual tone about Ophelia, so I felt sure they didn't carry any hint that would go outside it. Also, no doubt, the maids give the flower this unmentioned name "when they laugh alone," and here the Love of a maid did become Death and fumble at her, but there is a broader, and one might well say a prettier, suggestion behind all these hints at her desire; that nobody wants her to be frigid. A certain amount of teasing about the modesty required from her would be ordinary custom, but the social purpose behind both halves of this little contradiction is to make her a good wife. Indeed to struggle against these absurd theories about her is to feel as baffled as she did by the confusions of puritanism; it makes one angry with Hamlet, not only with his commentators, as I think we are meant to be. Being disagreeable in this way was part of his "mystery."

Turning now to the Queen: Mr. Dover Wilson argued that

159

the First Quarto was merely a perversion of the single play by
Shakespeare, with a less "subtle" treatment of the Queen. I do
not think we need at once call it subtle of Shakespeare to make
her into an extra mystery by simply cutting out all her explana-
tions of her behavior. The idea of a great lady who speaks
nobly but is treacherous to an uncertain degree was familiar on
the stage, as in Marlowe's *Edward II*, not a new idea deserving
praise. No doubt the treatment is subtle; several of her replies
seem unconscious proofs of complete innocence, whereas when
she says her guilt "spills itself in fearing to be spilt" she must
imply a guilty secret. But we must ask why the subtlety is
wanted. An important factor here is the instruction of the Ghost
to Hamlet, in the first Act, that he must contrive nothing against
his mother. I think this was supplied by Kyd; he would see its
usefulness as an excuse for the necessary delay, and would want
his characters to be high-minded. Also he had to give his Ghost
a reason for returning later, because the audience would not want
this interesting character to be dropped. In Kyd's first act, therefore, the Ghost said Claudius must be killed and the Queen
protected; then in the third Act, when Hamlet was questioning
her suspiciously, the Ghost came back and said she hadn't known
about his murder, supporting her own statement to that effect;
meanwhile he told Hamlet that it would be dangerous to wait
any longer about killing Claudius, because the Play Scene has
warned him. Hamlet had felt he still ought to wait till he knew
how much his mother was involved. The Ghost had already for-
given her for what she had done—perhaps adultery, probably
only the hasty re-marriage to his brother—but had not cared to
discuss it much; the tragic effect in the third act is that he clears
up too late an unfortunate bit of vagueness in his first instructions. This makes him a bit absurd, but the motives of Ghosts
seldom do bear much scrutiny, and he is better than most of
them. (On this account, Hamlet is still liable to have different
motives in different scenes for sparing the King at prayer, but

that seems a normal bit of Elizabethan confusion.) Thus there is no reason why Kyd's Queen should not have satisfied the curiosity of the audience fully; she would admit to Hamlet that her second marriage was wrong, clear herself of anything else, offer to help him, and be shown doing it. Shakespeare, in his first treatment of the play, had no reason not to keep all this, as the First Quarto implies; his problem was to make the audience accept the delay as life-like, and once Hamlet is surrounded by guards that problem is solved. But if we next suppose him making a minor revision, for audiences who have become interested in the mystery of Hamlet, then it is clearly better to surround him with mystery and make him drive into a situation which the audience too feels to be unplumbable.

Mr. Richard Flatter, in an interesting recent book (*Hamlet's Father*), has done useful work by taking this re-interpretation of the Ghost as far as it will go. He points out that the Ghost must be supposed to return in the bedroom scene to say something important, and yet all he does is to prevent Hamlet from learning whether the Queen helped in his murder; such then was his intention, though he had to deny it. After this Hamlet does up his buttons (stops pretending to be mad) and has nothing left but a high-minded despair about his duties to his parents; that is why he talks about Fate and refuses to defend himself. In effect, he can now only kill Claudius after his mother is dead, and he has only an instant to do it in before he himself dies, but he is heroic in seizing this moment to carry out an apparently impossible duty with pedantic exactitude. To accuse him of delay, says Mr. Flatter with considerable point, is like accusing Prometheus of delay while chained to the Caucasus. This result, I think, is enough to prove that the Flatter view was never a very prominent element in a play which hides it so successfully. He produces interesting evidence from stage history that her complicity in the murder was assumed as part of the tradition; but I can't see that the German version has any claim to echo a pre-Shakespearean play, whereas the First Quarto gives evidence that it was Shakespeare who first started this hare, in his revision of 1601. He goes on to claim that the theme of a Ghost who, so far from wanting Revenge, wants to save his un-faithful wife from being punished for murdering himself, wants even to save her from the pain of confessing it to their son, is an extraordinary moral invention, especially for an Elizabethan; and so it is, for a playwright in any period, if he keeps it so very well hidden. Here, surely, we are among the vaguely farcical "Solutions of the Hamlet Problem" which have been cropping up for generations. But we need also to consider why they crop up, why the play was so constructed as to excite them. I think the Flatter theory did cross the keen minds of some of the 1601 audiences, and was intended to; but only as a background pos-sibility in a situation which encouraged a variety of such ideas. I think the fundamental reason why the change was "subtle," to recall the term of Mr. Dover Wilson, was something very close to the Freudian one which he is so quick at jumping away from; to make both parents a mystery at least pushes the audience to-wards fundamental childhood situations. But it would have a sufficient immediate effect from thickening the atmosphere and broadening the field.

There is a question about the staging of the bedroom scene which opens out in interesting directions. By all the rules of an enthusiast for the balcony, Hamlet must scold his mother on the balcony; whereas a modern producer usually feels it absurd to put such a long and dramatic scene in such a remote cramped space. One side says: "Hamlet walks straight on through one private room (the inner stage, the King at prayer) to a still more private room (the Queen's 'closet,' the balcony); any-thing else would break the dramatic tension"; the other side says "How are you going to get four actors and a double bed and all the rest of it onto this balcony? How can the audience see them properly, let alone feel close enough to them?" We must also recognize and salute the splendid invention of J. C. Adams, a Globe Theatre in which the balcony was the most prominent stage, so that Desdemona could die on it actually touching the back wall of the whole building. This machine ought to be constructed, but the actual Globe could hardly be such a thrillingly specialized instrument; the plays had to be ready for use under rougher circumstances. I think there is evidence that, here and in other cases, Shakespeare wanted to use the balcony more than the Company would let him, but that, even so, he regarded it as a "distancing" stage, like the modern producer and unlike J. C. Adams.

The Folio, to begin the next scene, just says "Enter King," whereas Q2 says "Enter King and Queen with Rosencrantz and Guilderstern." Mr. Dover Wilson finds the Quarto odd here, because "not only is an entry for the Queen superfluous when she is already 'on', but Rosencrantz and Guilderstern are quite obviously in the way, so much so that the Queen has to get rid of them at once." However, they are called back in a moment to search for Hamlet, and Q1 brings them on here without bothering to move them out and back. Mr. Dover Wilson suggests an intervening scene cut by Shakespeare while revising his manuscript, but this I think only follows from his curious lack of interest in the Globe Theatre. Surely the Q2 version means that the inner-stage curtain is opened, "discovering" the King plotting with R. and G., and that the Queen at once walks downstairs from the balcony; the purpose of the Folio version, where the King walks into the bedroom alone and calls for R. and G. thirty lines later, is to keep the whole bedroom scene on the inner stage, not the balcony. This is a clumsy plan, because it forces the incident of the King at prayer out onto the apron stage, whereas how a King can be caught in private is one of the traditional lines of interest of Revenge Plays—here it happens because the Queen wants to speak to Hamlet privately just when the King urgently needs solitude to recover from the shock of the Mouse-Trap, and her room is only reached through his. This must also be how Hamlet can assume that the King has crept behind the arras in her room to spy on him. To make these points clear on the stage urgently needs two private rooms, and if the Company opposed using the balcony for such a definite purpose they must have opposed using it for any major scene. Now, on the theory of Mr. Dover Wilson about Q2 and F, this means that Shakespeare wrote the scene for the balcony but was never allowed to put it there. Presumably he had just built the instrument he wanted; he must have been on the committee about the technical requirements of the new Globe, as a major shareholder, and the wishes of the leading author about the shape of the balcony would have to be heard. It is an intriguing idea that, perhaps for the first big use of the Globe, he was not allowed to play with his toy as much as he wanted. One may suspect that the mysterious quarrel, which Mr. Dover Wilson can somehow smell in his dealings with *Hamlet,* was not about cuts in the text but about where to put the double bed.

There is a parallel case over the blinding of Gloucester in *King Lear,* with the opposite relation between Folio and Quarto. Here the Quarto is supposed to be a reconstruction of what was acted, the Folio to be mainly a record of Shakespeare's manuscript, and the Quarto but not the Folio gives a soliloquy of fourteen lines by Edgar before the blinding scene. The previous scene is a shed for hiding from the storm, so has to be the inner stage, and the curtain needs to open on a "bench" and some "joint-stools," one of them "warped." The next gives the blinding of Gloucester in his own castle, and the irony of this requires grandeur—his own coat-of-arms on a hanging cloth, and at least one grand chair facing away from the audience on which he is blinded. Edgar is ignored by the supporters of the now unconscious Lear but presumably leaves the hut when they do; so the back curtain can be closed behind him, and his speech is just long enough for a simple change of furniture. Neither scene requires the balcony. But his words are so clumsy that many critics have suspected interpolation, also they break the rule that he never talks sanely at length while dressed as mad; yet they make quite good dramatic irony and are obviously by Shakespeare. I think this is a decisive bit of evidence as far as it goes, apart from any theory about the Folio and Quarto; Shakespeare wrote these extra lines in cold blood for convenience in staging a performance without a balcony; therefore in his first draft, written in hot blood, he must have presumed the use of one for the blinding of Gloucester. But I am not sure how much we can build on this fact. If we suppose he had a major quarrel with the producer over the balcony in *Hamlet*, surely it is odd to have him running bull-headed into the same trouble six years later in *Lear*, when he can have been in no mood for negotiations with producers. The obvious view, it seems to me, is simply that the Company always required a version, less important than the one for the Globe Theatre, which could be acted where there wasn't a big balcony, for instance at Court. They wouldn't much care which version eventually hit print.

I cannot be decisive here but feel the questions need to be raised. It is clear from Q2 that Shakespeare wanted the bedroom scene in *Hamlet* on the balcony, because otherwise the peculiar requirements of that text would not have got written down. But are we to suppose that Kyd already had it on the balcony, or contrariwise that Shakespeare himself only wanted it there in his 1601 revision, as a way of adding to the general mystery? It seems probable that Kyd already had the crucial sequence of scenes here; first sparing the King at prayer, then testing the Queen and being interrupted by the Ghost. This requires the balcony already. Kyd had a balcony, but a small one used only for short scenes or as part of a general effect; if he used it for this scene he would not also kill Polonius on it. There is a direct theatrical or symbolical reason for putting the

scene on the balcony; Hamlet has drifted away from the obvious
necessity of killing Claudius, so he is next shown bellowing in
a remote place, and when the Ghost arrives the effect is like
some animal in the near-by bear-pit being driven back from a
hiding-place to its death in the ring. (It is thus a rehabilitation
for Hamlet when he fights his own way back from England.)
Besides, any stage Ghost is safer from ridicule when kept a bit
remote. So I think it likely that Kyd already had the scene
there, without Polonius and with less prolonged scolding by
Hamlet. Anyhow Shakespeare would have it there in his first
version, because it is required by his dramatic sequence, not
merely by his later desire to add extra mystery about the Queen.
Probably he told the Company he was only following tradition
by putting it on the balcony, whereas he had made the scene so
much bigger, to fit the new balcony of the Globe, that the effect
was quite different. I do not think the Folio is adequate evidence that they refused, but they may have done.

The more important question is what Shakespeare wanted
from his balcony, and therefore how we should build theatres
for acting him. There is a large practical difference between the
"distancing" theory of the balcony which is commonly assumed
and the theory of J. C. Adams that it was simply the most prominent stage. One must suppose a gradual development; no doubt,
the Globe of 1599 might have made a startling break with previous theatrical construction, but if so it is odd that that didn't
get mentioned. The current view of experts seems to be that the
balcony came to be used more and more in the seventeenth century, for the "public" theatres. The year before the theatres
were closed for the Rule of the Saints a hopeful man published
a play with a stage direction requiring *two* double beds and other
French farce material saying he *hoped* it could all be done on
the balcony, and this may encourage us to believe that the for-
ward-looking vision of Shakespeare was eventually justified.
Even the Folio text of *Lear* is generally supposed to be check-

ing its version by the Quarto etc., not copying a fifteen-year-old manuscript blindly; one could argue that the copyist in many of his cuts was leaving out the parts he knew were never spoken "nowadays"—for instance, you didn't want those tiresome extra lines for Edgar because nowadays the balcony was used. The whole subject is confusing, but my impression is that Shakespeare regarded his balcony as a "distancing" stage, even while arranging for a bigger one and trying to use it more. We tend to feel that the obscenity and jealousy of Hamlet towards his mother are in themselves unpleasant enough to be the better for "distancing," but squeamishness is not the main point; as I have tried to argue, there would already be a dramatic reason for putting it there in the 1580's, which Shakespeare might well want to carry further.   In the same way, we would prefer to feel farther off from the blinding of Gloucester, but also the function of the scene is to "sum up the eye imagery" and what not, rather than to emphasize his pain, since he does not become a major character till after it.   Of course, as so often happens in a quarrel about how to use a new object, both sides may have been wrong in making the same basic assumption; J. C. Adams may be right in saying that the balcony was in fact the most prominent stage of the 1600 Globe, and yet everyone concerned may have failed to recognize this at the time. I imagine there is a good deal yet to be discovered about the staging, which may help to clear up our views about the first audiences; this makes a contrast with what may be called the basic point of *Hamlet*, which does seem to have been pursued, in the last century and a half, about as far as it will go.

I ought finally to say something about the Freudian view of *Hamlet*, the most extraordinary of the claims that it means something very profound which the first audiences could not know about.   I think that literary critics, when this theory appeared, were thrown into excessive anxiety. A. C. Bradley had made the essential points before; that Hamlet's first soliloquy drives home (rather as a surprise to the first audiences, who expected something about losing the throne) that some kind of sex nausea about his mother is what is really poisoning him; also that in the sequence around the Prayer scene his failure to kill Claudius is firmly and intentionally tied up with a preference for scolding his mother instead. I have been trying to argue that his relations with the two women were made increasingly oppressive as the play was altered, but in any case the Freudian atmosphere of the final version is obvious even if distasteful. Surely the first point here is that the original legend is a kind of gift for the Freudian approach (even if Freud is wrong); it need not be painful to suppose that Shakespeare expressed this legend with a unique power. There is a fairy-story or childish fascination because Hamlet can boast of his secret and yet keep it, and because this crazy magical behaviour kills plenty of grown-ups; to base it on a conflict about killing Mother's husband is more specifically Freudian but still not secret. The Freudian theory makes a literary problem when its conclusions oppose what the author thought he intended; but it seems clear that Shakespeare wouldn't have wanted to alter anything if he had been told about Freud, whether he laughed at the theory or not. Then again, what is tiresome for the reader about the Freudian approach is that it seems to tell us we are merely deluded in the reasons we give for our preferences, because the real grounds for them are deep in the Unconscious; but here the passage to the underground is fairly open. A feeling that this hero is allowed to act in a peculiar way which is yet somehow familiar, because one has been tempted to do it oneself, is surely part of the essence of the story. There is a clear contrast with Oedipus, who had no Oedipus Complex. He had not wanted to kill his father and marry his mother, even "unconsciously"; if he came to recognize that he had wanted it, that would weaken his bleak surprise at learning he has done it. The claim is that his audiences wanted to do it unconsciously—that is why they were so deeply stirred by the play, and why Aristotle could treat it as the supreme tragedy though in logic it doesn't fit his case at all, being only a bad luck story. This position is an uneasy one, I think; one feels there ought to be some mediation between the surface and the depths, and probably the play did mean more to its first audiences than we realize. But Hamlet is himself suffering from the Complex, in the grand treatment by Ernest Jones, though the reactions of the audience are also considered when he makes the other characters "fit in." And this is not unreasonable, because Hamlet is at least peculiar in Saxo, and Shakespeare overtly treats him as a "case" of Melancholy, a specific though baffling mental disease which medical textbooks were being written about.

What does seem doubtful is whether his mental disease was supposed to be what made him spare the King at prayer. We may take it that Kyd already had the scene, and gave the reason (that this might not send him to Hell), and meant it to be taken seriously; and also meant its effect to be seen as fatal, a tragic failure of state-craft. A moral to this, that a desire for excessive revenge may sometimes spoil a whole design, would seem quite in order. But, by the time Shakespeare had finished raising puzzles about the motives, even the motive for this part, though apparently taken over directly, might well come into doubt; for one thing, the failure of Hamlet even to consider his own danger, now that the King knows his secret, is so very glaring. Even the wildly opposite reason suggested by Mr. Dover Wilson, that he feels it wouldn't be sporting though he can't tell himself so, might crop up among contemporary audiences; in any case, the idea that there was some puzzle about it could easily occur to them. And the idea of a man grown-up in everything else who still acts like a child towards his elder relations is familiar; it could occur to a reflective mind, not only be sensed by the Unconscious, as soon as behavior like Hamlet's was presented as a puzzle. The trouble with it if made prominent would be from making the hero contemptible, but Hamlet has many escapes from that besides his claim to mental disease. That his mother's marriage was considered incest made his initial disturbance seem more rational then than it does now; but his horror and jealousy are made to feel, as Mr. Eliot pointed out for purposes of complaint, a spreading miasma and in excess of this cause. I do not think Mr. Dover Wilson need have suspected that Mr. Eliot hadn't heard about incest, even for a rival effort at dodging Freud; there was admittedly an excess, because the old play was admittedly theatrical. Unconscious resistance to killing a *King* is what the audience would be likely to invent, if any; for Claudius to talk about the divinity that doth hedge a king is irony, because he has killed one, but we are still meant to feel its truth; there may be some echo of the current view of Hamlet, as a recent critic has suggested, in the grand scene of Chapman with the repeated line "Do anything but killing of a King." It would fit well onto the high-minded aspect of Hamlet, as having an unmentioned doubt about the value of his revenge. But none of this is a rebuttal of the Freudian view; the feeling about a King is derived very directly from childhood feelings about Father.

We have to consider, not merely how a play came to be written which allows of being searched so deeply so long after, but why it has steadily continued to hold audiences who on any view do not see all round it. The Freudian view is that it satisfies the universal Unconscious, but one feels more practical in saying, as Hugh Kingsmill did, that they enjoy the imaginative release of indulging in very "theatrical" behavior, which in this case is hard to distinguish from "neurotic" behavor. The business of the plot is to prevent them from feeling it as an indulgence, because the assumption that Hamlet has plenty of reasons for it somehow is always kept up. If we leave the matter there, I think, the play appears a rather offensive trick and even likely to be harmful. Indeed common sense has decided that people who feel encouraged to imitate Hamlet, or to follow what appear to be the instructions of Freud, actually are liable to behave badly. But the first audiences were being asked to consider this hero of legend as admittedly theatrical (already laughed at for it) and yet unbreakably true about life; in one way because he illustrated a recognized neurosis, in another because he extracted from it virtues which could not but be called great however much the story proved them to be fatal. So far as the spectator was tempted forward to examine the "reasons" behind Hamlet he was no longer indulging a delusion but considering a frequent and important, even if delusory, mental state, and trying to handle it. If one conceives the play as finally rewritten with that kind of purpose and that kind of audience, there is no need to be astonished that it happened to illustrate the Freudian theory. Indeed it would seem rather trivial, I think, to go on now and examine whether the successive versions were getting more Freudian. The eventual question is whether you can put up with the final Hamlet, a person who frequently appears in the modern world under various disguises, whether by Shakespeare's fault or no. I would always sympathize with anyone who says, like Hugh Kingsmill, that he can't put up with Hamlet at all. But I am afraid it is within hail of the more painful question whether you can put up with yourself and the race of man.

Marion Trousdale

CORIOLANUS

AND THE PLAYGOER IN 1609

In 'Flatcaps and Bluecoats: Visual Signals on the Elizabethan Stage', an essay that appeared in *Essays and Studies 1980*, George Hunter argued that on the Elizabethan stage 'the individual is given full meaning only when caught up into his social role' (p. 26) and that 'all the characters are understood first in terms of rank and function'. I do not so much disagree with this observation as wish to complicate it. Character as it relates to dress I wish to examine not only as it appears on the stage in what I am positing as the first production of *Coriolanus* in 1609,[1] but as we can imagine it appeared in the audience that attended that first performance at the Globe. My argument is that performance as a means of projecting character as a field of force, as Hunter describes it, is as characteristic of the society that frequented the theatre as it is of the actors who showed that society on stage. That suggests that the hierarchy we take for granted in Elizabethan society and which Hunter himself refers to as part of his argument is not hierarchy as we imagine it retrospectively — a received and inflexible structure within which social identity is a given and violence is cloaked with the acceptable garb of validating ceremony. Rather the markings of rank, like the topics of argument, were material and occasional. They could be assembled and were assembled in the society, as on the stage, to enable the performer in both instances by means of visible signs to present a persuasive show. Thus acting as successful performance not only put in question established degree, as others have pointed out; it also drew upon and validated deeply held social practices that themselves subverted established social position.

What then can we tell about the seventeenth-century audience at the Globe? Were we to imagine attending the Globe in 1609 for the first night, or rather the first afternoon, of *Coriolanus*, we would know, from Andrew Gurr's painstaking reconstruction in *Playgoing in Shakespeare's London*, to expect a mixed audience, and it would appear that all of the theatres were both crowded and noisy. Drayton describing the Rose, which we now know to have been quite small, mentions the 'thronged Theatre' and the 'Showts and Claps at ev'ry little pawse' (Gurr, 1987, 45, 215). We know that at the Fortune, as well as at other

172

theatres, the audience hissed to express their disapproval. 'Clapping or hissing is the onely meane,' William Fennor notes in 1616, 'That tries and searches out a well writ Sceane' (Gurr, 1987, 230), and Dekker in the Prooemium to *The Gvls Horne-booke* tells his readers that he sings like the cuckoo in June, 'hisse or giue plaudities, I care not a nut-shell which of either' (B1).

Obviously whoever was in that first audience, they actively participated in the action on the stage. The extent of that participation is indicated not only by the descriptions we have of the onstage audience rejecting the play the company has chosen to present as in *The Knight of the Burning Pestle*, but by the suggestion in the same play and earlier, in the performance of William Gager's *Ulysses Redux* at Christ Church, Oxford, that members of the audience felt important enough to consider themselves part of the action on the stage. Theatre, as Bruce Smith has remarked, is people talking to people, and as Gurr amply illustrates, in 1609 the talking went both ways. Whether standing in the pit, sitting in the lords' room, or sharing the platform with the actors, for the auditors at the Globe, going to the theatre was as active and public a performance as acting on the stage.

The response of a disappointed audience at the Hope Theatre on 17 October 1614 gives us some idea as to just how active an audience might be. The audience is described in some detail by John Taylor, the water poet, in *Taylor's Revenge*. He was to have had a rhyming contest with William Fennor who failed to appear. Taylor says that he personally stepped out on the stage to appease the crowd: 'But they all raging, like tempestuous Seas:/Cry'd out, their expectations were defeated/And how they all were cony-catch'd and cheated:/Some laught, some swore, some star'd & stamp'd and curst. . . . One sweares and stormes, another laughs & smiles,/Another madly would pluck off the tiles,/Some runne to th'doore to get againe their coyne.' But their response was not only vocal: 'For now the stinkards, in their irefull wraths,/Bepelted me with Lome, with Stones, and Laths,/One madly sits like bottle-Ale, and hisses,/Another throwes a stone, and 'cause he misses,/He yawnes and bawles, and cryes Away, away:/Another cryes out, Iohn, begin the Play/. . . .' One from the audience, he reports, 'valiantly stept out vpon the Stage,/And would teare downe the hangings in his rage.' Their active response Taylor sums up as the 'clapping, hissing, swearing, stamping, smiling,/Applauding, scorning, liking, and reviling' of what he calls the 'Hydra-headed multitude'. In desperation Taylor himself begins to act (145).

It is obvious that the stinkards, as Dekker among others described the

lowest of these playgoers, felt as entitled to judge and be listened to as
the gallant in the sixpenny box. It had been just such a presumption of
privilege as playgoer that had led the Merchant Taylors' school to cease
performances in 1573. 'Whereas at our Common Playes . . .', they
stated, 'everye lewd persone thinketh himselfe (for his penny) worthye
of the chiefe and most commodious place withoute respecte of any
other, either for age or estimacion in the comon weale, whiche bringeth
the youthe to such an impudente famyliaritie with theire betters that
often tymes greite contempte of Maisters, Parents, and Magistrats
followeth thereof' (Harbage, 1941, p. 13); and Dekker in 1609 suggests
that the sense of shared privilege among the public theatre audience had
become even more widespread. 'Sithence then the place,' he writes in
The Gvls Horne-booke in 1609, 'is so free in entertainment, allowing a
stoole as well to the Farmers sonne as to your Templer: that your
Stinckard has the selfe-same libertie to be there in his Tobacco-Fumes,
which your sweet Courtier hath: and that your Car-man and Tinker
claime as strong a voice in their suffrage, and sit to giue iudgement on
the plaies life and death, as well as the prowdest Momus among the
tribe of Critick' (Harbage, 1941, p. 13).

Coriolanus then, one might say, puts on stage the stinkards who
frequent the public theatres and puts them on stage in much the same
dress as they appeared in the audience at the Globe. They are aproned
men with caps who, in the words of the Merchant Taylors, thought
themselves 'worthye of the chiefe and most commodious place withoute
respecte of any other'. A company of mutinous citizens, according to
the Folio stage direction, begins the play, and Martius in his first
appearance characterises them in words reminiscent of Marullus in
Julius Caesar. Their opinion, in Martius' view, is worth no more than
their social position. 'Rubbing the poor itch of your opinion,' he tells
them, 'you make yourselves scabs' (Riverside Edn., I.i.165). It is a
remark that carries the same social judgement as Dekker's. Like Jonson,
Martius characterises the commoners as deficient in judgement while
assertive of their status. When stopped by the Tribunes in Act III when
the crowd has turned against him, Martius calls it 'a purpos'd thing . . .
To curb the will of the nobility . . . with such as cannot rule,/Nor ever
will be ruled' (III.i.38–41), and when they banish him, Martius curses
them as 'You common cry of curs! whose breath I hate,/As reek
a'th'rotten fens, whose loves I prize/As the dead carcasses of unburied
men/That do corrupt my air' (III.iii.120–3). It would appear to be such
commoners thronging the theatres that made the city fathers worry
about playhouses as places of public disturbance. If we ask what the first

audience of *Coriolanus* saw, we might say that what that part of the audience saw when they watched *Coriolanus* was, throughout all of the play, an unsympathetic if commonplace image of themselves.

But the audience was not made up only or even chiefly of aproned men, and although assertive of their own importance, it does not seem to have been principally aproned men who had the means to refashion themselves through dress. Told by Master Probee that he and Master Damplay have been sent 'unto you, indeed, from the people,' the Boy in *The Magnetic Lady* asks 'which side of the people' and is told 'Not the *Faeces*, or grounds of your people, that sit in the oblique caves and wedges of your house, your sinfull sixe-penny Mechanicks' (sixpence being the minimum price of admission to the Blackfriars Theatre); to which Damplay adds, '. . . the better, and braver sort of your people! Plush and Velvet-outsides! that stick your house round like so many eminences' ['Induction or Chorus'].

From the correspondence of Philip Gawdy it would appear that some of these people along with less distinguished members of the multitude were caught up in the impressment carried out in the playhouses by the city authorities in 1602 (Gurr, 1987, p. 66), and to judge from other letters he wrote to his family, these people came to the theatre as they went to Court, to show themselves in velvet and plush. Dekker advises his gallant that if he wishes to be taken for a gentleman, he should sit on the stage and 'talk loudly' to publish his 'temperance to the world' that he might appear 'as a gentleman to spend a foolish hour or two'. One must imagine that like such a gentleman as Philip Gawdy, Dekker's gallant was concerned as well with his dress. And that dress is assembled in imitation of betters. Whether the visible trappings Gawdy purchases are a saddle for his father, hose for his brother or a dress for his sister, the models are the accoutrements of those with power and place. 'For I can assure yow that bothe the quene, and all the gentlewomen at the courte weare the uery fashion of your tuff taffata gowne with an open wired sleve and suche a cutt, and it is now the newest fashion,' he writes to his sister Anne in December 1587 (Gawdy, 28). In December 1593, he writes to his brother: 'I have boughte the a sadle with the furniture coryspondente no other then my L. of Essex, Sr. Charles Blunt, Sr Roger Williams and such other cavilleros at this hower do vse. The footclothe bought of a clothe dyed out of a blewe blankett, which neuer will change coller for any weather garded not after the old fashion but the newest in request and most profitable, for lace therwith is alderman lyke and suche as will hange vppon euery taynter' (Gawdy, 77). He makes a similar observation about the hose he has bought. 'Thy hose I haue bought of the mallard coller. It will holde well a perfecte wynter coller, paved and rowled just according to the fashion. I will not saye that very greate men I tooke the pattern from them [*sic*].' Even in Redenhall near Halston in Norfolk, Gawdy's family seat, the great men in the court are the arbiters of fashion, and as Gawdy copied Cecil or Essex or Blunt, so the lesser gentry and indeed those who were not gentry copied such gentry as Gawdy.

George Hunter, in the essay I mentioned earlier, points out in a different context that clothes, in a way in which we are unaccustomed to marking, were the means by which the society and the individual constituted themselves. Using the example of the apprentice Quicksilver in *Eastward Ho*, Hunter shows the extent to which clothes, as they say, make the man. Quicksilver, who claims to be of gentle parentage, keeps a chest of clothes with the usurer Security, and in Act II, using what he calls his finery, he changes his appearance from that of an apprentice, charged by statute to wear only the appropriate clothes provided by his master, into that of a nobleman. Hunter sees in this change 'a breach with social reality . . . an outside without an inside' (31). Losing his clothes in a shipwreck when escaping to Virginia, he is press-ganged for the army and subsequently ends up in gaol. His return at the end to a proper sense of clothing Hunter sees as the 'visual sign of social self-knowledge and mental balance'. But identity as we have examined it so far does not appear to be that stable, and although one can argue that Quicksilver's sense of self is represented by his awareness of the importance of how he is dressed, his attitude toward that dress and toward the social codes such dress embodies reveals not only the extent to which dress is felt to determine identity but the ways in which social rank in the period is attached to what one wears. Gawdy is a gentleman by birth. That does not keep him from associating status with fashion. Rather, like the actors that dressed up in expensive garments in order to draw the crowds to the theatre, Gawdy sees clothes as a means of social identity and seeks for himself and his family through fashionable dress a position enhanced by its exterior association with the powerful men at court.

To judge from such pamphleteers as Philip Stubbes and Stephen Gosson, and the repeated proclamations enforcing the sumptuary laws, Quicksilver's attraction to finery in the way of dress was characteristic of the society at large. 'How often', Stephen Gosson asks in *The School of Abuse* in 1579, 'hath her majesty, with the grave advice of her honorable councell, sette down the limits of apparell to every degree, and how soone againe hath that pride of our harts overflowen the

channel?'; and he observes that 'overlashing in apparel is so common a
fault, that the very hyerlings of some of our players, which stand at
reversion of vi.s by the weeke, jet under gentlemens noses in sutes of
silke' (p. 39). The decree of 1582 ordering people of all degrees to obey
the sumptuary regulations which specified what each was entitled to
wear, observes that the luxury of the times had 'greatly prevailed among
people of all degrees in their apparel' (Baldwin, 231). The decree issued
in 1588 observes that no reformation in dress had followed the earlier
decrees (Baldwin, 226). Francis Baldwin, after looking closely at all of
the sumptuary proclamations, remarks that 'even the queen's high
indignation was not sufficient to terrify offenders against the sumptuary
laws' (226). The sumptuary decrees show us what Quicksilver shows
us. If it is felt that how you dress is meant to tell us who you are, then
changing clothes can change status. This is the double bind of the fact
that how you dress tells us who you are.

We can see the kind of social dilemma this creates in the remarks of
Philip Stubbes. He is at once fascinated with dress — he describes it in
minute detail — and offended by it. His descriptions of what he
identifies as abuses are the descriptions of someone who could not tear
his eyes away from the magnificence of what he saw. Of the notorious
ruffs he remarks that they 'are eyther clogged with golde, siluer, or silke
lace of stately price, wrought all ouer with needle work, speckled and
sparkled here and there with the Sonne, the Moone, the starres and
many other Antiques straunge to beholde. Some garments are wrought
with open worke downe to the midst of the ruffe and further . . . some
with purled lace so cloyd, and other gewgawes so pestred. . . . Sometimes,
they are pinned vp to their eares, sometimes they are suffered to hang
ouer their shoulders, like flagges or Windmill sayles fluttering in the
wind, and thus euery one pleaseth her selfe in her foolish deuices' (43).
Of their doublets he observes: 'The women also there haue Doublets
and Jerkins as men haue here, buttoned vp the breast, and made with
wings, weltes and pinions on the shoulder pointes, as mans apparel is in
all respectes' (44). His admiration for what he is ostensibly condemning
can be seen in the detailed way in which the clothes are described. 'If the
whole gowne be not Silke or Velvet, then the same must be layd with
lace, two or three fingers broad all ouer the gowne, or els the most part.
Or if not so . . . then it must be garded with great gardes of Veluet,
euery garde foure or sixe fingers broad at the least, and edged with
costly lace' (45). The ambivalence of Stubbes' attitude toward the
extravagant dress he condemns in such loving detail can be seen even
more clearly in the way in which the sheer magnificence of the

garments he describes is itself, to him, a source of national pride:

> 'But I haue heard them say, that other nations passe them for
> exquisite finenesse and brauery in apparell: as the Italians, the
> Athenians, the Spaniards, the Chaldeans, Helvetians, Zuitzers,
> Venetians, Muscouians, and suchlike: . . . The Muscouians,
> Athenians, Italians, Brasilians, Affricanes, Asians, Cantabrians,
> Hungarians, Ethiopians, Dutch, French, or els what nations soeuer
> vnder the Sunne, are so farre behinde the people of England in
> exquisitnesse of apparell, as in effect, they esteeme it little or
> nothing at all . . . for it is manifest that all other nations vnder the
> Sunne, how strange, how new, how fine, or how comely soeuer
> they thinke their fashions to be, when they bee compared with the
> diuers fashions, and sundry formes of apparel in England, are most
> unhandsome, brutish and monstrous. And hereby it apeareth, that
> no people in the worlde are so curious in newfangles, as they of
> England be' (9–10).[2]

Other documents confirm Stubbes' boast. It would appear from a
complaint of one Thomas Gylles against the Yeoman of the Revels
in 1572 that even earlier the demand for extravagant clothes was
such that both independent tradesmen and the Yeoman of the Revels
had clothes for hire. The garments for hire by the Yeoman of the
Revels were garments that belonged to the Queen. Gylles' complaint
states:

> 'Wheras the yeman of the quenes Magestyes revelles dothe vsuallye
> lett to hyer her sayde hyghnes maskes to the grett hurt spoylle &
> dyscredyt of the same to all sort of parsons that wyll hyer the same
> by reson of wyche comen vsage the glosse & bewtye of the same
> garmentes ys lost & canott sowell serve to be often allteryde & to be
> shewyde before hyr hyghnes . . . for ytt takythe more harme by
> ounce werynge Into the cytye or contre where yt ys often vsyd then
> by many tymes werynge In the cowrt by the grett presse of peple &
> fowlnes bothe of the weye & wether & soyll of the wereres who for
> the most part be of the meanest sort of mene to the grett dyscredytt
> of the same aparell which afterwards ys to be shewyd before her
> heyghnes & to be worne by theme of grett callynge.'

He had complained before with no results 'by reson that the sayd
yeman havynge alloen the costodye of the garmentes dothe lend the
same at hys plesuer ffor remedy heroff . . . And your orator shall praye
vnto allmyghty gode for your honores longe lyffe & prossperytye for
your orator ys grettlye hynderyde of hys lyvynge herbye who havynge
aparell to lett & canott so cheplye lett the same as hyr hyghnes maskes

be lett as knowytt god who ever preserv you In honor & felycytye'
(Feuillerat, 409).

It is interesting to put beside the preoccupations of Stubbes the
accounts in Henslowe's diary which show how important dress was to
the actors on the stage. The list of playing apparel written in the hand of
Edward Alleyn (291–4) includes a scarlet cloak with gold laces and gold
buttons down the side, a scarlet cloak with silver lace and silver buttons,
a short velvet cloak embroidered with gold and gold spangles, a damask
cloak with velvet, a scarlet [cloak?] with buttons of gold faced with blue
velvet, a black velvet gown with white fur, a crimson robe stripped with
gold faced with ermine, a coat of crimson velvet cut in panes and
embroidered in gold, a carnation velvet jerkin laced with silver. Like the
members of the audience who by acquiring the right clothes could
acquire at the same time a social identity, the actors on the stage
projected the character they wished to represent by means of elaborate
dress. And Alleyn's list, like Stubbes's description, reveals a similar
ambiguity in its definitions of that social identity. 'Daniels gowne' like
'will somers cote' at least suggests the possibility of character established
by recognisable dress, and we know from other inventories (317, 321)
that at least some well-known stage personalities (Tamburlaine, Henry
V) have particular garments associated with the part. Thus the expensive
clothes in Alleyn's wardrobe could project character, suggesting self-
fashioning. At the same time established characters are imagined as
fixed. Tamburlaine is not so much created as recognised by means of
what he wears.

What would such an audience see as they watched *Coriolanus* on the
stage? They would see in the first instance a Roman who questioned the
belief that dress could be the means of giving or assuming a local
habitation and a name. Coriolanus changes clothes three times during
the course of the play. During most of his time on stage he is the Roman
warrior who safeguards the city from the Volscians. Wearing the short
Roman kirtle and using what was taken to be Roman armour,[3] the actor
playing the character of Coriolanus paradoxically is playing a man for
whom identity is not something one can put off with one's clothes. This
can be seen very clearly when he wears the toga of humility in order to
win the necessary voices. 'May I change these garments?' he asks
Sicinius after pleading for the plebeians' voices, and told that he may,
remarks that he'll 'straight do; and knowing myself again,/Repair to the
senate-house' (II.iii.144). Like the ideal posited by the sumptuary laws,
Coriolanus' continuing sense of himself is of one whom clothes cannot
change. Even when returning to Rome as the hero of the Volsces and

presumably dressed like a Volsce, Coriolanus in the presence of his
kindred and at the intercession of his wife and mother allies himself
with Rome. He is the citizen Hunter describes, the one for whom
clothing is the visual sign of social self-knowledge. Change in Coriolanus'
eyes is a sign of weakness. It is the fact that the crowd can be wooed as
well as the fact that they are cowardly that makes him have no respect
for the crowd. This is then a man who, we might imagine, represents on
stage an Elizabethan ideal. He is unfailingly courageous, and in his
death, as Cavell remarks, the city loses the best hero it ever had. Like
Jonson's his standards never vary. As the best of the playwrights, he
refuses to appease the hydra-headed multitude.

Yet fame for a playwright or a soldier, like the status of a citizen,
exists only when publicly inscribed. Like the clothes for which the
populace hungered and which consumed the wealth they were meant to
display, Coriolanus' constancy consumes him. His inability to woo the
mob means that he fails to gain that fame he hungers for, for that only
the mob can bestow. Stubbes reports that

> 'So farre hath this cancker of pride eaten into the body of the
> common welth, that euery poore yeoman his Daughter, euery
> Husband man his daughter, and euery Cottager his Daughter will
> not spare to flaunt it out, in suche gownes, petticots, and kirtles, as
> these. And notwithstanding that their Parents owe a brase of
> hundredpounds more than they are worth, yet will they haue it. . . .
> For they are so impudent, that all be it, their poore Parents haue
> but one cow, horse, or sheep, they will neuer let them rest, til they
> be sould, to maintain them in their braueries' (46).

Although with more cause because of greater public worth, Coriolanus
is similarly impudent, and similarly imprudent. Unable to fashion
himself as both auditory and actors did, unable to indulge a love of
finery, or even to understand it, unable in a consciously histrionic
society to play more than one part, Coriolanus is destroyed. More
accurately, like Narcissus whom he resembles in self-love, Coriolanus
destroys himself.[4]

I draw several conclusions from this. *Coriolanus* on the stage in 1609
affronts the audience on whom its popularity depends. But a closer look
suggests a deeper sympathy with an auditory that expected to be known
by their clothes. In addition to wearing a Roman kirtle, Coriolanus it
would appear has a beard and wears a hat. This makes him not only a
Roman but an Elizabethan Roman, one for whom the ability to act a
part with the props at hand was as important as being able to sway a mob.

My concern in this essay has been with what the audience saw in

1609, if the play did have an audience in that year. And I have confined my attention to the ways in which a deep and abiding concern with dress might be thought to tell us something about the contemporary reception of the play. But dress as we see it used in *Coriolanus* and in Stubbes attaches itself to a broader spectrum of values, one in which the honor and integrity of the military man can only be compromised in a society in which the values and the voices of the common man have a commanding say. Dress in this context coexists with ideas of valour, and some idea of at least one man's perception of that valour is described by Edward Grimstone, once secretary to Sir Edward Stafford, the English ambassador in Paris.

Grimstone dedicates his *Generall Historie of the Netherlands* to Robert Cecil and prefaces what he excuses as a translation with observations about the relationship between a country and its sovereign. 'The one is when as the prince seekes to haue a full subiection and obedience of the people, and the people contrariwise require, that the prince shold maintaine them in their freedoms and liberties, which he hath promised and sworn solemnly vnto them, before his reception to the principalitie' (781). He mentions Philip II in this regard, but as the history continues, it is the Earl of Leicester as governor of the Netherlands who objects to the traditionally democratic rule. Leicester complains that all instructions from the Council of Estates 'were no other in effect, then limitations of his commission. . . . In the end (to content his Excelency) the deputies of the states sayd, that hee should not bee bound to those instructions, but that they were made for the Councell of Estate, and that his Excelency was not to bee bound to conclude, any matter of importance by plurality of voices.' Grimstone reports that 'To this resolution the Estates were hardly to bee drawne, as well foreseeing, that hee not beeing tide to any instructions might easily bee seduced by bad Counsell' (911).

Coriolanus too refuses to be bound by voices, and to give public acknowledgement to the estates on whom his office depends. Like Essex who followed in the footsteps of Leicester, he sought the sole distinction of military glory. What the histrionic inscribes as a social norm is a questioning of such traditionally noble values as givens and prescribed. The classical prototype Grimstone mentions is not the story of Coriolanus but that of Lucrece. Tarquin's banishment, he points out, brings the republic into being. We might see in the 1609 performance of *Coriolanus* at the Globe an affirmation of the social code of Quicksilver and his clothes.

Notes

1 1609 is an arbitrary date. Philip Brockbank in the Arden edition places the play's composition between 1605 and 1610. Plague occurs in each of those years. Brian Parker who is editing the play for Oxford believes it might have been performed originally at Blackfriars. The argument of this essay assumes a performance at the Globe.
2 Frank Whigham makes a similar point in his discussion of sumptuary legislation and the social attitudes toward dress. See *Ambition and Privilege: The Social Tropes of Elizabethan Courtesy Theory*, Berkeley: University of California Press, 1984, pp. 154–69.
3 See Moelwyn Merchant, 'Classical Costume in Shakespearian Productions', *Shakespeare Survey*, 10, 1957, pp. 71–6.
4 This is documented in the excellent essay by Stanley Cavell, '*Coriolanus* and Interpretations of Politics', *Themes out of School: Effects and Causes*, Chicago: University of Chicago Press, 1988, pp. 60–96.

References

Baldwin, Francis Elizabeth (1926) 'Sumptuary Legislation and Personal Regulation in England', *Johns Hopkins University Studies in Historical and Political Science*, 44, Baltimore: Johns Hopkins Press, pp. 1–282.

Dekker, Thomas (1609) *The Gvls Horne-book*, London.

Feuillerat, Albert (1908) *Documents Relating to the Office of the Revels in the Time of Queen Elizabeth*, London: David Nutt.

Letters of Philip Gawdy, ed. Isaac Herbert Jeayes (1906) London: J. B. Nichols & Sons.

Gosson, Stephen (1579) *The School of Abuse*, London.

Grimstone, Ed[ward] (1608) *A Generall Historie of the Netherlands . . . Continued vnto this present yeare . . . 1608*, London.

Gurr, Andrew (1987) *Playgoing in Shakespeare's London*, Cambridge: Cambridge University Press.

Harbage, Alfred (1961) *Shakespeare's Audience*, New York: Columbia University Press.

Henslowe's Diary, ed. R. A. Foakes and R. T. Rickert (1961) Cambridge: Cambridge University Press.

Herford, C. H. and Simpson, Percy and Evelyn (1938) *Ben Jonson*, vol. VI, Oxford: Oxford University Press.

Hunter, G. K. (1980) 'Flatcaps and Bluecoats: Visual Signals on the Elizabethan Stage', *Essays and Studies*, ed. Inga-Stina Ewbank, London: John Murray, pp. 16–47.

Shakespeare, Riverside edition (1974) Boston: Houghton Mifflin.

Smith, Bruce R. (1988) *Ancient Scripts and Modern Experience on the English Stage 1500–1700*, Princeton: Princeton University Press.

Stubbes, Philip (1595) *Anatomie of Abuses*, London.

Taylor, John (1868) *Works Reprinted from the Folio Edition of 1630; Part II*, printed for the Spenser Society.

Joel B. Altman

"PROPHETIC FURY": *OTHELLO* AND THE ECONOMY OF
SHAKESPEAREAN RECEPTION

"For that which we reveal is logos, but logos is not substances and existing
things. Therefore we do not reveal existing things to our neighbors, but logos,
which is something other than substances."
   —Gorgias, *On Nature*[1]

"Words, words, mere words, no matter from the heart"
   —*Troilus and Cressida*, 5.3.108[2]

I want to begin with a postulate that may seem self-evident. Underlying the
various kinds of theatrical language we have distinguished in Shakespeare's texts—
languages of gesture, of place and time, of voice and body, of metatheatrics and
extratheatrics (contemporary allusion)—there is an ur-language that we might
call the language of theatrical potentiality. This language is potential insofar as it
is incomplete in itself and must coalesce with labile thought- and feeling-struc-
tures in an auditor's mind in order for it to produce the powerful, temporary
satisfactions that we call meaning.[3] In the theatrical experience of Shakespeare's
audience, it was this tendentious, interactive process that gave shape to a dramatic action that might, if scanned analytically, actually resist intelligibility.[4]

Such a claim may seem conventional at best and not worth pursuing. After all,
Renaissance thinkers, heirs to a cognitive and psychological tradition traceable to
Aristotle, knew as well as we do that the mind works upon that which lies outside
it and transforms external stimuli into ideas upon which it can act. An equally
venerable rhetorical tradition depended upon this assumption.[5] Still, this language of theatrical potentiality is worth our inquiry, for Shakespeare seems to
have deliberately engaged its capacities in his scripts and problematized it for his
audiences. By this I mean that he exploited the psychagogic force of the enacted
word—its power of marshaling the intellectual and emotional energies that produce belief—but he also deconstructed both word and belief and thematized that
deconstruction. Thus he made the factitiousness of such language a principle of
the composition and a condition of the reception of his plays. In theory, any truly
historical account of Shakespearean reception must take as its starting point this
language of theatrical potentiality, an irreducibly occasional language constituted
at the intersection of speaking and hearing, acting and seeing, during every moment of performance in Shakespeare's theater.

I say "in theory," acknowledging the impossibility of actually reconstructing
the reception of dramatic enunciations. The futility of such an enterprise is understood as we go about the task of second-level historicizing—conjecturally su-

183

turing contemporaneous events, explicit social and political concerns, and inferred cultural strategies to the words that are their only remaining traces. But if full historical retrieval is beyond our means, it is possible to light up the historical grounding of Shakespearean language by pointing to its factitious nature as this is disclosed upon emergent occasions. We will then be in a better position to appreciate the significance of the epideictic ironies that so frequently resonate from Shakespeare's texts—ironies that remind us not simply that we are watching a play or that "all the world's a stage," but that the world represented on the stage is contiguous in its communicative and cognitive processes with the world of audience and actors present in the theater. We might hear better the linguistic hermeticism in Lear's "Which of you shall we say doth love us most?"; the histrionic claustrophobia of Macbeth's "poor player, / That struts and frets his hour upon the stage, / And then is heard no more"; and the poignant expression of lost referentiality when Troilus exclaims "Words, words, mere words" and rejects the final linguistic performance of Cressida, whose life has been a series of improvisations upon circumstances, as being false because performed. Troilus, one might say, longs to capture an essence whose unavailability is made most apparent by the theatrical medium in which he exists. The caution of the sophist Gorgias, quoted above, may stand as a corrective to this longing—and as an epigraph to Shakespeare's own awareness that what he conveys in the theater to his audience is precisely what the people in his imitated world onstage—and, a fortiori, in his offstage audience—convey to one another: words not substances.

In these pages, I want to explore the essentialist impulses urged into action by the inessential medium of theater and the way Shakespeare exploits these impulses in audiences both real and imitated. Correlatively, I shall suggest that he recognized that dramatic performance and reception provided the exemplary model of the communicative factitiousness that governs lives outside the theater. His interest in these phenomena is widely evident, increasingly so in the major tragedies and the tragicomedies, and most instructively in *Othello*, to which I will devote the larger portion of this essay.[6]

I. "What was done to Elbow's wife?"

I shall begin by pointing out some examples of the language of theatrical potentiality at work. One that comes readily to mind is the colloquy in *Richard II* that follows immediately upon Richard's departure for Ireland—a passage of some seventy-five lines in which Northumberland, Ross, and Willoughby discuss first the commons' grievances against the king, then his latest injury to the banished Duke of Hereford (accomplished only moments before), and finally Hereford's imminent arrival in England to redress these wrongs (2.1.224–300). The impossible conjunction of these events—expounded consecutively by the trio—has inspired speculation about Bolingbroke's character and motive, and has especially cast doubt upon his claim to have returned "But for his own," as Northumberland tells York (2.3.148–9). Indeed, from the perspective afforded by subsequent events, Bolingbroke's unauthorized landing at Ravenspurgh appears to have been planned prior to Richard's seizure of his inheritance, which act was then appropriated retroactively as the justification for invasion. But this construction is made possible—even probable—by Shakespeare's releasing into the air at a crucial moment in the action certain fragments of speech joined together by their synchronic function as dialogue yet sundered by the diachronic nature of the news being imparted. The chorus thus provides crazed information that contains, depending upon how we piece together its intelligence, various meaning-possibilities. An audience's disagreement over the actualization of these meaning-possibilities is bound to follow as a structural necessity. By inserting such linguistic material at this time, Shakespeare has artificially induced the kind of skepticism we entertain in actual life regarding almost any action we hear about, for we often acquire our information piecemeal and are not in a position to calculate the temporal relationship of the information to the event. This gives rise to just such questions as gather about Bolingbroke's premature return to England and acquisition of the crown: was it propter-hoc or merely post-hoc? Does post-hoc have a way of turning into propter-hoc in the natural course of events? Or does propter-hoc, in the course of events, turn into something else entirely, something anticipated by neither the agent nor his supporters, as is claimed on different occasions by both Henry IV and the Percies during reflective, explanatory moments in the two subsequent plays of the Henriad?[7] Given their origin in the language of the choral trio, these questions suggest that it is part of Shakespeare's craft precisely to solicit the meaning-making faculties of his audience by simulating the incomplete and anachronistic evidentiary offerings present in actual life, thereby leading that audience inevitably into controversy about the meaning of his dramatized action.

A somewhat different issue is opened by Shylock's revenge. Here we are not offered information on what has passed, what is happening now, and what is anticipated by the allies of an exile. Instead, we witness the behavior of the exile himself—an internal exile, in this instance—as we meet Shylock expressing his hatred for Antonio. It seems he hates him because he is a Christian; moreso, because he brings down the usury rate in Venice. We hear, too, his desire to catch Antonio "once upon the hip" to "feed fat the ancient grudge I bear him" (1.3.74–7). But we also notice more ambiguous gestures: the sharing of an ancient family story ("When Jacob graz'd his uncle Laban's sheep"); an attempt to make Antonio aware of the human dimension of the financial transaction he seeks ("it now appears you need my help"); a self-demeaning protestation ("I would be friends with you. . . . This is kind I offer") (1.3.71–90, 114, 142). These contradictory strands may represent tactical variations upon a fixed ground of antipathy or a series of communicative openings enabled by Shylock's perception of Antonio's sudden vulnerability. It is hard to say. But they all lead to the merry bond that concludes the scene and that turns out to be the trap in which Shylock himself is caught. Although the dark, comic release of the action depends upon an audience feeling that the purpose of the plotter has been defeated by one who can outwit him at his own device ("This bond doth give thee here no jot of blood" [4.1.306]), that very darkness may make us wonder if the merry bond was undertaken purposefully to feed fat Shylock's ancient grudge. That is, does it represent Shylock's intention to kill Antonio? Or is it rather a receptacle for the aggregate of meaning-possibilities issuing from Shylock's ambiguous representation of himself—an outrageous improvisation whose outcome cannot be foreseen distinctly—by Shylock, Shakespeare's audience, or perhaps, in its particularity, even by Shakespeare? To put it another way, Shakespeare allows Shylock's mixed signals to pose the problem of how individuals (dramatic characters and real persons) behave in a future-oriented way without deliberately planning to perform a specific act and how that originating promise, which is void of intention in the usual sense, holds the possibility of doing the things such persons do. There is something sporting in this merry bond because it is a verbal bundle whose meanings, not yet unpacked, can only be realized in the future circumstances that elicit them.[8]

A more radical example of the language of theatrical potentiality will introduce its workings in *Othello*. In this instance Shakespeare does not demand that his audience configure data to establish evidence of motive and character or ponder the contingent relations of pact and act; rather, he allows it to believe in an event that never takes place. I refer to Iago's promise that he will devise a means to bring Cassio within range of Roderigo's revenge at a specified hour:

> He sups tonight with a harlot, and thither will I go to him; . . . he knows not yet of his honourable fortune: if you will watch his going thence, which I will fashion to fall out between twelve and one, you may take him at your pleasure. (4.2.232–7)[9]

Now Iago knows Cassio will be at Bianca's because he overheard her invite him there after she testily returned the handkerchief he had asked her to copy. He himself had urged Cassio to make up to her: "After her, after her" (4.1.158). When Cassio then tells him he plans to dine with Bianca, Iago plainly says, "Well, I may chance to see you, for I would very fain speak with you"—to which Cassio replies, "Prithee come, will you?" (4.1.162–4), and Iago assures him he will. Within a few lines Shakespeare creates the impression that Iago will be on hand when Cassio sups with Bianca. Iago's subsequent promise to Rodigero confirms this impression, and further suggests that he will actually be present at the supper and in a position to make sure that Cassio leaves Bianca at the right time to walk into Roderigo's ambush. But of course this doesn't happen. Cassio leaves Bianca's house when he is supposed to, but not because Iago was there to usher him out. When Iago seizes Bianca as a suspect in the attack upon Cassio and tells Emilia to find out where Cassio had taken supper, he observes Bianca shaking and extracts from her the confession that Cassio had supped at her house. There is no suggestion in this exchange that Bianca recognizes Iago as Cassio's supper companion. He simply wasn't there. Rather it was his expressed intention that enabled him to place Cassio in the right place at the right time so that Roderigo could stab him. That is, a piece of speech has taken on agency and made the assassination attempt possible, for that is all the audience needed to understand how a certain action could come about.

Shakespeare parodies this propensity to substitute the word for the action in Elbow's comical arraignment of Pompey and Froth before Angelo and Escalus in Act II of *Measure for Measure*. Doing his best to bring "two notorious benefactors" to justice, Elbow characterizes Pompey as a "parcel-bawd" and Mistress Overdone's bathhouse as a "naughty house," and darkly hints of a lewd overture made to his wife in that place by Froth. Pompey denies any impropriety, takes over the narrative from Elbow, and proceeds to pack it with a mass of detail about Mistress Elbow's pregnancy, her longing for prunes, Froth's consumption of and payment for all but two of the prunes, his preference for the room called "the Bunch of Grapes," their gossip about a venereal acquaintance, the death of Froth's father, and so forth—until the action that his narrative had presumed to relate literally disappears in a welter of circumstantial description. As a result, the answer to Escalus's repeated question, "What was done to Elbow's wife?" (2.1.116, 139, 146) is indefinitely postponed. Pompey concludes his defense by presenting Froth's face as proof of his innocence, and the irate Constable corroborates his charge by rehearsing his circumstances: "the house is a respected house; next, this is a respected fellow; and his mistress is a respected woman" (2.1.162–64). The alleged misdeed having been lost in these verbal ambages, Escalus's only possible judgment is to offer some prudent advice: "Truly, officer, because he hath some offenses in him that thou wouldst discover if thou couldst, let him continue in his courses till thou know'st what they are" (2.1.185–88).

Now it is not at all clear from the language of this scene that anything was done to Elbow's wife. All we know is that this "respected person" was in Mistress Overdone's house and that she encountered Froth and Pompey. It is all Elbow himself seems to know, though he transforms the facts of place and person into evidence of wrongdoing, just as Pompey employs Froth's face as evidence of harmlessness. What is Shakespeare up to here? Clearly he is dramatizing, in an absurd register, the problematic of inference that concerns him from the Duke's opening charge to Angelo—"There is a kind of character in thy life / That to th'observer doth thy history / Fully unfold" (1.1.27); but written into that remark and, even more pointedly, into Escalus's bemused audition of Elbow's and Pompey's testimonies, is a directive that calls attention to precisely the task imposed upon the audience—of constructing the fact and quality of events and persons from words and images. In this instance, Shakespeare makes us feel that within the vivid presence of these spoken words there lies a hollow space in which meaning is being formed by fumbling desire; something must have happened, but what it is, of what nature and what name, is yet to be determined. The strange impression that testimony is antecedent to event is strengthened by Escalus's final advice, which is taken by Elbow as tantamount to a conviction. "Thou art to continue," he triumphantly tells Pompey, as if the tapster's subsequent action will surely reveal the answer to Escalus's reiterated question.

I have been suggesting in these examples that Shakespeare is often a dramatist of shreds and patches, providing for his audience disparate strands of verbal and visual material that must be woven by them into an intelligible fabric. This process is not only internal to his dramaturgy but is often the object of his dramatic representation. It actualizes an epistemology and an ontology that can only be described as theatrical: what you see and what you hear are nothing but images and words. Their meaning is to be found in the soul of the auditor: there lies the substance. He seems to have known, both objectively and intuitively, that fragmentary, promissory, and even contradictory utterances are the raw materials of collaborating minds, which shape them into intelligible and coherent accounts of observed actions that are not always in agreement with one another—*tot homines, quot sententiae*—but are always derived from that combination of idiosyncratic and communal appropriation of exteriority that constitutes individual experience. And he knew this, I shall further suggest, not only from his observation of how theater works but also from his own practice of composition, which depended upon a theater of the mind in which meanings came together in often unexpected ways.

II. Sibylline Leaves

One of the most haunting sentences in the Shakespeare canon is the one Othello utters when describing the lost handkerchief: "there's magic in the web of it" (3.4.67). From the first inklings of *Othello* criticism this small handkerchief, with which Desdemona attempts to cure Othello's headache by binding his brow, has been felt to carry a significance beyond its function as plot device, even one so emotionally invested. "So much ado, so much stress, so much passion and repetition about an Handkerchief!" wrote Thomas Rymer, the seventeenth-century critic. "Why was not this call'd the Tragedy of the Handkerchief? What can be more absurd than (as *Quintilian* expresses it) *in parvis litibus has Tragoedias movere?*" (Rymer 160).

Rymer is answered proleptically, of course, by Othello himself, when he describes the history of the handkerchief to Desdemona:

A sibyl, that had number'd in the world
The sun to make two hundred compasses,
In her prophetic fury sew'd the work;
The worms were hallow'd that did breed the silk,

188

And it was dyed in mummy, which the skilful
Conserve of maidens' hearts. (3.4.68–73)

The handkerchief possesses not only a sacred origin but also an intimate human genealogy. It was given Othello's mother by an Egyptian charmer, who "could almost read / The thoughts of people" and told her that it would subdue Othello's father entirely to her love while she kept it but if she lost it, "my father's eye / Should hold her loathly." Dying, Othello's mother gave it to him and he, on marrying, passed the talisman to Desdemona: "Make it a darling, like your precious eye, / To lose, or give't away, were such perdition / As nothing else could match" (3.4.64–66).

So much for Rymer's complaint. In a sense he could not appreciate, Othello is indeed the Tragedy of the Handkerchief.[10] But why? Whence this mantic handkerchief and its extraordinary history and power? In Cinthio, Shakespeare's primary source, we find only that "il qual pannicello era lavorato alla moresca sottilissimamente, & era carissimo alla Donna & parimente al Moro" (this handkerchief was made ever so subtly in the Moorish fashion and was most dear to the lady and equally to the Moor).[11] The Moor frequently asked to see it, Cinthio implies, because it was his wedding gift to his wife. The handkerchief is a memento not to be idly given away, but hardly the charismatic token of Othello's imagining. From the phrase "prophetic fury," however, we learn that Shakespeare may have conflated Cinthio's little handkerchief "alla moresca" with a much larger fabrication, the extraordinary pavilion provided by the magician Melissa for the nuptial celebration of Ruggiero and Bradamante in Ariosto's *Orlando Furioso* (Muir 183; Smart 183, n. 1). This elaborate tent was sewn by none other than Homer's Cassandra, who presented it as a gift of her own hand to her brother Hector:

Una donzella de la terra d'Ilia
ch'avea il furor profetico congiunto,
con studio di gran tempo e con vigilia
lo fece di sua man di tutto punto. (XLVI, 80, 2–5)

[A damsel of the city of Ilium, in whom prophetic fury was joined with toil long practised and with sleepless nights, made every whit of it with her own hand.][12]

Although not the work of a seamstress who had counted "two hundred compasses" of the sun, this tent had been embroidered nearly two thousand years ago (*anni appresso . . . duo milia*), and was taken from Hector at his death by Menelaus who carried it to Egypt in his train, where he traded the pavilion to the Egyptian king Proteus in exchange for Helen, whence it passed down through the Ptolemies

189

to Cleopatra, who lost it to the Romans at the Battle of Actium.[13] The later history of the pavilion does not concern us; what should be noted is that it serves as the "maritale albergo" (nuptial chamber) of Ruggiero and Bradamante, in the midst of which "il genial letto fecondo" (the fertile genitive bed) is placed on the wedding night, and that an epic tradition carried it to Egypt where it remained long domiciled before it returned to circulation in the West. Now, if it is at all important that Shakespeare borrowed a phrase from Ariosto (nothing like it appears in Harington's translation), that importance lies in the imaginative process such borrowing suggests. Two different textual fragments came together momentarily in Shakespeare's mind and spoke to one another: Cinthio's little handkerchief appeared to him the vehicle for the tenor of Ariosto's pavilion, which underwent in his imagination a metonymic transformation from primal scene to fetishistic object. The "pannicello . . . lavorato alla moresca" was impregnated, as it were, by the "genial letto fecondo" and emerged from the obscure encounter as the handkerchief "spotted with strawberries" that denotes a foregone conclusion.[14]

Lest this sound utterly fanciful, it should be observed that the handkerchief is not even mentioned in the play until after Othello and Desdemona have consummated their marriage, if we may infer that act from Othello's words at 2.3.8–10 ("The profit's yet to come 'twixt me and you") and from Iago's voyeuristic account at 2.3.171–5 of the brawl between Cassio and Montano that roused the lovers from their bed ("In quarter, and in terms, like bride and groom . . . In opposition bloody"), a simile extended by Othello himself when he addresses Montano at 2.3.186–7 ("That you unlace your reputation thus, / And spend your rich opinion"). It follows that if Shakespeare has introduced the handkerchief post-coitally, as it were, at 3.3.290, revealed its spots at 3.3.442, and explicitly identified the conjunction of two texts at 3.4.70—then his own practice of composition adumbrates the meaning-making activity of his audience. That is to say, he and they fabricate significances as their play of interests construe them, and then explain their readings post-hoc. This suggests that meaning, though it appears to coalesce presently before the mind's eye, has a retroactive dimension. It exists potentially before it is fashioned and is acknowledged only after that fashioning has occurred.[15]

This cognitive process is represented in the action of the play itself. Desdemona loses the handkerchief by accident as the result of a loving act. "Your napkin is too little," Othello tells her, as he pushes it from his brow, and at his injunction it remains on the ground as they depart for dinner. It is at this moment that the handkerchief's "deep history" begins, for Emilia finds it and informs the audience that Iago has "a hundred times / Woo'd me to steal it," adding that Desdemona not only has sworn to keep it but indeed treats it as a fetish, kissing and talking to it as though re-enacting her lovemaking with Othello. In Cinthio, of course, the handkerchief is lost not by accident but as the result of the ensign's calculated theft: it is literally his "plot device." Shakespeare, who is more interested in the way future-oriented behavior void of intention and plot issues in particular acts, supplies Iago's desire for revenge with its instrument retroactively. When Emilia offers it to him, its existence seems to come as a complete surprise:

> *Emil.* What will you give me now,
> For that same handkerchief?
> *Iago.* What handkerchief?
> *Emil.* What handkerchief?
> Why, that the Moor first gave to Desdemona,
> That which so often you did bid me steal. (3.3.309–13)

Useful news indeed. Once persuaded that Emilia has the long-sought handkerchief that only a moment ago he couldn't recall, Iago assimilates it to his latent design:

> I will in Cassio's lodging lose this napkin,
> And let him find it: trifles light as air
> Are to the jealous, confirmations strong
> As proofs of holy writ; this may do something. (3.3.326–29)

The handkerchief, that is to say, is released as a datum that retroactively becomes the object of Iago's intention, just as he will "lose" it in Cassio's lodging so that it may "do something." This is part of a repeated gesture in the play whereby inchoate "tendencies" are expressed (2.1.304: "'tis here, but yet confused"), particular things noted before their relevance is recognized (1.3.390: "Cassio's a proper man, let me see now"), and then hazarded in the expectation that they will be found to signify. This is most explicitly thematized as first Emilia, then Cassio, expresses the desire to "ha' the work ta'en out" of the handkerchief (3.3.300, 3.4.198, 4.1.148–150). If there is a design in these actions, it is to undesign—to provide supplies for recirculation and recontextualization in which a new meaning may be found. Emilia puts it well when she describes the indeterminacy of her passing the handkerchief to Iago. "Heaven knows, not I," she says, "I nothing know, but for his fantasy" (3.3.303). She surrenders a known meaning for a design-to-be, and in so doing rehearses the continuous reconfiguration of meaning that is the work of both characters and audience.[16]

We must now seek the figure who underlies this impulse to deconstruct and retexture. Cassandra may have been a prophetess, but how did she become a sibyl? Behind the wedding pavilion of Ruggiero and Bradamante stands the wondrous tent of Brandimarte in Boiardo's *Orlando Innamorato*, which he is carrying on his ship when he encounters a tempest and is forced to debark on the coast of North Africa near the site of ancient Carthage with his wife Fiordelisa. This tent, too, is prophetic, in that it reveals the heroic deeds of the twelve Alphonsos of Aragon and Castile:

> Una Sibilla, come aggio sentito,
> Gia stette a Cuma, al mar napolitano,
> E questa aveva il pavaglione ordito
> E tutto lavorato di sua mano.
> Poi fo portato in strane regione,
> E venne al fine in man de Dolistone. (II, xxvii, 51, 3–6)

> [I understand a Sibyl in
> Cumae, upon the Bay of Naples,
> Had fabricated it by hand—
> She had embroidered it herself—
> Then it was brought to foreign lands.
> King Dolistone owned it last.] (Boiardo 705)

Ariosto's *padiglione* is an imitation of Boiardo's *pavaglione*, and it would be exciting to discover that this imitation was duly noted in the elaborate 1584 edition of the *Furioso* published by Francesco dei Francesci in Venice and consulted by Harington, for then we would seem to have caught Shakespeare at his standish, assimilating the stitchery of the ancient prophetess to that of Hector's mad sister, whose work had already been woven into Cinthio's handkerchief. I can offer no such evidence. But even if we knew that Shakespeare was conflating Cinthio and Ariosto, then checking both against Boiardo, that fact would not explain what imaginative imperative determined this singular handkerchief to be the handiwork of a sibyl. By a more obvious logic Cassandra, lovelorn and without credit, would appear to be the more suitable seamstress of the gift destined for Desdemona. There are indications, however, that Shakespeare was already thinking of the Cumaean sibyl before composing the scene in which Cinthio's handkerchief assumes the symbolism and history of Ariosto's pavilion. From the moment of their entrance in Act III, Scene iii, Othello and Iago are shown together engaged in close dialogue, Iago's every remark attracting Othello's sharp attention:

> *Iago.* Ha, I like not that.
> *Oth.* What dost thou say?
> *Iago.* Nothing, my lord, or if—I know not what.
> *Oth.* Was not that Cassio parted from my wife? (3.3.35–38)

We usually read this as Shakespeare's rendering of an informal conversation. It is possible, however, that what we are seeing and hearing is not conversation at all but rather an attentive, dialectical consultation, begun in the unseen, unheard time between Scenes ii and iii, when Iago meets Othello on the "works" (3.2.1–4). For the silent referent of Iago's "that" is picked up instantly by Othello, and Iago's reply, "Cassio, my lord?"—which echoes and emphasizes Othello's word—releases a signifier that becomes associated, by negation, with the idea of subterfuge and crime ("I cannot think it, / That he would sneak away so guilty like"), and thus demands a new resolution (3.2.39–40).

In this instance it is Desdemona who finds a home for the signifier by echoing once more Cassio's name and confirming that it was indeed he who "went . . . hence now." Together with "I like not that" and "sneak away so guilty like," the name so lodges in Othello's troubled spirit that he will not engage the issue of appointing a time for Cassio's recall as Desdemona urges, but recasts his refusal as an index of his devotion to her: "I will deny thee nothing" (3.3.77, 84). Immediately Iago arrests the words just released by Desdemona: "Did Michael Cassio, when you woo'd my lady, / Know of your love?" (3.2.95–96). He wants this information, he says, "But for a satisfaction of my thought," as though he were absorbing intelligence in order to bring an idea to fullness. This initiates the series of verbal echoes (Indeed/Indeed, Honest/Honest, Think/Think) that Othello hears as reverberations upon doors barring him from the contents of Iago's mind ("As if there were some monster in his thought, / Too hideous to be shown"), and as he rehearses the exchange just completed he imagines Iago's thoughts as mental hoardings ("And didst contract and purse thy brow together, / As if thou hadst shut up in thy brain / Some horrible conceit")—Iago's brain having become a room or treasury that must be laid open. "Show me thy thought," he demands (3.2.111–12, 118–19, 120).

The direction of my argument may be growing apparent. Iago is functioning in this scene as a desacralized sibyl, the sibyl-cum-ensign who distributes ambiguous words and signs from an evacuated interior that only appears to be full of knowledge. But in doing so he actually imitates Virgil's sibyl, that fearsome prophetess whose cryptic, disordered words the inspired Helenus warns Aeneas to circumvent:

huc ibi delatus Cumaeam accesseris urbem
divinosque lacus et Averna sonantia silvis,
insanam vatem aspicies, quae rupe sub ima
fata canit foliisque notas et nomina mandat.
Quaecumque in foliis descripsit carmina virgo,
digerit in numerum atque antro seclusa relinquit.
illa manent immota locis neque ab ordine cedunt;
verum eadem, verso tenuis cum cardine ventus
impulit et teneras turbavit ianua frondes,
numquam deinde cavo volitantia prendere saxo

193

ne revocare situs aut iungere carmina curat;
inconsulti abeunt sedemque odere Sibyllae. (III.441–52)

[And when, thither borne, thou drawest near to the town of Cumae, the haunted lakes, and Avernus with its rustling woods, thou shalt look on an inspired prophetess, who deep in a rocky cave sings the Fates and entrusts to leaves signs and symbols. Whatever verses the maid has traced on leaves she arranges in order and stores away in the cave. These remain unmoved in their places and quit not their rank; but when at the turn of the hinge a light breeze has stirred them, and the open door scattered the tender foliage, never does she thereafter care to catch them, as they flutter in the rocky cave, nor to recover their places, nor to unite the verses; uncounselled, men depart, and loathe the Sibyl's seat.] (Virgil 1.376–79)

A modern authority on the Cumaean sibyl, H. W. Parke, writes:

the general picture of the Sibyl's procedure is that her responses were frustrating and difficult to grasp. Even the Vergilian picture of her voice booming out of a hundred mouths from an inner cavern certainly suggested to ancient commentators that different words came out of different openings and were hard to combine. Similarly, but much worse, the fluttering leaves each carrying a separate word baffled the enquirer. All this was part of the popular notion that the Sibylline prophetess's utterances were teasing and evasive. (Parke 83)

As if attempting to avoid the odium the sibyl incurs as a result of the incoherent intelligence fluttering from her cave, Iago issues a disclaimer for his "close denotements, working from the heart, / That passion cannot rule":

I entreat you then,
From one that so imperfectly conjects,
You'ld take no notice, nor build yourself a trouble
Out of my scattering and unsure observance;
It were not for your quiet, nor your good,
Nor for my manhood, honesty, or wisdom,
To let you know my thoughts. (3.3.148–58)

Othello's response is instantaneous. "Zounds!" he exclaims and, rather than be placated, he again insists, "By heaven, I'll know thy thought!" In this dialectic of scattered inferences and demands for direct disclosure, Shakespeare seems to be recasting the scene of anticipated obscurity and hard-won revelation described in Virgil. For, knowing the sibyl's disinclination to reunite her disordered verses,

Helenus warns Aeneas not to be satisfied with the prophetess's fluttering leaves but to "plead that she herself chant the oracles, and graciously open her lips in speech." Aeneas does precisely this when he meets the sibyl:

> "foliis tantum ne carmina manda,
> ne turbata volent rapidis ludibria ventis;
> ipsa canas oro." (6.74–7)

> ["Only trust not thy verses to leaves, lest they fly in disorder, the sport of rushing winds; chant them thyself, I pray."] (Virgil 1.511)

Shakespeare's scene is different, of course, since Iago is not a divine prophet and resists Othello's vow to know his thought: "You cannot, if my heart were in your hand, / Nor shall not whilst 'tis in my custody" (3.3.165–67). But Othello seems to have caught the Virgilian note even as he rejects Iago's cryptic warning against jealousy:

> . . . exchange me for a goat
> When I shall turn the business of my soul
> To such exsufflicate and blown surmises
> Matching thy inference . . . . (3.3.184–87)

The Arden and New Cambridge editors observe that "exsufflicate" is a nonce-word and assimilate it to "blown"; for Ridley, it suggests "fly-blown," for Sanders "rumored." In the context of sibylline leaves, however, the doublet has a far more literal meaning: Iago's surmises are "blown forth" and, for the moment, at least, Othello rejects such disconnected inferences as insufficient grounds for jealousy.

Whither has this light breeze stirred us? It would appear that yet another literary element has been mingled with Cinthio's original. As long ago as 1694, Charles Gildon perceived a likeness between Aeneas's tale to Dido and Othello's to Desdemona, and other critics have from time to time concurred; it should come as no surprise, then, that Shakespeare's "extravagant and wheeling stranger" should owe something to the *perfidus* ("faithless pirate"), the *externus* ("stranger") (7.362, 424) whom Lavinia's mother tries to keep from marrying her daughter.[17] What concerns us, though, is less the discovery of another model than what is implied by its presence in Shakespeare's play. This Virgilian reminiscence suggests several related hypotheses: that in the sibyl Shakespeare found a figure for the source of wisdom his hero seeks; that in Othello's world, this figure has been emptied of wisdom and only "imperfectly conjects"; that the fluttering sibylline leaves, with their cryptic signs and symbols, represent the crazed information from which the inhabitants of this world must infer meaning; that in so adapting Virgil Shakespeare was registering his own practice of composing disparate pieces of language; that his composition adumbrated his audience's reception. If this reticulation of ideas is plausible, then it holds important thematic consequences for the play that bear a relation to the magic in the web with which we began our inquiry. That magic is there, Othello tells Desdemona, because the sibyl put it there in her prophetic fury when she sewed the work of silk bred from hallowed worms and dyed in maiden mummy. In thus explaining the significance of the handkerchief, he is insisting upon a pristine wisdom with transhistorical powers in a play whose internal and external filiations all indicate that only historical, ingenious inferences are available. This is what makes Othello the hero so vulnerable and, correlatively, what gives the play its distinct feeling of nostalgia.[18]

III. "Pageant[s] to keep us in false gaze"

Othello is a tragedy both of lost origins and of compensatory substitutions. Lost origins because there is no pristine wisdom to be had, but only historically constituted experience, desire, and anxiety. Compensatory substitutions because stable origins are wanted and must be fabricated. This accounts for that "hunger for narrative" recent critics have detected in the play.[19] The sibyl without a secret casts her shadow many times in the action, through narratives that appear to have deep histories but are actually psychagogic instruments enabling present acts. Hence their historic resonances function like perspectives in Renaissance paintings, where figures represented on flat surfaces appear to recede in space toward hypothetical vanishing points.[20] In *Othello*, time is the illusory dimension, and the beginning of an action the putative point of origin. The primal history, as we have seen, is that of the handkerchief, transmuted for the occasion from marriage token to object of sacred manufacture. But there are three other occasions on which Othello seems to reach into time past to satisfy present needs.

The first occurs when he defends his right to marry Desdemona:

> 'tis yet to know—
> Which when I know that boasting is an honour,
> I shall provulgate—I fetch my life and being
> From men of royal siege . . . . (1.2.19–22)

This is a claim that is forever yet to know—literally a piece of speech presented as evidence of Othello's social acceptability. By means of this verbal matter the hero "thickens other proofs," to adapt Iago's words, "That do demonstrate thinly" (3.3.436–47). He shows cause to himself for confidence in his own merit and to his audiences to build their confidence in him. Indeed, the lines serve the same rhetorical function for both character and audience, for they are never verified and have no more authority than Iago's "scattering and unsure observances," which, we may remember, ought not be used to "build yourself a trouble." They, too, are "pageant[s] to keep us in false gaze," creating the illusion of authenticity. They have no depth.[21]

The second instance of Othello's reach into history is the "round, unvarnished tale" he tells the Senators in Act I, Scene iii, when, by means of indirect speech, he retells the tale told first to Brabantio and then to Desdemona. This thrice-told tale clearly has multiple origins, its matter encompassing not only the heroic events in Othello's life but the rhetorical occasions on which he recounted them. That it is capable of profoundly affecting audiences is attested by its reception in the play itself and by the subsequent reception history of *Othello*. Its structure, however (I refer specifically to the version given the Senators), is much like the grammatical deferral of Iago's "I dare presume, I think that he is honest" (3.3.129), where the ontological "is" lies weakened behind the destabilizing forces of "dare," "presume," and "think." Which is to say that the origins and being of Othello's history lie not in the events described but in its performative moments, as Othello himself suggests when he says, "I ran it through, even from my boyish days, / To the very moment that he bade me tell it" (1.3.132–33). In each of those moments Othello's life is reborn as verbal matter that is subject to further regeneration.

Its materiality is felt as Othello recalls how Desdemona would "with a greedy ear / Devour up my discourse," a hunger that is linked to the cognitive temptation of the fluttering sibylline leaves. For Othello adds that he drew Desdemona, who had been only an intermittent listener to his tale, to ask

That I would all my pilgrimage dilate,
Whereof by parcel she had something heard,
But not intentively . . . . (1.3.153–55)[22]

"Intentively," usually glossed as a synonym for "attentively," is cognate with "intention" and "intending," and refers not only to Desdemona but also to the "tendency" of these pieces of sibylline speech—the trajectory whereby they are shaped into meaning by Othello—of which Desdemona pleads ignorance. In Othello's mind, it seems, these bits of speech have already assumed a shape, for he describes the events he represented to Desdemona as elements in a pilgrimage—his word, chosen now—for such a shape is not likely to have been discerned by one hearing "not intentively." As elsewhere in the play, meaning is shown to be retroactive, fashioned in the telling. Othello's life acquires a teleology as he recapitulates it, first to Brabantio, then to Desdemona, and finally to the Council. We don't know its initial ending, but we do know its second and third. From Desdemona he learns that it was "wondrous pitiful," the adjectives applied

197

to the experience of a tragic hero; before the Council, the random incidents of an adventurous life—disastrous chances, moving accidents, hairbreadth escapes, captivity, slavery, and redemption—are shaped as a pilgrimage to a saint's shrine.[23]

The third instance of apparent historical research by Othello is heard at the end of his final speech. Again he fashions himself in narrative, but this time the performative origin of that self is explicit. He directs Lodovico to "relate . . . these unlucky deeds" in such a way that the acts constituting them are enunciated in a series of character references:

> then must you speak
> Of one that loved not wisely, but too well:
> Of one not easily jealous . . .
> of one whose hand . . .
> of one whose subdued eyes . . . (5.2.345ff)

As always, Othello is addressing multiple audiences here. For himself, he reconstructs the "he that was Othello" whom he has lost (5.2.285). For his stage and theater audiences he attempts to explain the quality of his actions by reference to a third person against whom these audiences might bear no animus. To all audiences he is presenting evidentiary fragments of a moral nature that are then "collected" in an apparent afterthought— "And say besides, that in Aleppo once"— that is offered as a confirmation of the predicated character references. Did he ever kill a turban'd Turk? We don't know. What is important about this "remembrance" of an allegedly historical act is that the inference to be drawn from the spoken character references is not only rehearsed in a narrative that Lodovico is asked to repeat—it is actually performed; performed, that is, in the dramatic present where the inference most urgently needs to be believed. This is the salient moment when the apparently historical, that which reaches back into time, bleeds onto the surface of the present, as if a flat canvas on which we saw the heroic encounter at Aleppo in the middle distance were suddenly to ooze from that spot. But is it blood or paint that flows? It is paint, made to appear blood by such presencing words as "All that's spoke is marred" (5.2.358), words which impart substance to the rhetorical gesture being performed before our eyes. What are we to make of this double displacement in which words that seemed to refer to the past are revealed to coincide with the present, as historical origin is translated into current performance and performance assumes the substance of history?

For Othello, the recitation-turned-performative enunciation re-attaches a life story to one "who was Othello," thus allowing him to regain his narrative identity and make manifest his moral credentials. For the audience onstage it produces a vertiginous threshold moment, like the one in *The Winter's Tale* when the statue comes to life. But here the response is horror. The theater audience shares that moment but must also be aware of the epideictic character of the act. That is, it

198

must be both absorbed by and admiring of the tour de force it is witnessing, for its response is shaped by an awareness that it is in a theater, and in a theater one can anticipate irruptions into illusion. Othello's is the latest version of that dizzying trick, by means of which playing kills, that Thomas Kyd had introduced to the London stage. Logos may convey logos, not substances, but the word can appear to be made flesh by abruptly traversing the distance between an apparent past and an apparent present, an apparent playing and an apparent doing. The result is to collapse any absolute distinction between representation and actuality.

IV. "Put money in thy purse"

I have been arguing thus far that *Othello* is a tragedy of lost origins and compensatory substitution, of sibylline speech detached from its mantic center and displaced onto reception, as its scattered leaves take root in the soil of an auditor's mind and there develop intellectual coherence, historical depth, and moral complexity. Now I want to address, if only briefly, the difficult issue of agency in this process. What follows, then, is a sketch—I would even call it a scattering—of some useful elements that should come into play in considering this matter.

If Shakespeare takes a certain pleasure in foregrounding the flat ontology of dramatic representation even as he exploits its power to induce in audiences the illusion of dense reality, constructed from pieces of speech mouthed before the eye and floated past the ear, is he also interested in representing the psychagogic energy that enables this to happen? We find this interest expressed, I believe, in the sibyl's continuator, the Egyptian charmer who "could almost read / The thoughts of people" (3.4.55–56). This charmer is the genius standing outside the door to the sibyl's cave. If the sibyl in her carelessness allows the *janua* to swing open and scatter her prophecies, the charmer gathers them up, tidies them, specifies them. Which is to say she persuades, smoothing rough bits and pieces into a contiguous whole. How does she do this? For a useful explanation, let us return to the sophist whose conception of speech has such an affinity to Shakespeare's theatrical practice. In his richly suggestive *Encomium of Helen*, Gorgias defends Helen of Troy by speculating that she may have betrayed her husband and country for several reasons: either she was fated to do so, or was the victim of physical violence, or was seduced by words, or was obsessed by love. He lingers longest on the third alternative, which has unsuspected filiations with the other three.

"Speech is a powerful lord," he declares, "which by means of the finest and most invisible body, effects the divinest works." He illustrates this claim by referring to the effects of tragic poetry: "Fearful shuddering and tearful pity and grievous longing come upon its hearers, and at the actions and physical sufferings of others in good fortunes and evil fortunes, through the agency of words, the soul is wont to experience a suffering of its own."[24] Gorgias touches here upon the ethical dimension of dramatic response, for an auditor experiencing the suffering of another becomes philanthropic; but it is the psychic economy by which this interpersonal circuit is completed that is of special interest to us. For the two accompaniments to lordly speech that effect its closure are *apate* (deception) and *peitho* (persuasion).

The word *apate*, Thomas Rosenmeyer explains, refers not to something objectively false—*pseudos*—but rather to two kinds of falsification involved in human communication. One is a linguistic falsification best described as incompleteness, and it may be contrasted with the divine communication characterized in the Heraclitean fragment, "The Lord of Delphi neither speaks out nor conceals, but gives a sign." There is a mysterious fullness in such communication—it is ambiguous, metaphoric, potentially contradictory—that cannot be conveyed by ordinary human speech (Rosenmeyer 230). In its second, more positive sense, *apate* refers to a "trick" imposed upon an audience by a skillful composer of discourse in order to convey a meaning of his own. This is the implication of an anecdote in Plutarch, in which Gorgias is said to have observed that tragedy produces a "deception . . . in which the deceiver is more justly esteemed than the non-deceiver, and the deceived is wiser than the undeceived."[25] Here, the worker of deception is the man who imposes his own configuration upon disparate *logoi* ["external" principles and "internal" opinions or attitudes], linking them in harmony and forging meaning out of what hitherto had only been meaning-possibilities. In Mario Untersteiner's words, the poet "must set before himself as his aim the knowledge of the right moment (*kairos*), that is, of the instant in which the intimate connection between things is realized," and through this artful reticulation "arrange the things he knows in the right place and in accordance with their significance" (Untersteiner 111). A postsocratic way of putting this is that the poet arranges speeches and actions according to the rules of decorum, calculating the conjunction of his matter, his audience's mental disposition, and the moment of performance in such a way as to enable his public to "see things his way."

This passage from Plutarch was familiar in Shakespeare's England. It supplied the text for one of the gratulatory sonnets printed in the quarto edition of Jonson's *Sejanus*, a play acted by the King's Men (among them Shakespeare) in 1603:

Thy Poeme (pardon me) is meere deceat.
   Yet such deceate, as thou that dost beguile,
   Are juster farre then they who use no wile:
And they who are deceaved by this feat,
More wise, then such who can eschewe thy cheat.
   For thou hast given each parte so just a stile,
   That Men suppose the Action now on file;
(And Men suppose, who are of best conceat.)
   Yet some there be, that are not moov'd hereby,
   And others are so quick, that they will spy
Where later Times are in some speech enweav'd;
   Those wary Simples, and these simple Elfes:

They are so dull, they cannot be deceav'd,
These so unjust, they will deceave themselves. (Jonson 7)

The writer of the poem is clearly aware of the Gorgianic themes: the poetic deceiver edifies the deceived by shaping the random thoughts of his auditor in relation to his matter and also that artful dramatic speech induces the illusion of
presence in the auditor's imagination. One is tempted to suspect that the "Philos"
who signed the piece was Jonson himself, so neatly does he adapt the fragment to
Jonson's obsessive interest in controlling his own material and to his fear that
audiences will misconstrue him. For the dull-conceited, the deception doesn't work;
for the overly quick-witted, it works too well, since representation of the past
invites expropriation by the *logoi* of the present—a phenomenon that led Jonson
before the Privy Council to answer charges of slander. He was so skillful in following Gorgias' primitive rhetoric of intersubjective collaboration that contemporaries fused material representing the Rome of Tiberius with their own latent
ideas about Jacobean London and turned informer.[26]

If *apate* (deception) is the means by which undetermined opinions acquire
significance through the imposition of *kairos* in artful speech, then *peitho* (persuasion) is the force or violence that empowers this work. Peitho has the "form of
necessity," according to Gorgias, and is wont to "impress the soul as it wishes"
(B11.12–13). It has this form, Charles Segal explains, not only because it imposes on human beings from outside but also, paradoxically, because of its volun-
tarist complexion. As it is absorbed by the psyche, it becomes the instrument of a
powerful internal impulse of organization that has its own dynamic. It works like
a fearsome spectacle that can upset the normal disposition of the soul and produce unexpected behavior:

> an external sense-datum—a visual one acting upon the *opsis* [sight] or *logos*
> [speech] having *metron* [aural figuration] upon the hearing . . . creates an
> impression upon the psyche which in turn results in a physical action. It is
> thus implied that the psyche itself responds to the physical structure of the
> word or vision with emotional impulses which, if strong enough, result in a
> total *ekplexis* [sudden yielding] and a concrete action of the unexpected,
> nonrational type. The *logos*, therefore, if properly calculated, can through its
> "impression" on the psyche lead the hearer into lines of action hitherto not
> considered or beyond or in violation of its "habituation" or "nomos." (Segal
> 107–08)

In the case of Helen of Troy, either verbal persuasion or visual demonstration may
have constrained her to act the way she did, for both work in the same way.
Gorgias illustrates this process with reference to the emotional response we have
to the formal qualities of works of art: "Whenever pictures perfectly create a
single figure from many colors and figures, they delight the sight. . . . If, there-

fore, the eye of Helen, pleased by the figure of Alexander, presented to her soul eager desire and contest of love, what wonder?" (B11.18–19). Alexander's *kairos*—the single configuration he assumed at the moment—appeared to Helen's *opsis* in such a way that it was eroticized and presented its desire to her psyche, which yielded, just as it would have responded to painterly or rhetorically organized colors and figures.

Peitho was a figure affiliated with Aphrodite in fifth-century and sixth-century Greek thought, sometimes as her daughter, sometimes as her handmaiden. She is associated with Eros in Aeschylus and Pindar, and in her accession to political persuasion she never loses her older connotation as goddess of amorous seduction (Lain-Entralgo 64–67). In Gorgias's view, then, the schemes and tropes of rhythmic speech must have possessed an erotic capability which stimulated the disconnected "opinions" of the psyche to a powerful cathexis in which the meaning-configuration imposed by the speaker was apperceived by the auditor with a discharge of pleasure in the process of his being "convinced."

The relevance of *apate* and *peitho* to the workings of *Othello* should be apparent. One need only think of the brief passage between Othello's assertion, "I'll see before I doubt, when I doubt prove" (3.3.194) and "Now do I see 'tis true" (3.3.451)—a passage in which he has "seen" nothing but the verbal images Iago has collocated before his mind's eye—to discern the powers of poetic deception and persuasion engaging his latent desire to be convinced of Desdemona's infidelity.[27]

But there are further connections. *Peitho* is also associated with magic and medicine. Gorgias offers as an example of verbal persuasion the epode or magic charm: "Sacred incantations sung with words are bearers of pleasure and banishers of pain, for merging with opinion in the soul, the power of incantation is wont to beguile it and persuade it and alter it by witchcraft" (B11.10). In the early sixteenth century Erasmus repeats the association of *peitho* and magic charm in his *Paraclesis*. As he exhorts his readers to study the Scripture, he prays for "an eloquence which not only captivates the ear with its fleeting delight, but which leaves a lasting sting in the minds of its hearers, which grips, which transforms, which sends away a far different listener than it had received." He commends "the entreaties which the Greeks called epodes," and says "if there were any such kind of incantation anywhere, if there were any power of song which could truly inspire, if any Pytho [sic] truly swayed the heart, I would desire that it might be at hand for me" (Erasmus 98). But he is also alert to the potential mendacity of such power. In the *Ciceronianus*, his spokesman Bulephorus complains:

> your rhetoricians permit the orator to lie on occasion, to magnify humble matters (*res*) with words, and to depreciate important ones, which is truly a kind of magic (*praestigii*), penetrating insidiously into the mind of the listener.[28]

This linking of persuasion and magic charm is widespread in the Renaissance; Spenser, Chapman, Donne, and Milton make the connection, and it is not surprising to find it in Shakespeare as well.[29] "Is there not charms, / By which the property of youth and maidhood / May be abused?" cries Brabantio, upon discovering Desdemona's escape (1.1.171–3). At the Sagittar he insists his daughter would never have run away with Othello "If she in chains of magic were not bound" (1.2.65), and though the charge of black magic is dismissed, the chains that bound Desdemona turn out to have been the discursive links of Othello's narrative history. When Iago tells Roderigo, "Thou knowest we work by wit, and not by witchcraft" (2.3.362), he is phrasing as antithesis what is in actuality an apposition.

Peitho has yet another hold on *Othello*. Historically it is also likened to medical therapy: "The effect of speech upon the condition of the soul is comparable to the power of drugs over the nature of bodies. For just as different drugs dispel different secretions from the body, and some bring an end to disease and others to life, so also in the case of speeches, some distress, others delight, some cause fear, others make the hearers bold, and some drug and bewitch the soul with a kind of evil persuasion" (Gorgias, B11.14) Pedro Lain-Entralgo has shown how ideas about *goeteia* and *pharmacia* come together in the fifth and fourth centuries in writers discussing persuasive speech. During this period the word *epode* takes on a metaphoric significance, just as drug therapy becomes associated, among the presocratics, but also in Plato and Aristotle, with a kind of discursive psychotherapy (Lain-Entralgo 69). Again the connection persists, and we find Erasmus prescribing a course of logotherapy for sixteenth-century Christians (Boyle 47–48). When Iago murmurs, "Work on, / My medicine" (4.3.43), he taps an ancient tradition in which the irrationality of linguistic cogency is explicated as occult empirical physic.

Thus the Egyptian charmer who "could almost read / The thoughts of people" is a deeply overdetermined figure in *Othello*. Given her textual location, she is probably associated with Cleopatra, the last eastern possessor of the pavilion-cum-handerkerchief, and consequently with eros, the charm, and the drug. But her function is that of the poetic deceiver who shapes her words, engaging the power of *peitho*, to the just meridian of the listener. Her work complements that of the sibyl. While the sibyl scatters and allows the hearer to compose, the charmer binds and imposes. These activities proceed reciprocally in the play and inform its rhythm, just as the design of the handkerchief is "ta'en out" and reworked on the level of theme and plot. Often the roles of sibyl and charmer are associated with the same character. The central sibylline scene at the beginning of Act III, Scene iii, where Othello plays Aeneas to Iago's prophetess, is recast in the brothel scene when Desdemona, bewildered by Othello's cryptic irony, implores: "Upon my knees, what does your speech import? / I understand a fury in your words, / But not the words" (4.2.30–32). Similarly, Othello's account of his tale to Desdemona, "Whereof by parcels she had something heard, / But not intentively," casts him as charmer to the young girl's curiosity, while his role is reversed as Iago repeats and corroborates Brabantio's inferences about Desdemona's apparent perversity before his rapidly weakening resistance (3.3.210–47).

Although the act or threat of charming is distributed among several figures in the play, it is most often attached to Iago who, Janus-faced, is also the principal sibyl. Like the rhetorical necromancer described by Erasmus, who magnifies humble matters and depreciates important ones, Iago speaks the language of magical illusionism from his first incitement of Roderigo:

> though that his joy be joy,
> Yet throw such changes of vexation on't,
> As it may lose some colour. (1.1.69–73)[30]

Iago concedes he cannot alter the reality of Othello's good fortune, but he can diminish it by giving it a new gloss. He later uses the same device to color Desdemona's advocacy for Cassio:

> I'll pour this pestilence into his ear,
> That she repeals him for her body's lust;
> And by how much she strives to do him good,
> She shall undo her credit with the Moor;
> So will I turn her virtue into pitch. . . . (2.3.347–50)

The most explicit demonstration of Iago's illusionism occurs when Iago informs Othello how to interpret his coming encounter with Cassio:

> but encave yourself,
> And mark the jeers, the gibes, and notable scorns,
> That dwell in every region of his face;
> For I will make him tell the tale anew,
> Where, how, how oft, how long ago, and when,
> He has, and is again to cope your wife:
> I say, but mark his gesture . . . . (4.1.81–87)

Here he provides a definitive gloss on the pantomime about to take place, creating an a priori configuration that is calculated to the exact pitch of Othello's emotional state, with the result that the encaved auditor emerges from the performance determined to see it his way: "How shall I murder him, Iago?" (4.1.165).

In the Folio text, "changes of vexation" reads "chances of vexation," and whether or not this represents a Shakespearean variant, it reveals the ontology of Iago's power. For Iago's coloration is "accidental," not "essential"—logos conveys logos, not substances—and though it ultimately succeeds, Othello does not allow it to overshadow his own perception of Desdemona without a struggle. This is seen in his peculiar exchange with Iago just after he has witnessed the glossed panto-mime:

> *Oth.* I would have him nine years a-killing; a fine woman, a fair woman, a sweet woman!
> *Iago.* Nay, you must forget.
> *Oth.* And let her rot, and perish, and be damned to night, for she shall not live. . . . O, the world has not a sweeter creature, she might lie by an emperor's side, and command him tasks.
> *Iago.* Nay, that's not your way.
> *Oth.* Hang her, I do but say what she is. (4.1.175–83)

This is crazy talk. But it plays out the contradiction Othello feels between his own construction of Desdemona's purity—"what she is"—and Iago's "chances" of vexation, which have darkened her virtue and made Othello's name black as his own face.[31] This clash between ingenuously discovered and disingenuously im-posed satisfactions leads to the increasingly schizophrenic perception in the mur-der scene, when Othello refuses to shed her blood,

> Nor scar that whiter skin of hers than snow,
> And smooth, as monumental alabaster;
> Yet she must die, or else betray more men. (5.2.4–6)

Stanley Cavell has interpreted the contradiction expressed here as an insoluble double bind: to sustain his sense of Desdemona's involate otherness, Othello must believe that he has not sullied her purity, hence her virginal whiteness; to revenge her betrayal of him, he must believe she is soiled by others and deserving of death (Cavell 133–38). We can assimilate this insight to the dramaturgic processes of the play if we realize we are witnessing a primal scene of *peitho*—that eroticized reception of an image through whose agency Helen yielded to Alexander—in Othello's insistence upon maintaining his original, historical encounter with the heavenly Desdemona, even as he struggles with the calculated *apate* of Iago, which itself works by means of a persuasive force that engages Othello's craving to be pure—if not by association with Desdemona, then by dissociation from her. That he succumbs to the poetic deceiver shows how well Iago has woven the net in which he will enmesh them all—for Desdemona's denial and her lament for Cassio only intensify the colors he has laid on her, and she dies an accused strumpet.

The net, the web, the handkerchief in which magic reposes— each is a reticulation in which the charmer's toil is realized. But there is an actual reticule also associated with Iago. In the opening lines of the play Roderigo says,

> I take it much unkindly
> That thou, Iago, who hast had my purse,
> As though the strings were thine, shouldst know of this. (1.1.1–3)

From the beginning, then, Shakespeare represents Iago as one who holds the purse strings. If the purse is initially a symbol of Roderigo's generous if imprudent friendship, however, it soon becomes apparent that it figures far more importantly. It is both a source of profit for Iago and a repository of meanings that can be filled, emptied, and replenished. When Roderigo voices despair at Desdemona's departure for Cyprus, Iago gives him new purpose—accompanied by a refrain:

> Put money in thy purse; follow these wars, defeat thy favor with an usurp'd beard; I say, put money in thy purse. It cannot be that Desdemona should long continue her love unto the Moor . . . put money in thy purse, . . . nor he to her; it was a violent commencement, and thou shalt see an answerable sequestration: put but money in thy purse. . . . These Moors are changeable in their wills . . . fill thy purse with money. (1.3.340–48)

It is a strange speech. The rhythmic, repetitive command alternates with information and advice, as though Iago himself were filling the purse with currency. This is perhaps the most sustained incantation we see him perform, and it is immediately effective. "I am chang'd," declares Roderigo, and (in the Folio) "I'll sell all my land." Roderigo is a different man—the man Erasmus had hoped to create through his *epode*—now that he is filled with Iago's charming prognostication. "Thus do I ever make my fool my purse," Iago confesses a moment later, instantly turning London coney-catcher. But if Roderigo's purse holds potential wealth for Iago, that wealth will be expended not on commodities but on interpretations—choral commentaries of ostensible value to him. As burses tend to be, it is a site of exchange, and what is purchased is poetic deception.

If this were Jonson's play, not Shakespeare's, we might be disposed to hear in Iago's "Put money in thy purse" a perverse exhortation to the audience to pay and be gulled, and to discern in Iago a refraction of the avaricious author or player. But we never see, as we do in *Volpone* or *Bartholomew Fair*, any gold, jewels, or coins change hands. Something less material and perhaps more interesting is going on here. In this play Roderigo's purse is the metaphoric source of the activities of gathering, collating, and imparting verbal intelligence. Iago is the chief dispenser of poetic deception, and the audience is privileged to observe how he distributes and fashions his goods. When his deceits are finally revealed to his victims and he is punished, Shakespeare's auditors are confirmed in their belief that they have all along—unlike most of the characters in the play—enjoyed an untampered vision of reality. They have witnessed the factitiousness of Iago's *apate* and the force of *peitho* in Othello, "unshunnable, like death" (3.3.279). Yet somewhere along the way Shakespeare has surreptitiously entered this scene of lucidity and meddled with the time frame. He has scattered pieces of speech that indicate "long time" into the "se'nnight's speed" of the action without anyone noticing it—silently conflating the roles of sibyl and charmer even as Iago was thematizing these roles and being scapegoated for practicing arts inhibited. Roderigo's purse, it seems, was the audience's as well—used sometimes, if we may paraphrase Othello, to "unlace . . . and spend [one's] rich opinion," sometimes to "contract and purse . . . together" some horrible conceit, according to the cognitive laws of supply and demand. The question of "long time" versus "short time" is a vexed one in Shakespeare criticism (it creates an interpretative problem, as we have noticed, in *Richard II*, and it takes an even more bizarre form in *Measure for Measure*[32]); its presence in Othello, however, should now be intelligible enough. It is a dramaturgic extension of the process of scattering and charming that is represented within the play itself: "This only is the witchcraft I have used" (1.3.169).

If, on the basis of this practice, one may venture an opinion of Shakespeare's "world view," it is that all the world is indeed a stage—not simply in the sense that all human beings play roles or that, as Jaques has it, human life may be formulated as seven acts; rather, it is so in the sense that human beings understand one another and the events in which they mutually engage in much the way one writes, acts, and auditions a theatrical manuscript. The magic in the web is our own desire for coherence, and it is this libidinal energy that Shakespeare engages to his scattering and sure observances.

NOTES

[1] Frag. B3.84, trans. George Kennedy, in Sprague 46.

[2] Citations from plays other than *Othello* refer to *The Riverside Shakespeare* and will appear in the text.

[3] I. A. Richards' notion of an historical "play of interests" present in the reader, which is engaged by the poet's "play of interests," is a useful analogue of the intersubjectivity I have in mind, though I am concerned not with a norm of reading but of playgoing—with a specifically audio-visual encounter and the fragmented language that constitutes it. For Richards, see *Science and Poetry* 506–11.

[4] The earliest record of such a reflective moment is probably Thomas Rymer's discovery of "double time" in *Othello*. See Rymer 151, and Altman, "Preposterous" 148–49.

[5] The locus classicus is Aristotle, *De Anima* 433a; for a detailed account of this tradition, see Eden (esp. 62–111).

207

[6] Critics have noted that problems of understanding shown in Shakespeare's plays often mirror those of the audience listening and watching. Norman Rabkin, Stephen Booth, and Stanley Cavell have addressed this issue in different ways, and recently James Hirsh has argued the case for *Othello* in terms of syllogistic reasoning and in relation to the binary either/or model Rabkin uses in his discussion of *Henry V*. I take a somewhat different view of the cognitive activity represented and elicited by Shakespeare. Described in the early modern period as the work of *ingenium*, it involved a more or less tendentious reception of disparate stimuli, followed by the transformation of these stimuli into significance through the noetic insight of "ingenious inference." Put simply, one asks the question, "What has this to do with that?" and makes meaning in much the way a metaphor is fashioned. For discussion of *ingenium* in rhetoric and philosophy, see Grassi 20, 92–96; for its relation to metaphor, see Ricoeur 197–98; for its work in *Othello*, see Altman, "Practice" 487–91.

[7] *Henry IV, Part I*, 3.2.39–84, 5.1.30–71; *Henry IV, Part II*, 3.1.60–79, 183–212.

[8] In the Aristotelian tradition, one cannot act intentionally without the deliberation of the practical reason and this entails filling in the steps between the desire to accomplish something and its enactment (Joachim 100–05). Shylock does not do this, though the play itself provides the necessary circumstances in Lorenzo's seduction of Jessica, the harrassment of Solanio and Solario, the trade of Leah's ring for a monkey, etc. A similar engagement to vague futurity governs Iago's actions in *Othello*.

[9] Citations from *Othello* refer to Ridley's edition.

[10] A point frequently made by critics who confute Rymer by arguing that it is the handkerchief's spiritual, sentimental, romantic, exotic, or erotic significance that makes it so apt an instrument of Othello's destruction. I risk belaboring the point once more to argue an ur-significance: that Shakespeare develops the handkerchief as the site of stable meaning for Othello.

[11] Giraldi (182), my translation.

[12] Ariosto (ed. Segre), 1227; Ariosto (trans. Gilbert), 826.

[13] Stanzas 81–83. Ariosto draws on the story transmitted by Herodotus and others that Helen was taken from Paris by King Proteus and kept safe in Egypt, where Menelaus claimed her and his treasure at the end of the Trojan War.

[14] This would be the literary genealogy of the cultural understanding of the handkerchief expounded by Boose, who relates the spots to the folk tradition of displaying nuptial sheets stained with hymeneal blood.

[15] I am presuming an "historical" process of composition here, wherein the writing of an episode begets inchoate ideas that could not have been engendered without that prior event and whose possibilities are realized only as composition proceeds—much as Shylock's merry bond holds possibilities of action that can only be elicited by subsequent events. When these events occur, they confer meaning on previous meaning-possibilities, which will then appear to have been motives or intentions all along.

[16] Othello stands out starkly in opposition to this pattern. He continually seeks "circumscription and confine," whether it be in the form of eschatological finality ("If it were now to die, / 'Twere now to be most happy" [2.1.189–90]) or of ancient custom ("A liberal hand; the hearts of old gave hands, / But our new heraldry is hands, not hearts" [3.4.42_43]).

[17] For Gildon, see Vickers (2.72); Shakespeare's interest in Virgil has been studied at length by Brower, Bono, Miola, and Hamilton, but only Major sees any extensive connection between the *Aeneid* and *Othello*, and he limits his discussion to Dido and Desdemona. A more thorough study of Shakespearean imitation is needed to account for transformations such as these, along the lines suggested by Pigman.

[18] Stanley Cavell has remarked that Shakespearean heroes come belatedly into a world in which Christian faith has ebbed and the fideist gamble of Cartesian skepticism is only dimly realized. It is an insight that brilliantly illuminates Othello's virtual apotheosis of Desdemona and Antony's transformation of the riggish Cleopatra. It also explains the transvaluation of sibylline wisdom found in *Othello* and why, as we shall see, the play is farced with theatrical, factitious histories.

[19] Greenblatt 234–39; Parker 60.

[20] An interesting example of the visual representation of narrative is seen in the engravings made for Harington's *Orlando Furioso*. In his Advertisement to the reader Harrington writes: "The use of the picture is evident, which is that (having read over the book) you may read it (as it were again) in the very picture, and one thing is to be noted which every one (haply) will not observe, namely the perspective in

every figure. For the personages of men, the shapes of horses, and such like, are made large at the bottome and lesser upward, as if you were to behold all the same in a plaine, that which is nearest seems greatest and the fardest shews smallest, which is the chief art in picture" (17). In each book (reversing the order of my hypothetical model), the earliest events are shown in the foreground, with later ones receding into the distance.

[21] Shakespeare inscribes an antidote to credulity in Iago's nostrum for Roderigo: "mark me, with what violence she first lov'd the Moor, but for bragging and telling her fantastical lies; and will she love him still for prating?" (2.1.221–23).

[22] Parker has demonstrated the importance of "dilation" in the play, especially regarding amplification by circumstances. I would emphasize the occasional and tendentious character of such dilation, as in the second version of the handkerchief story, which Othello fashions to parallel his own situation (5.2.217–18). Moisan is useful here: "To the extent . . . to which Othello's 'story' draws our attention to the narrativity of the play, it also helps to inscribe the play as a discourse ever revising itself and improvising its own text" (66). I see such revisions and improvisations as continuous attempts to fix meaning.

[23] For the common translation of Aristotle's "pity and fear" as "commiseration and admiration," see Cunningham 142–63; for the progress of Othello's pilgrimage, see his arrival at Cyprus after the storm (n. 18); his perusal of Desdemona's body, white and smooth as "monumental alabaster" (5.2.5); their imagined meeting "at count" (5.2.274), which will hurl him from heaven.

[24] Frag. B11.8–9 in Sprague 52. Citations will appear in the text.

[25] Frag. B23, "On the Fame of the Athenians," in Sprague 65. This is reproduced in "How the Young Man Should Study Poetry."

[26] Had Jonson miscalculated the *logoi*? Or had he, as he claimed in a later play, "writ it just to his meridian" who would be politic? It is hard to tell at this distance, but the uncanny way in which the accusations levelled at the historian Cordus in the play were reproduced against the author of the play suggests that Jonson shaped *Sejanus* so as to demonstrate the poetic theory whose dangerous realization is attested by the "Philos" poem.

[27] Snow persuasively elaborates the heterosexual disgust experienced by Othello, which finds symbolic representation in the handkerchief and wedding sheets and demands purification.

[28] Cited in Cave 158; cf. Breen 395.

[29] Spenser, *F. Q.* 3.2.15; Donne, *Satyre II* ll. 17–20; Chapman, *Bussy D'Ambois* (4.2.84–88); Milton, *P.L.* (2.556, 566–69).

[30] "Colour" is a rhetorical term for the particular "slant" or "theme" one gives to the events one speaks about, and thus is a persuasive formal element. See Quintilian (IV.ii.88). It is the antithesis of the "unvarnish'd tale" by which Othello purports to represent his sincerity.

[31] The persistence of Othello's original perception speaks to the profundity of his outsider's need to be "put into circumscription and confine" by the white Venetian lady: "She lov'd me for the dangers I had pass'd, / And I lov'd her that she did pity them" (1.3.167–68).

[32] Cf. Mariana's assertion that the Duke, just recently disguised as Friar Lodowick, "Hath often still'd my brawling discontent" (4.1.3).

WORKS CITED

Altman, Joel. "Preposterous Conclusions: Eros, *Enargeia*, and the Composition of *Othello*." *Representations* 18 (1987): 129–57.

———. "The Practice of Shakespeare's Text." *Style* 23 (1989): 466–500.

Ariosto, Ludovico. *Orlando Furioso*. Ed. Cesare Segre. Rome: Mondadori, 1976.

———. *Orlando Furioso*. Trans. Sir John Harington. Ed. R. McNulty. Oxford: Clarendon, 1972.

———. *Orlando Furioso*. Trans. Alan Gilbert. 2 vols. New York: Vanni, 1954.

Boiardo, Matteo. *Orlando Innamorato*. Trans. Charles S. Ross. Berkeley: U of California P, 1989.

Bono, Barbara. *Literary Transvaluation: From Vergilian Epic to Shakespearean Tragicomedy*. Berkeley: U of California P, 1984.

Boose, Linda E. "Othello's Handkerchief: The Recognizance and Pledge of Love," *ELR* 5 (1975): 360–74.

Booth, Stephen. "On the Value of *Hamlet.*" *Reinterpretations of Elizabethan Drama*. Ed. Norman Rabkin. New York: Columbia UP, 1969.

Boyle, Marjorie O'Rourke. *Erasmus on Language and Method in Theology*. Toronto: U of Toronto P, 1977.

Breen, Quirinus. "Giovanni Pico della Mirandola on the Conflict of Philosophy and Rhetoric." *JHI* 13 (1952): 384–426.

Brower, Reuben. *Hero and Saint: Shakespeare and the Graeco-Roman Tradition*. Oxford: Clarendon, 1971.

Cave, Terence. *The Cornucopia Text*. Oxford: Clarendon, 1979.

Cavell, Stanley. *Disowning Knowledge in Six Plays of Shakespeare*. New York: Cambridge UP, 1987.

Cunningham, J. V. *Tradition and Poetic Structure*. Denver: Swallow, 1960.

Eden, Kathy. *Poetic and Legal Fiction in the Aristotelian Tradition*. Princeton: Princeton UP, 1988.

Erasmus, Desiderius. *Christian Humanism and the Reformation*. Ed. John C. Olin. New York: Fordham UP, 1987.

Giraldi, Giovanni Baptista Cinthio. *Gli ecatommiti ovvero cento novelle*. Firenze: Borghi, 1834.

Gorgias. *On Nature; Encomium of Helen*. Sprague 42–47, 50–54.

Grassi, Ernesto. *Rhetoric as Philosophy: The Humanist Tradition*. University Park: Pennsylvania State UP, 1980.

Greenblatt, Stephen. *Renaissance Self-Fashioning*. Chicago: U of Chicago P, 1980.

Hamilton, Donna. *Virgil and* The Tempest: *The Politics of Imitation*. Columbus: Ohio State UP, 1990.

Hirsh, James. "Othello and Perception." Vaughan and Cartwright 135–59.

Jonson, Ben. *Sejanus*. Ed. W. D. Briggs. Boston: Heath, 1911.

Lain-Entralgo, Pedro. *The Therapy of the Word in Classical Antiquity*. Ed. and trans. L. J. Rather and John M. Sharp. New Haven: Yale UP, 1970.

Major, John M. "Desdemona and Dido." *SQ* 10 (1959): 123–25.

Miola, Robert S. "Vergil in Shakespeare: From Allusion to Imitation." *Vergil at 2000: Commemorative Essays on the Poet and His Influence*. Ed. John D. Bernard. New York: AMS, 1986.

Moisan, Thomas. "Repetition and Interrogation in *Othello*: 'What needs this Iterance?' or, 'Can anything be made of this?'" Vaughan and Cartwright 48–73.

Muir, Kenneth. *The Sources of Shakespeare's Plays*. London: Methuen, 1977.

Parke, H. W. *Sibyls and Sibylline Prophecy in Classical Antiquity*. London: Routledge, 1988.

Parker, Patricia. "Shakespeare and rhetoric: 'dilation' and 'delation' in *Othello.*" *Shakespeare and the Question of Theory*. Ed. Patricia Parker and Geoffrey Hartmann. New York: Methuen, 1985.

Pigman, G. W. "Versions of Imitation in the Renaissance." *Renaissance Quarterly* 33 (1980): 1–32.

Quintilian. *Institutio Oratoria*. Trans. H. E. Butler. London: Heinemann, 1921.

Rabkin, Norman. *Shakespeare and the Problem of Meaning*. Chicago: U of Chicago P, 1981.

Richards, I. A. *Science and Poetry*. In *Criticism: The Foundations of Modern Literary Judgment*. Ed. Mark Schorer et al. Rev. ed. New York: Harcourt, 1958.

Ricoeur, Paul. *The Rule of Metaphor*. Toronto: U of Toronto P, 1977.

Rosenmeyer, Thomas G. "Gorgias, Aeschylus, and *Apate*," *AJP* 76 (1955): 225–60.

Rymer, Thomas. *Critical Works*. Ed. Curt A. Zimansky. New Haven: Yale UP, 1956.

Segal, Charles. "Gorgias and the Psychology of the Logos." *Harvard Studies in Classical Philology* 66 (1962): 99–155.

Shakespeare, William. *The Riverside Shakespeare*. Ed. G. Blakemore Evans et al. Boston: Houghton Mifflin, 1974.

_____. *Othello*. Ed. M. R. Ridley. New York: Vintage, 1967.

_____. *Othello*. Ed. Norman Sanders. London: Cambridge UP, 1984.

Smart, John S. *Shakespeare: Truth and Tradition*. London: Arnold, 1928.

Snow, Edward. "Sexual Anxiety and the Male Order of Things in *Othello*." *ELR* 10 (1980): 384–412.

Sprague, Rosamund Kent, ed. *The Older Sophists*. Columbia: U of South Carolina P, 1972.

Vaughan, Virginia M., and Kent Cartwright, eds. Othello: *New Perspectives*. Rutherford, N.J.: Fairleigh Dickinson UP, 1991.

Vickers, Brian, ed. *Shakespeare: The Critical Heritage*. Vol. 2. London: Routledge, 1974.

Virgil, Publius Maro. *Virgil*. Trans. H. Rushton Fairclough. 2 vols. London: Heinemann, 1954.

Garrick, Colman, and *King Lear:* A Reconsideration

ARTHUR JOHN HARRIS

HE belief has prevailed since the early nineteenth century that David Garrick is chiefly responsible for the initial steps in the restoration of Shakespeare's *King Lear* to the stage. The accepted opinion has been that, while Garrick began his career with the Nahum Tate version of Shakespeare's tragedy, he was thereafter gradually restoring Shakespeare's lines to his acting text and that in 1756 he presented a partially restored version of the play much as it is to be found in the text published in London, 1773, by John Bell. Hence, Garrick's work in the restoration of *King Lear* has been given precedence over that of his rival, George Colman, whose more complete restoration was both printed and performed in 1768. The intention of this essay is to challenge Garrick's primacy in the restoration of Shakespeare's text to the stage and to assert the importance of Colman's work on the play.

The evidence that Garrick made substantial restorations of Shakespeare's text to his acting version as early as 1756 rests largely on the testimony of two early nineteenth-century critics. James Boaden in 1831 makes a general assertion in the introduction to his edition of the correspondence between Garrick and his contemporaries:

> The season of 1756-7 opened propitiously enough. . . . On the 28th of October, Mr. Garrick improved his *Lear,* by striking out the sophistications of Tate, and using Shakespeare's own language, whenever it was practicable to do so—that is, consistently with the love interest of Edgar and Cordelia, and the allowing old Lear to be a King again.[1]

Unfortunately, Boaden does not reveal the source of his information, and there is nothing in the correspondence itself to indicate that Garrick at that time made extensive restorations. As we shall later see, Boaden may have been influenced either by Garrick's prompters' diaries or playbills or both. It was Genest, however, who seems to have been the first to conjecture that the restorations of 1756 were anything like those found in the Bell edition:

> Oct. 28. [1756] King Lear—with restorations from Shakespeare. Lear— Garrick: Cordelia—Mrs. Davies; the alteration of King Lear which Garrick made at this time, probably did not differ materially from King Lear as published by Bell in 1772 or 1773 from the Prompt-book of D. L.[2]

[1] *The Private Correspondence of David Garrick with the Most Celebrated Persons of His Time; Now First Published from the Originals, and Illustrated with Notes. And a New Biographical Memoir of Garrick,* ed. James Boaden (London, 1831-32), I, xxxii-xxxiii.

[2] John Genest, *Some Account of the English Stage* (Bath, 1832), IV, 475.

These two early theater historians, then, were the initiators of an idea which modern historians have generally held to. Odell, for example, repeats Genest in his assumption:

> On October 28, 1756—the year of his versions of *The Winter's Tale*, *The Taming of the Shrew*, and *The Tempest* as an opera—Garrick played King Lear with restorations from Shakespeare. The version used was not printed at the time, but was probably very like that included in Bell's Shakespeare, 1773.[3]

"Probably" echoes Genest and at the same time indicates Odell's general tendency to qualify all that he says about the Bell text as regards its being Garrick's work. What undoubtedly dismayed him was the discrepancy between a serious attempt at restoration of Shakespeare's text of *King Lear*, claimed to have been made in 1756, and the fact that Garrick was at that very time making, as Odell puts it, such "onslaughts on the Shakespearian drama", cutting mercilessly and rewriting to suit the tastes of his age.

Following his predecessors' beliefs about Garrick's work on *King Lear*, though perhaps with more assurance, George Winchester Stone refers to Garrick's "extended revision of the acting text, which he performed on 28 October 1756." His evidence for this comes from the records kept by Garrick's prompters, the Cross-Hopkins Diaries, now in the Folger Shakespeare Library at Washington, D.C., which record for the night of October 28, "KING LEAR—with restorations from Shakespeare." Later, however, he states more tentatively: "The texts of *King Lear*, identical in Bell's 1773 and 1774 printings, may well represent accurate transcriptions of Garrick's 1756 play.[4]

Charles Beecher Hogan, on the other hand, in his introductory paragraph to a summary of Bell's text, states unequivocally: "This alteration was made by David Garrick, and was first acted in 1756 (but not then printed).[5] Kalman F. Burnim, in his recent study of Garrick as manager-director-artist, is also quite positive: "Finally, Garrick propitiated the god of his idolatry on October 28, 1756, by announcing "KING LEAR—with restorations from Shakespeare." He too refers to the Cross-Hopkins Diaries.[6]

So the belief that Garrick in 1756 restored Shakespeare's text much as we find it in the Bell edition of 1773 had its beginnings with Boaden and Genest and has now been accepted as fact by modern theater historians, whose only evidence seems to be a note in a prompter's diary. It might have been observed, incidentally, that in defense of tradition there are Garrick playbills in the collection of The Royal Shakespeare Theatre Library for both the 28th and 30th of October, 1756, which announce, as in the Diaries: "With Restorations from Shakespeare". It may well have been upon these that the initial references of Boaden and Genest depended.

Even these, however, would be dubious proof, for they offer no evidence that whatever restorations were made at that time were in any way comparable to the considerable restorations found in the Bell text. Indeed, if one is to depend

[3] George C. D. Odell, *Shakespeare from Betterton to Irving* (New York, 1920), I, 377.

[4] George Winchester Stone, "Garrick's Production of *King Lear*, A Study in The Temper of The Eighteenth-Century Mind", *SP*, XLV (January 1948), 91, 95, 96.

[5] Charles Beecher Hogan, *Shakespeare in the Theatre 1701-1800* (Oxford, 1952), II, 334.

[6] Kalman A. Burnim, *David Garrick, Director* (Pittsburgh, 1961), p. 144.

upon playbills, there is evidence to suggest that, at the beginning of Garrick's career during his first full season at Drury Lane, 1742-43, an event took place that not only questions his position as "restorer" but goes far to suggest that other actors—in disputing his sudden eminence—offered a challenge *on the basis of* restorations. On 10 January 1743, and on the 23rd and 26th following, an anonymous "Gentleman" performed Lear at Lincoln's Inn Fields, as the bills record: "With Restorations from Shakespeare." Ironically, this was Giffard's company of actors among which Garrick had risen to fame the preceding season at Goodman's Fields; several of the same names as those in Garrick's first performances appear in the cast lists, including Giffard, Mrs. Bambridge, and Mrs. Giffard, with one notable addition, Theophilus Cibber, Garrick's arch-enemy, in the part of Gloucester. The anonymous gentleman may well have been the obscure actor Christopher Perry, who was the only other player to perform Lear the following season, this time at Covent Garden, "At the desire of several persons of quality for the Benefit of Mr. Perry".[7] Again the bills read, "With Restorations from Shakespeare".

Was Theophilus Cibber in any way responsible for this competitive Lear "with restorations"? And were there, in fact, "persons of quality" who opposed Garrick's use of Tate? The first question remains only a suspicion, but the second demands further exploration, for as the legend of Garrick as "restorer" has grown, so has the wider belief that Joseph Addison was a lone voice in opposition to Tate.

Addison's pronouncement is famous in eighteenth-century Shakespearian criticism:

> The English Writers of Tragedy are possessed with a Notion, that when they represent a virtuous or innocent Person in Distress, they ought not to leave him till they have delivered him out of his Troubles, or made him triumph over his Enemies. . . . *King Lear* is an admirable Tragedy of the same Kind, as Shakespeare wrote it; but as it is reformed according to the Chymerical Notion of Poetical Justice, in my humble Opinion it has lost half its Beauty.[8]

These are the lines to which Professor Stone refers when he speaks of Addison as the beginning of "a thin voice of critical opposition"; but Dr. Burnim has gone farther in insisting that:

> Except for the one weak voice of Addison protesting that in this now "chimerical notion of poetic justice" Shakespeare's admirable tragedy had lost half its beauty, the adaptation was accorded highest praise by eighteenth-century moralists.[9]

While Addison may have been the earliest known critic to express disapproval, he was unquestionably not the "one weak voice" in the eighteenth century to protest the use of Tate's adaptation. Early in 1747, Samuel Foote published a pamphlet entitled "A Treatise on the Passions", in which he

[7] *The London Stage 1660-1800. A Calendar of Plays, Entertainments & Afterpieces Together with Casts, Box-Receipts and Contemporary Comment Compiled from the Playbills, Newspapers and Theatrical Diaries of the Period. Part III, 1729-1747*, ed. Arthur H. Scouten (Carbondale, Illinois, 1961), p. 1138.
[8] *The Spectator*, No. 40, 16 April 1711.
[9] Stone, p. 90; Burnim, p. 142.

criticizes Garrick's performance of Lear, the general excellence of which he cannot deny, though he takes pleasure in fault-finding. His final jab is relevant:

> I have promised to mention no more of his Faults, I shall be silent, and am, for once pleased with Tate's Alteration of Shakespear, because it has prevented my commenting on Mr. G's Manner of Dying, about which, I am afraid, we should have some Disputes.[10]

Following Addison's opinion, then, Foote is not generally pleased with Tate; indeed, he seems to take this displeasure for granted.

On the heels of this opposition to Tate came a pamphlet, written by Dr. Benjamin Hoadly, to which he attached: "A Word of Advice to Mr. G-ar-ck". He mocks Foote by pointing out that:

> He quotes a Passage that is not in SHAKESPEAR.
>
>   Ungrateful as they were,
> Tho' the Wrongs they have heaped on me are numberless,
> I feel a Pang of Nature for 'em yet.
>
> Is it not surprizing that this great Critick and Man of Taste, should propose Lines for your Consideration, which are in the Vile Alteration by Tate? and which only mark that Tenderness and Affectation, which in other Parts of his Pamphlet he condemns in you, as no Ingredients of the Character?[11]

Although Hoadly attacks Foote for mistaking Tate for Shakespeare and contradicting himself in another passage, he shares Foote's distaste for Tate's "vile Alteration", an opinion which he later rephrases as "the unhallow'd Pencil of Tate". Did Garrick agree? Possibly, but by this time he had already performed thirty-two of his eighty-seven performances.

Nor was it only argumentative pamphleteers who were offended by Tate. Mrs. Montagu, the acclaimed queen of London's blue-stocking society, received a letter from her dear friend, Mrs. (Anne) Donnellan, friend of Dean Swift, 17 November 1747:

> I went with Mrs. Southwell on Saturday to "King Lear" to see Garrick and Mrs. Cibber, both performed extremely well. I think he took the part of the old testy madman better than Hero [Quin?], and Mrs. Cibber is the soft, tender Cordelia in perfection. I am only provoked that they have altered Shakespear's plain, sincere, artless creation into a whining, love-sick maid. I would have an Act of Parliament, at least of Council, that nobody should add a word to Shakespear, for it makes sad patchwork.[12]

Addison, then, while perhaps first among the critical minds of his age, was hardly alone in his condemnation of Tate.

[10] [Samuel Foote], *A Treatise on the Passions, so far as they regard the Stage; with a critical Enquiry into the Theatrical Merit of Mr. G---K, Mr. Q---N, and Mr. B---Y. The first considered in the Part of Lear, the two last opposed in Othello* (London [n.d.]), p. 24.

[11] Dr. Burnim assigns this to Foote, along with "A Treatise", but this seems unlikely, and the British Museum copy has "Benjamin Hoadly" in pencil on the title page: *"An Examen of the New Comedy, call'd The Suspicious Husband. With Some Observations upon our Dramatic Poetry and authors; To which is added, A Word of Advice to Mr. G-ar-ck; and a Piece of Secret History* (London, 1747), p. 26.

[12] *Mrs. Montagu, "The Queen of the Blue-Stockings," Her Correspondence from 1720 to 1761*, ed. by her great-great-niece, Emily J. Climenson (London, 1906), I, 253-254.

There was good cause, then, for Garrick to work towards the restoration of Shakespeare's text to the stage. Professor Stone has pointed out that as early as 1753 Joseph Warton heard Garrick deliver, "O me, my heart! my rising heart!—but down", a line not to be found in Tate.[13] And certainly in late 1755 and the early months of 1756 pressures were brought to bear upon him that might have induced him to restore more. The first arose out of the greatest disaster of Garrick's career: the devastation to his purse, his prestige, and the physical structure of Drury Lane caused by the riots over *Les Fêtes Chinoises,* an extravaganza Garrick had brought over from Paris. Political sentiments against the French ran high, and the theater-going public did not take kindly to his efforts to import something of the exquisite beauty of the Parisian theater. The result was riot. Out of this frightening, and for Garrick heart-breaking, experience arose the opportunity for his enemies to attack. Theophilus Cibber delivered a lecture at the Haymarket:

> Were Shakespeare's ghost to rise, would he not frown indignation on this pilfering pedlar in poetry, who thus shamefully mangles, mutilates and emasculates his plays? *A Midsummer Night's Dream* has been minc'd and fricasseed into a thing called *The Fairies, The Winter's Tale* mamoc'd into a droll, and *The Tempest* castrated into an opera.[14]

While it may seem strange that this kind of attack should come from the son of Colley Cibber, whose *Richard III* rivals Tate's mutilation, it must have given pause to Garrick, the professed idolator of Shakespeare.

One other event more assuredly had a powerful effect upon Garrick's considerations about *King Lear*. This was Spranger Barry's performance of Lear at Covent Garden three months after the Chinese disaster. Playing the part half-a-dozen times after opening on 26 February 1756, he was an immediate success. Garrick, on the other hand, had performed Lear on February 12th but did not take up the part again until more than two months after Barry's final performance of the season. Even so, the town was abuzz with comparisons: although the public recognized Garrick's superiority in the role, here was certain challenge. Two long-remembered ditties went round the town:

> The town has found out different ways
> To praise the different Lears.
> To Barry they give loud hazzas,
> To Garrick—only tears.

or again:

> A King, nay, every inch a king,
> Such Barry doth appear,
> But Garrick's quite a different thing,
> He's every inch King Lear.[15]

---

[13] See Stone, pp. 93-94; for the Warton reference, see *The Adventurer,* 4 December 1753.

[14] Theophilus Cibber, *Two Dissertations on the Theatres, with an Appendix in three Parts. The Whole Containing a general View of the Stage, from Earliest Times, to the Present* (London, 1756), quoted by Odell, I, 365.

[15] *Theophilus Cibber, to David Garrick, Esq.; with Dissertations on Theatrical Subjects* (London, 1759) Second Dissertation, p. 43, and William Cooke, *Memoirs of Charles Macklin, Comedian, with the Dramatic Characters, Anecdotes, etc. of the Age in which he lived: forming an History of the Stage during almost the Whole of the last Century and A Chronological List of all the Parts played by Him* (London, 1806), p. 162.

In acting, the cup still seemed to be Garrick's, if only precariously. But the competition only added fuel to the fire of his detractors over textual matters. Although Mrs. Frances Brooke, the novelist and playwright, could praise his acting, she allowed herself to indulge in what Garrick was later to term "female Spite", when on 13 March 1756, she reviewed Barry's performance:

> It has always been a matter of great astonishment to me, that both the houses have given Tate's wretched alteration of King Lear, in preference to Shakespear's excellent original; which Mr. Addison, the most candid, as well as judicious of critics, thinks so infinitely preferable, as to bear no degree of comparison; and one cannot help remarking particularly, and with some surprise, that Mr. Garrick, who professes himself so warm an idolator of this inimitable poet, and who is determined, if I may use his own words, in the prologue to The Winter's Tale, "To lose no drop of this immortal man," should yet prefer the vile adulterated cup of Tate, to the pure genuine draught, offered him by the master he avows to serve with such fervency of devotion.[16]

Addison's opinion, then, remained, not as one thin voice of criticism, but the standard of taste for many later critics, who could appreciate "Shakespear's excellent original".

It was in this climate of riot, competition, and criticism, therefore, that in the autumn of 1756 Garrick presumably restored some lines from Shakespeare to the acted version of the play. That these revisions, however, were in any way extensive—as Garrick scholars have come to believe—seems highly unlikely. Only Tate Wilkinson, who favored Garrick, recorded in his memoirs: "Mr. Garrick's Lear seemed to have gained additional strength, lustre, and fashion"; while at the rival theater in Covent Garden: "This season opened rather languid.—Mr. Barry's Lear was not attractive."[17]

This would hardly seem sufficient evidence to claim that Garrick made such extensive revisions as those found in the Bell text. Only Samuel Derrick, in 1759, offers any indication of what Garrick had done before that year to restore Shakespeare's King Lear to the stage. After a defense of poetic justice, using Tate's alteration as a good example, Derrick continues:

> In some things it were injustice not to own that Tate has changed Shakespeare's plot for the better. . . . But Tate, to make amends for his judicious emendations, lest too much merit should acrue to him from them, has left out some of the finest speeches in the character of Lear, which Mr. Garrick has properly restored; and they are, I believe, retained by other performers.[18]

Derrick, then points out that Garrick had restored some of Shakespeare's lines to his own speeches, but if he had done more with the text than just this,

---

[16] Frances Brooke, The Old Maid, by Mary Singleton [pseud.], No. XVIII, 6 March 1756, p. 105; quoted by Robert Gale Noyes in The Thespian Mirror (Brown University, 1953), p. 173n. Little and Kahrl, in their edition of Garrick's letters, note that her "spite was not great"; but they seem to miss the tone of the above passage, nor do they seem to recognize what it must have meant to Garrick to be reported as acting, in his greatest role, a "vile adulterated cup". See The Letters of David Garrick, ed. David M. Little and George M. Kahrl (Cambridge, Mass., 1963), II, 461-462.

[17] Tate Wilkinson, Memoirs of His Own Life (London, 1790), IV, 221.

[18] [Samuel Derrick], A General View of the Stage (London, 1759), p. 31; attributed on the title-page to Thomas Wilkes, but see note in Lowe's Bibliographical Account of English Theatrical Literature (London, 1888), p. 87.

Derrick, in writing a general view of the stage, would most certainly have mentioned it.

If in 1756 Garrick did not restore Shakespeare's text as we find it in the Bell edition of 1773, this awakens new interest in George Colman's alteration of 1768, a work which has received relatively little attention because it has for so long been considered at best only an extension of the supposed Garrick revisions. If it can be shown that Colman's work precedes any major restorations made by Garrick this places an entirely new light on the relative merits of Colman and Garrick as restorers of Shakespeare's *King Lear* to the stage.

As Colman states in his Advertisement at the front of the text, his main objection to Tate was the banality of the love scenes between Edgar and Cordelia:

> The distress of the story is so far from being heightened by it, that it has diffused a langour and insipidity over all the scenes of the play from which Lear is absent; for which I appeal to the sensations of numerous audiences, with which the play has been honoured.

The uneven quality of the typical eighteenth-century production is well known; what concerned Colman, then, was the impact of Tate's love scenes upon the total impression of the tragedy: they detracted from rather than contributed to the impact. Audiences, he believed, would attest to this. "The embraces of Cordelia and the ragged Edgar", if they had not been incorporated into some of Shakespeare's finest scenes, would have been too ridiculous to be believed. He argues that although love was "the soul of Tragedy as well as Comedy" in Tate's time, Tate was "so devoted to intrigue, that he has not only given Edmund a passion for Cordelia, but has injudiciously amplified on his criminal commerce with Gonerill and Regan, which is the most disgusting part of the original." In Shakespeare, at least, there was some motive for their conduct; in Tate, there is none.

> In all these circumstances, it is generally agreed, that Tate's alteration is for the worse; and his King Lear would probably have quitted the stage long ago, had not the poet made "the tale conclude in a success to the innocent distressed persons." Even in the catastrophe he has incurred the censure of Addison: but "in the present case," says Dr. Johnson, "the publick has decided, and Cordelia, from the time of Tate, has always retired with victory and felicity."

Colman here assesses, perhaps more clearly than any later critic has done, the contemporary critical opinion of Tate's work: it was "generally agreed" to be "for the worst", except in its happy ending. Even the ending had been called in question, but Colman calls upon the mighty Johnson for his defense in retaining it: the public had decided.

Colman's major objective, then is clear: "To reconcile the catastrophe of Tate to the story of Shakespeare". The love scenes were cut entirely and the order of Shakespeare's scenes was largely restored in the earlier part of the play. Gloucester's fall, however, was omitted, though Edgar's description of the cliff was preserved. Tate, it may be remembered, had kept this piece of stage business; Colman rejected it as "utter improbability". Colman objected to the horror of Gloucester's blinding (also kept by Tate) and would have cut the scene if possible, but he found it so interwoven with the story that he could not see how to remove it.

His final consideration has significance with regard to Garrick's position concerning restoration. Colman concludes: "I had once some idea of retaining the character of *the fool;* . . . yet, after the most serious consideration, I was convinced that such a scene 'would sink into burlesque' in the representation, and would not be endured on the stage." If he "had once some idea" of such an ambitious restoration, then it would seem that he had been considering his alterations before he broke his partnership with Garrick at Drury Lane the preceding year, 1767. Had he discussed his proposed alterations with Garrick? Had he wanted Garrick to restore the text, further than in those lines which Garrick himself delivered? From the following evidence, the answer to these questions would seem to be in the affirmative.

Davies, writing in 1785, long after the fact, offers the picture from this angle:

> It was once in the contemplation with Mr. Garrick to restore the part of the fool, which he designed for Woodward, who promised to be very chaste in his colouring, and not to counteract the agonies of Lear: but the manager would not hazard so bold an attempt; he feared, with Mr. Colman, that the feelings of Lear would derive no advantage from the buffooneries of the parti-coloured jester.[19]

Woodward was at Drury Lane from about 1751 to about 1763, after which he appeared at Covent Garden. This means that Colman had considered his alteration of *King Lear* at least as early as 1763 while working with Garrick.

There is no indication, however, that Colman had an opportunity to experiment with his new text until after his defection to Covent Garden in 1768. Quite the contrary, there is, even in his "Advertisement" to his published text, the subtle suggestion that Garrick had piqued him by restraining him from acting upon his plans for the restoration of Shakespeare's text:

> In this kind of employment, one person cannot do a great deal; yet if every Director of the Theatre will endeavour to do a little, the Stage will every day be improved, and become more worthy attention and encouragement.[20]

But the proof-positive, hitherto unnoticed in Garrick studies, that Garrick had restrained Colman in his efforts, appears in an obscure and otherwise irrelevant pamphlet of 1768, written by Colman in defence of himself in a dispute with his new fellow-managers at the Garden:

> If the celebrated manager of Drury Lane had ever attempted to execute my projected plan of altering King Lear, my labours on this occasion would undoubtedly have been superseded.[21]

[19] Thomas Davies, *Dramatic Miscellanies: consisting of critical observations on several Plays of Shakespeare: with a review of his principal characters, and those of various eminent writers, as represented by Mr. Garrick, and other celebrated comedians, with anecdotes of dramatic facts, actors etc.* (London, 1785), II, 267-268.

[20] See Colman's text, p. iv.

[21] George Colman, *A True State of the Differences Subsisting between the Proprietors of Covent-Garden Theatre; in answer to a false, Scandalous, and Malicious Manuscript Libel, exhibited on Saturday, Jan. 23, and the two following Days; and to a Printed Narrative signed by T. Harris and J. Rutherford* (London, 1768), p. 40.

Here, then, is specific contemporary evidence that Garrick had been adamant in his determination not to restore Shakespeare's text as Colman had proposed.

But the most important evidence in support of the assertion that Garrick did not extensively restore Shakespeare's text in the early part of his career comes from *The Dramatic Censor,* published by Francis Gentleman in 1770. One of the essays in this collection is an interesting comparative evaluation of the two alterations of *King Lear* made by Tate and Colman. Gentleman in the essay does not mention a third alteration; yet if Garrick had been using a revision anything like the Bell text, which is much more like Colman's than Tate's text, Gentleman would surely have noted it.

On the contrary, after weighting and considering the relative merits of the Tate and Colman texts, he rather favors Tate, but would like, ideally, to find a happy medium:

> ... for the credit of SHAKESPEARE, TATE, COLMAN, and advantage of the stage, we wish an able critic, Mr. GARRICK, for instance, would undertake a third alteration upon medium principles, between the latitude of TATE, and the circumscription of Colman.

Quite clearly, Gentleman here, in 1770, is requesting from Garrick a text that, since the time of Genest, is believed to have been first acted by him in 1756.

It only remains to establish, if possible, an authoritative date for the first acting of this text, later published by John Bell; and, thus, to set a terminal date for Garrick's revisions along "medium principles". Garrick had not acted Lear since his departure for the continent in 1763, probably because of the competition he would have shared with William Powell, the young actor whom he had left in his place at Drury Lane. Powell, young and ambitious, had opened as Lear in 1765, while Garrick was still in Europe. He played Lear at the Lane until 1768, when he deserted Garrick and went over to Covent Garden, only to be followed by Colman, where they soon presented Colman's restored text. Powell continued to play Lear until his sudden and premature death in the summer of 1769; then, on 21 February 1770, Garrick appeared again as Lear. The cast lists for this and subsequent performances that season indicate no departure from the Tate text.

During the following season, however, on 31 October 1770, Barry appeared as Lear at Garrick's theater, with one highly significant addition to the cast lists—"Curan", a name, apparently invented by Garrick, for the gentleman who accompanies Kent on the heath. Curan appears only in the Bell text of 1773, and not in either Tate or Colman. What happened seems obvious: after the appearance of Gentleman's criticism in 1770, Garrick, or at any rate someone at Drury Lane, altered the text of the play along the lines that Gentleman had advised. Garrick, however, did not appear, but sent Barry in his place. Was he testing? Garrick had long ago given up new parts, and although Lear would by no means be new to him, a *new text* would be a distinct challenge, especially in picking up cues, since so much had been restored to the other characters. Moreover, Garrick's health was not what it once had been: it is easy to understand why he might hesitate to attempt to a new version of his old favorite.

Garrick, in reworking *King Lear,* seems to have attempted to satisfy Gentleman's request for a text along "medium principles, between the latitude of Tate, and the circumscription of Colman." His success may be measured by the conclusion drawn by Gentleman, who contributed the introduction and notes to the new version:

> This tragedy originally is, in many places, too diffuse, and in others ob-scure. TATE, in his alteration, has properly curtailed, and, in general, polished it: however, we think the following edition, as performed at the theatre in Drury-lane, by judiciously blending of TATE and SHAKE-SPEARE, is made more nervous than that by the Laureat; and much more agreeable than Mr. COLMAN's late alteration.

Gentleman, however, did not have a hand in the task of editing, for he noted on the first page of the text that he favors Tate's beginning with Edmund's soliloquy over the original scene from Shakespeare, as found in both Colman and the new version.

The major difference between Colman's and Garrick's texts, of course, is that the latter retains the love scenes that Colman and others had found so excruciating in the theater. Both were in agreement, however, about the final scene, for this remained as in Tate: a prison, with Lear in final triumph over his adversaries and the ascension of Cordelia and Edgar to the throne. Hence, Garrick's new text was still far removed from Shakespeare's original; it did not hold the stage for long; and when Kemble came to perform the play nearer the end of the century he reverted to an essentially Tate text. It was Edmund Kean who first restored the tragic ending in 1823, and, more signi-ficantly, William Charles Macready, in 1834 and 1838, who restored first a Tate-free text and later, with much trepidation, restored the Fool.[22]

In conclusion, then, contrary to established belief among theater historians, Garrick did not initiate a return to Shakespeare's text of *King Lear*. Indeed, at the very outset of his career, his archenemy, Theophilus Cibber, seems to have been responsible for a competitive production "with restorations". While Garrick, in the years ahead, restored some lines to his own role of Lear, he did not in 1756, as has been traditionally believed, restore any sizable portion of Shakespeare's text. Rather, it was George Colman who pressed Garrick to restore more of the original and, failing to persuade his friend, produced his version at Covent Garden in 1768, a version which prompted Francis Gentle-man to request of Garrick a text along "medium principles" between Tate and Colman. This Garrick gave his audiences, with Spranger Barry in the leading role, in 1770. Garrick himself did not appear in his new Lear until 1773, three years before his retirement. Hence, Garrick's reputation as prime mover in the restoration of Shakespeare's text of *King Lear* to the eighteenth-century stage is no longer tenable. Colman's work, therefore, emerges as per-haps the most important single contribution towards the restoration of the original text between the time of Tate and the early nineteenth century.

Eastern Michigan University

---

[22] There is amusing irony here, in that, while Colman attempted to "reconcile the catastrophe of Tate to the story of Shakespeare", Kean merely attached the catastrophe of Shakespeare to the earlier four acts of Tate. This experiment, too, failed.

WRITING FOR THE METROPOLIS: ILLEGITIMATE PERFORMANCES OF SHAKESPEARE IN EARLY NINETEENTH-CENTURY LONDON

JANE MOODY

'A kingdom for a stage, princes to act, / And monarchs to behold the swelling scene.'[1] Such was Shakespeare's description of the theatrical space in which he wished his plays to be performed. Or rather, so Thomas Morton, a reader of plays at Drury Lane, sought to defend the existing system of dramatic regulation in nineteenth-century London. Shakespeare's plays, he claimed, should be performed 'only in the noblest temples of the Muses'.[2]

Until 1843, theatrical legislation permitted only Drury Lane and Covent Garden (the 'patent' theatres) to perform Shakespeare within the metropolis.[3] This article discusses certain 'illegitimate' performances of Shakespeare which took place at the London 'minor' playhouses. These establishments included the Royal Circus/Surrey in Southwark, the theatre in Tottenham Street, the Pavilion and Garrick theatres in Whitechapel, and perhaps most importantly, the Coburg theatre, now the Old Vic. Often converted from other non-cultural uses – an old clothes factory, a shop or a disused chapel – these new playhouses attracted not only the local gentry, but also *petit bourgeois* and artisan spectators: butchers, shopkeepers, sugar bakers, tailors and mechanics as well as hackney coachmen, sweeps and dustmen.

The commercial survival of local playhouses depended on their ability to target the interests of spectators from the neighbourhood. Nevertheless, managers also wished to encourage the lucrative patronage of genteel theatre-goers from Westminster. What deterred such spectators were the unrespectable neighbourhoods in which the minor theatres were often situated, and the 'vulgar' social constituencies which attended them. Reviewers too perceived the world of Whitechapel or the New Cut as a theatrical *terra incognita*: distant, exotic, primitive, and sometimes threatening. If ever the English Emperor or Empress were to visit the Coburg, commented one, it would be necessary 'to imitate the Roman potentate, by drenching the audience with rose-water to neutralize certain vile odours arising from gin and tobacco, and bad ventilation'.[4]

Accounts of minor performances of Shakespeare often read like theatrical travelogues of native culture for the amusement of a genteel readership. Although certain reviewers admired these performances, others laughingly dismissed popular Shakespearian consumption. Their derision seems to mask a pervasive anxiety about this theatrical disintegration of

---

[1] *Henry V*, Prologue, 3–4.

[2] *Report and Minutes of the Select Committee on Dramatic Literature*, in Parliamentary Papers, *Reports from Committees*, 18 vols., vol. 7, para. 3897.

[3] The Little Theatre in the Haymarket was permitted to perform 'legitimate drama' in the summer months only. See further, Watson Nicholson, *The Struggle for a Free Stage in London* (London, 1906) and Dewey Ganzel, 'Patent Wrongs and Patent Theatres: Drama and the Law in the Early Nineteenth Century', *PMLA*, 76 (1961), 384–96.

[4] F. G. Tomlins, *A Brief View of the English Drama* (London, 1840), p. 60.

established cultural and social hierarchies. The presence and visibility of 'vulgar' spectators at these performances, and their capacity to influence the choice of dramatic repertoire, seemed to threaten the stability and the integrity of the cultural state.

In order to avoid prosecution, the minor theatres needed to circumvent the illegality of their Shakespearian productions. House playwrights were therefore hired to adapt and recast the plays in accordance with the regulations governing illegitimate performance. At the same time, these playwrights reinvented Shakespeare for popular dramatic constituencies. Critics have recently claimed that the early nineteenth century is the cultural moment when a 'populist' Shakespeare becomes politically unpalatable.[5] Illegitimate productions of Shakespeare offer a different perspective on these arguments. My exploration of how theatrical practice and cultural politics map on to each other seems to make possible a more eclectic description of Shakespeare's cultural capital in nineteenth-century London.

The most obvious ruse by which Shakespeare could be staged was by reinventing his plays as burlettas or melodramas.[6] Playbills therefore advertised a 'serious Melo-dramatic Burletta, founded on a favourite and popular Tragedy to be called *The Mantuan Lovers, or Romeo and Juliet*' or 'a new grand historical spectacle' entitled *The Death of Caesar; or, the Battle of Philippi*.[7] These compilations usually retained the 'principal incidents' of Shakespeare's play, often adding a few extra characters for a comic subplot. Reviewers interpreted these changes in terms of the theatrical interests of the spectators at a particular playhouse. An account of *The Death of Caesar* reported for example that the adapter had 'introduced something of his own, which is probably better understood by the Surrey audiences'.[8]

The geographical location of the East-End theatres ensured them some immunity from the litigious eyes of the patentees. On the south bank of the river, however, the Surrey and Coburg theatres ran a much greater risk of prosecution. Glossop, manager of the Coburg, was prosecuted and subsequently fined £50 for representing *Richard III*, starring the controversial tragedian Junius Brutus Booth.[9] In 1828, the Coburg was threatened with prosecution by Drury Lane for proposing to stage what seems to have been an unadulterated version of *Macbeth, King of Scotland! or the Weird Sisters*. On this occasion, the new manager was keen to avoid a confrontation. Having protested against 'so inordinate a Claim to the Intellectual Monopoly and Domination', he withdrew the piece and a version of *Hamlet* based on Jean-François Ducis's adaptation was staged instead.[10]

The Royal Circus *Macbeth* of 1809 carefully signposted its own illegitimacy.[11] The opening address, spoken by Elliston, wryly pointed out

---

[5] See Annabel Patterson's discussion of Coleridge in *Shakespeare and the Popular Voice* (Oxford, 1989), pp. 5–7; John Collick, *Shakespeare, Cinema and Society* (Manchester, 1989), pp. 19–20.

[6] Burletta had become an umbrella term for performances at the minor theatres which for legal purposes included five or six songs in each act. See Joseph Donohue, 'Burletta and the Early Nineteenth-Century English Theatre', *Nineteenth-Century Theatre Research*, 1 (1973), 29–51.

[7] Surrey playbills, 4 March 1823; 26 December 1823. All playbills cited can be found in the collections of the Theatre Museum.

[8] *Mirror of the Stage*, vol. 3, no. 12 (5 January 1824), p. 185.

[9] Middlesex Sessions, 6 and 19 January 1820. See *Morning Chronicle*, 10 February 1820; *British Stage and Literary Cabinet*, vol. 4, no. 34 (March 1820), 140–1.

[10] For the controversy over *Macbeth*, which was to have been staged on 15 and 16 February, see playbills for 11, 15 and 18 February 1828.

[11] *The History, Murders, Life and Death of Macbeth* (London, 1809). The theatre was not prosecuted, but Elliston's interpretation of the law was raised at a meeting between Sheridan and the Lord Chamberlain. 'The Justice was in a fury. Much was said about the illegality of your Circus Macbeth, when Sheridan slily observed, the greatest violation was to the bard, in *your* attempting the impersonation!' See George Raymond, *Memoirs of Robert William Elliston*, 2 vols. (London, 1844), vol. 1, p. 437.

that the performers were 'not indulged with fullest pow'rs of speech'. Here, the manager cautiously set out the theatrical terms under which he proposed to negotiate the law and yet apparently keep within the terms of his licence. The play was staged in dumbshow, with occasional rhymed dialogue. Linen 'scrolls' or banners carried by the characters and bearing such announcements as 'Macbeth ordains a solemn Banquet' or 'Destruction to the Tyrant' (Macduff's banner at Birnam Wood) translated or supplemented the events narrated in dumbshow. What in the patent houses would have been communicated to the audience primarily by linguistic means was presented at the Royal Circus in a non-verbal affective code.

Music accompanied the stage action almost throughout. One notable exception was Act I, Scene 7, after the retirement of Macbeth's guests, and Banquo's presentation of the ring to Macbeth. The next part of the play bears the specific stage direction, 'very solemnly and strikingly performed without music'. The music stops, as if to express the encroaching evil, and eerie silence, broken only by the sound of the bell tolling, prevails throughout a dumbshow version of the dagger scene:

Lady Macbeth descends and listens at Duncan's door, and finds all quiet, she then enters. Macbeth and attendant descend. Macbeth discharges him, and moves lightly about. Enter Lady Macbeth. A struggle between her and Macbeth, he being afraid to execute the deed. Lady Macbeth then leaves him. An illusion of a spirit holding a dagger appears, which he endeavours to seize, but it vanishes when he makes the attempt. A bell tolls.

MACBETH Hear not that Duncan; for it is a knell
That summons thee to Heav'n, or to hell.
[Exit]

By the 1820s, however, caution had been thrown to the winds, at least as far as banners were concerned. Nevertheless, the presence of musical accompaniment continued to provide a theoretical safeguard against prosecution as well as an important theatrical language in itself. We

know that the Coburg production of *Richard III* in 1819–20 was accompanied by music because of the testimony provided by Doobey, an assistant in the Covent Garden box office who had been sent to spy on the performance. Doobey stated that the Coburg *Richard III* resembled the Covent Garden production with the exception of an occasional, and almost inaudible musical intrument. According to one reviewer, a Surrey production of *Othello* as late as 1831 was 'interspersed with melo-dramatic music, in order to render it legitimately illegitimate'.[12]

Managers employed their house dramatists to adapt or 'melodramatize' Shakespeare for a particular playhouse. My argument is that this process of adaptation began primarily as a legal safeguard but also provided an opportunity to translate Shakespeare for popular consumption. Glossop defended his production of *Richard III* on the grounds that he had employed Moncrieff to 'melodramatize' the play; he claimed that the production therefore came within the terms of the Coburg's licence. Indeed, the extant evidence would suggest that the Coburg play differed only in its penchant for gory sensation. Doobey remarked that the scene featuring the murder of the children in the Tower (which took place off stage at Covent Garden), was staged at the Coburg in full view of the audience, accompanied by music whose purpose Doobey conjectured was 'to drown the cries'.[13] Moncrieff's adaptation seems to have catered to the notorious taste of Coburg audiences for 'blood-tub' drama.

In the wake of this prosecution, the Coburg management exercised more caution, and not a little ingenuity, in their Shakespearian productions. One tactic was to stage a different version of the story altogether. Milner's adaptation of *Hamlet* – staged 'at the request of

12 *Figaro*, no. 7 (21 January, 1831), p. 82.
13 *British Stage*, p. 141. Compare the Surrey *Macbeth*, where Macduff's children were murdered 'very properly off the stage' (Act 2, Scene 6).

numerous Frequenters of the Theatre' – was therefore based on Ducis' version of Shakespeare's play. The playbill somewhat gleefully emphasized that the piece 'is neither founded on Shakespeare's admirable Tragedy of the same name, nor is it for one moment purposed to be thrust into a mad competition with that sublime production'. The story of *Hamlet*, it was announced, provided 'a multitude of powerful Situations, capable of being Melo-Dramatically treated'; the resulting melodrama would be 'as interesting, impressive, moral, and terrific, as was ever produced in a Minor Theatre'.[14]

Ducis had transformed Shakespeare's tragic plot into a gothic melodrama.[15] The hero whose prevaricating introspection seemed to epitomize a certain kind of Romantic idealism becomes a decisive military hero who has returned in triumph after his victory over the Norwegians. Having dispensed with the *confidantes* for Gertrude and Hamlet, introduced by Ducis in accordance with neo-classical convention, Milner closely followed the plot of the French play. At the 'SPLENDID BANQUET Given in honor of Hamlet's Victory', Hamlet presents his mother with the poisoned cup, ordering her to '*Pledge his Father's Memory*'; her horror convinces him that she is guilty. She later confesses her crime at the elder Hamlet's tomb; Hamlet is on the point of killing her when he is forbidden to do so by the ghost's 'SUDDEN APPEARANCE'. Finally, Hamlet is put on trial in the 'GRAND HALL OF AUDIENCE' for his father's murder, and the attempted murder of his mother. On the point of being condemned, he is absolved by the Queen's confession. The conspiracy of Claudius is '*defeated by the Zeal and Loyalty of Horatio*' and Hamlet is proclaimed King.

It is clear from the language of the playbill that the fear of prosecution lay behind the Coburg's decision to stage Ducis's version of *Hamlet* rather than Shakespeare's. Ducis provided Milner with a convenient theatrical short cut enabling the Coburg to stage a play which was both Shakespearian and not Shakespearian,

legitimate and illegitimate. But the melodramatic framework of Ducis' play may also have appealed to the Coburg dramatist. For Ducis recasts Shakespeare's plot within that familiar moral economy where the good are rewarded, and the evil punished in a last-minute reversal. The French play reinvented *Hamlet* in such a way that it would dovetail neatly with the values and ideology of the Coburg's non-Shakespearian repertoire.

Magna Charta; or, The Eventful Reign of King John was Milner's most distinctive adaptation.[16] Here a popular melodramatic subplot was woven into a Shakespearian narrative. Comic subplots were frequently interpolated in performances at the London fairs in the eighteenth century.[17] What is distinctive about Milner's translation is that it makes a hero out of a lowly French servant. In addition, Magna Charta, an event scarcely mentioned in Shakespeare's account, is placed in Milner's play at the heart of the plot.

Milner's *Magna Charta* was grandiose in scale and visually spectacular. The 'splendid and characteristic scenery' included an 'exact Representation of the Arms, Armorial Bearings, and Warlike Accoutrements of those Ancient times (1215)' in the final scene; it had been painted for the occasion by Wilkins, Walker, Pitt and others. The play's attractions included 'a DESPERATE COMBAT between the French and English kings MOUNTED ON

---

[14] Playbill for 28 January advertising a forthcoming performance on 4 February 1828.

[15] J. F. Ducis, *Hamlet*, Tragédie en cinq actes (Paris, 1769, new edition, 1815).

[16] My reading of the performance is based on a playbill for 5 May 1823 and a juvenile drama text published by Hodgson. It cannot be assumed that this play script is a faithful record of the Coburg production. Nevertheless, it does provide a textual skeleton from which we can to some extent reconstruct *Magna Charta*.

[17] Stanley Wells discusses eighteenth-century booth adaptations of *The Winter's Tale* including the history of *Doratus and Fawnia* in 'A Shakespearean Droll?' *Theatre Notebook*, 15 (1961), 116–17.

SUPERB WAR HORSES' and a 'GORGEOUS banquet' 'embracing the entire extent of the Stage'.

In *Magna Charta*, a comic melodrama of mistaken identities involving two French couples – Celine and Henrique, Louise and Basil – is incorporated into the story of the barons' demand for a charter. The hero of Milner's play is Henrique, Baron Falconbridge's faithful French servant. Henrique is a loyal and patriotic character who vows to sell his cottage and garden and to shed 'the last drop of my blood' fighting for his country. It is Henrique and the Baron who try to prevent Arthur's death; in its aftermath Baron Falconbridge is responsible for the creation and signing of Magna Charta. Watched by all the barons, Falconbridge brings the dead Arthur out of the moat; the demand for a charter to protect their rights and liberties begins from the contemplation of Arthur's death:

See this, ye noblemen of England, and lament for ever! – here is your lawful prince inhumanly murdered! – Follow me, brave Barons, and let us swear never to sheath our swords till John shall grant us a charter to secure our rights and liberties.[18]

At Runnymede, King John capitulates in desperation and signs the charter in a last-ditch attempt to hold on to his crown. But the disguised Henrique (rather than an anonymous monk) offers him a poisoned goblet: the King drinks and dies, having accepted the justice of his fate as melodramatic convention dictates. Milner thus makes a poor Frenchman the author of the gesture which transforms Britain into 'the land of liberty'.[19]

Popular subtexts sometimes took the form of miniature plots as in *Magna Charta*; in other performances the addition of a single character seems to introduce a kind of ideological change or disturbance. Consider a Coburg performance of a favourite Shakespearian plot: *The Battle of Bosworth Field; or, the Life and Death of Richard III*. The standard acting version of the play incorporated part of Rowe's tragedy, *Jane Shore*. In a Coburg playbill for 1827, Shore, in an 'EXTREMITY OF DISTRESS' is 'on the point of DYING with HUNGER in the Streets'. Here however, she is rescued by a 'BENEVOLENT BAKER', who is promptly arrested for his trouble.[20] It seems that the Coburg compiler suddenly detected an opportunity to include a tragic version of the melodramatic rescue formula starring a humble character with whose status and heroism a Coburg audience might readily identify.

I want to turn now from the adaptation of texts for performance to the broader context in which illegitimate productions of Shakespeare were being presented. The meanings and functions of these performances were varied and distinctive: rivalry with the patent establishments, defiant flouting of theatrical legislation, signs of cultural legitimacy. Certain benefit performances conspicuously deployed Shakespeare as a weapon in metropolitan theatrical politics. *Othello* was performed in support of the Bill 'to relieve the Minor Theatres from unjust oppression, and thus give the Public an opportunity of seeing the regular Drama performed at other than the Major Houses'.[21] John Kemble Chapman, the manager of the New City, also staged *Othello* in order to help pay the fine which he had incurred at the suit of the patentees for having illegally performed legitimate drama at the Tottenham Street theatre. Although commercial considerations were obviously paramount in the selection of repertoire for such a benefit, the choice of Shakespeare for these performances also drew public attention to the fact that, according to law, Shakespeare could not be represented at the minor playhouses.

Playbills announced that certain Shakespearian performances had been 'requested' by the

---

18 Act 2, Scene 12.
19 Chorus, Act 3, Scene 18.
20 See playbills for 29 January and 5 February 1827.
21 Surrey playbill, 27 January 1832.

audience. A Surrey bill for 1832 described the proprietor having been 'waited on by a Deputation of Gentlemen, and others' from the neighbourhood requesting the performance of 'some part of the NATIONAL DRAMA'.[22] A later bill emphasized that the chosen burletta 'interspersed with Melo-dramatic Music, founded on Shakespeare's Othello! TO BE CALLED THE VENETIAN MOOR' was to be staged 'solely in compliance with the above request, and not in opposition to the existing laws, which it is his HUMBLE PETITION, and that of HUNDREDS OF THOUSANDS of this vast and enlightened Metropolis, may be forthwith altered and amended'.[23] Were these tactics a democratic subterfuge for circumventing dramatic regulation, or simply an ingenious dramatic puff designed to emphasize the management's determination to please its consumers even if it meant staging illegal performances?

A Surrey playbill advertising the 'highly popular burletta founded upon King Richard III' announced the inclusion of an unusual interlude during the Battle of Bosworth Field:

MR COOKE will (accoutred in a REAL) FRENCH CUIRASS, STRIPPED FROM A CUIRASSIER, ON THE FIELD OF BATTLE AT WATERLOO, and which bears the Indenture of SEVERAL MUSKET SHOT AND SABRE CUTS go thro' the Evolutions of the **Attack and Defence, with a Sword in each Hand!**[24]

Here, a Shakespearian battle becomes a sign of a war outside the playhouse; the performance of Richard III a patriotic event. By putting on a French cuirass, did Richard/Cooke (the archetypal representative of the British tar) become in the minds of the Surrey spectators a British soldier at Waterloo? The cuirass seems to be advertised not so much as a cue for patriotic display as an authentic, yet almost supernatural spoil of war. A visual sign of the war with France outside the theatre, the cuirass was also a piece of exotic booty.

Shakespearian performances were a crucial

way of signalling a theatre's aspirations towards cultural legitimacy. Playbills cited the performance of Shakespeare and other legitimate playwrights as evidence of the theatrical 'march of intellect', and the substitution of 'decorum' for 'jingling doggerels ... riot and confusion'.[25] When the Coburg was prosecuted for representing Richard III, the manager's defence hinged on the argument that the patentees were trying to suppress cultural improvement and theatrical respectability. Glossop argued that to force the theatre back to 'ribaldry, nonsense, scrolls, and orchestra tinklings' would be 'an outrage on the intellectual character of the nation, an injury to public order and christian morality'.[26] By linking the minor theatres' dramatic past with immorality and disorder, the manager cleverly insinuated that theatrical democracy and the performance of legitimate plays were necessary conditions for popular cooperation in the social order.

Staging Shakespeare with a famous patent performer like Junius Brutus Booth or Kean also challenged the supposed dramatic supremacy of the patent houses. The Regency theatre in Tottenham Street even had the audacity to invite the patent proprietors to a representation of Othello to witness the superiority of their own actor 'on the above extraordinary occasion'.[27] But the most notorious example of an attempt at cultural legitimacy which backfired was the engagement of Edmund Kean at the New City theatre in Milton Street, Finsbury, and the Coburg theatre in 1831.

---

[22] 16 January 1832.
[23] Surrey playbill, 30 January 1832.
[24] 11 September 1815. The bill added that the Cuirass belonged to 'a Gentleman just arrived from the Continent, who has kindly lent it to Mr Cooke FOR THIS NIGHT ONLY'.
[25] Surrey playbill, 15 September 1832.
[26] 'Attempt to Suppress the Minor Drama' in the Theatrical Inquisitor, vol. 16 (February 1820), 99–103, 102. See also the Morning Chronicle for 8 and 14 January 1820.
[27] The Times, 10 January 1815.

Kean's engagement was presented by these playhouses as an incontrovertible sign of their dramatic respectability. Davidge's playbill alluded to Southwark's glorious theatrical history and the manager's pride 'in reflecting that the Preference for the first Appearance of Mr KEAN on this side of the Water ("the side on which the olden Theatres once stood, where Shakspeare, Massinger and Ben Jonson wrote and acted") had been given to his Theatre'.[28] In order to capitalize on the profits anticipated during Kean's engagement, the Coburg redesigned its theatrical space so as to provide stall seats. The playbill promised that those who had seen Kean at the patent theatres would 'find their Admiration and Delight at his splendid powers tenfold increased by embracing the present opportunity of seeing them exerted in a Theatre of moderate Dimensions, allowing every Master Look and fine tone of the Artist to be distinctly heard and seen'. Ironically, Kean's performance as Othello at the Coburg was marked by disruption as spectators loyal to Cobham, a favourite local actor, expressed their disapproval that Kean had invaded the native performer's territory. The *Tatler* commented somewhat wryly that Davidge's 'laudable ambition' of introducing Shakespeare, 'and his present best interpreter, KEAN', at the Coburg was unlikely to be realized 'till his audiences learn to abate much of their boisterousness, and approach nearer to his own good taste in these matters'.[29]

Reviewers flocked to the New City and the Coburg partly in order to gloat at the contrast between Kean's once glorious career and his descent to what they regarded as a theatrical Hades. Both these playhouses were perceived as plebeian and therefore unrespectable cultural spaces. Their neighbourhoods offered a distinctive collection of social and cultural signs through which critics interpreted Kean's performances. As the *Satirist* remarked, Kean must surely realize 'it will be transportation to no one but himself to exhibit at such a place'.[30] And whilst 'by no means for monopoly . . . we

certainly *do* consider Mr Kean's present itinerary derogatory to himself, and degrading to the drama at large'.[31]

What was the significance of Kean's performances? Several recent prosecutions had highlighted the precarious legal position of the minor playhouses; the campaign to abolish the theatrical monopoly was now gaining momentum. At the New City, Kean – whether out of conviction or as a politic dramatic role we cannot tell – explicitly supported the cause of the minor theatres. He alluded to the declining state of the patent houses and 'their monopolizing spirit' and announced his determination to make the New City 'the rival of the large ones in talent, though not in style'.[32] Kean's appearance might not have fulfilled its financial promise; it did however provide more incidental ammunition for the minor theatres' cause.

We can see from the comments surrounding Kean's engagement that the status and 'respectability' of these theatres dominated reviews. Just as the tastes of popular theatregoers were being incorporated into Shakespearian adaptations, so these consumers and their insalubrious neighbourhoods were relentlessly inscribed on critical descriptions of illegitimate Shakespearian performances. Both critics and playwrights were deploying Shakespeare to write for and about the nineteenth-century metropolis. Since

---

[28] Coburg playbill, 1 July 1831. Cf. *Tatler*, no. 260 (4 July 1831), p. 11.

[29] *Tatler*, no. 276 (22 July 1831), p. 80.

[30] *Satirist*, vol. 1, no. 12 (26 June 1831), p. 94.

[31] *Age* (3 July 1831), p. 213.

[32] *Tatler*, no. 225 (24 May 1831), p. 900, signed 'F.F.'. Whilst engaged at the New City, Kean was asked to appear at Drury Lane. He accepted, but insisted, much to the amusement of reviewers and supporters of the minor theatres, that the Drury Lane playbill should mention his appearance at the patent house 'by kind permission of John Kemble Chapman'. According to the *Age* (12 June 1831), p. 189, the Drury Lane management instituted an inquiry into the inclusion of this reference.

the minor theatres continued to be regarded as artisan domains, the interpretation of these plays was inevitably preoccupied with questions of popular cultural consumption. Cast adrift from the familiar territory of Westminster, critics tried to come to terms with the changing configuration of urban and cultural space in London – and the apparently inexplicable sight of Whitechapel butchers watching Shakespeare.

On the one hand, some reviewers welcomed what they perceived as improvements in the repertoire and productions of the Surrey or the Pavilion theatres. For others, however, these productions violated not only established social and cultural hierarchies, but Shakespeare himself. The claim that *Hamlet* and *Macbeth* 'are but little calculated for the multitude' was simply a convenient way of displacing into liberal paternalism the more determinedly conservative argument that Shakespeare should not be available to the populace at all.[33] We can identify these concerns in the critical antipathy which greeted the Surrey *Macbeth* of 1809. One reviewer accused Elliston of having transformed Macbeth into 'a musical retailer of eight line verses' and the manager was indicted for 'administering to the ignorance or depravity of the multitude'.[34] The *Theatrical Inquisitor* called for the theatre to return to its former repertoire of ballets of action and pantomimes, which suggestion produced an indignant reply from a local theatregoer congratulating Elliston on behalf of the Surrey inhabitants for his improvements to the theatrical culture in the neighbourhood.[35]

Illegitimate Shakespearian productions provided genteel reviewers with comic and satirical ammunition. One critic remarked that Farrell's performance as Macduff at the Whitechapel Slaughter House (*alias* the Pavilion) resembled that of a Whitechapel butcher.[36] Reviewers alluded darkly to the 'murdering' of Shakespeare at certain minor theatres, or the 'conspiracy now going on at the Queen's against Shakespeare's immortality' in the presence of 'a

selection from the Tottenham Court Road sweeps, and the Saint Giles' vagabonds'.[37]

Laughing at plebeian consumption of Shakespeare was another more oblique method of policing those social constituencies which had, or should have access to 'high' culture. The rhodomontades which posed as reviews of these performances allowed their writers to replay as comedy anxieties about the consequences of these cultural changes. Burlesquing minor Shakespeare, and its spectators in particular, provided a textual form for critics to express, and simultaneously to dismiss genteel fears about the social and political consequences of popular education and knowledge.

Reviewers drove an aesthetic wedge between a 'genuine' representation of Shakespeare, and the travesty they had condescended to patronize at the Surrey or the Pavilion in order to recover some ideological ground and to shore up their cultural élitism. Shakespeare's own authority provided a convenient weapon for these manoeuvres. An account of *King Lear* starring David Osbaldiston at the Surrey for example scored its pejorative critical goal by invoking Hamlet's instructions to the players:

When he repeated 'This is not Lear', the whole house, or rather those who knew what *Lear* ought to be, bore evidence of the truth of the exclamation. Whatever approbation he might have elicited from the generous shopkeepers who knew no better, his whole performance had the effect of making the 'judicious grieve'.[38]

This account is founded upon the gap, half comic, half disturbing, between an 'authentic'

[33] *Theatrical Inquisitor*, vol. 5 (December 1814), p. 403.
[34] *Theatrical Inquisitor*, vol. 2 (April 1813) p. 136, signed 'H'. in vol. 16 (January 1820), p. 34; the journal concluded that Lawler 'broke SHAKESPEARE upon the wheel by versifying him, and Mr. ELLISTON gave him the *coup de grace* by performing his *Macbeth*'.
[35] *Theatrical Inquisitor*, vol. 1 (October 1812), 68–70, signed 'Veritas'.
[36] *Columbine*, no. 4 (25 July 1829), p. 30.
[37] *Figaro in London*, no. 90 (24 August 1833), p. 136.
[38] *Satirist*, vol. 1, no. 19 (14 August 1831), p. 150.

Shakespeare, and a popular travesty. The reviewer is of course alluding to Hamlet's objections about that style of acting which 'though it make the unskilful laugh, cannot but make the judicious grieve'.[39] Hamlet's distinction between a 'judicious' theatrical constituency and those groundlings to which a 'periwig-pated fellow' might play for cheap laughs, is seen to have its nineteenth-century parallel in the Surrey performance. Here, the spectators can be divided into the 'judicious' (who share with the reviewer the right to make critical judgements) and the 'generous' (who can never be culturally enfranchised). A popular Shakespearian event is neatly and conclusively dismissed.

That broader nineteenth-century debate about social and cultural hierarchy, the nature and function of cultural provision, often breaks through the cracks of these critical accounts. Watching Shakespeare at a minor theatre was an unfamiliar and jarring experience to reviewers precisely because these performances made visible the theatrical interests of 'generous shopkeepers'. These playhouses were neither unequivocally genteel nor unequivocally plebeian places. Illegitimate performance seemed to resist assimilation into either the language of moral and biological contagion in which the middle classes sought to characterize the social 'other', or indeed the emerging discourse of social respectability. The old moral topographies in which the metropolis had been defined were losing their authority, but new interpretive maps which might have made these cultural spaces legible and familiar had not yet replaced them. And what was threatening about theatres like the Coburg or the East-End playhouses was that they made available cultural capital to social groups which until now had been theatrically disenfranchised. That Shakespeare was popular, and even commercially successful at these playhouses challenged existing assumptions that, as Thomas Morton would have put it, princes acted, whilst monarchs beheld. The presence of mixed social groups watching these performances no doubt seemed all the more incomprehensible in view of the increasing segregation of domestic and cultural spaces by class taking place outside the theatre.

I have argued here that the iconographic conventions of minor Shakespeare – banners, music and song – originated from specific legal circumstances. However, it has been suggested that these various adaptations and translations of Shakespeare must also be interpreted in terms of the social identity of their consumers. Moncrieff and Milner adapted and reworked Shakespearian material for particular local audiences. Melodrama – the prevailing theatrical form in the minor repertoire – offered a set of theatrical conventions and moral values through which Shakespeare was mediated and transformed. The critical ambivalence surrounding these performances reveals the way in which theatrical practice, and in particular popular consumption, disturbed existing assumptions about the control, dissemination and patronage of dramatic culture in the metropolis.

---

[39] *Hamlet*, 3.2. 25–6.

Shakespeare, Illustrated: Charles Kean's 1857 Production of *The Tempest*

MARY M. NILAN

IN our century *The Tempest* has assumed a special prominence, many modern critics contending that through this work Shakespeare presented mankind with a "new vision" or at least with the playwright's "final vision" of the world. E. M. W. Tillyard suggests that the play embodies the theme of "regeneration" in which "Ferdinand and Miranda sustain Prospero in representing a new order of things that has evolved out of destruction."[1] For Mark Van Doren, the play is an attempt "to fix a vision . . . Shakespeare is telling us for the last time about the world. . . . *The Tempest* does bind up in final form a host of themes with which the author has been concerned."[2] And G. Wilson Knight observes that the play "repeats, as it were, in miniature, the separate themes of Shakespeare's greater Plays. . . . It yet distils the poetic essence of the whole Shakespearian universe."[3]

In the first half of the nineteenth century, however, *The Tempest* was not accorded such a significant role in the Shakespearean repertoire; it was considered by most literary critics of the period as a more or less delightful romantic fantasy and little more. It was for Samuel Taylor Coleridge, "a specimen of the purely romantic drama";[4] for William Hazlitt, a "fantastic creation" where "the real characters and events partake of the wildness of a dream";[5] for Thomas Campbell, "a comparatively grave counterpart to *A Midsummer Night's Dream* . . . for its gayety is only less abandoned and frolicsome."[6]

Why this disparity in views from one century to the next? The answer may be at least partially discovered through a study of nineteenth-century stage presentations of *The Tempest*. Professional Shakespearean productions have tended to influence contemporary concepts about the significance of individual characters and about the overall meaning of any given drama. For example, Hazlitt, writing in 1820, noted with regard to *The Merchant of Venice*:

> When we first went to see Mr. Kean in Shylock, we expected to see, what we had been used to see. . . . We were disappointed because we had taken our idea from other actors, not from the play. . . . But so rooted was our habitual impression of the part from seeing it caricatured in the represen-

[1] E. M. W. Tillyard, *Shakespeare's Last Plays* (London: Chatto & Windus, 1938), pp. 49–58.
[2] Mark Van Doren, *Shakespeare* (New York: Doubleday, 1939), pp. 178–85.
[3] G. Wilson Knight, *The Shakespearian Tempest,* 3rd ed. (London: Methuen, 1964), p. 247.
[4] Samuel Taylor Coleridge, *Shakespearian Criticism,* ed. Thomas Middleton Raysor, 2nd ed. (New York: Dutton, 1960), I, 118.
[5] William Hazlitt, *The Characters of Shakespeare's Plays* (London, 1817), p. 116.
[6] Thomas Campbell, *Dramatic Works of Shakespeare* (London, 1838), p. 87.

tation, that it was only from a careful perusal of the play itself that we saw our error.[7]

Hazlitt was certainly not the only critic influenced by theatrical representations rather than the literary text. As Charles Shattuck comments in his introduction to *The Shakespeare Promptbooks*:

> It does not matter very much, practically, whether the original author of the play was Francis Bacon or Edward de Vere; it has often mattered greatly that the "effective" authors have been . . . all the Garricks and Guthries whose stage imagery has spread upon the plays the form and pressure of their separate generations.[8]

Thus what the critic as well as the general public has at times accepted as "Shakespeare's intention," has only been what a leading producer believed that intention to be.

With this in mind, it is interesting to analyze one major production of *The Tempest* in the mid-nineteenth century, one which was really the culmination of a long-established trend toward emphasizing the purely theatrical aspect of the work while deemphasizing the text itself. Early in the nineteenth century, Coleridge had commented on this tendency in *Tempest* productions:

> Although the illusion may be assisted by the effect on the senses of the complicated machinery and decorations of modern times, yet this sort of assistance is dangerous. For the principal and only genuine excitement ought to come from within,—from the moved and sympathetic imagination; whereas, where so much is addressed to the mere external senses of seeing and hearing, the spiritual vision is apt to languish, and the attraction from without will withdraw the mind from the proper and only legitimate interest which is intended to spring from within.[9]

Coleridge notwithstanding, the trend toward theatrical emphasis continued, reaching a peak with Charles Kean's staging of the piece.

By 1857 Kean was already noted as a Shakespearean producer who spared no effort or expense and insisted on historical accuracy in costumes, properties, and decorations. In preparing *The Tempest* for its 1 July opening at the Princess Theatre, however, he apparently felt himself free from the confines of any specific historical period and at liberty to exercise his unrestrained imagination. John William Cole, the producer's contemporary biographer, probably summed up the concept which guided Kean when, in *Bell's Weekly Messenger* of 4 July 1857, he said:

> In a fanciful creation, such as *The Tempest*, in which the exhaustless genius of the poet has soared beyond existing worlds and imagined new ones, no boundaries are defined and no restrictions are imposed. In transferring this majestic drama to the stage, an outline is sketched by the original inspira-

---

[7] Hazlitt, pp. 276–77.
[8] Charles Shattuck, *The Shakespeare Promptbooks* (Urbana: University of Illinois Press, 1965), p. 1. (In his descriptive catalogue Shattuck assigns a number to each of the primary source materials he lists as available to the researcher. Where applicable, these numbers will be cited.)
[9] Coleridge, I, 118.

tion, the details of which may be filled up according to the extent, comprehension and understanding of kindred tastes.[10]

The critic for the *Morning Chronicle,* writing 3 July 1857, defended this concept:

> No objections can possibly be raised to the employment of the utmost extent of scenic efforts or artistic accompaniments in the representation of those fairy productions of the genius of Shakespeare. A world of dreams, of fairies, of haunted woods, and enchanted caves has to be made visible to the spectator, and the play of human passions is subordinate.

Assuming that Shakespeare sketched only an "outline" and that the producer was to fill the void, Kean spared no effort or expense in meeting the challenge of making visible to the spectator the "world of dreams, of fairies, of haunted woods, and enchanted caves."

Kean's opening shipwreck scene followed the example of Samuel Phelps' 1847 rendition in making use of a large practical ship on a truck; Kean far outdid the earlier producer, however, by employing various special lighting effects in order to pinpoint specific pictures in the overall darkness of the scene.[11] Thus the audience was left with the memory of a series of vivid tableaux within the total moving picture. The scene was pictured in detail by the reviewer for the *Era* of 5 July 1857:

> The whole available space of the stage is devoted to a representation of the ocean lashed into boiling fury by the howling tempest, while filling up the center is the royal galley, with lamps suspended round her poop, dashed hither and thither by the waves off a lee shore. . . . To the utter helplessness of the ship is added the wild half-smothered shrieks of the sailors as they are, from time to time, revealed by the fitful lightning in groups or seen in the lurid beams from the poop lamps. Ariel flits among the frantic mariners as with flashing axe they hew the mast. Ariel is seen darting into the cabin, surrounded by white globules of ethereal fire contrasting admirably with the mortal red of the lamps and the clear blue of the levin. The wild plunges of the ship . . . the boom of the falling masts, and the sharp crack as she splits and rends on the rocks, forms a picture of grand and startling illusion.

This opening sequence became an "act" in itself or, as the playbill termed it, a "prologue" to the play.[12] At the close of the scene the curtain fell and the orchestra played the overture.

The curtain then rose to reveal the mist of the storm gradually dispersing and the sun slowly ascending. Prospero was seen "superintending the effect of

[10] All reviews quoted are from the "London Scrapbooks—Princess Theater" (3 vols.), in the collection of the Folger Shakespeare Library.

[11] The details of this production can be ascertained from a study of the promptbooks at the Folger. Except when specifically attributed to another source, information concerning Kean's staging is taken from the "souvenir promptbook" (Shattuck, p. 19) which was compiled in 1859 by the prompter, T. W. Edmonds and includes 14 small watercolor renderings of the settings to guide the scene painters, Mr. Grieve and Mr. Telbin. The Folger also possesses the "rehearsal workbook" as well as a "cuebook for *Richard II* and *The Tempest*" (Shattuck, pp. 21 and 22) both by George Ellis, the stage manager. (For a more detailed account of this and other source material see Shattuck, pp. 453–54.)

[12] Playbill for 1 July 1857 in "*The Tempest* Scrapbook," in the Theater Collection of the New York City Public Library.

his art" from the pinnacle of a rock which jutted out over the sea. Miranda stood beside him as she begged her father to "allay" the waters; in response to his daughter's request, the magician stretched forth his hands and the waves began to recede from the shoreline, revealing the "yellow sands." By the time the dialogue of the scene between father and daughter was concluded, the waves were hushed, the tide had receded, and a glorious flood of sunlight poured over the sands.

For Ariel's first entrance, Kean made use of William Macready's "business" in which a "ball of fire" was hurled from the flies above into an open stage trap below. The trap, in Kean's production, was masked from the audience's view by a scenic bush, and thus, after his fiery entrance, the sprite appeared to rise up from this bush. At the close of his scene with Prospero, Ariel suddenly disappeared and was then seen "rising from the sea at the back of the stage on the back of a dolphin." As the spirit bade adieu to his master, the dolphin appeared to "sink" beneath the receding "waves." In the final scene of the act, Ariel was seen making a skimming flight across the beach, beckoning towards Ferdinand, while the stage became filled with the sounds of an invisible chorus singing the airs which Shakespeare had assigned to the sprite alone. Throughout the play many scenes were permeated with music from an invisible orchestra as well as from a chorus, so that the island was indeed "full of sweet airs"; Ariel was relieved from singing any solos, a duty "too material," Kean felt, for the airy spirit.[13]

Act II, when compared with the parade of spectacles in the prologue and Act I, was relatively simple. The scenes, of course, offered no real opportunity for elaboration, but there was a new scenic display: "a view of the interior of the island with basaltic columns of rock piled on each other in fantastic forms" against a background of sea and high white-capped mountains. In this setting both scenes of the second act were played. In the first, Ariel actually floated above the nobles playing on a lyre, so that "a general drowsiness seems to pervade all on stage." After Ariel wakened the group, they left the stage, and Caliban, Trinculo, and Stephano arrived to provide some comedy. While there were no memorable theatrical innovations here, Kean may well have desired his audience to have a momentary respite between the breathtaking effects that had preceded and those still to come in the ensuing acts.

For the banquet scene Kean was apparently guided by the theme of "metamorphosis." As the comic conspirators left the stage and the shipwrecked nobles arrived, the scenery itself seemed to become animate. The set, consisting of two bare trees and a number of barren rocks, had remained constant throughout an abbreviated version of Act III, but now, in the words of the *Daily Telegraph* (2 July 1857):

> Gradually the effect of fertilization grows upon the spectator. Little by little, the solid rocks give place to blooming herbiage and the leafless trunks of trees burst into foliage and blossom. Slowly, and by degrees, the evidence of luxuriant vegetation arises on every side while at length, from the land dividing, a river flows forth through the scene and fountains of clear crystal-like water spring up from where formerly all was dry and inanimate.

[13] See John William Cole, *The Life and Theatrical Times of Charles Kean* (London, 1859), II, 220.

In the fertile landscape naiads arrived to dance on the surface of the undulating waters. Satyrs and wood nymphs who had, in the words of Kean's playbill "taken the place of the ludicrous and unmeaning monsters hitherto presented," came on stage laden with baskets of fruits and flowers. Then in the words of the *Times* (3 July 1857):

> The old fashion of making a table arise from a trap is abolished, and the Nymphs, who carry baskets of fruit on their heads, bring them together, so that they themselves form the banquet table, the illusion being perfected by the festoons of flowers [deposited in a ring by the satyrs] that conceal their figures while they crouch beneath the load of conglomerated dainties.

Once the banquet circle was formed, Ariel as "the harpy," was hoisted up in the center in a basket of fruit. From this position, to the accompanying roll of thunder, he pronounced his dire prediction and, as thunder crashed, the stage darkened. The harpy and festive baskets disappeared through a trap; as the lights returned, the nymphs and satyrs scattered about the stage so that the banquet table actually appeared to "break up" before the eyes of the astonished nobles. The scene then concluded with what the *Morning Advertiser* (2 July 1857) described as "a dance of fauns and satyrs that realizes all Theocritus could suggest or Poussin paint."

Just as the banquet scene represents the focal point for Act III, the masque does the same for Act IV. Phelps had set the precedent for treating this sequence in the manner of a court pageant, and Kean continued and elaborated on this idea. The act opened with a view of the interior of Prospero's cave; gradually the back wall dissolved, revealing a view of clouds and the heavens. Iris opened Kean's masque by appearing stage right, riding on a cloud drawn by doves who were driven by Cupid. The second vision, which appeared stage left, depicted a far-off view of Eleusis, the shrine of Ceres, surrounded by nodding cornfields and prolific gardens, and attended by the goddess herself, who was surrounded by all the attributes of peace and plenty. The final climactic vision, completing the triptych effect, took place center stage: Juno appeared suspended high up in her chariot with, in the words of the *Era* (5 July 1857), "her peacock steeds half lost in rosy-lighted clouds, while arching round her head, hang the circling Graces in robes of ruby, sapphire and changing opal." Directly over Juno's head, Hymen appeared; below her, on stage level, seven water nymphs were seen sporting in a crystal clear pool, and rainbow arches encircled the completed vision.

After Juno and Ceres had ended their song (the only air not reinforced by a chorus), the vision dissolved through enveloping clouds and the rocky wall of Prospero's cave was seen again. As the vision disappeared, rolling thunder was heard and continued in the background until the act ended with the routing of the comic conspirators in an anti-masque. Kean had announced in his playbill that "to preserve the mythological tone throughout, the principal demons and goblins commanded to torture the brute Caliban and his drunken associates, Trinculo and Stephano, at the close of the fourth act, are copied from Furies depicted on Etruscan vases." These were supervised by Ariel, "flying on a Bat's back and setting them on."

Shakespeare had provided no indication of a spectacle with which to close

Act V; Kean, however, began his presentation with a scenic prologue and apparently felt that, in order to maintain the self-imposed framework, there should be a fitting scenic epilogue. He therefore devised a series of tableaux within a total moving picture with which to close the production. According to the directions:

> Clouds rise and fall. Night descends. The Spirits, released by Prospero, take their flight from the island into the air. An invisible Chorus of Spirits sings "Where the Bee Sucks." Clouds close in on the Spirits and rise again, discovering a ship in a calm, prepared to convey the King and his companions back to Naples. The epilogue is spoken by Prospero from the deck of the vessel. The ship gradually sails off. The island recedes from sight and Ariel remains alone in mid-air, hovering over the sea, watching the departure of his late master. A distant Chorus of Spirits is heard singing, "Merrily, Merrily."

Thus Kean's *Tempest* ended with a spectacular finale, far more elaborate than that conceived by any previous producer.[14] In earlier presentations the Neapolitan fleet usually had been simply "seen in the distance"; in Kean's version, however, an actual ship appeared on stage to carry off Prospero at the conclusion of Shakespeare's epilogue. Ariel was thus left alone, both literally and figuratively "in the limelight."

Despite the fact that the play was, in Kean's words, "an imaginative drama," the producer's penchant for historical accuracy evidenced itself at several points. The ship, for example, was an exact replica of an Italian one of circa 1294–1330 with the insignia for the kingdom of Naples painted on her sails.[15] The tempest, the movement of ship and crew during the storm, was made as life-like as possible. Even Ariel's initial meteoric appearance was, in the words of the playbill, "in accordance with an ancient omen of a tempest." Moreover, since Shakespeare stipulated no precise time for his action, Kean supplied an historical context: "I have taken the liberty of selecting the thirteenth century as a date."[16] The producer's costume books reveal that pictures of Italian noblemen from this century served as models for the dress of Prospero and the shipwrecked courtiers, while sketches of mythological figures on Greek vases inspired the costumes for the goddesses, harpy, satyrs, naiads, and wood nymphs. Miranda and Ariel's attire resembled that of the nymphs.

Kean's revival, more than any previous one which actually used Shakespeare's text, emphasized theatrical elements, including scenery, properties, costumes, invisible music, and other aural effects.[17] According to the *Morning Post* (2 July 1857) on opening night Kean made the following appeal to his audience:

> The kind indulgence of the public is requested should any lengthened delay take place between the acts during the first representation of *The Tempest*.

---

[14] The history of earlier productions is recounted in my unpublished doctoral dissertation, "*The Tempest*: A Question of Theatricality" (Northwestern University, 1967).

[15] Watercolor sketches, with some notations by the Hamilton Smiths, for the vessel as well as costumes, are found in "The Kean Costume Books" (Shattuck, pp. 25, 26), at the Folger.

[16] From the playbill.

[17] There were, of course, adaptations based on Shakespeare's play including the comedy of John Dryden and William Davenant in 1667, and the later Shadwell operatic version of 1674, as well as various other operatic alterations in the eighteenth century.

>This appeal is made with great confidence, when it is stated that the scenic appliances of the play are of a more extensive and complicated nature than ever yet been attempted in any theatre in Europe, requiring the aid of above 140 operatives nightly, who (unseen by the audience) are engaged in working the machinery, and in carrying out the various effects.

It was well that Kean made such a special plea, because the *Morning Advertiser* (2 July 1857) noted that the opening-night audience, arriving at 8:00 P.M., was not to leave the theater until nearly 1:00 A.M., after a total of some five hours. One week later, on 8 July 1857, the *Morning Post* reported that "this magnificent play is now shortened a full hour, by the rapidity with which practice has brought the working of the machinery."

Although the finished production ran four hours, prior to opening night Kean found it necessary to prune much of Shakespeare's text in order to allow sufficient time for his various theatrical displays.[18] While he omitted no scene, he did make liberal cuts within scenes and within speeches. All dialogue was deleted in I. i and the exposition sequence of I. ii was pared down to the barest essentials. The first meeting between Miranda and Ferdinand was condensed. The two scenes of Act II were combined into one with about two-thirds of the dialogue among the nobles deleted (II. i), although the subplot comedy sequence (II. ii) was left intact. Each subsequent act then focused on a particular spectacle: Act III, on the elaborate banquet scene; Act IV, on the masque; Act V, on the scenic epilogue. Dialogue not connected directly with the focal sequence of the particular act was condensed in order to save time for the major displays. Still the playbill boasted that Shakespeare's "original text" had been preserved with the proper sequence of scenes and with "only occasional" cuts.

While most critics praised the entire production, most echoed the sentiments of the *Saturday Review* critic (4 July 1857), who commented with reference to the acting that "there is not much room for it," and the *Globe* critic (2 July 1857), who contended that "the acting, with such illustrations, is secondary." But apparently in the eyes of most reviewers, excitement over Kean's theatrical displays far outweighed any sense of loss regarding the poetry or the opportunities for acting. The presentation was accorded unanimous raves by the critics, only one periodical, the *Saturday Review* (4 July 1857), offering any reservations, and these expressed only after many paragraphs of praise for the various displays:

>There is no attempt made by Mr. Kean to draw the attention of the audience from what is seen to what is said. Their eyes, not their ears are consulted. . . . As a series of spectacles illustrating a drama of Shakespeare, it is in every way to be praised and admired. Still, no beauty of scenery, and no success in contrivance and decorations can entirely content us.

But that is the central question: If Shakespeare had had all the resources of mid-nineteenth century stagecraft available to him, would he have wished *The Tempest* to be so produced? Although the playwright did have all the resources devised for court masques at his command, there is no indication in the Folio

---

[18] It should be noted that Kean did rely on Shakespeare's original text and that, despite very liberal "cuts," the version presented was uncontaminated by the Davenant-Dryden comedy or by the Shadwell opera.

text that the original production made more than an occasional use of the theatrical devices available. Certainly Shakespeare intended to appeal to the ear at least as much as to the eye; it is obvious that the playwright expected the spoken word to be given an emphasis equal to or surpassing that of the theatrical display, else he would not have endowed *The Tempest* with some of his most beautiful poetry nor used this drama as the vehicle to convey what some modern critics have termed his "new vision" or his "final vision" of the world.

While he was Charles Dickens' houseguest in England, Hans Christian Andersen attended Kean's *Tempest*. Although his commentary on the presentation in the Danish daily, *Berlingske Tidende* (a series printed from 24 January through 2 February 1860), indicates his obvious fascination with the spectacles and particularly with investigating the specific techniques used to create them, he concludes:

> Everything was afforded that machinery and stage direction can provide, and yet after seeing it, one felt overwhelmed, tired, and empty. Shakespeare was lost in visual pleasure: the exciting poetry was petrified by illustrations; the living word had evaporated. No one tasted the spiritual banquet—it was forgotten for the golden platter on which it was served. . . . A work of Shakespeare performed between three simple screens is for me a greater enjoyment than here where it disappeared beneath the gorgeous trappings.[19]

Almost as if in response to this kind of commentary, the *Art-Journal* for 16 August 1857 attempted to reply to any would-be critics of Kean's highly theatrical production:

> We must offer a few words of comment on a question which has been raised as to the propriety of this large amount of illustration applied to the works of the dramatic poet in general and Shakespeare in particular. The objection proceeds on an intimation that the poetry of the scene painter is substituted for the poetry of the poet; and that he who undertakes to illustrate Shakespeare assumes to supplant him. Without insisting on the not very flattering want of faith in Shakespeare on the part of the objector himself, when he hints at the possibility of the mechanist thus putting out the poet, we confess that we do not see how he is able to maintain his argument, unless he forbids the use of scenic illusion altogether. What the manager does in this respect constitutes the exact difference between stage representation and closet reading; if he may assist the illusion of his text at all by material realization of the times and places, why may he not do so on a sufficient scale? Where will the objector divide the principle, or draw the line of its application?

Almost twenty years earlier, when discussing Macready's presentation of *The Tempest*, the critic for *John Bull* (21 October 1838) had discussed the very problem which the *Art-Journal* now raised and had concluded at that time that a producer was not wrong in making use of theatrical devices to assist the illusion of the play, as long as these remained "subservient to the spirit of the scene."[20]

---

[19] Commentary quoted (in his own translation) by Frederick J. Marker, in "The First Night of Charles Kean's *The Tempest*—from the Notebook of Hans Christian Andersen," *Theater News*, 25 (1970), 23.

[20] Review quoted in George C. D. Odell, *Shakespeare from Betterton to Irving* (New York: Scribner, 1920), II, 218–19.

By this criterion Kean's elaborate spectacle would have had to be condemned, for he made an assault on the auditor's senses but apparently not on his mind. The 1857 reviewers, almost to a man, bemoaned the fact that the beauty of the production was "fleeting" and, once withdrawn from the boards, would be lost for all time. The *Morning Post* for 3 July echoed the feelings of the other papers when it stated: "The only regret is what [sic] we may safely affirm that it will never again be equalled on the stage in our time." Commentators described various displays in detail yet quoted no memorable lines. Apparently Kean had not hinged his theatrical delights on the sound framework of Shakespeare's poetic thought. Theatricality had not assisted the dramatic illusion but had instead supplanted it, so that, in the words of the *Saturday Review,* the production became "a series of spectacles illustrating a drama of Shakespeare." The opening shipwreck sequence became something Shakespeare had never intended, a separate prologue piece. To complete the framework, Kean then created a scenic epilogue so spectacular in its effect that it obscured the textual epilogue Shakespeare had written. Furthermore the presentation imparted a feeling that Ariel, rather than Prospero, was the central figure of the drama, as the *Times* (3 July 1857) noted: "As Ariel is the ever-prominent personage throughout the action, so does he remain sole occupant of the stage at the end of the play." Indeed Ariel was both literally and figuratively in the limelight, and much of the presentation focused on the effects of his magic-making.

In the final analysis, of course, the audience was treated to a fairy tale, viewed through the larger-than-life illustrations of a childhood imagination—a wonderful piece of art in itself, but hardly what Shakespeare had intended. Yet, while the production may not have remained subservient to the spirit of its author, Kean's version was extremely popular in its day, holding the boards for a total of eighty-eight performances, a lengthy run for any production in that period and more than half again the number accorded Macready's very successful revival twenty years earlier. There was not to be another major professional presentation in England until that of Herbert Beerbohm Tree at the turn of the century. In the meantime, for those who had missed Kean's staging, the printed acting edition of the 1857 version was available.[21]

Charles Kean must certainly be listed (to quote Shattuck) as one of those "effective authors" who shaped the concept of Shakespeare in their era.[22] It must also be repeated, however, that this highly theatrical rendition of the play was simply the culmination at mid-century of an already well-established trend towards "theatricalizing" presentations of *The Tempest.* The influence of such productions on nineteenth-century readers and critics should be obvious.

St. John's University

[21] *Shakespeare's Play of The Tempest, arranged for representation at the Princess Theatre, with historical and explanatory notes by Charles Kean, as first produced on . . . 1 July 1857 . . .* (London: J. K. Champman & Co., n.d.).
[22] Shattuck, *The Shakespeare Promptbooks*, p. 1.

Theatrical Shakespearegresses at the Guthrie and Elsewhere: Notes on "Legitimate Production"

Thomas Clayton

THIS ESSAY BEGAN as a response to a complex challenge issued in a call for papers on Shakespeare's plays that "should investigate the subject of contemporary productions: do such non-traditional approaches"—with Ariel as an "androgynous punk," for example—"enhance the characters, the text, the beauty, the point of the plays, or have some directors distorted the plays in making them more accessible to wider audiences?"[1] The question is appropriately ambiguous, because the answer is, I think, "both." And M. H. Abrams's classic coordinates in *The Mirror and the Lamp* seem to me pertinent for the purpose: first, the artist (playwright, director, designer, and so forth); second, the audience(s); third, the "workitself"; and an implicit fourth, the "world." Equally pertinent are such questions as *what, where,* and *when* is a play? Is it in the conception and composition of the playwright? So most have thought, more or less, some emphasizing the playwright and others the conception and composition. In the eyes, mind, and viscera of the beholder? So most have been bound also to think, from ordinary spectators to reception theorists. In some kind of mimetic relationship between the play and the phenomenal world? "Probably," somehow, by common consent if not by the consent of solipsists and language prison-housekeepers. Or, with particular reference to theater, is it in the performance and/or the eyes of the director and company? Also yes, notwithstanding Aristotle, who may have been right in theory about the distance between "spectacle" (i.e., performance) and dramatic art (i.e., script) but who did not foreclose upon the actualities of aesthetic and theatrical Realpolitik, where all definitions and evaluations have their *practical* essence and descent. There, I take it, is a primary rub.

These issues have of course been persistently controverted. Two pertinent recent discussions taking opposed positions in effect are those of Charles Marowitz in his Introduction to *The Marowitz Shakespeare,* and Alan C. Dessen in "Shakespeare's Scripts and the Modern Director."[2] Dessen's position is that there is "much virtue in the original conventions and the original logic of presentation," and that we

241

should "really trust Shakespeare's know how and skills to the extent that we feel a responsibility to *discover* and *recover* his techniques and meanings" (64, italics his), a partly archaeological project. Marowitz, introducing his "Adaptations and Collages" of *Hamlet, Macbeth, The Taming of the Shrew, Measure for Measure,* and *The Merchant of Venice,* proceeds from the position that

the question is not, as it is so often put, what is wrong with Shakespeare that we have to meddle with his works, but what is wrong with us that we are content to endure the diminishing returns of conventional dramatic reitera- tion; that we are prepared to go to the theatre and pretend that what dulls our minds and comforts our world-view is, by dint of such reassurances, cul- turally uplifting; not to realise that there is nothing so insidious as art that perpetuates the illusion that some kind of eternal truth is enshrined in a time-space continuum called a "classic"; not to challenge the notion that its theatrical performance is *automatically* an experience because our presump- tion of a play's established worth guarantees us this experience. We all dupe ourselves in the theatre because we have been sold a bill of goods for a quarter of a century before we enter. (25)

Dessen speaks temperately for a species of scholarly respect for the "original" meanings and techniques; Marowitz's reconstructive icono- clasm is characteristically impatient. There is something to be said for both positions, but Marowitz's position is paradoxically easier to de- fend, because it is concerned not primarily with reproducing Shake- speare but ultimately with adapting, in effect replacing, Shakespeare, as in his own collages, a species of creation in which Shakespeare's script is both assumed and subsumed in a work substantially and for- mally not of his making. Although Marowitz advocates replacing An- cients with Moderns, defense of adaptation does not entail categorical rejection of "the classics," and the case for new works is self-made regardless of their sources, even without invoking Ulysses' ironical analysis in *Troilus and Cressida:*

> One touch of nature makes the whole world kin,
> That all with one consent praise new-born gawds,
> Though they are made and moulded of things past,
> And give to dust that is a little gilt
> More laud than gilt o'er-dusted.
> The present eye praises the present object. . . .
>
> (3.3.175–80)

Perhaps there never was such an entity as "the play itself," even more than there no longer is "the poem itself," because outside of closet drama the play does not exist, except hypothetically and potentially, short of performance and audience reception: those are the ends—the final cause—of the script. Thus the latter are easily, or perhaps facilely, granted autonomy and permitted to be what they will—that is, as director and audience will have them. In such cases the script may be all but irrelevant, a mere source of boundless performance, while the latter is what counts—as suggested by the stage direction of Ionesco's *Macbett* for the opening dialogue between Glamiss and Candor: *"the text serves only as a basis for their mounting anger."*[3]

Directors' "distortions" are otherwise, because distortion itself implies a systematic relationship between the intermediation—the director's designs and the performances—and the script intermediated. In fact, among the few alternatives to a systematic relationship between script and production are psychodrama, the happening, and Living Theater, a form of histrionic activity involving collective and extemporaneous interaction between actors and audience that was especially prominent in the late sixties. In such cases, whatever scenario there may be soon dissolves into spontaneous and autonomous activity, the collective theatrical equivalent of stream of consciousness. John Russell Brown notes of performing act three, scene one of *Hamlet* that "the action of this scene, the bearing, movements and gestures of its two figures," Hamlet and Ophelia, "can give Shakespeare's words almost opposite effects. Which is the more 'true' depends on how the whole play has been brought alive in continuous relationship to Shakespeare's text,"[4] however few or many are responsible for the relationship and whatever its principles of coherence. Script and performance may perhaps best be seen as different manifestations of the same dramatic work, visible from many angles but beyond comprehending, at any rate beholding, as a whole.

In formal production "enhancement" and "distortion" are not strict antitheses; in fact, in some relations distortion effects enhancement. But they do correspond with positive and negative value judgments, and for most practical purposes those are all that matter. A script is "enhanced" when its performance accomplishes the ends of those primarily and immediately concerned, namely, the persons of the theater on and behind the stage, and the persons of the theater in front of or around the stage, the audience. Whether it has been "distorted" is a critical or sociopolitical enquiry, very often both, since the two can hardly be disjoined, as some contemporary critics never tire of reminding us. And any academic critic in his or her very real social and economic worlds is bound to recognize the practical if not the theoretical force of both of these.

What matters in a primary critical perspective—one that is not vocationally a reviewer's, a theater person's, or a politico's—is not a production's realizing the originality and inventiveness of the director and company, or causing the generalized excitement or boredom of the audience during or at the end of a given performance. It is rather the relationship, the fit, of the performance with the script in terms of what the script can properly yield from its own text(s) and its contexts. "Properly" may seem unusual in present usage, but it points up an important distinction. Translators use *proper*—sometimes misleadingly—for two different but related ideas in Aristotle's Greek, *to prepon* (what is appropriate, fitting, proportionate, seemly) and *idios* (one's own, integral, distinctive, peculiar). The distinction helps to clarify differences between what "belongs to" a script and what is appropriate or necessary for an audience. A script so remote from an audience's experience as to be scarcely intelligible, however lucid and distinguished in its own terms and for its specificity, would demand "distortion" to become comprehensible in popular presentation (academic study of the "same" play is a different matter). When works of any kind are remote from prospective users, something has to be done to one or the other, or both, to reduce the distance: by educating the audience or translating the work. Translation is a form of distortion, and cultural "translation" is sometimes no less necessary than linguistic translation. Educating the audience is itself a form of translation, and it can be accomplished by the theater as well as by external preparation to understand the theater.

A script's contexts include current history and the circumstances of performance, which are unavoidably part of its realizable potentiality as well as of its pressures for communication. A striking example of a script's communicating more of its potentialities than its performers intended, in an unpolemic production, is revealed in an anecdote of Ian McKellan given in John Barton's *Playing Shakespeare:*

> Let me tell you a story. In 1969 I played Richard II in a production which we took round England and then briefly to Europe and we went to Czechoslovakia. The costumes were of the actual period of Richard II but the scenery was minimal because it was a touring production. . . . On the whole we concentrated on the humanity of the characters rather than their political nature. We thought of the political factions as a family, Richard II as a man with cousins and uncles and other relatives, and I think it was in that sense that we looked at the politics in it.
>
> However, we landed in Czechoslovakia only six months after the Prime Minister, Dubcek, had been removed by his neighbouring allies, the Russians. One result of this political change was that they didn't want visiting foreigners with their plays. They tried to stop our visit, but it was too late. . . . We only played two nights and the houses were full, although all our posters

had been pulled down. So perhaps the audiences were ready to see this visit as a special occasion and indeed a political occasion, in that we were coming from the West.

When I came to the speech where Richard II returns from Ireland to discover that his nation has been overrun by his cousin Bolingbroke, and he kneels down on the earth and asks the stones and the nettles and the insects to help him in his helpless state against the armies who had invaded his land, I could hear something I had never heard before, nor since, which was a whole audience apparently weeping. It shakes me now to think about it, because in that instant I realised that the audience were crying for themselves. They recognized in Richard II their own predicament of only six months previously when their neighbours and as it were their cousins had invaded their land, and all they had were sticks and stones to throw at the tanks.

I would never have talked about the play in those terms. We hadn't seen it as directly relevant to any modern political situation. Shakespeare couldn't have known about communism, about the East or the West. Afterwards I said to one of the new men, the anti-Dubcek faction, to one of their leaders who was in the audience, "Who did you side with in the play, Richard II or Bolingbroke? The man on the ground or the invader?" And he said, "Both right, both wrong."[5]

The response is one that Shakespeare arguably did "intend," in the sense that the causes of such emotional response are clearly in the play: Richard's love of country and deeply felt sense of loss entail sympathetic responses in an emotionally responsive audience. Obviously such a response is at odds with those aimed at by Brechtian alienation effects, which are, however, quasi-cathartic in seeking a particular effect, political consensus and programmatic action.

That is partly where the question tends, "have some directors *distorted* the plays in making them more accessible to wider audiences?" —that is, more familiar and a la mode in relation to conventions of contemporary sound and spectacle, which *may* make the sense of the script even less accessible by the intermediation; it might or might not seem so, depending upon who is seeing Peter Brook's famous (and notorious) production of *A Midsummer Night's Dream* and what he or she brings to the performance by way of experience and expectations. The same is true to a greater degree of a recent London musical adaptation, *The Dream,* performed in a reggae-punk rock-and-roll idiom by the Hempen Homespuns with the bass player doubling as Bottom.[6] No doubt such productions differ in their aesthetic organization of demands and rewards, but both bring to the theater données as well as assumptions recognizable from their contexts of origin and conventional conditions of performance as circus, concert, disco, and so on.

II

Even if strict "fidelity to the script and playwright" were desirable as such, it is impossible to achieve except in the immediate theatrical circumstances in which it originated and came to realization; it is difficult even there, certainly in our own day as it probably was in Shakespeare's. As shareholder and active participant in productions as well as playwright, he must have had more of a controlling hand as well as interest in his plays and their playing than playwrights of our day ordinarily have, but he cannot have been much less subject to circumstances—the slings and arrows of audience, box office, fellow members of the company, rival playwrights; dark ladies, and Bankside and Blackfriars socioeconomics generally. How complicated such issues may be, even when as relatively simple as this, is suggested by Tom Stoppard's Author's Note to *Jumpers*, a text of multiple applicability:

In preparing previous plays for production I have tried with some difficulty to arrive at something called a 'definitive text', but I now believe that in the case of plays there is no such animal. Each production will throw up its own problems and very often the solution will lie in some minor change to the text. . . . What follows is a basic version of *Jumpers*. . . .

POSTSCRIPT (February 1973): . . . [His spaced periods.] And indeed after some months' absence *Jumpers* returned to the National Theatre in a slightly altered form. This edition incorporates the changes because they seem to me an improvement on the original. . . .[7]

Aristotle's advice to tragic playwrights applies equally well to the exigencies of production: "the example of good portrait-painters should be followed. They, while reproducing the distinctive form, make a likeness which is true to life and yet more beautiful."[8]

The acceptability of a production depends inescapably upon its socioeducational context. In volatile or early-revolutionary social circumstances, anything goes—for a while; where "prohibition" or its counterparts prevail, not much passes muster: it is a long way from Reinhardt and Dieterle's Mendelssohnian Disney World *Midsummer Night's Dream* to Peter Brook's, not to mention the 1984 reggae-punk musical version of *The Dream*. The case of *The Tempest's* Ariel as "androgynous punk" seems roughly thus: "he/she" would probably offend sheltered audiences as outrage for the sake of outrage, which of course it might be by design for such audiences; an audience of "androgynous punks" would tend to find more ironical amusement than matter for offense or painful "self-recognition."[9] At the performance I saw of *The Dream*, about a third of the audience—mostly the older third—disappeared at the interval; probably most of those who left had come for the Shakespeare and many of those who stayed had come for the music, but those who left apparently had a lower level of tolerance for the alarums and excursions, too, though plainly heralded in advertisements and program. The major problem with all adaptations is that they *are* adaptations—restylings, translations, transformations—of old or otherwise alien scripts to new purposes and circumstances, hardly in itself a critical problem so long as the intention of adaptation is generally made clear as such. Charles Marowitz's position is flawless in this way. So are such proximate adaptations as John Barton's *Wars of the Roses* and Giorgio Strehler's *Das Spiel der Mächtigen*, not least because "one can scarcely hope to mount the three parts of *Henry VI* in their entirety."[10] And much the same is true of the Falstaff saga, enacted or referred to in five of Shakespeare's plays, that became Orson Welles's film *Chimes at Midnight*. But when production is claimed, those intimate with the script rightly object when adaptive uses made of the language and its contextual implications result in distortion, misrepresentation, and downright confusion by the confounding of primary intentions incorporate in the script.

Three representative test cases from the Tyrone Guthrie Theater's repertoire in the late sixties and early seventies are a notorious Banana Republic *Julius Caesar*, a *Measure for Measure* in nineteenth-century Viennese and Austro-Hungarian idiom, and a "conventional" *Merchant of Venice*.

Julius Caesar was so generally condemned for persistent conflict between the design and the dialogue that, when one of the styrofoam statues of Caesar caught fire during a performance, a critical act of God was suspected in some quarters. The Latin-American overlay—culture upon culture as well as costume over costume—virtually insures conflict and multiple confusion, and in that way failure of production. This was the case of a bright idea with severely limited application: analogy acknowledged, out goes the candle, and we—and the production—are left darkling. The contrast between the effect of this production, which strove for "relevance," and the "politically neutral" *Richard II* performed in Czechoslovakia is as striking as it is instructive: the relevance is *in* the text—action, character, dialogue, design; what is willfully imported, when no systematic relationship to the script is possible, suppresses or confuses what was already there, a case of substantial negative distortion.

There was no problem in the congenial resetting of *Measure for*

Measure, which has no received and entrenched conception with entailed responses for a midwestern American audience—like many
other "postmodern" audiences—to react to as such; and the doctrinal
matter is unobjectionable in post-theological circumstances. The
Austro-Hungarian uniforms and setting, after initially impressing,
became subliminal. Especially interesting about this production was
that "the play" ended differently on different nights. On most it
ended on a note of temperate happiness, with the novice nun Isabella
modestly but evidently pleased by the prospect of finding a new vo-
cation in a marriage to the Duke, who had saved her from Angelo's
hypocritical attempts to seduce her. On a few it ended ominously,
with Isabella blocked in the same position, vis-à-vis the Duke, in
which she had earlier confronted Angelo, now removing her wimple
with an air of apprehension, as though the Duke himself were about
to inflict marriage upon her in the sinister spirit of Angelo, with a
strong hint of women perennially at the mercy of a dark "brotherhood" of exploiting men. To the extent that Shakespeare's tempted
and fallen Angelo and the once remiss but self-reforming Duke are
made to seem interchangeable, we have a counter-Gordian final solution that forces the equating of dramatic antitheses, the would-be villain with the must-be hero.[11]

   The power of suggestive performance to achieve electrifying effect
in this *Measure* could hardly be gainsaid, but that is a given: kinesiolo-
gists have sufficiently demonstrated that body language speaks
louder than words, as professional actors have always known; and, as
a rule of bitten thumb, the more welcome or provocative the message, the more eloquent the gesture.[12] But the question is not
whether "the spectacle has, indeed, an emotional attraction of its
own" (in Aristotle's phrase), but whose senses take priority in a production, a question of ethics, politics, and economics as well as of
aesthetics and semantics. A "supertext" that cannot count on the
script for much countenance may find it readily enough in acceptability to favorably disposed audiences and critics. What this amounts
to is the power of the production values as such, or the congeniality
of the overlay in itself, or both. Whether such playing falsifies the
script is one question, answerable in the affirmative; whether playing
and script *should* take a particular position is two other questions, to
be answered in terms of what is seen as necessary or appropriate contemporary satisfactions.

   From the Guthrie *Measure for Measure* to *The Merchant of Venice* was
the distance from general acceptance to wholesale controversy, provoked by one of the local reviewers and outraged members of the
public. This *Merchant,* despite a deftly balanced and complex Shylock,
was the focal point of protracted debate, some but not most of it in

the Jewish community and much of it arguing that the play is anti-Se-
mitic in effect, despite acknowledged efforts made in this production
to defuse the imputed anti-Semitism. So the question became
whether *Merchant* should be allowed to be performed at all, as
written. One answer, in the form of "found meaning," was offered
first by Edmund Kean in 1814, elaborated by Sir Henry Irving (1879)
and others, and employed recently by Jonathan Miller in his 1970
stage production and later film, with Lord Olivier as a sympathetic
victim-hero Shylock. There is clearly an ethical and social case for this
kind of treatment, founded on a need to counteract persisting anti-
Semitism in the culture where the performance originates, but the
script will not yield it without systematic distortion: gone from
Miller's production, for example, was Shylock's self-characterizing soliloquy beginning,

> How like a fawning publican he looks.
> I hate him for he is a Christian.
> But more, for that in low simplicity
> He lends out money gratis, and brings down
> The rate of usance here with us [usurers] in Venice.
>
> (1.3.36–40)

Whether rewriting *The Merchant of Venice* is even a particularly effective—let alone otherwise justifiable—way is twice open to question, but Miller and many members of his audience answered with a
resounding yes. The "success" had to rest not on production as such
but on adaptation not identified as "Miller's (and Olivier's) *Merchant
of Venice*," which in fact it is. Distinctions of this kind are matters of
degree, no doubt, and edges will feather, but reversing the main
thrust of a script is clearly different from producing it. No such furor
attended the productions of *The Merchant of Venice* at the Royal
Shakespeare Theatre in Stratford-upon-Avon in 1981 and 1984, the
first with a Shylock in general not unlike the Guthrie's, the second
with a mostly unsympathetic figure, but neither a comic butt nor a
Jew of Malta. All three productions operated well within the scope of
tenable script-based production, and such usual reviewers' differences as there were centered not on Shylock but on other aspects,
particularly in the 1984 Royal Shakespeare Company *Merchant*, a
production marred by the excesses of the designer, increasingly a
second principal responsible for *auteur* production as the composer is
coming to be a third through programmatic scoring.[13]

The Guthrie's *Measure for Measure* was given a feminist final turn,
and Jonathan Miller's *Merchant of Venice* was reconstituted from the
remains of Shakespeare's *Merchant* surviving amputation: not merely

epater la bourgeoisie but by social imperatives' dictating the terms of production, which entailed remaking Shakespeare. Though some sociohistorical critics tend to reduce Shakespeare to the countermeasure of Ben Jonson's "he was not of an age, but for all time," Shakespeare is arguably a better tutor than his directors and critics, but he clearly needs interpreting for our own latterly historical eyes. And there is another rub: the academic and the theatrical interpreter, individual or collective, are cut in part from the same cloth, and designs play a substantial part in the action, designs not only semantic and aesthetic.

III

In a Guthrie symposium on "Staging Shakespeare Today" held in connection with the 1982 production of *As You Like It*, there was about an even division between proponents of "conservative" and of "liberal" production—useless terms for specific applications, but sufficiently differential. The respective representation was perhaps a little surprising. On the liberal side were two academics, together with Michael Lupu, one of the dramaturgs and Director of Outreach at the Guthrie and a Rumanian like the director, Liviu Ciulei. On the conservative side were two actors—an Englishman David Warrilow, the Beckett specialist, who played Jacques, and Ken Ruta, who played the Dukes—together with a third academic, a sometime dramaturg, who inveighed against (Continental) "concept" production.[14]

The actors were such proponents of fidelity to the text that Samuel Johnson would have been at home in their company, as a typical Enlightenment spokesman for the well-heard play. "A dramatick exhibition is a *book recited* with concomitants that encrease or diminish its effect," he wrote in 1765 in the Preface to his edition of Shakespeare; spectators come "to *hear a certain number of lines recited* with just gesture and elegant modulation" (my italics). Warrilow held that the text speaks best for *itself*, when allowed to, through cultivated articulation of the demonstrable sense and music of the words. It would be difficult for a *reader* of Shakespeare not to agree, since interpreting what a text says is practically subject to as well as theoretically circumscribed by the relative norms of the language(s) the text was written in. And intelligible production of a play is not less beholden to the script. Even if it is true that all texts cannot help but be misread if not mismapped in the reader's own way, there is a tacit social and moral obligation to try to read it accurately, *if* one purports to be representing its sense as more or other than one's own. This obligation does not preclude doing anything one pleases with a text after it has been assigned the status of a point of departure and made the basis of an adaptation. Nahum Tate can no more be faulted than Charles Marowitz for his confessed adaptations to the perceived needs or expectations of his audience, but producers may reasonably be faulted who come close enough to reflect and nevertheless falsify their scripts simultaneously.

But much depends upon the audience addressed. Those very familiar with the canon, like substantial numbers in Royal Shakespeare Theatre audiences, can recognize departures and approve or disapprove according to their lights. Those less familiar (like the ones addressed by the BBC-Time/Life television series) are not unlikely to accept as Shakespeare's whatever they see, and understandably ascribe to the playwright idiosyncrasies originating elsewhere. If *Timon of Athens* is performed in Jacobean dress to stress the raging waste and conspicuous consumption of the court of James I, the play has been made emphatically a document of an age, and of an ideology to the extent that the tacit referent is the Rise of Capitalism, while the "universality" anchored in Shakespeare's Athenian setting is cut loose and cast adrift. If the Athenian setting designed by the playwright cannot convey the significance desired by a director, "restoring" production to the period of composition is not likely to improve upon it, especially for a modern audience. Ron Daniels's imaginative *Timon* and Richard Pasco's powerful Timon at The Other Place in Stratford-upon-Avon in 1981 achieved much of their effect by the production's spare "Athenian" setting as well as by proximity to the audience—all (Western) time and space as one, as it were. The reference of the dialogue is preserved in such a setting, whereas much may be made "problematic" by leaving the dialogue in place but not the setting when that matters as certainly as it does in the tragedies set in classical antiquity—not as dead museum pieces but as actions vital and enlightening as historic (or retrojected) archetypes. Greece and Rome remain foundations of archetypal reference in Western culture, and Shakespeare used them sparingly but deliberately; directors do well to think carefully before they abandon the moorings to look for new ones.

Timon is a practical case in point, where abstract discussion of such issues as "fidelity to the text" leads mainly to synonymity (e.g., "loyalty") and as often to obscurity. Many favor "correctness," but far from all agree on what correctness is, much less how to recognize it. The philosopher David Hume is still instructive in cases of this sort:

. . . it is very difficult, if not impossible, to explain by words where the just medium lies between the excesses of simplicity and refinement, or to give any rule by which we can know precisely the bounds between the fault and the beauty. A critic may discourse not only very judiciously on this head without instructing his readers, but even without understanding the matter perfectly himself. . . . However different the tastes of men, their general discourse on these subjects is commonly the same. No criticism can be instructive which descends not to particulars, and is not full of examples and illustrations. It is allowed on all hands that beauty, as well as virtue, always lies in a medium; but where this medium is placed is a great question, and can never be sufficiently explained by general reasonings.[15]

Critics of production must eventually come to cases, and it is inevitably the principles and ends of re-creation and the particulars and means of re-production that determine the judgment.

For another example take a recent Royal Shakespeare Company *Twelfth Night* (1983–84)[16] as reviewed by Irving Wardle in *The Times:*

Quite a deal of poison has been *seeping into* this play over the past few years, but John Caird's is the first I have seen that *projects Twelfth Night* as an all-out dark comedy. This is good news not only for jaded old spectators who have seen the piece too often. There is a limit to the amount of fun that can be extracted from the drinking scene and permutations of Malvolio's letter in a play that was never more than intermittently uproarious. And there is everything to be said for muting the comedy *for once* and giving full attention to the central matter of the illusions and frenzies of love.[17]

This review is revealing. It is no doubt a long way from here to *The Revenger's Tragedy* and what Vindice calls the "spendthrift veins of a dry duke, / A parched and juiceless luxur," but those "jaded old spectators" evidently need some new kicks—or even a touch of flogging—to get the cathartic juices flowing. And of course the "illusions and frenzies of love" are so much a fashion if not a fact of our time and place that they *would* be the "central matter" of *Twelfth Night.* Other phrases acknowledge the extraneous origin of the gathering gloom, the pressure for novelty ("for once"), and the presence of tacitly uncharacteristic because only intermittent "uproariousness."[18] Comparable recent redactions of *Twelfth Night,* all three on the brighter side of this once "Joyous Comedy," are Ariane Mnouchkine's at *Le Theatre du Soleil* in Vincennes, Paris (1982–1984); a small-scale production by the Actors Touring Company, performed in the spring of 1984 in London in various fringe venues, including Fenton House garden; and Liviu Ciulei's at the Guthrie in October and November of 1984. All three were "Joyous" productions in which Feste was made the choice and master spirit, the "intermittent uproariousness" was allowed prominence, and Malvolio was the vain spoilsport and comic butt of the script (for most, but currently being controverted), not without shading or a measure of sympathy but with firmness: he was duly exorcised as he is in the script, for "thus the whirligig of time brings in his revenges."

Also enlightening in this perspective are a pair of West Indies-set productions with all-black casts performed in London in the spring of 1981, one a low-budget reggae production of *The Tempest* staged at the Oval in Brixton, and the other—which I chanced to see the following night—a lavish production of *Measure for Measure* staged in the National's Lyttelton Theatre. The first was received with immense enthusiasm by a mostly black audience salted with punks and others. The second had a mixed reception by both reviewers and spectators, a typical National Theatre crowd of affluents, buffs, students, and tourists.

As he wrote in his Director's Notes to the Cast, Michael Rudman set his National Theatre *Measure for Measure* "on a *mythical* Caribbean island. A mixture of Haiti and Trinidad. Mainly West Indian, because there are a lot of very good West Indian actors. Mythical because I don't want too many specific political parallels." He wanted to "place the characters in a political context that is familiar yet remote. . . . The point you want to touch in Shakespeare is where remoteness and accessibility meet. Setting the play outside Europe makes it easier, for example, to believe in the fervour of Isabella's Catholicism." But perhaps most important of all: "If the events of *Measure for Measure* were to happen in closed rooms, they would not be so effective. I'm prejudiced toward public behaviour in Shakespeare. One should get a feeling . . . that everything important that happens is going directly from the market-place to the nerve-ends of the State. . . . That's one reason for choosing to set the play on a Caribbean island. One senses, when Castro speaks to a market-place full of people, that everything he says is going immediately into the bloodstream of the country." In the event, what confronted the audience was an open plaza surrounded by balconies on which colorful supernumeraries were constantly lounging and milling about, Lucio in panama hat and Palm Beach suit sipping frozen daiquiris "on the stem," a great fat madam of a Mistress Overdone turning up at Marina's moated grange to play a whorehouse piano and sing the erstwhile Boy's song "Take O take those lips away," and so on. The production was undoubtedly original and visually appealing, and the Director's Notes to the Cast were persuasive enough. But such notes are not seldom partial, descriptive in the round, and remote from the details and entailed effects of production. If the intentional fallacy

lives, it is found more often in the relation between director and production than between writer and script.

There seems little ground for objecting in theory to Rudman's
treatment, though the Director's Notes are not auspicious. What was
mainly wrong, owing to the gratuitous foregrounding, was that so
little of the profoundly personal and ethical in *Measure* made it
through the filter, which emphasized a languid tropical haze of pervasive corruption very much a part of Shakespeare's script—except
for the "languid tropical haze"—but far from all of it. In fact, Isabella
seemed twice anomalous in a setting of such massive and amorally
cheerful cupidity, and that was *not* part of Rudman's announced
design.

By contrast, the mostly nonprofessional but exuberant cast of Michael Armitage's "*The Tempest* / Reggae Shakespeare," with "Reggae,
Carnival, African dance & drumming / Music by Wasimba"—
breathed real creative life out of Shakespeare's *Tempest* without piti-
fully disastering the script despite the disparity between stage-setting
and script-setting, probably because the European reference was tacitly mythologized as the background it already is in Shakespeare's
script. The audience as a whole received it warmly. The setting was
village Afro-Caribbean, with Prospero as headman/shaman, a burly,
deep-voiced, benevolent tyrant who ruled his world with an assured
and genial balance of firmness and compassion. Ariel was played by
the lead singer of Wasimba, with hilarious refractoriness in an idiom
consonant with Shakespeare's Ariel's: told to "Go! Hence with dili-
gence!" (1.2.304), he sauntered off at leisure with an afro-comb
sticking out of a back pocket and still later—with "I'll fetch them, *sir*"
(5.1.32)—sticking out of his bikini. A droll way of dealing with colo-
nialism and (in)subordination in the play, the pertinent places, and
the production, which ended with a thoughtfully abbreviated epilogue well attuned to the collective spirit: "But release me from my
bands, / With the help of your good hands"—the cast and musicians
joined in concert by an audience that clapped in time to this final
refrain for a full ten minutes. With such community there needs no
applause. It is not easy to get at the exact causes for the success of this
production and the weaknesses of the National's *Measure,* but the systematic relationship between production and audience is surely
prominent—and easier come by when the audience is a smaller and
homogeneous subset than a larger sampling from decidedly hetero-
geneous communities. Aside from that important consideration, the
impression conveyed was that the reggae *Tempest* had been thought
out of, toward the audience, and the calypso *Measure* had been
thought into, by the director—a state of affairs suggested by

Rudman's being "prejudiced toward public behaviour in Shakespeare," perhaps.

The reggae *Tempest* was clearly not a scholar's "authentic" production or a comprehensively nuanced contemporary one like Liviu Ciulei's at the Guthrie in the same year, but it exploited its own (implicit) "concept" very successfully for its audience and in itself; an alien familiar with the play could recognize both the script as written and read, and the reciprocal presence of the script in the production and the production in the script. Rudman's *Measure,* by contrast, persistently elicited awareness of ingenuity straining to stretch the script over an epic stage that dissipated much of the text in its recesses, an effect complemented by parts of the dialogue being all but inaudible, an accidental but "integral" circumstance. The less professional but more effective *Tempest* was a festive production that made a harmonious community of audience and players, and went far in its own way toward expressing, both with words and without, a persistent view of the potentialities of human kindness and its capacity for sympathetic imagination that is characteristically Shakespearean and especially *Tempest*atic. In such cases, a useful distinction may be found between the letter-faithful production of conventional staging, and a spirit-faithful production that systematically maintains the tone, attitudes, and interior relationships of the script, with the latter realizing "subtext" in faithful translation and the former in literal fidelity.

IV

In Liviu Ciulei's productions at the Guthrie, the production "concepts," though distinctive, have not been radically remote, and they do not automatically suggest the bent and detail of playing throughout; *or,* though their hallmarks are distinctive and memorable, they are still not the master key to details of performance and delivery. His productions characteristically begin with a provocative and enigmatic set, confronting the audience as soon as they enter the theater. For *The Tempest* (1981) a moat of blood surrounded the thrust stage, with various objects afloat in it symbolizing the history of human endeavor, its arts, sciences, and conflicts, some of these on the stage as well: the trunk of a suit of armor with the legs on stage and the upper body in the moat, for example. Conceived as the archetypal artist-scientist, Prospero was dressed by turns in a cardigan or smock-cum-lab coat, late Victorian and twentieth century, externally nondescript creativity personified. His identity was established at once in scene one by his carrying from backstage a ship

model like the storm-tossed ship projected on a large screen, beginning small, growing to fill the screen, sinking, as the characters on
shipboard played out the scene while Prospero sat on the Dali-esque
remains of a rowboat and contemplated the model. The ship (of
state) like the island played its prominent physical part in the production as well as in the script: it merged with the human condition
partly by virtue of its "deck" (1.1), which became the interior of Prospero's study—a magical room in which window, doorway, and a
mirror in the raised cover of a miniature harpsicord opened on
brightly lighted, Magritte-like azure seascapes on different planes,
suggesting the "problematics" of nature, art, and science; this effect
of enchantment was both heightened and erased when full lighting
came up to reveal window and door as themselves an illusion, mere
frames in a metal grillwork.

Ciulei was trained as an architect, and his productions always have
an architectonic dimension that speaks for itself but also blends with
the dialogue and action. The dialectic of art and nature in *As You Like
It* was conveyed at first sight by a center-stage Palladian-style gazebo
of light wood, on the upper story of which musicians played Renais-
sance-style music and from which various characters watched others
perform unawares. Second and more strikingly, the dialectic was
conveyed by a chorus of ten anthropomorphic trees—or dendro-
morphic masquers—costumed after Inigo Jones's designs for
Thomas Campion's *Lords Maske* of 1603. These were sometimes more
humane than the humans themselves; for example, they read Orlando's pathetic verses to themselves rather more sympathetically
than Rosalind and Touchstone read them aloud with a hoot and a
holler. Carts of the same wood as the gazebo were used liberally,
changing "form" by virtue of application and flexibility of convention—function, in short. Hawsered winches prominently visible on
stage right and left appeared to shift the gazebo in its occasional
movements a few feet downstage and back, a constant reminder that
all was done by manifold efforts and inventions, seen and unseen (I
am not sure this added much to the obvious, but it was consonant and
unobtrusive enough not to detract). To an occasionally very comic
Duke Frederick were contributed a bathtub that proved to be bottomless when he arose and walked backstage with it around him (2.2),
and in a long red cape which fell to the ground at his departure to
expose the Duke in long johns, his emperor's new clothes (3.2). All
these contributions enhanced the action and significance; though not
in the script, they were wholly consonant with the spirit and sense of
what is. The same was true of the at once bittersweet and richly comic
1984 production of Ciulei's *Twelfth Night* in a "distillation-of-circus"
idiom partly inspired by *The Clowns* and by Fellini generally.

Ciulei's first three Shakespeare productions effectively made of Shakespeare's scripts something our-timely and artfully timeless, too, at least as those who are prepared to speak of timelessness measure it at the moment. A major means was his allowing the script to speak for itself through careful and faithful articulation of the dialogue, something that he did rather less in his 1985 production of *A Midsummer Night's Dream*, his last before his resignation as Guthrie artistic director was to take effect in March of 1986. This *Dream* was a dark comedy about power politics and patriarchal abuses of power in particular, a reading prescribed by the imperatives of our time, according to Ciulei. The Guthrie press release had it that "the play's festive tone, celebrating the bliss of a wedding and the rites of summer, contrasts sharply with a male-dominated social order," and it certainly did in this production, which was epitomized in the dumb show preceding the beginning of Shakespeare's script. From a darkened entrance at the back of the stark Chinese-red-vinyl-covered stage, two white-clad attendants carried a lighted brazier down front, strolling back whistling, until stifled by two entering representatives of Authority, also in white. Then, flanked by guards in white, a black Hippolyta in dark fatigues and with Grace Jones crewcut stalked in defiantly, high-heeled boots clicking, eyes flashing, and nostrils flaring. Expressionless female attendants in white ripped off the fatigues, threw them on the brazier, and dressed her in a floor-length white gown and vast cape. Next a condescending Theseus and his courtiers entered in white and politely applauded the duchess-to-be in her new clothes. Finally, Theseus's "Now fair Hippolyta, our nuptial hour / Draws on apace," and so on.

For one ecstatic reviewer, the production "sends your mind and emotions reeling into vertigo," but "there are *loose ends of course, the chief one here probably inherent in the script.* At play's end the glaring, icy Hippolyta does join in and adjourn with Theseus. They aren't arm in arm, and we still suspect it will be an uneasy night, but she is no longer resistant, and the play gives us no reason for her change in temper" (my italics). This inchoate adaptation had no means of tying up the loose ends without adding sufficient threads to complement the ones contributed at the beginning.

V

An extraordinary example of contemporary unorthodoxy in Shakespearean production is to be found in the work of Ariane Mnouchkine and her company of *Le Theatre du Soleil*, in the Cartoucherie, Vincennes, just outside Paris. In 1982 she had in repertory

Twelfth Night and *Richard II* (performed in Los Angeles in 1984 in connection with the Olympic Games). These have since been joined by the First and Second Parts of *Henry IV*. In some ways her stage work resembles Akira Kurosawa's Noh-influenced film adaptation of *Macbeth,* which uses very little dialogue but has justly been called the best film yet made of a play by Shakespeare. Mnouchkine's productions are appropriately but inadequately described as "exotic." *Twelfth Night* was classical East Indian kathakali in costume, movements, gestures, and music. The Japanese idiom of *Richard II* combined elements of Kabuki, Noh, and Bunraku. Her productions use most of Shakespeare's dialogue, in her own French verse translations, but they express meaning especially through spectacle and nonverbal gesture: relentless energy manifested in gymnastics, mime, and constant movement punctuated by moments of charged and eloquent stillness; exotic settings analogical enough to beguile and suggest without annihilating sense; specially composed music attuned to the mode of dramatization and performed on a large variety of exotic instruments in plain sight, in a defined space at audience right, as an integral part of the spectacle; and dialogue chanted with emphatic pitch variation.

Delivery of the dialogue studiously avoids "realism" and is at times addressed directly to the audience by actors aligned before them; it retains the cognitive and emotive force of the original not by verisimilitude but by rhetorical stress and theatrical framing: the script is clearly there, in a systematically adjusted, not distorted, perspective. The ambience and settings are world-enough-and-time-wide eclectic: a production idiom at first glance remote from the "reality" of the script world that in the event can be seen as an organically integrated "part" of it. The experience of Shakespeare in *Le Theatre du Soleil* irresistibly enlarges one's conception of the range of performing idiom Shakespeare's plays can sustain and even demand. The difference between Banana Republic *Julius Caesar* and Japanesque *Richard II* is one apparently of degree that is in fact a difference in kind: changing only the setting and costumes in the former case emphasizes the disparity; in Mnouchkine's versions, total refraction in performance crystallizes the script anew in what is paradoxically a production and an adaptation simultaneously. A major difference is in the strain on the script in the former case and the script in relief in the latter.

Such productions need not, in my view should not, take the place of those more conventional, but they are invaluable parts of a larger performing whole that includes them: they explore the worlds of Shakespeare, art, and the human community together. Innovation in theater as elsewhere is an imperative of our time, any time, not merely because it is a demand of passing fashion and economic imperatives, though often it is both, but because, as Heraclitus lately might have said, the times they are a-changing always already. And it is fitting that Shakespeare, like Falstaff in *Henry IV, Part 2*, should be not only witty in himself but the cause that wit is in other persons. The whole of the periphery, the off-off, and the fringe of conception and production can be accommodated, should even be welcomed, provided there is somewhere a gravitational center, preferably in regular active performance as well as in widespread familiarity and general understanding of what is going on in and through the script. That is, the script must be recognized in detail for something of what it was, and in altered cultural circumstances still is, in order to be coherently what it can be imaginatively in contemporary realization.

VI

The drift of this excursion is "purist" to the extent that respectful —not necessarily reverent, still less slavish—adherence to the inferably integral meanings of the script seems to me to have priority over every other aspect of production. Obviously these meanings are not writ in neon, but they can be localized within reasonable limits by attending first to the script and its internal relations, second to the complex of its times and historical relations, and *then* to apparent resemblances between a play's "objects of imitation" and the events and persons of our own times, proceeding with a calculus that though it *cannot* exclude the pressures of the present does not prematurely aggrandize the third at the expense of the first two. "If indeed Shakespeare crafted his plays according to a set of conventions or a sense of design that we ignore or make no effort to understand, how can we expect to realize the full extent of his characters, images, and meanings?"[19] Or how can we expect to realize our own designs sufficiently if we do not understand the means and ends of a script being used as a means to present ends? If dialogue does not make consistent sense in performance, owing to cuts, reorientation, gratuitous emphases, persistent disparity between setting and dialogue, and the like, the resulting "production" will falsify Shakespeare's play, rarely "improving" upon it unless adaptation has been carried so far—as by Charles Marowitz or the many who have made musicals of Shakespeare's plays—that a substantial (re)composition results, a state of affairs we can applaud both on its own terms and for what more we can see of the original at the same time. *Rosencrantz and Guildenstern*

Are Dead is the joint creation of Shakespeare and Tom Stoppard, and we understand *Hamlet* the better in many ways by virtue of this offspring, which owes much also to "our time" in general and to the influence of Samuel Beckett in particular.

The Merchant of Venice affords an example of almost every kind of stress and strain, and also serves as a focal point for addressing variations in production that convey, intensify, or falsify the designs of the script. Two crucial moments of script and production will illustrate, the treatment of either being something of a touchstone of interpretation at large and invariably implying the correlative playing of Shylock, the central problem of performance, because he can never again be quite the *shalach*, or cormorant, he was in Shakespeare's London (though never so simply in his script). The moments are the Casket scene (3.2), in which Bassanio chooses the lead casket with Portia's picture in it, and the delivery and staging of the play's final lines. The first epitomizes the relationship and character of Portia and Bassanio, and by implication Antonio and the rest of the Venetians, and Shylock by contrast; the second determines the harmony or discord of the whole in the concluding notes. J. C. Trewin succinctly describes the casket situation. "We cannot guess ourselves how those caskets will be displayed at Belmont. In my first *Merchant* [seen in the English provinces as a child] they were obviously old cigar boxes, indifferently concealed. Most directors and designers work hard on them. I have known them huddled on a table, hidden behind tapestry, arranged on a flowerpot stand, wheeled in on a trolley, held by kneeling servants, disposed about the room, and once, and weirdly, enclosed in what resembled an automatic machine: we waited for Morocco to insert a ducat before the machine worked."[20]

The 1984 Royal Shakespeare Company production was remarkable chiefly for the designer's heavy hand and did not transfer to the Barbican in 1985. The set was defined by a huge oriental carpet as background that dominated continuously, as though the entire action took place within the casket, an effect complemented by the omnipresence of the caskets at the front of the set. These, the size and shape of British postboxes on pedestals, were held high on cantilevers that dropped them bouncing into place when needed for the choosing by Morocco, Arragon, and Bassanio, and when wanted otherwise to be seen to impinge upon the action. The point was evidently to convey—in effect throughout—that "so is the will of a living daughter curb'd by the will of a dead father" (1.2.23–24) who tyrannically forecloses on posterity. Two huge manned pipe organs were regrettably reminiscent of Terry Jones's naked piano-playing in some episodes of *Monty Python's Flying Circus*. The actors found it both difficult and necessary to perform *against* a set so oppressive.

Trewin continues, "Komisarjevsky's singer of 'Tell me where is fancy bred', at Stratford in 1932, heavily stressed the rhymes to 'lead' —'bred', 'head', 'nourished'. It could not have been sillier, for in this scene, at the very centre of the Belmont story, Bassanio knows, Portia knows, and we know."[21] But *how* do—we get shown that—they know? A question to be asked, and a complicating factor for any director, is the ambiguous stage direction calling for "A song *the whilst* Bassanio comments on the caskets to himself" (3.2.62 f., my italics). But the purport and effect are much the same whether the song is sung *while* he speaks audibly "to himself" the speech beginning "So may the outward shows be least themselves" or, while the song is sung, he is seen but not heard to comment "to himself" before beginning aloud with "So may," etc. The operative phrase is "to himself."[22] However the choosing is staged, the script evidently has Bassanio at some distance from Portia when it takes place:

> *Away then!* I am lock'd in one of them,—
> If you do love me, you will find me out.
> Nerissa and the rest, *stand all aloof,*—
> Let music sound while he doth make his choice,
> Then if he lose he makes a swan-like end,
> Fading in music. . . .
> *Now he goes. . . .*
>
> (3.2.40–45, 53; my italics)

Representative treatments, opposed in tenor but neither extreme, are those of Jonathan Miller's film with Olivier as Shylock, and Michael Langham's production at the Guthrie. In Miller's film, the caskets are on pedestals arranged in lazy-susan fashion. As Bassanio approaches them, two elderly women enter and begin singing "Where is fancy bred?" flanking and framing the lead casket during most of the song, in which the rhyme words are emphasized, with supporting glances at the lead casket by the singer nearest Bassanio. For a Bassanio thus surely if not blatantly instructed which to choose, his speech of deliberation following the song might seem both hypocritical and redundant. In Langham's production, the song was sung softly at stage rear, unattended by Bassanio, who deliberated *"whilst"* the song was being sung. Ways of dramatizing Bassanio's trial abound, but a crucial difference is made by the presence or absence of an apparently deliberate hint confounding in a trice the integrity of Portia—"I could teach you / How to choose right, but then I am forsworn, / So will I never be" (3.2.10–12)—and the percipience and psychic affinity of Bassanio—"Away then! I [Portia] am locked in one of them,— / If you do love me you will find me out" (3.2.40–41). The following five stage endings of *Merchant* convey something of the range of possibility more or less countenanced by Shakespeare's script at the second of these two crucial moments, the least countenanced coming first.

1. Antonio is left alone on stage as melancholy as he was at the play's beginning. This ending typically has Antonio in unrequited love with Bassanio, making him anomalous in several ways and very prominent as such: at the expense of all the other principals, his melancholy and its cause assume centrality in conclusion.

2. Jessica lingers after the others leave, while the kaddish—the Jewish lament for the dead—is heard. Thus Shylock is finally given memorial fixation and primary consequence in an ending almost inevitable in Miller's film, which centralizes him.

3. In a combination of 1 and 2, in effect, first Bassanio and Portia, then Gratiano and Nerissa, leave by couples, in that order; next Lorenzo and Jessica leave, the latter pensive and holding in her hand what could be the "merry bond" or, more likely, the will Shylock was obliged to sign by the settlement of act four, scene one; finally, Antonio remains, discarding with apparent indifference the letter of good news Portia had just given him of his ships' coming safely to harbor. So ended the Chichester Festival Theatre production (Summer 1984), with Sir Alec Guinness as a dignified, subdued, and sympathetic but rather "neutral" Shylock in a production of indeterminate, apparently undetermined, position.

4. Gratiano is last to leave, as in a *commedia dell'arte* production performed in London by Shared Experience and the Crucible Theatre of Sheffield in 1981: with Nerissa over his shoulder, posterior to audience, Gratiano delivered the play's last lines, "Well, while I live, I'll fear no other thing / So sore, as keeping safe Nerissa's ring," making an appropriate literal and symbolic gesture with a "ring" of thumb and index finger. Gratiano does, after all, have the last lines in *The Merchant of Venice* as we have it, in an authoritative Quarto text based on copy very close to Shakespeare's manuscript. In the most recent revival of the play by the Royal Shakespeare Company at Stratford-upon-Avon in 1984 Gratiano again had the concluding words and emphasis.

5. *"Exeunt"*—*they* leave—the concluding stage direction and last "line" of the authoritative Quarto text. The nearest to this are the *commedia* and Royal Shakespeare Company productions (4), since Gratiano's words are not erased by a subsequent impression. There are few performing spaces from which all the actors present could leave together, abreast, and arm in arm, as it were; hence the variation in who goes last, and how in accordance with whom. But whatever we may choose to make of Shakespeare's *Merchant*, he himself

apparently ended it without Shylock but with virtually all others present—including Antonio—together and in evidently festive spirit.

VII

> Well then,
> Legitimate *Edgar*, I must haue your land,
> Our Fathers loue, is to the Bastard *Edmond*,
> As to th'legitimate: fine word: Legitimate.
> Well, my Legittimate, if this Letter speed,
> And my inuention thriue, *Edmond* the base
> Shall to'th'Legitimate: I grow, I prosper:
> Now Gods, stand vp for Bastards.[23]

In the preceding discussion I have been concerned all along with the issue of "legitimate production" of classic plays as an issue of currency and concern for the many constituencies of contemporary theater, where often enough "novelty is only in request."[24] If there is a finite range of "legitimate productions" of Shakespeare's plays, it is not easily defined, because theatrical performance involves at least two orders of analysis and evaluation that do not necessarily and in practice very often do not coincide: they center on the meaning(s) of the script and on the significance of performance. E. D. Hirsch's terms point usefully in the right direction: what a play meant for its playwright and original audiences, what a play in production signifies in contemporary performance, and how far a modern production is consonant with, and an extension of, the play as originally conceived and performed—so far as we know and can reasonably infer.[25] In fact, the dialectic of meaning and significance must come into play at a premiere production, since there is invariably some tension between script and performance that has finally to be resolved in favor of the latter; the greater the distance of the playwright from his or her performers and audience, both metaphorically and in actual production, the greater the tension is likely to be.

In the case of Shakespeare's plays, the issues are further complicated by the fact that there is continuing disagreement over what many of the plays mean. Without a consensus about a given play, how can we define a range of legitimate productions? The answer is, in part, I think, that such a range includes, in varying degree, any tenable interpretation of a play, and there are sufficient *un*tenable interpretations about, by responsible consensus, that one may hypothesize about a tenable remainder. If *Hamlet* is not necessarily a play chiefly about Oedipal complications, those can hardly be excluded from the realm of possibility while they retain psychological explanatory power in a culture, especially when the Oedipus complex has recently been argued to be culturally specific and fairly narrowly so, and arguably correlative with the development of a nuclear family—in the Renaissance, for example. On the other hand, Shakespeare's play is *not* about a woman in disguise, though so played by Asta Nielsen on film in 1920, where "she" is discovered by Horatio's opening Hamlet's doublet to ease "his" last gasp. Such playing is "provocative" (and in this event irresistibly risible), but it is "from the purpose of playing," which has tacit obligations to hold the mirror up to the nature of its script as well as to such "reality" as a representational script may be said to imitate. This is bound to vary somewhat from its own to our time as humors psychology gives way to ego psychology and so on.

Much contemporary production of classics seems to be concerned less with producing scripts than in seeing what those scripts may yield by way of the unexpected. Motives could be found in many quarters, including *auteur* and explorers' impulses, the imperatives of "relevance," the attractions of "concept" production, the demand of audiences for variety, and box-office pressures, but the effect is in general the same: novelty arrived at by departure from the script. In particular, of course, "departure" is a matter of degree: if Shakespeare's comedies are performed with various "circus" redactions, as *The Comedy of Errors* was by the Royal Shakespeare Company in 1983 and 1984 and *Twelfth Night* by the Guthrie in 1984, its essentials of human action, character, and dialogue need not be confounded by the new compounding; the scripts themselves are charged with tongue-in-cheek implausibilities, and the identity crises and losses of temper that constitute their serious matter are already tinctured in the plays as written. Comedy in general lends itself readily enough to excesses without losing its essential nature, but its particular meanings may be another matter, as in *A Midsummer Night's Dream*, which has been much set upon in productions of the past twenty years: its orders of magic and hallucination seem to solicit psychogenetics and hallucino-genetics of every kind, and its depths are rather easily muddied by contemporary stirrings.

The problems of evaluating idiosyncratic production are due in large part to the elementary fact that relationship to the script is usually but sometimes erroneously assumed to be one of (re)production, realizing the script. Presentation distant from the script will accordingly be faulted by those who see the latter lost in the former. "Adaptations" acknowledged as such—like Charles Marowitz's Shakespeare collages—explicitly invite entirely different perspectives, interpretations, and evaluations. A recent instance at the Guthrie was a "production" that, if it had been called "Lucien Pintilie's [Adaptation of] Chekhov's *The Seagull*," could hardly have been faulted for what was never attempted: conventional production. "Lucian Pintilie's dismembered and rearranged version of 'The Seagull' had Guthrie patrons firmly divided—some muttering about the rape of Chekhov and others glowing with the pleasure of seeing an *inventive reconstruction* of a play from the standard repertoire."[26] The production was in its own way both original and parasitic: whether the new work of theatrical art was better or worse than the original, or separate but equal, was the appropriate question, but it was seldom asked because of uncertainty about the work's status.

If this were a matter merely of accurate truth-in-labeling, and generally understood as a case of caveat emptor, it would be a matter of limited consequence. But in cultural circumstances where scripts are seldom or never available in conventional production, their sense and form are lost to all but readers, who themselves have only abbreviated experience of the play. This is a cultural as well as dramatic loss of a serious order. It is to the credit of the sometimes gratuitously maligned BBC-Time/Life series of television films of Shakespeare's plays that on the whole they have striven for conventional production. If some of the productions are not very good, it is doubtful whether conventionality as such is responsible. There is substantial agreement if not unanimity, for example, that the conventional *Romeo and Juliet* is lifeless and dull, while *Measure for Measure* is vigorous and engaging.

The anchorage of conventional production is in any case not very difficult to identify in general. It consists in a play's action, characters, dialogue, settings, and sound effects, musical and otherwise, as the script presents them and a receptive reader finds them, and its "meanings" as a compound of entailed affects and cognitions, both progressive and cumulative. A reader of a play loses much more, no doubt, than effects peculiar to performance, but a competent reader has every chance of a sound grasp of what it is "about" in relation to those realities of human action and passion it has stylized. Such a reader may be self-tutored or taught by others, but the effect should be much the same: a prepared spectator.

Among the obstacles to agreement on whether there is "legitimate production" and what its boundaries are, two seem all but insurmountable if any sort of comprehensive consensus is sought. First, contemporary theater in practice is often "driven" by one of two motive forces or both together—box office and deliberate ideology. To the extent that either is allowed prior claims on production, they are the criteria of "legitimacy": if a production brings in audiences and makes a profit, or is made to say or do what is politically correct according to whatever faction determines correctness, it *is* "legitimate" because prescribed. Second, the irreconcilability of apparently decimated and certainly beleaguered "liberal humanist" critics and audiences, on the one hand, and their legion entrenched opponents, on the other.[27]

If "seeking to establish a continuity between the past and the present" and "focusing on 'universal' themes such as justice, chastity, appearance vs. reality, love and marriage, freedom vs. restraint, folly, avarice, time, order vs. chaos, deception, good vs. evil, and so on" are reprehensibly "idealist" in abstracting "the play from its history and the material conditions of its production,"[28] there is not much latitude for the position of John Barton and his Royal Shakespeare Company actors as represented in *Playing Shakespeare*. There a primary question for both is "the pragmatic one, 'how does Shakespeare's text actually work?' " (3). This project proceeds from the assumption that "we are of today but the text endures" (182), and in the conviction that "Shakespeare is timeless in the sense that he anatomises and understands what is in men and women in any age, and what he has to say is always true and real. It is this element that is truly contemporary and which the wise actor or director will try to bring out" (190). If there are norms of signification within a script that may be observed with more or less propriety and clarity, of the sort that Barton finds firmly in Shakespeare's plays, for example, then there is a hypothetical range of legitimate production. It will not yield an instant gauge of individual productions, but it does provide a conceptual basis for interpreting and evaluating theatrical interpretations—with due allowance, too, for legitimate differences. Touchstone has something in "Your If is the only peacemaker; much virtue in If."[29]

UNIVERSITY OF MINNESOTA

NOTES

1 Call for Papers for the 1983 MMLA meeting, with thanks to the Chair, Professor Louis R. Barbato of Cleveland State University. "Shakespearegresses" includes both "regresses" and "egresses." I am indebted to Professor Jay L. Halio of the University of Delaware for reading this essay in draft and making corrections and suggestions that I have acted on too gratefully to wish him held responsible for the parts he graciously spared.
2 Charles Marowitz, *The Marowitz Shakespeare* (New York, 1978), pp. 7–27; Alan C. Dessen, *Shakespeare Survey 36* (Cambridge, 1983), pp. 57–64; hereafter cited in text.
3 Eugène Ionesco, *Macbett*, tr. Charles Marowitz (New York, 1973), p. 3.

4   John Russell Brown, *Discovering Shakespeare* (London, 1981), p. 61.

5   John Barton, *Playing Shakespeare* (London, 1984), pp. 191–92; hereafter cited in text.

6   Performed at the Half Moon Theatre in May of 1984.

7   Tom Stoppard, *Jumpers* (New York, 1972–73), p. 11.

8   *Poetics*/15.8/1454b10.

9   "Androgynous punks" is likely to express a user's (though not Professor Barbato's) intention to depreciate by both terms, though "punk" is by now generically descriptive and neutral as "unisex" is and "androgynous" could be but rarely is.

10   Ralph Berry, *On Directing Shakespeare: Interviews with Contemporary Directors* (London, 1977), p. 18. Berry understandably "know[s] of no general criteria for judging such adaptations: each one is a separate enterprise, and will be judged on the skill and tact with which the adaptor interprets and re-animates the vital essences of the original text," *when*, I should add, the purposes of adaptation are as they are here said to be ("faithful," in effect) and in practice were in the *Henry VI* adaptations. In *Modern Shakespeare Offshoots* (Princeton, 1976), Ruby Cohn "use[s] a looser and more neutral word, 'offshoot,' for the 'array of names' by which 'rewriting of Shakespeare' is known" (p. 3). She classifies "offshoots that are close to a Shakespearean text by the process that molds them: *reduction/emendation*. . . . *Adaptation*, probably the most overused term for a Shakespeare offshoot, will constitute the second group," characterized by substantial cuts, "much alteration of language," and—in a definition supplied by Christopher Spencer—one or more "important (or scene-length) additions. . . . Invention will be the basis for the third grouping, *transformation*" (pp. 3–4).

11   In Roman Polanski's film influenced by Jan Kott's *Shakespeare Our Contemporary* (London, 1964), there is an emphatic instance of Kott's Grand Mechanism come full circle: near the beginning, Macbeth is first seen riding horseback along a mountain trail where he meets the three witches (1.3); at the end, after Malcolm's soliloquy, Donalbain—in Shakespeare's script not seen or mentioned again after he announces his departure for Ireland in 2.4—is seen riding along the same trail.

12   Another access is provided by Michael Green's study of *The Art of Coarse Acting*, rev. ed. (New York, 1981), first published as *Downwind of Upstage* (London, 1964).

13   Two discussions of particular interest in this connection are Norman Rabkin's "Meaning and *The Merchant of Venice*" in *Shakespeare and the Problem of Meaning* (Chicago, 1981) and a dialogue between Royal Shakespeare Company director John Barton and two recent Royal Shakespeare Company Shylocks, David Suchet and Patrick Stewart, in "Exploring a Character: Playing Shylock," in *Playing Shakespeare*.

14   "Concept" has as much inflammatory power for some as it has explanatory power for others. The term is used in effect to refer to the novelty dimension, especially when pronounced; a "concept" of some sort is implicit in any production that has a systematic relationship to the text.

15   David Hume, "Of Simplicity and Refinement in Writing" (1741), *Philosophical Works* (Boston and Edinburgh, 1854), III, 213–14.

16   Performed at the Royal Shakespeare Theatre in 1983 and at the Barbican in 1984.

17   Irving Wardle, *The Times*, 21 April 1983. My italics.

18   The production may have "lightened" somewhat between Stratford-upon-Avon and its rebirth at the Barbican in August 1984, when it struck more of a balance between the comic and overtly serious, the latter taking the elegiac part of its keynote from Feste's concluding song and its refrain, "For the rain it raineth every day." The melancholy mood was conveyed partly by the prominent, almost cinematic music, together with sound effects associated with the weather, and partly by the set, which had the action taking place in front of a hillock with frowning clouds and lowering sky in motion almost throughout.

19   Alan C. Dessen, *Elizabethan Stage Conventions and Modern Interpreters* (Cambridge, 1984), p. 162.

20   J. C. Trewin, *Going to Shakespeare* (London, 1978), p. 111.

21   Trewin may seem precipitate in dismissing the protracted debate over the hint, but he has the support of Occam's razor as well as the reasons given with succinct comprehensiveness by John Russell Brown in the New Arden Edition (1955; corr. rpt. London, 1959), p. 80.

22   "There are some directions which probably only Shakespeare could have written. A book-keeper in the theatre would not think of adding that . . . Bassanio comments on the caskets 'to himselfe' "; J. R. Brown, New Arden edition, p. xiv.

23   *King Lear* 1.2.15–22 (TLN 349–56); Folio (1623), sigg. qq3^{r+v}.

24   Duke Vincentio's entire speech is pertinently pointed: "None [i.e., 'news abroad in the world'], but that there is so great a fever on goodness that the dissolution of it must cure it. Novelty is only in request, and it is as dangerous to be aged in any kind of course as it is virtuous to be constant in any undertaking. There is scarce truth enough alive to make societies secure, but security enough to make fellowships accursed. Much upon this riddle runs the wisdom of the world. This news is old enough, yet it is every days news" (*MM* 3.2.212–20).

25   E. D. Hirsch, "Meaning and Significance Reinterpreted," *Critical Inquiry*, 11 (1984), 202–25; Hirsch's modifications usefully enlarge upon the terms he first advanced in 1960.

26   David Hawley, reviewing Pintilie's subsequent production—adaptation—of Moliere's *Tartuffe* in *St. Paul Pioneer Press*, 3 August 1984.

27   See Terry Eagleton: "Liberal humanism has dwindled to the impotent conscience of bourgeois society, gentle, sensitive and ineffectual." *Literary Theory: An Introduction* (Minneapolis, 1983), p. 199.

28   Derek Longhurst, " 'Not for all time, but for [sic] an Age': an approach to Shakespeare studies," in *Re-Reading English*, ed. Peter Widdowson (London, 1981), p. 157. In "Dialectical Immaterialism," *American Scholar*, 54 (1985), 449–65, Frederick Crews finds the Achilles heel on the other foot: "the loyal Marxist is precisely someone who identifies *himself* with an ordained class of people to whom 'history' has granted extra liberties, and thus he will be unlikely to recognize that the theory is undemocratic and mischievous in its essence. Instead, he will appease his conscience by blaming 'the capitalists' for thwarting history's wishes and goading the international Left into regrettable overreactions" (452). "If, as we are told, Western Marxism is now in general retreat, we might expect the Marxist theorizing that finds its way into the Anglo-American academy to be a humble and academic affair. Among the more conscientious radical professoriat, that is indeed the case. The atmosphere of Left Eclecticism, however, constitutes a temptation to wanton posturing. Under that dispensation, and more particularly in the absence of the passé assumption that theories are supposed to account for data more parsimoniously and cogently than their rivals, a Marxist academic need only skirt the classic dilemmas of his tradition—making sure, however, to identify his claims as avant-garde in provenance and affinity—to gain a place at the banquet table of radical pan-theoreticism" (458).

29   *As You Like It* 5.4. 103–04.

Acknowledgments

Barry, Jackson G. "Shakespeare with Words: The Script and the Medium of Drama." *Shakespeare Quarterly* 25 (1974): 161–71. Reprinted with the permission of the Folger Shakespeare Library.

Orgel, Stephen. "Shakespeare Imagines a Theater." *Poetics Today* 5 (1984): 549–61. Reprinted with the permission of Duke Unviersity Press.

Gurr, Andrew. "The Bare Island." *Shakespeare Survey* 47 (1994): 29–43. Reprinted with the permission of Cambridge University Press.

Urkowitz, Steven. "'I am not made of stone': Theatrical Revision of Gesture in Shakespeare's Plays." *Renaissance and Reformation* 10 (1986): 79–93. Reprinted with the permission of the Canadian Society for Renaissance Studies.

O'Connell, Michael. "The Idolatrous Eye: Iconoclasm, Anti-Theatricalism, and the Image of the Elizabethan Theater." *English Literary History* 52 (1985): 279–310. Reprinted with the permission of Johns Hopkins University Press.

Knapp, Jeffrey. "Preachers and Players in Shakespeare's England." *Representations* 44 (1993): 29–59. Reprinted with the permission of the University of California Press.

Empson, William. "*Hamlet* When New." *Sewanee Review* 61 (1953): 15–42. Reprinted with the permission of the editor. Copyright 1953, by the University of the South.

Empson, William. "*Hamlet* When New (Part II. " *Sewanee Review* 61 (1953): 185–205. Reprinted with the permission of the editor. Copyright 1953, by the University of the South.

Trousdale, Marion. "*Coriolanus* and the Playgoer in 1609." In *The Arts of Performance in Elizabethan and Early Stuart Drama: Essays for G.K. Hunter*, edited by Murray Briggs, Philip Edwards, Inga-Stina Ewbank, and Eugene M. Waith (Edinburgh: Edinburgh University Press, 1991): 124–34. Reprinted with the permission of Edinburgh University Press.

Altman, Joel B. "'Prophetic Fury': *Othello* and the Economy of Shakespearean Reception." *Studies in the Literary Imagination* 26 (1993): 85–113. Reprinted with the permission of *Studies in the Literary Imagination*.

Harris, Arthur John. "Garrick, Colman, and *King Lear*: A Reconsideration."

Shakespeare Quarterly 22 (1971): 57–66. Reprinted with the permission of the Folger Shakespeare Library.

Moody, Jane. "Writing for the Metropolis: Illegitimate Performances of Shakespeare in Early Nineteenth-Century London." *Shakespeare Survey* 47 (1994): 61–69. Reprinted with the permission of Cambridge University Press.

Nilan, Mary M. "Shakespeare, Illustrated: Charles Kean's 1857 Production of *The Tempest*." *Shakespeare Quarterly* 26 (1975): 196–204. Reprinted with the permission of the Folger Shakespeare Library.

Clayton, Thomas. "Theatrical Shakespearegresses at the Guthrie and Elsewhere: Notes on 'Legitimate Production.'" *New Literary History* 17 (1986): 511–38. Reprinted with the permission of John Hopkins University Press.